Arabs and Young Turks

Arabs and Young Turks

Ottomanism, Arabism, and Islamism in the Ottoman Empire, 1908–1918

Hasan Kayalı

UNIVERSITY OF CALIFORNIA PRESS

Berkeley / Los Angeles / London

University of California Press
Berkeley and Los Angeles, California

University of California Press, Ltd.
London, England

Some parts of this book have been published previously in somewhat different form. Parts of various chapters: "Greater Syria under Ottoman Constitutional Rule: Ottomanism, Arabism, and Regionalism", in *The Syrian Land in the 18th and 19th Century*, ed. Thomas Philipp, 27–41 (Stuttgart: Franz Steiner Verlag, 1992).

Part of chapter 5: "A Note on Railway Construction Schemes in the Hijaz During the Second Constitutional Period of the Ottoman Empire", *Arab Historical Review for Ottoman Studies* (Tunis), no. 5–6 (1992): 39–43.

Library of Congress Cataloging-in-Publication Data

Kayalı, Hasan.
    Arabs and Young Turks : Ottomanism, Arabism, and Islamism in the Ottoman Empire, 1908–1918 / Hasan Kayalı.
      p.   cm.
    Includes bibliographical references and index.
    ISBN 0-520-20444-1 (alk. paper). — ISBN 0-520-20446-8 (pbk. : alk. paper)
    1. Arab countries—Foreign relations—Turkey.   2. Turkey—Foreign relations—Arab countries.   3. Turkey—Politics and government—1909–1918.   I. Title.
DS63.2.T8K39   1997
327.56017'4927—dc20
                                                     96-11474

Manufactured in the United States of America

9 8 7 6 5 4 3 2 1

To Ayşe, Murat, and Nihal

Contents

Acknowledgments

I owe a special debt to Feroz Ahmad, who has shared with me over the years his wealth of knowledge and insights on the Young Turk period. I am fortunate to have received inspiration and guidance from the late Albert Hourani. The doctoral dissertation that anteceded this book was supervised by Zachary Lockman, who has graciously supported my work since. Engin Akarlı, Chuck Allen, Selim Deringil, Stephen Humphreys, William Ochsenwald, Roger Owen, and an anonymous reader kindly read and commented on parts or the whole of drafts.

I would like to acknowledge the financial and institutional support of the Harvard Center for Middle Eastern Studies; the History Faculty at the Massachusetts Institute of Technology; the American Research Institute in Turkey; the American Council of Learned Societies; the Department of History, the Academic Senate, and the Hellman Family Foundation at the University of California, San Diego. Thanks are also due to the staffs of the Başbakanlık Archives (İstanbul), the Public Records Office (Kew Gardens, London), the Auswärtiges Amt Archives (Bonn), Haus-, Hof-, und Staatsarchiv (Vienna), Archives du Ministère des Affaires Etrangères (Paris), the archives of the Turkish General Chief of Staff (Ankara), the Widener Library and the Geisel Library (especially Library Express).

I am indebted to Philip Khoury, Thomas Philipp, and Leila Fawaz for supporting my academic endeavors over the years. In this regard, I wish also to express my gratitude to L. Carl Brown, Renata Coates, Ali Gheissari, Şükrü Hanioğlu, Kemal Karpat, Rashid Khalidi, Walid Khalidi, Avigdor Levy, Michael Meeker, Donald Quataert, Bassam Tibi, Judith Tucker, and Mary Wilson.

Lynne Withey of the University of California Press took an early interest in the manuscript and sponsored it with grace and efficiency. Tony Hicks directed the production of the book, and Lynn Meinhardt copyread the text.

The cheerful company of the RC, Mufundi, and İTÜ fellows and friendships that grew over countless cups of tea at the Başbakanlık made the writing of this book less of a lonely experience.

I owe by far the largest debt to my wife, Ayşe Kayalı, and to my parents, Reşid and Mihriver Kayalı, for all the sacrifices they have made.

La Jolla
May 1996

Note on Sources

Two considerations governed the choice of primary material for this project. First, the objective being to investigate trends, attitudes, and policies in İstanbul in their "imperial" context, particular attention was given to documents of the central government, parliamentary proceedings, and the capital's contemporary daily press. Second, as far as non-Ottoman primary material is concerned, the unbeaten track of German and Austrian consular correspondence was explored, in addition to French, American, and the extremely rich (and equally well exploited) British Public Record Office collections. Each of these collections has proved to have different degrees of usefulness for different periods. For instance, for periods of strict censorship, the Ottoman press loses much of its utility. For the years of World War I, the value of German, Austrian, and American sources increases as British and French consular reports cease.

The following abbreviations have been used in the text:

Archival Sources

AA	Auswärtiges Amt, Bonn
ATASE	Askeri Tarih ve Stratejik Etüt Dairesi (Archives of the Turkish General Chief of Staff, Ankara)
BBA	Başbakanlık Osmanlı Arşivi (Ottoman Prime Ministry Archives), İstanbul

BEO	Bab-ı Âli Evrak Odası
DH	Dahiliye (Ministry of the Interior)
DUIT	Dosya Usulüne Göre İrade Tasnifi
FO	Foreign Office
HHS	Haus-, Hof-, und Staatsarchiv, Vienna
IJMES	*International Journal of Middle East Studies*
İ.Um.	İdare-i Umumiye
KMS	Kalem-i Mahsus
MAE	Archives du Ministère des Affaires Etrangères, Paris. Correspondance politique et commercial, 1908–1918
MMZC	Meclis-i Mebusan Zabıt Cerideleri (Proceedings of the Ottoman Parliament, 1908–1918)
MTV	Muhaberat-ı Umumiye İdaresi Mütenevvia Kısmı
PA	Politisches Archiv
PRO	Public Record Office, London
SYS	Muhaberat-ı Umumiye Dairesi Siyasi Evrakı
TCTA	*Tanzimat'tan Cumhuriyet'e Türkiye Ansiklopedisi* (Encyclopedia of Turkey from the Tanzimat to the Republic)
US	Records of the U.S. Department of State Relating to Internal Affairs of Turkey, 1910–1929

Note on Transliteration

Lest I appear to concur with T. E. Lawrence's dictum that "I spell my names anyhow, to show what rot the systems are," a word of explanation is needed about spelling. Arabic and Turkish words that are familiar to the reader in their Anglicized versions are rendered as such and not in transliteration or in italics (e.g., vizier). Only an incomplete system of transliteration is used for Arabic words. Most marks that are not on an English keyboard are omitted. Only the *hamza* (') and *'ayn* (') are indicated.

I have chosen to use Turkish renderings of words that are common to Middle Eastern languages and regions, as most of the non-Western texts I used were Ottoman or modern Turkish. The transliteration of personal names poses a more substantive problem and may prejudge important issues in the present study, which touches on questions of ethnic identification. Personal names common to Arabs and Turks (often Arabic in origin) have identical rendering in Ottoman Turkish and Arabic. However, in their modern Turkish rendition some Arabic names become unrecognizable (e.g., *Esat* and *As'ad*). I have had to make a decision between the Turkish and Arabic versions of a transliteration of a personal name on a case-by-case basis. (Thus, for instance, *Mahmud Shawkat Pasha* has been preferred to *Mahmud Şevket Pasha*.) If certain transliterations appear unusual, they should be evaluated within the context of the arguments.

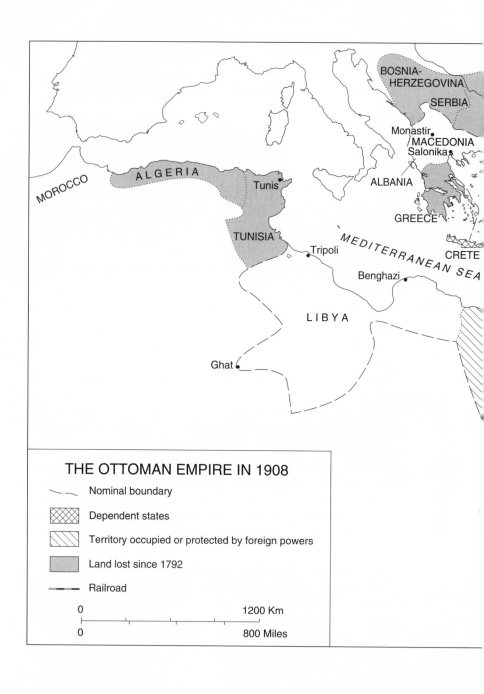

THE OTTOMAN EMPIRE IN 1908

- - -   Nominal boundary

Dependent states

Territory occupied or protected by foreign powers

Land lost since 1792

━━━ Railroad

0   1200 Km

0   800 Miles

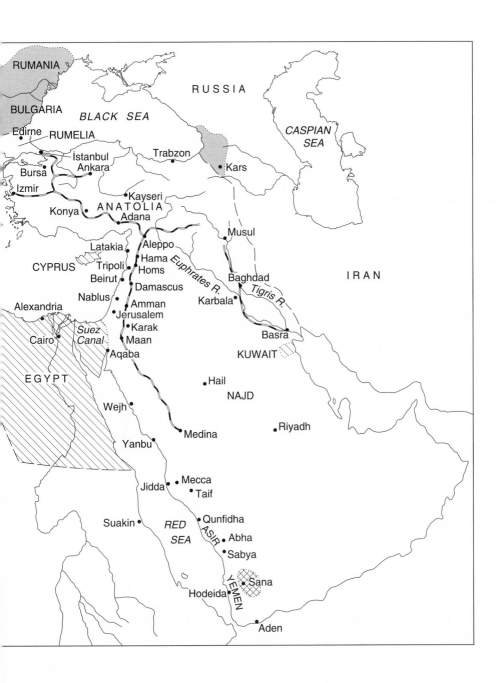

Introduction

We know by now something of what the British thought about the Arabs, and of what Arabs thought about the British and Turks, but what the Turks, and in particular the Turks of the Committee of Union and Progress, thought about the Arabs is still largely an unanswered question.[1]

Fifteen years after they were written, Albert Hourani's words remain valid. This study addresses the very void Hourani mentioned. Its purpose is to illuminate not so much what the Turks *thought* about the Arabs (for the preoccupation with mutual perceptions only produces sterile and polemical analyses),[2] but what the policies of Ottoman governments were in the Arab-populated parts of the empire, as well as how these policies were refashioned at the beginning of the twentieth century, specifically during the last decade of the Ottoman state. An examination of Ottoman government and the Arabs also has to address the genesis and development of Turkish and Arab nationalism, because nationalist discourse is salient in the established scholarship on the period in general and the topic of the Arab policy of the "Young Turk" governments in particular.

The reinstatement of the Ottoman constitution (first promulgated in 1876 but suspended within two years by Sultan Abdülhamid II) on 23 July 1908 marks the beginning of the second constitutional period of the empire. Though only a brief episode when viewed against the vast span of Ottoman history, the second constitutional period (1908–18)[3] was marked by extraordinary social and political transformations. The Young Turk Revolution of 1908 introduced parliamentary rule and lib-

erties that recast social, political, and cultural life in the wake of the long
autocratic reign of Abdülhamid. The revolution, however, failed to arrest the rapid territorial dissolution of the empire. In Europe, the events
of July 1908 prompted Bulgaria's declaration of independence, Crete's
decision to unite with Greece, and the Austrian annexation of Bosnia-
Herzegovina. Within four years the Ottoman government ceded Libya
and the Dodecanese Islands in the Aegean Sea to Italy and virtually all
remaining European territories except İstanbul's Rumelian hinterland to
the Balkan states. It confronted insurgencies in Syria, Albania, and Arabia (i.e., the Arabian Peninsula). The second constitutional period also
encompasses World War I, the major watershed in the history of the
modern Middle East.

One may argue that less is known about the second constitutional
period than the earlier periods of Ottoman history. In spite of its significance and the presumable ease of treating a fairly recent period, this
era of constitutional monarchy has escaped systematic examination and
consequently has suffered from misrepresentation. There are a number
of reasons for the historians' neglect of the period.

First, there is the elusiveness of Ottoman official documents for these
years. This is partly explained by the disarray of documentary sources
due to disruptions caused by revolutionary change, the administrative
inexperience of the newly forged governing elite, the succession of unstable governments after the revolution, and the continual state of war
in which the Ottomans found themselves from 1911 on. Important de-
positories of official documents were lost, while some remained in the
hands of individuals.[4] Government documents pertaining to the period
after 1914 remained classified until the nineties and are gradually being
opened to research. Occasional memoirs produced by the period's statesmen make scant use of documents and treat the events of the period
haphazardly and defensively.

A further problem in scholarship on the second constitutional period
can be described as a case of losing sight of the forest for the trees. Some
of the most important questions of the subsequent history of the Middle
East originated in this period as a result of conditions created by the
war and, to a large degree, of the involvement of European powers in
Middle Eastern affairs in order to promote their wartime aims. This
Western involvement, in particular Britain's deceptive and conflicting
pledges to the Arabs and Zionists, has had momentous consequences
for later Middle Eastern history. An attempt to better understand contemporary Middle Eastern political and social events has generated dis-

proportionate interest in the study of Britain's relations with its wartime allies and local agents and has emphasized the wellsprings of selected problems having contemporary relevance. The broader Ottoman context of the issues has failed to attract scholarly attention.

The general neglect of the period also has to do with the ideological attitude that there is little value in studying an era that was a relatively brief interlude before the inevitable downfall of a once illustrious empire led by one of the longest-ruling dynasties in history. In fact, the Ottoman Empire's collapse was hardly apparent until the late stages of World War I. The Ottoman state—"Sick Man" though it may have been— actually had more resilience in its last decade than historians generally credit it with.

A generalization that has survived without critical scrutiny against the failure to examine this era in its own right pertains to the Committee of Union and Progress (CUP), the conspiratorial constitutionalist society that engineered the 1908 Revolution. The prevalent view of the CUP is as a military oligarchy (the favorite term is "triumvirate") that governed throughout the second constitutional period with a commitment to promote, overtly or covertly, Turkish nationalism. The CUP, however, neither adhered to a coherent agenda nor always succeeded in exerting its will in imperial politics during this period. Initially, its inexperience led to excessive dependence on the statesmen of the old regime. Subsequently, it was challenged vigorously by its decentralist opponents and even briefly lost power to them. When the Committee finally attained power in January 1913, it exercised a collective leadership that was not decisively dominated by military officers.

Even more problematic and pervasive in existing studies of the second constitutional period is a prejudice that has distorted the social and political picture of that era: the nationalist bias shared by Western observers contemporary with the period as well as by later Middle Eastern historians.

Contemporary European eyewitnesses viewed the prewar Middle East with their own nationalist perspective. They portrayed nationalism as a major, if not *the* major, political force in this late phase of the Ottoman Empire, even though for most Muslims the notion of belonging to a nation (much less to a nation-state) had no meaning at the time. Often Western European observers looked at the Balkan Christian communities that were experiencing nationalist movements and drew parallels between them and the Muslim communities. Their perceptions were occasionally shaped not only by uninformed extrapolations but also by an element of wishful thinking, especially in the appraisal of domestic unrest in the empire.

Central Europeans maintained a more discerning perspective on the nationalities question. We find that German and Austrian observers did not as a rule view Middle Eastern events through the prism of nationalism. They offered different insights compared to their Western European counterparts, perhaps not only because nationalist ferment in the Ottoman Empire did not usually serve German or Austro-Hungarian political interests but also because they were more familiar with the realities of a multiethnic empire.

The use of the term "Young Turk" has reinforced nationalist-minded interpretations of the period under study. It is an expression coined by Europeans to refer to the constitutionalist opposition to Abdülhamid. In addition, the second constitutional period is alternatively referred to as the Young Turk period. The designation is an unfortunate misnomer, because it implies that the group of liberal constitutionalists called Young Turks consisted exclusively of Turks, or even of Turkish nationalists. The Young Turks, in fact, included in their ranks many Arabs, Albanians, Jews, and in the early stages of the movement, Armenians and Greeks. Even Karl Deutsch, a keen observer of nationalism, described the 1908 Revolution as a Turkish nationalist affair and also linked it to the Kemalist Revolution, noting that "Turkey had a revolution that overthrew Sultan Abdülhamid and put the Young Turk nationalists in power by 1908, and a second installment of this Revolution followed in 1918 when Kemal Pasha came to power."[5] It would be wrong to view the 1908 Revolution as a nationalist revolution, though the argument can be made that it set afoot political and social changes, which, after many transformations, facilitated a revolution of the Kemalist kind. The Young Turks wanted to preserve the empire and its main institutional underpinning, the monarchy. More accurate is Cyril E. Black and Carl Brown's recent appraisal that

although the Young Turks can now be seen as the penultimate link in the historical chain leading to the establishment of the Turkish Republic it would be anachronistic to argue that the Young Turk leadership after 1909 was prepared to do what Atatürk did 14 years later—abolish the empire and establish a Turkish nation-state.[6]

Western accounts and archival sources also informed indigenous Middle Eastern scholarship after World War I[7] and reinforced the nationalistic ideological concerns of official histories in the successor states of the Ottoman Empire. Often historians made selective and distorted use of the Ottoman past. The Young Turk period did not cater well to the needs of postwar projects of imagining and constructing political communities. Turkish Republican historians sought the beginnings of Turkish nationalism in the pre-Ottoman period, in the steppes of Central Asia, and among the Hittites of Anatolia. While they appropriated the glorious periods of the Ottoman Empire, they viewed the Young Turk era as the sorrowful period when Balkan and Middle Eastern peoples treacherously rebelled against the Turks, who for centuries had shed their blood to defend them from the very foreign enemies with whom these peoples colluded. Arab historians, on the other hand, dwelled on what they saw as the four-centuries-long oppression[8] of the Arabs (and, to be sure, of the Lebanese, Syrians, Iraqis, Palestinians, etc.) under tyrannical Turkish rulers, who exploited their ancestors and usurped Islam. The Young Turks were portrayed in this conception of Arab history as pan-Turkist dictators desirous of eliminating the Arab national identity and "Turkifying" all under their rule. Thus, twentieth-century Middle Eastern historians have tended to see the beginnings of particular nationalistic movements (be they Arab or Turkish) in a more distant past than may historically be justified. They have viewed the second constitutional period in retrospect as one in which conflict and separation had already occurred, and Arab and Turkish nationalism had already defined political discourse. While the mutual misperceptions ingrained by nationalist writings continue to this day, in the last three decades a succession of historians have refined the interpretation of the development of Arab nationalism.

In this regard, attempts at a systematic reexamination of early Arab nationalism have far outweighed similar efforts to understand the origins and maturation of Turkish nationalism. The interest in Arab nationalism has been inspired by the turbulent course nationalism has taken in the Arab Middle East since World War I. Large parts of the Arab world remained under imperialist rule, which gave new and diverse turns to Arab nationalist thought and activity. Confronting Israel has posed new questions about the meaning and scope of Arab nationalism in the past and the present. If dynastic and other hegemonic claims on the leadership of the "Arab nationalist movement" have recently waned, tensions between regionalism and pan-Arabism, on the one hand, and secular nationalism and Islamic formulations, on the other, are still ripe and stimulate interest in the origins and growth of Arab nationalism. It is probable that the recent challenges to Turkish Republican nationalism from the Kurdish autonomist and Islamist movements will awaken interest in the essence and early manifestations of Turkish nationalism. Turning to the past with contemporary problems, though, poses the peril of "plundering the past." [9]

No reappraisal of Arab nationalism can start without reference to George Antonius's seminal work, *The Arab Awakening*.[10] For more than two decades after it was published in 1938, this account of an awakening, or *nahda*, constituted the definitive history of the Arab nationalist movement. Antonius placed the beginnings of Arab nationalism in the first half of the nineteenth century. He saw in the activities of a Beiruti literary and scientific society composed of liberal Arabs exposed to missionary influences, mostly Christians but also including Muslims, the first expression of national consciousness developing in response to long and oppressive Turkish domination. Relying on the testimony of postempire nationalists, he traced the progressive development of the Arab national idea from the mid–nineteenth century to World War I, culminating in the Arab Revolt of 1916, and beyond.

Our understanding of early Arab nationalism today is more accurate than the picture drawn by Antonius, thanks to the interest that a new generation of scholars rekindled during the sixties in the origins and content of Arab nationalism through research in works of Arab intellectuals, prosopography, and diplomatic sources. More recently, in the last two decades, scholars who have come to be known as the "revisionist" historians of Arab nationalism further refined our understanding of early Arab nationalism by promoting the research agenda in directions that included local archives and journalistic sources.

Zeine Zeine was the first to challenge Antonius's idea of a secular and liberal Arab awakening as well as the notion of a tyrannical Ottoman rule that catalyzed this nationalist awakening.[11] He accurately, though superficially, identified the role of Islam in the development of Arab political consciousness. He pointed to the allegiance of most Arabs to the Islamic caliphate embodied in the Ottoman sultans. According to Zeine, the critical phase in the development of Arab nationalism was the second constitutional period, when the overly secular Young Turks broke with established Ottoman practice and enforced Turkish nationalist policies. "[S]eparation was almost forced upon some Muslim Arab leaders by the short-sightedness and chauvinistic Pan-Turanian policy of the Young Turks."[12]

Albert Hourani[13] and A. L. Tibawi[14] further explored the origins of

Arab nationalist consciousness and substantiated Zeine's conclusions about its Islamic thrust. They questioned the political content and significance of the activities to which Antonius referred, as well as the latter's contention that the Arabs educated in missionary schools, where they acquired a secular and pro-Western outlook, were the forerunners of Arab nationalism. Hourani examined the ideas of Islamic modernist intellectuals of the late nineteenth century, which later ignited an Arab ethnic consciousness among the Muslim youth in the Arab provinces. The concern of the Islamic modernists with the glories of early Islam was conducive to an exaltation of the Arabs as the carriers of the Islamic faith. Islamic modernism was formulated as a response to imperialist encroachments and as such stressed Islamic unity against Europe. Therefore, while Islamic modernist ideas led to an enhanced Arab consciousness, this consciousness did not translate into a political agenda that undermined the legitimacy of the Ottoman state.

Hourani wrote that historically "there were no lines of exclusion which kept the Arabs out" of the Ottoman state and society.[15] He also analyzed the linkages between the Arab provinces and the Ottoman center, İstanbul, within his paradigm of the "politics of notables." He concluded that a large segment of Arab leaders became integrated into the Ottoman ruling elite during the Hamidian period, but subsequently, "under the Young Turks and then the Mandatory governments, the idea of Arab nationalism provided them with a new instrument of resistance."[16] Like Zeine's, this analysis suggested that the overthrow of the Hamidian regime by the Young Turks resulted in Arab alienation and, again, coupled with nationalistic policies of the CUP, politicized Arabism.

More recently, another historian of Arab nationalism, 'Abd al-'Aziz Duri, further focused on historical internal developments among Arabs. Duri corroborated Tibawi and Hourani's arguments with respect to the Muslim component of Arab nationalist consciousness. However, his stress on the formation of Arab identities in the early Islamic period undermined not only any decisive Western influence but also the long Ottoman legacy in the historical development of the Arab nation.[17] Thus, according to Duri, the Arab nation existed since the Prophet's time. It "gained momentum . . . when the Turks clearly displayed their inability to stand up to Europe, and similarly, when the Unionists introduced a grave provocation by opposing the Arab language and adopting a policy of Turkification."[18]

The most radical departure from these analyses is Ernest Dawn's. In a series of articles he began to write in 1958,[19] and in particular in his "Rise of Arabism in Syria,"[20] Dawn analyzed Arab nationalism in the second constitutional period in the context of a social conflict within the Damascene elite and as a function of the ability of the members of this elite to attain government positions. Dawn's two basic arguments are, first, that the ideological foundations of Arabism, which owed a lot to Islamic modernism, were well established before 1908 and cannot be viewed as a reaction to the Turkish nationalism of the CUP; and, second, Arabism failed to break out of the realm of narrow elite politics into a movement with popular appeal until the end of the empire.[21]

Dawn's views, in turn, have been questioned by Rashid Khalidi, who sees a growing middle class of merchants, intellectuals, and lower-level bureaucrats in Syrian cities during the second constitutional period as the vanguard of modern Arab nationalism.[22] Khalidi argues that Arab cities closer to the Mediterranean have been ignored by students of Arab nationalism, who have focused on Damascus, the traditional cultural center of the Arab world. He points to journalistic writing and consular reports from towns such as Jerusalem and particularly Beirut, which were experiencing rapid demographic and economic changes at the turn of the century, and argues that a public sphere conducive to the growth of popular Arabism was emergent in these urban centers.

Opinion differs as to the significance of the Arab movements before World War I. Dawn's revisionism about the scope and strength of Arabism has been noted in more recent scholarship.[23] In contrast, his conclusion about the unlikely role of Turkish nationalism in the development of Arab nationalism has not received similar attention. The view still prevails that the 1908 Revolution gave a most significant impetus to Turkish nationalism in the Ottoman polity, which in turn elicited a response in kind from the Arabs. To be sure, there is more recently the realization of the need to modify this view in two directions: by differentiating more precisely between Turkification and perceptions of centralization, and by focusing on the impact of European colonialism (on the rise during the Young Turk period) as another important factor in the growth of Arab nationalism.[24] In the absence of research in Ottoman sources, however, Turkish nationalism and "Turkification," as systematic policies of the Young Turk governments, have remained immune to serious revisionist scrutiny.

Critics of nationalist-minded historiography have not modified the prevailing common wisdom. With respect to the early modern period,

for instance, Rifaʿt ʿAli Abou-el-Haj aptly comments, "[W]e must research, think, and write less within the parameters of an inevitable but
exclusive nationalist model, and more along the lines of an inclusive,
universalist culture and society."[25] In the epilogue of his book, Abou-el-
Haj looks beyond the period he examines to remark, "The nineteenth
century Ottoman state took on other characteristics of the modern state,
including a new ideology, Ottomanism, an uneasy mix of the old ideology (Ottoman culture and Islam) and modern nationalism." He proceeds to conclude (and to converge with conventional wisdom), however, that "in the early twentieth century some Ottoman cultural
elements and Islamic elements were abandoned in favor of Turkism, a
more potent device based on an ethnic identity and dependent on a
language-based nationalism."[26]

It is reasonable to assume that the Western-oriented segments of the
Ottoman elite were drawn to the concept of the nation-state in the late
nineteenth and early twentieth centuries, but not in any ethnic sense.
Şerif Mardin argues that in their attempts "to build a state modeled after
the nation-state" these elites confronted three problems, all of which
"brought into play the relations of the center with the periphery": the
integration of non-Muslim peoples, the integration of the Muslim periphery (which consisted in large part of the Arab provinces), and the
incorporation of these two elements into a modern political system.[27]
The steady loss of largely non-Muslim-dominated regions made the integration of the Muslim periphery even more imperative. The creation
of an inclusive society and polity based on consensus rather than coer-
cion remained as the objective, to which an ethnic agenda would be
anathema.

Eric Hobsbawm describes "belonging to a lasting political entity" as
"the most decisive criterion of protonationalism."[28] The Young Turks
envisaged the creation of a civic-territorial, indeed revolutionary-
democratic, Ottoman political community by promoting an identification with the state and the country through the sultan and instituting
representative government. Though they remained committed to the
monarchy within the constitutional framework, they conceived of an
Ottoman state and society akin to the French example in which religion
and ethnicity would be supplanted by "state-based patriotism."[29] While
it would be easy to dismiss the notion of a voluntaristic "Ottoman nation" based on rights of representation at this juncture, a quest for political integration that was premised on such a conception was perhaps
not much more naive than were French revolutionary postulates about

integration, as analyzed by Eugene Weber.[30] The Young Turks did promote state-patriotism and clearly recognized the political risks, hinted
by Hobsbawm, of blending it with "non-state nationalism."[31]

As prototypes of what we recognize as Arab and Turkish
nationalism today, the terms Arabism and Turkism, despite (or perhaps
because of) their indeterminacy, have served a useful purpose in thinking about early forms of Arab and Turkish nationalism. It would, however, be useful to bring more clarity to these terms, particularly because
they do not have entirely parallel connotations.

The most common use of Arabism and Turkism is with respect to
Arab and Turkish cultural and literary sentiments and currents. Cultural
Arabism and Turkism, as they emerged in the late nineteenth century,
signified more than an articulation of the distinctness of Arab or Turkish
cultural markers. Rather, they represented the activation of cultural elements by intellectuals responding to social, political, and economic currents of the second half of the nineteenth century. Arabism and Turkism
resulted from the mobilization of latent as well as newly forged elements
of identity. Since Ernest Dawn identified Arabism as an oppositional
cultural-political identification to Ottomanism, historians have referred
to Arabism in describing a variety of political movements and currents
among Arabs short of demands for Arab sovereignty. The range of connotations that Turkism has conveyed, in contrast, has remained rather
narrow.

Arabism did not evolve into political nationalism during the period
under study. To argue this on the basis of Ernest Gellner's conception
of nationalism as "a principle which holds that the political and national
unit should be congruent"[32] would, of course, not be of much value in
studying the empire. Somewhat more nuanced is John Breuilly's conception that views a movement as a nationalist one if it seeks to secede
from the state, to take it over, or to unite it with another state.[33] Despite
their denunciation of the Ottoman government, viewed as Turkish and
Turkifying, most Arabists did not disavow the monarchy and lacked a
clear conception of the territorial basis of a national Arab unit. Nevertheless, Arabism was closely connected to politics. Even if one does not
subscribe to Dawn's instrumentalist representation of Arabism, its relationship to empire-wide political agendas needs to be appraised in
addressing it as Arab protonationalism.

Hobsbawm, who subscribes to a similar approach in the study of
nationalism as Gellner by privileging its relationship with the nation-

state, distinguishes three phases in the development of national movements (following Miroslav Hroch).[34] Phase A is "purely cultural, literary
and folkloric [with] no political or even national implications." In phase
B militants and activists engage in political propaganda to mobilize the
cultural group. Finally, in phase C "nationalist programmes acquire mass
support, or at least some of the mass support that nationalists always
claim they represent."[35]

The first phase of Arabism and Turkism in Hroch and Hobsbawm's
terms predated the second constitutional period. Starting in the late
nineteenth century there was an increased consciousness of an ethnic
community among the Muslim groups. On the one hand, readily iden-
tifiable (primordial) group attributes were activated under the influence
of enhanced communications, education, and commerce. On the other
hand, there was the formulation and embellishment of these group attributes as new constructs. This did not occur under the direct influence
of European cultural or political nationalism, rather as independent indigenous responses to reform and relative decline. Phase B of the Arab
movement started in the second constitutional period, spurred by new
freedoms of expression and beginnings of politics. Turkist trends in this
period lagged in the category of phase A. Extrapolations of Turkism in
the form of pan-Turkism did not impart to it a political content that had
relevance to imperial political realities. Arabism, on the other hand,
nourished political agendas that fit in with broader imperial patterns of
political contestation, though it did not engender a coherent exclusionary or separatist Arab nationalist program. Its proponents vied for political goals and enhanced recognition within the imperial system. Politicization of Arabism did not lead to nationalism in the sense defined
by Gellner or Breuilly, nor did it culminate in Hobsbawm's phase C.

This volume portrays the political, social, and ideological
currents in the Arab-populated periphery of the Ottoman Empire in
relation to transformations in the imperial center, İstanbul. It pursues
Ernest Dawn's critique of existing scholarship further and attempts to
nuance the inert view of the center shared by most scholars by intro-
ducing evidence about political contestation and shifting imperial alliances and their repercussions in several Arab provinces. The premise is,
first, that processes in İstanbul and Arab linkages to this center have
shaped Arab trends in important ways; and, second, that political and
social processes in the Arab areas contributed to imperial policy making

and ideology. Thus, this study seeks to move beyond established historiographical paradigms.

In general studies of the late Ottoman Empire, scholars have devoted very little attention to the Arab regions. Similarly, as mentioned above, the Arab regions have been studied with inadequate reference to the rest of the empire and to the issues confronting governments in İstanbul. The reason for this fragmentation has to do with particularist and nation-state oriented ideological preoccupations of historians and the implicit, but mistaken, assumption that the two approaches are complementary. An artificial compartmentalization of the subject matter has developed between Arabist and Ottomanist, which today is not just methodological but also ideological and is more rigid than the corresponding division of labor in nineteenth-century Orientalist scholarship. The implications of this dichotomy go beyond the study of the second constitutional period, but are particularly acute for this period, which many consider the critical and decisive phase of the unfolding of the history of Middle Eastern nation-states rather than the denouement of the history of empire.

Arab nationalism has so far been viewed exclusively from the vantage of the provinces, whereas it, too, should be examined with an integrative approach that takes into account both the local perspective and the central imperial one. The methodological concern here will not be with a particular Arab province, region, or town but with the entirety of those Arab-populated parts of the empire that were not colonized at the beginning of the second constitutional period. As it will be evident, this general approach is informed on the one hand by the scrupulous monographic studies of Arabists who have illuminated social and political trends in late Ottoman Damascus, Beirut, Hijaz, Iraq, Palestine, or Transjordan, and on the other by the work of Ottomanists who have examined the social, political, and economic history of the core regions of the empire. The present study makes inquiries into the power structure in İstanbul, the workings of Parliament, party politics, the ideological basis of the empire, and political and social change. Its central concern is to demonstrate the interactions between the center and the Arab periphery and to situate the genesis of nationalist currents among Ottoman Muslims in the imperial context. It makes use of documentation on the Arab provinces in the Ottoman archives, hitherto unexploited by Ottomanists or Arabists for reasons pertaining to problems of access and organization mentioned earlier.

A main proposition of this study is that among the chief Muslim groups of the Ottoman Empire political nationalism was not a viable force until the end of World War I. Appeals to religion, which constituted a significant component of individual nationalist ideologies, paradoxically prevented nationalism from becoming the primary focus of allegiance for Muslim peoples, and as such actually defused nationalism. It is further proposed that if Young Turk policies fostered the growth of Arab nationalism, it is more appropriate to seek the explanation in the processes of socialization that the revolution set in motion. The introduction of mass politics, a liberal press, and greater educational opportunities enhanced ethnic communal consciousness among certain groups, whereas they were promoted by the government with the purpose of achieving greater societal integration and administrative amalgamation. As Edward Shils has argued in his classic essay "Center and Periphery," processes of social and political integration on the one hand imparted "the central value system . . . a wider acceptance than in other periods of history," and on the other "increased the extent . . . of active 'dissensus' or rejection of this system."[36] Historians, particularly when their outlook is affected by nationalist biases, tend to focus on instances of "rejection" and conflict and not sufficiently on consent.

Chapter 1 examines the impact of the administrative, social, and political restructuring of the Tanzimat (1839–76) and Hamidian (1876–1908[37]) eras on the Arabs and the Arab provinces of the empire. In this period, Ottoman governments subscribed to different interpretations of Ottomanism as a supranationalist outlook transcending communal divisions and focusing on the institution of the sultanate-caliphate. The glimmerings of a cultural nationalist consciousness emerged in this period as a result of (1) the central government's attempts to project its rule to the imperial periphery, (2) the incorporation of the Ottoman economy to that of Europe, and (3) the entry of Western modes of thought as well as social and political organization. However, among Arabs *and* Turks this new consciousness failed to supersede the parochial allegiances on the one hand and the imperial-universalist ones on the other. Since the role of Arab deputies in Ottoman parliaments after 1908 is examined in some detail in later chapters, the short-lived Parliament of 1877–78, and Arab representation within it, is analyzed in the first chapter as a basis for comparison. In discussing the background to the second constitutional period, the opposition to Abdülhamid's regime is stressed, because it is from the ranks of this constitutionalist opposition that the political cadres and agendas of the second constitutional period emerged. Arab elements, particularly intellectuals and middle-class groups, were active in this opposition. Finally, the chapter's general examination of the Tanzimat and Hamidian eras illustrates not only the changes that came about after 1908 but also the often unnoticed continuities from the preceding era of reform.

The new conditions that the 1908 Revolution brought about in both the capital and the Arab provinces are dealt with in chapter 2. The revolution initiated a new level of political discourse with the reopening of Parliament and the lifting of restrictions on the press. The disappointment of unrealistic expectations, the inexperience of the CUP, and a unified effort of all opposition forces contributed to a counterrevolutionary movement that could be crushed only with the help of the army. The ensuing restrictions on certain freedoms and the initiation of a determined policy of centralization caused widespread unrest and resulted in the formation of political parties rival to the CUP and with significant Arab representation in them.

Centralizing administrative measures gave rise to accusations of a CUP-led "Turkification" campaign. The claim that the governments of the Committee of Union and Progress carried out a methodical policy of Turkification often goes together with the contention that they rendered support to extreme notions of Turkish nationalism and to fantastic schemes, such as a political union of all Turks throughout the world. In fact, the CUP subscribed to the supranational ideal of Ottomanism. There is no convincing evidence that it formulated or pursued a Turkish nationalist cultural or political program.

During 1910 and 1911 the CUP strengthened its control over the government machinery, while its liberal political opposition organized along party lines and formed a rival bloc in Parliament. A significant segment of Arab deputies was active in the ranks of this opposition. Chapter 3 addresses the issue of Turkification and the clash between the CUP and the opposition over central issues that concerned the Arabs and the Arab provinces: the concession to the British Lynch Company on the Tigris and Euphrates, Italian occupation of Libya, and Zionist immigration into Palestine.

In chapter 4, the reform movements in the Arab provinces are analyzed in the context of the political contest between the CUP and its decentralist rival, the Liberty and Entente Party, and with reference to growing Great Power interest in the Arab districts. After the CUP consolidated its power in 1913 and neutralized the reform movements in the Arab provinces, a new compromise was reached between İstanbul and the Arab leaders. It was accompanied by a growing emphasis on Islam in the ideology of an Ottoman state now much diminished in size as a result of the Balkan Wars (1912–13). The analysis here contrasts with the more widely accepted view that, following the Unionist takeover in 1913, Turkish nationalism played a growing role in the state ideology and that the Arab element was increasingly estranged. When Ottomanism, the secular state ideology that called for a multiethnic and multireligious empire in which political equality and representative government would foster an imperial allegiance, failed, the Young Turks did not turn to Turkish nationalism but rather to Islamism as the ideological underpinning that would safeguard the unity and continuity of what was left of the empire. Islam became the pillar of the supranational ideology of Ottomanism, with religion imparting a new sense of homogeneity and solidarity.

The province of the Hijaz is presented in chapter 5 as a case study of Young Turk rule in an Arab province. There are several reasons for choosing the Hijaz, a province that stands out from the other Arab provinces because of the differences in its social and political organization. The Hashemite family has received considerable attention because of Sharif Husayn's alliance with Britain, which influenced the shape that the Arab Middle East took in the aftermath of the war. Nevertheless, very little scholarly attention has been devoted to the study of the Hijaz as part of the Ottoman Empire. Sharif Husayn's term as emir of Mecca started with the Young Turk Revolution and continued until 1916. An assessment of his relations with the central government during this time illustrates the nature of the interaction between prominent local dignitaries and İstanbul and the thrust of İstanbul's centralizing policies and their provincial repercussions. The focus on the Hijaz also allows the examination of the increased attention given to religion in the formulation of political ideologies, not only at the center of the empire but also in the provinces.

The last chapter addresses the strains on the Arab policy that World War I ushered. On the eve of the war the CUP had established itself as unquestionably the strongest political group in the empire. Once the war broke out, Sharif Husayn initiated the Arab Revolt (which "Lawrence of Arabia" and his fans later helped to popularize and romanticize around the world), because Husayn felt that rendering support to the Ottoman government would lead to his political demise given the empire's weak defenses against the British in the Red Sea. The Arab Revolt was not so much the culmination of Arab nationalist activity or a rejection of the refashioned Ottomanist ideology, but a convergence of dynastic ambition and strategic exigency that contributed to the eventual political separation of Arabs and Turks.[38] Husayn's revolt under British promises of an independent Arab state and the hardships arising from the war embittered the relations between the Unionist government and the Arabs. Once the empire had disintegrated and the European powers had imposed their will in the reshaping of former Ottoman territories contrary to the wishes of the indigenous peoples, Turks and Arabs sought renewed possibilities for cooperation. A significant portion of the Arab elites in towns like Damascus, Beirut, and Jerusalem hesitated before embracing Arab nationalism. The consequences of Anglo-French victory were to prove anything but sweet for the Arabs, who were forced to confront the prospects of direct European rule. The potency of the supranational ideology of Ottomanism is reappraised in this chapter against the background of imperial collapse and foreign occupation.

Arabs and Arab Provinces in the Evolution of the Young Turk Movement

Islamic cultural and political traditions with a strong Arab imprint had guided the Ottoman state since its foundation in western Anatolia in the thirteenth century and during its subsequent expansion into southeastern Europe. The Arabs themselves, however, entered the stage of Ottoman history in the sixteenth century, first with Sultan Selim I's (r. 1512–20) conquest of Egypt and Syria in 1516–17, and then with Sultan Süleyman's (r. 1520–66) campaigns to Mesopotamia starting in 1534, followed by his establishment of Ottoman suzerainty over most of North Africa and the Arabian Peninsula. The extension of Ottoman rule to the Arab lands may have had a greater impact on the conquerors than the conquered. For the Arabs, the conquest signified the replacement of one Muslim dynasty by another and the superimposition of imperial authority over local authority. For the Ottoman state, however, it meant a role as a world empire, dominating intercontinental trade routes and coming into contact with new imperial rivals, the Portuguese in the southern seas and the Safavids to the east in Iran.

The conquest of the historic heartlands of Islam and the symbolic establishment of suzerainty over the Muslim holy places in Arabia reinforced the religious ideological underpinnings of the Ottoman state, now ruling over a predominantly Muslim realm.[1] The Arab lands became an integral, though not entirely well-integrated, part of a Muslim Ottoman imperial system. In the seventeenth and eighteenth centuries, with regional variations, local families or provincial potentates maintained local authority, but often they recognized the sultan's overlordship and sought his protection against rivals or external foes.[2] Even as territorial losses occurred in Europe at this time, Ottoman suzerainty prevailed in the Arab world despite sporadic challenges.

In the nineteenth century Sultan Mahmud II (r. 1808–39) undertook a set of institutional changes to forestall domestic and international threats to the integrity of the Ottoman state. Mahmud's policies gave renewed emphasis to centralization and entailed a conscious commitment to restructure Ottoman institutions on a Western pattern. In the late 1830s a series of institutional changes collectively known as the *Tanzimat* [3] accelerated the processes of centralization and Westernization in the empire, as a reform-minded group of high-level officials took the reins of government in İstanbul. They endeavored to concentrate all political, financial, and military power in a refurbished bureaucracy. Centralization, they hoped, would arrest the demands for autonomy and bring all imperial possessions under İstanbul's direct rule for firmer political and economic control. Enhanced European involvement in the empire's economy, as ensured with trade treaties after 1838, reinforced Western interests in Ottoman territorial integrity above and beyond those dictated by balance-of-power considerations.

Tanzimat Centralization, Arabs, and Ottomanism

The Gülhane Decree of 1839 gave the empire's non-Muslims legal status equal to Muslims, and Ottoman statesmen expected—in vain—that this concession would reinforce the loyalty of the traditionally autonomous non-Muslim communities to the state. Instead, the Western powers quickly made use of their newly strengthened extraterritorial rights, known as the capitulations, to promote Christian merchants as their protégés and secure for them tax exemptions and immunity from the due process of Ottoman law. In the predominantly Christian-populated Balkan Peninsula the centralizing measures of the Tanzimat, particularly in the sphere of taxation, contributed to social unrest and nationalist movements.[4]

In the Muslim areas of the empire, including the Arab provinces, the political and economic dislocations that centralization and Western economic penetration caused did not have immediate nationalist or separatist implications. The Tanzimat policies expedited the integration of the provinces into the central administration. In the Asian provinces, as in the Balkans, the local notables who controlled the land resented the Tanzimat regulations. However, they found ways of promoting their interests in the newly founded provincial councils.[5] The predominance of local power continued within a centralizing administrative system that in the beginning provided for the appointment of provincial governors with limited powers.[6] Even as the 1838 treaty hurt Muslim trade, and secular Westernizing reforms (along with the enhanced status of non-Muslim groups) reflected negatively on the sultan's image as the binding force of an Islamic empire, Muslims questioned neither the unity of the empire nor Islam as its source of legitimacy. In 1864 a more confident leadership in İstanbul reorganized the provincial administration to strengthen the provincial governors, and the notables lost some of their political prerogatives and autonomy. When in the 1880s Sultan Abdülhamid (r. 1876–1909) imposed his personal authority on the government and further reinforced centralization, many local notables were forced to seek new ways of preserving or recovering their power and prestige by linking it to the central administration.

In contrast to the gradual transformation in the provinces, the bureaucratic machinery in İstanbul underwent fundamental reorganization early in the Tanzimat. The balance of power within the ruling elite resolved itself in favor of a group of reformist high-level bureaucrats, who made use of resources at hand in staffing the expanding bureaucracy. The imperial capital had long been a cosmopolis where people of various ethnic and religious backgrounds intermingled and assimilated into the Ottoman imperial culture. Its population, educationally more advanced compared with the rest of the empire, was exposed to European political, economic, and cultural influences, and thus provided the human resources needed for an expanding bureaucracy committed to Westernization. Most Tanzimat men were İstanbul-born, and many were sons of prominent officials,[7] even if the families derived from elsewhere. The more prominent statesmen started their careers in the Translation Bureau, a creation of Mahmud II and a breeding ground for reformers, where they received their language training and basic experience in government service.

Despite diminishing opportunities for mobility, it was theoretically possible for any Ottoman with some formal education to join and rise in the ranks of the civil service.[8] Social position was helpful to the extent that it facilitated access to the dispensers of patronage, but those on the lower rungs of the social ladder were not categorically denied opportunities for advancement.[9] A difference in education and training more than social background set the Tanzimat men apart from the members of the pre-Tanzimat ruling elite and distanced them further from the common people.[10]

Arabs were conspicuously absent in top government positions throughout Ottoman history, and the processes of elite recruitment during the Tanzimat reproduced the preexisting trend. According to Danişmend, of 215 Ottoman grand viziers (prime ministers) none is known to be Arab, although 3 "may have been," as compared to seventy-eight Turks and thirty-one Albanians. The roster of *kaptan-ı derya*s (admirals of the fleet) includes no Arabs, that of *başdefterdar*s (chief finance officers) one, and that of *reisülküttab*s (chief secretary–foreign ministers) four.[11] Although Muslim Arabs were traditionally prominent in the judicial administration of the empire,[12] the upper echelons of this religious hierarchy, too, were occupied by those trained in İstanbul and connected to high offices.[13] Moreover, the gradual secularization of the legal system starting with the Tanzimat undermined the role of the ulema, the religious scholars and officials, though many ulema proved to be resilient in the face of these changes, and those close to government gave their imprimatur to new laws.[14]

It is impossible to appraise the degree of representation of the various Muslim ethnic groups in the Ottoman bureaucracy. Official sources do not indicate the ethnic background of Muslim government functionaries, as the ethnicity of a Muslim had no pertinence in the Ottoman polity. Reliable means of ascertaining ethnic roots of Muslim officials do not exist; and even where there is ample biographical information, the criteria used in classification tend to be subjective.[15] Danişmend's classification is no exception. For example, he apparently does not view the two grand viziers of the second constitutional period, Mahmud Shawkat Pasha and Sa'id Halim Pasha, as Arabs. Both men were Ottomans with a principal Arab cultural affinity. Mahmud Shawkat was the scion of a Georgian family who had settled in Baghdad, and Sa'id Halim was a grandson of the Egyptian khedive Muhammad 'Ali. The ambiguity in the following authoritative description of as celebrated a personality in Arab history as Muhammad 'Ali points to the extraneousness of queries pertaining to ethnicity: "an obscure Turk from the city of Kavala [in Albania] (although some believe he was a Kurd)."[16]

Inferences from scant data and educated guesses about the ethnic background of Muslim government officials in the Ottoman service run the risk of imputing to the Ottoman political elite a prejudice of which it was not conscious. If the Tanzimat leaders did at all address themselves to the concept of equality of opportunity, what they had in mind was equality in rights and duties between Muslims and non-Muslims only.[17] Arab underrepresentation in the Ottoman central bureaucracy may be explained by historical factors such as the relatively late incorporation of the Arab provinces into the empire; the effective closure of one avenue of elite integration due to the gradual obsolescence of the *timar*[18] system by the time of the conquests of Arab lands;[19] the distance of the Arab regions from the capital; and the continuation of autonomous rule, particularly in tribal areas.

While the Tanzimat created a central bureaucratic elite keenly aware of its interests as a group and increasingly more independent of royal power, the provinces felt the impact of the reorganization only gradually. Many regions of the empire, including wide areas inhabited by Arabs, were not touched by İstanbul's reform measures until the second half of the nineteenth century. Yet, it was not solely via İstanbul that the provinces opened up to Western influences and ideas of reform. European merchants had penetrated some Arab lands long before the Tanzimat reformers. Syria had already experienced a period of reform under Egyptian rule. The region's early contacts with the West later affected the cultural and political life of the province. Trade, missionary activity, and emigration had exposed Mediterranean Arab towns to European culture and modern political ideals and brought about a climate of opinion sympathetic to what the Tanzimat stood for.

Cairo, autonomous under Muhammad 'Ali since the first decade of the nineteenth century, had a head start on İstanbul in acquiring a first-hand knowledge of European ideas, administrative ways, and technological advances. It implemented its own version of Tanzimat, as thinkers like Rafi' al-Tahtawi gave ideological expression to political and social change brought about by Muhammad 'Ali's policies. Further west in Tunis, a semiautonomous province of the empire closely linked to Europe, a Tunisian high-level bureaucrat took a keen interest in modernization. Khayr al-Din Pasha, who was Circassian by origin but culturally an Arab, praised and emulated the Tanzimat policies and statesmen before actually entering the service of the central government.[20]

The Tanzimat also had adherents in Arab provinces under the direct control of İstanbul. Yusuf al-Khalidi has been described as "a Palestinian representative of the Tanzimat."[21] He was born in 1842 to the Khalidi family, one of the oldest notable families in Palestine. Yusuf went to İstanbul to attend the medical school and the newly founded American Robert College before he returned to Jerusalem at the age of twenty-four. He secured a decree from the *vali* (governor) of Syria to set up a secular Tanzimat-style *rüşdiye* (middle school) in Jerusalem. After a nine-year career as president of the reorganized municipality of Jerusalem, he was appointed to the Translation Bureau. He served as consul in the Russian town of Poti before he returned to Jerusalem in 1875. In İstanbul, both Yusuf and his brother Yasin had close links with the Ottoman reformers, particularly Foreign Minister Raşid Pasha, who was born and raised in Egypt;[22] and the Khalidi family acquired a reputation as adherents of the "reform party."[23] A contemporary of Yusuf al-Khalidi was Khalil Ghanem, a Maronite Christian Arab from Beirut. As an employee in Beirut's provincial administration, Ghanem attracted Governor Esat Pasha's attention. Esat's patronage won Ghanem a job as translator at the grand vizierate, after Esat's promotion to that office.[24] He assisted Midhat Pasha in drafting the constitution.[25] Like Yusuf al-Khalidi, Khalil Ghanem was elected to the First Parliament in 1877. He was later to play a crucial role in the incipient Young Turk movement.

Neither Khalidi nor Ghanem nor any other bureaucrats of Arab descent, however, could break into the inner circle of the Tanzimat leadership, which remained restricted to a small group of İstanbul officials of an older generation. Like most political aspirants of their generation in İstanbul, these Arab functionaries were relegated to secondary positions by high-level bureaucrats who had consolidated their power at the critical juncture after Sultan Mahmud's death. Thus, it came as no surprise that Yusuf al-Khalidi and Khalil Ghanem later distinguished themselves in the Parliament of 1877–78 by their strong criticism of the government and opposition to senior statesmen.

A literary and political group that coalesced in the capital under the name of New Ottomans (better known as Young Ottomans) in 1867 embodied the main organized opposition to the Tanzimat regime. This group came into existence as the decline of Muslim trade and onerous foreign loans brought the Ottoman economy to the brink of collapse. Its grievances centered on the personal rule of a small bureaucratic elite, excessive foreign interference in the political and economic affairs of the empire, and European cultural domination. The Young Ottomans shared the Western orientation and social and professional background of the Tanzimat leaders. They criticized, however, the oligarchic Tanzimat elite for adopting only the superficial aspects of Western culture instead of its political institutions and principles.

The Young Ottomans insisted that reforms had to be consistent with the precepts of Islamic law (*şeriat* or *sharia*).[26] They advocated the establishment of constitutional government in the Ottoman Empire and argued that Islam, with its emphasis on consultation (*meşveret*), not only justified but called for parliamentary government. The Young Ottomans wrote profusely on constitutionalism, freedom, and patriotism, both in İstanbul and in European exile, where the London-based newspaper *Hürriyet* (Liberty) was their principal organ. While their liberal ideas reached only few in the provinces, sympathetic provincial officials assigned from İstanbul gradually transmitted and promoted their teachings.[27] Due to the absence of a cohesive political organization, the potential of the Young Ottoman movement remained unfulfilled until its ideas found sympathizers among a new generation of statesmen in the Tanzimat tradition.

Later in the nineteenth century, some Arab intellectuals stressed Islamic ideas in a different modernist vein. Their forerunner Muhammad ʿAbduh and his disciples, many from the ulema (unlike the prominent Young Ottomans), addressed more systematically the compatibility of liberal ideas with Islam. ʿAbduh's Islamic modernism (*salafiyya*) developed in response to similar social, economic, and political grievances that had nourished Young Ottoman thought (though Young Ottoman influences on this Arab movement have not been established). The *salafiyya* modernism flourished in Egypt and Syria in the post-Tanzimat period, thus also addressing the political and social malaise of the Hamidian period and intersecting with the later phase of the liberal movement against Abdülhamid.[28]

In addition to the Islamic modernist trend, the Tanzimat engendered the growth of a secular movement in Syria led by Christian intellectuals under the auspices of the Syrian Scientific Society, founded in 1857, and hailed by Antonius as "the first outward manifestation of a collective national consciousness" and "the cradle of a new political movement."[29] The society exalted the Arab race and language, possibly inspired by the romantic nationalist current in Europe. One of its Christian leaders, Butrus Bustani,[30] gave expression to the notion of a Syrian fatherland, but the society did not seek to rally the Syrian people around a sociopolitical platform, nor did it espouse secessionist aims, despite its criticism of the government. It remained as a secular literary society until the civil conflict of 1860 brought an end to its activities.[31]

Antonius also suggests that missionary schools, which many Christian leaders of the Syrian Scientific Society attended, promoted an interest in the Arabic language and thus helped kindle the flame of Arab nationalism. Arabic was emphasized in the missionary curriculum in order to attract students from different segments of Syrian society, but this effort had little success in attracting Muslims until later in the century.[32] Muslims preferred to send their children to new government schools that competed with the missionary secondary schools and offered instruction in Ottoman.[33]

The state schools represented a social institution that contributed to the beginnings of a civic allegiance. The Tanzimat principle of political equality begot the concept of Ottomanism, a common allegiance of all subjects in equal status to the Ottoman dynasty. Tanzimat Ottomanism was premised on a reciprocity between the subject and the state but was not upheld by integrative political institutions. Nevertheless, formal equality before the law, coupled with secular restructuring of social institutions and centralization, provided the framework upon which an identification with country and people that transcended the immediate corporate group could be built by stressing the powerful symbol of the dynasty of a historical political entity.

The Young Ottomans infused the Tanzimat notion of Ottomanism with an ideological component that was intended to strengthen the relationship of the subject to the state.[34] Indeed, in 1869 a citizenship law was passed that posited Ottoman subjects as Ottoman citizens. The Young Ottomans also promoted the concepts of legal representation and popular sovereignty that would erode the intercommunal divisions within the empire and focus the loyalty of Muslim and Christian alike on a geographical fatherland comprising Ottoman territories as well as on the ruling Ottoman dynasty. Having provided an Islamic basis to their ideas, the Young Ottomans believed that their vision of the Ottoman state would be readily acceptable to Turks and Arabs, while non-Muslim groups would be "bound by common interests to the common fatherland."[35] The constitution of 1876 was a consummation, as well as a test, of the Young Ottomans' notion of Ottomanism.

The Constitution, Parliament, and
Arab Representation

As domestic and international crises intensified in the mid-1870s, a group of high-level bureaucrats, influenced by Young Ottoman thought and led by former grand vizier and president of the State Council, Midhat Pasha, saw a constitutional regime as the new hope for reform, revival, and indeed survival.[36] Emboldened by their ability to manipulate the sultans in the crisis of succession in 1876, they prevailed upon the new sultan Abdülhamid to approve a constitution that called for a parliament.[37]

The new charter was not the product of a popularly elected representative assembly. The members of the First Parliament, which convened in March 1877, were determined, as stipulated in the provisional electoral regulations, by previously elected provincial administrative councils instead of popular suffrage.[38] Once Parliament opened, the outbreak of war with Russia and the defeats incurred paralyzed the government machinery and also required that caution and restraint be exercised in parliamentary proceedings.[39] The constitution had left Parliament at the mercy of the sultan, and the war provided him with the excuse to prorogue the assembly in 1878.

Despite its shortcomings, the constitutional experiment of 1876–78 was a landmark in late Ottoman history. It whetted appetites for constitutional rule that Abdülhamid could neither satisfy nor successfully suppress. Until 1908 the demand for the restoration of the constitution and Parliament served as a focal point that crystallized and unified the liberal opposition to the sultan.

The Parliament of 1877–78 deserves attention on the basis of its own merits, notwithstanding its short life and lack of concrete achievements. It served as a forum in which the Ottomanist ideal found expression. Elite and upper-middle-class provincial representatives from diverse parts of the empire came together for the first time to discuss issues varying from the appropriate official language of the empire to provincial reorganization, freedom of the press, tax collection, and Westernization.[40] Blocs not tied to religious and ethnic lines emerged. It was the scene of sophisticated deliberations on imperial and local issues in which government policy could be criticized—at times vehemently. The deputies from the Arab provinces were some of the most vocal, and often critical, in the Chamber of Deputies.[41]

Parliamentary government inducted the Arab provincial elites into the political vicissitudes of the capital. This first rudimentary experiment with participatory politics provides a reference point to situate the Arab provinces and Arabs in the imperial context toward the end of the nineteenth century.

Of the 232 incumbencies during the two terms of the First Parliament,[42] 32 belonged to Arabs.[43] The Arab provinces of Aleppo and Syria, historically better incorporated into the empire because of their proximity to the center and their commercial importance, were slightly overrepresented in relation to their respective populations. In contrast, Baghdad, Basra, and Tripoli (Libya) were underrepresented.[44] The *sancak* (subprovince) of Lebanon was invited to send deputies, but declined to do so to underscore the special autonomous status (*mümtaz mutasarrıflık*) that it had obtained in the aftermath of the civil strife of 1860–61. There is no evidence that any of the Muslim deputies from the Arab provinces were not Arab,[45] although at least one of the Christian deputies representing the Arab provinces was not.[46]

The Arab deputies were among the youngest members of the Chamber.[47] This suggests that the Arab notables in the provinces viewed parliamentary government as an experimental venture, one for which local position should not be sacrificed. The choices of administrative councils fell on younger members of leading families, who often had a modern education and familiarity with the new order in İstanbul. At the beginning of the second session in December 1877, Nafi' al-Jabiri of Aleppo was twenty-nine; Khalil Ghanem, now a deputy from Beirut, was thirty-two; and Ziya al-Khalidi, who had left his position as the head of the Jerusalem municipality to come to İstanbul, was thirty-five.[48] Khalidi vehemently attacked in one of the earliest meetings of the Chamber the principle of seniority so entrenched in the Ottoman social and political tradition.[49] He argued that the ablest rather than the oldest should be brought to leadership positions within Parliament, and he added that the young were better educated and more predisposed to liberal and constitutional ideas than the old, who held on to outmoded ones.

Khalidi's young, urban, professional outburst took the assembly by surprise and set the tone of his radicalism in the Chamber.[50] Nafi', and in the second session Khalil Ghanem, joined him. The three emerged as the staunchest supporters of the new parliamentary regime and sought to strengthen the position of the Chamber of Deputies vis-à-vis the

cabinet. Yusuf Ziya proposed that an absolute majority replace the stipulated two-thirds majority to enable the Chamber to interpellate a minister.[51] He declared that the cabinet circumvented the constitution in
appealing to the sultan in the case of a disagreement between it and the
Chamber.[52] He also criticized the censorship of the minutes.[53]

Khalil Ghanem, in turn, attacked the government for using the war
with Russia to temper its parliamentary opposition. In his early
speeches, Ghanem exposed the contradiction in the government's foreign policy when he inquired why the ostensible allies of the Ottoman
state, namely England and France, were not coming to its aid.[54] On a
later occasion, he pointed to procedural bottlenecks and complained that
Parliament's procrastination in passing reform legislation brought the
interference and pressure of foreign powers upon the state.[55] Khalil Ghanem did not refrain from attacking the government, and indirectly the
sultan, on the sensitive issues of the banishment of Midhat Pasha and
the imposition of the state of siege.[56] He argued that the emergency
powers only served the government to neutralize its domestic opposition.

Nafi', the only deputy elected to both the 1877 and 1908 Parliaments,
was from the prominent religious family of the Jabiris and the son of
the *müftü* of Aleppo. He thus differed in background and outlook from
the other two. He was in agreement with Ghanem on most issues but
was less vituperative in his criticism. He condemned the government
with regard to the state of siege, disapproved of the arbitrary banishment
of religious students, but made no mention of Midhat.[57] Nafi' became
the first deputy to offer an interpellation in Parliament when he called
on the minister of finance to provide an explanation of the general conditions and the prospects of the government's finances. In December
1877, when the Russian fleet seized an Ottoman commercial vessel in
the Black Sea, Nafi' offered a second interpellation[58] and took the minister of the navy to task.[59] He displayed a militant position on the subject
of interpellations, arguing that ministers should not be informed about
the subject matter of the interpellation prior to their appearance in the
assembly.[60] Meanwhile, he defended the rulings of the *şeriat*, opposed
any criticism of the sultan,[61] and disapproved of the secularization of
regulations governing property ownership, inheritance, and disposal.[62]

While Yusuf Ziya al-Khalidi, Khalil Ghanem, and Nafi' al-Jabiri were
among the most active and outspoken deputies in Parliament, several
other deputies from the Arab provinces distinguished themselves by
their extensive participation. They were Sa'di and Manuk of Aleppo;

'Abd al-Razzaq of Baghdad; and Nikula Naqqash, Nawfal, and 'Abd al-Rahim Badran of Syria. It was not uncommon for the Arab deputies to dominate the floor, even in discussions that did not directly or exclusively concern the Arab provinces.[63] The Arab representatives did not act as a bloc,[64] but the deputies from Aleppo and from Syria taken as a group participated in the proceedings more actively than perhaps any other provincial contingent. Even the Hijazi deputies, unlike their counterparts thirty years later, expressed themselves frequently.[65]

The deputies representing the Arab provinces articulated local concerns regularly and elaborately. A petition submitted by Manuk Karaja shows the specific nature of the demands that were made for reform in a province: the opening of a bank in Aleppo, the building of a road between two locations in the province, the elimination of swamp lands in Alexandretta, the setting up of a commercial court in the same town, and even the transportation of a broken bridge from İstanbul's Galata district to Birecik (near Aleppo) for installation over the Euphrates.[66] On different occasions the Iraqi deputies pointed to the exceptional land regime of Iraq and questioned the applicability of land reforms in their province.[67] Further appeals of Arab deputies for their constituencies often applied to other provinces as well. For instance, Nawfal voiced the Syrians' concern about personal security after the mobilization of the police forces for the war effort and asked for a local militia to be formed as a security force.[68] Badran referred to the same problem, asserting that the common people were indifferent to most legislative issues, such as the press law then before Parliament, but were first and foremost worried about their security.[69]

There were no clear common interests or an "Arab idea" that unified and distinguished the Arab deputies. They seemed to perceive themselves as the representatives of the empire in its entirety, and beyond that their interest was for their immediate constituencies. The issue of the creation of a new province of Beirut underscored the primacy of parochial rather than "Arab" or regional (e.g., Syrian) concerns. Beirut's deputies demanded the carving out of a province, with its center in Beirut, from the existing province of Syria (*Suriye* or *Şam* [Damascus]), pointing to the commercial and diplomatic importance of the city and to its distance and separation from Damascus, the Syrian provincial center. The remainder of the deputies of the province of Syria and Aleppo's deputies indicated that the creation of a new administrative center, sought by the Beiruti delegates in the expectation of boosting local commerce, would be costly for the imperial treasury. They also played down the distance between the two cities, especially now that the two were telegraphically linked.[70] Parliament closed without resolving Beirut's bid, as it had with most matters that had come before it.

After Abdülhamid prorogued Parliament in the spring of 1878, ten deputies regarded as dangerous were ordered to leave İstanbul for their hometowns.[71] Half of these were from the Arab provinces: Yusuf Ziya (Jerusalem), Ghanem (Syria), Nafi' (Aleppo), Manuk (Aleppo), and Badran (Syria). None of the ten were charged with a specific offense. The Council of Ministers sent a note to the sultan containing vague accusations about these deputies' actions against the state and the sultan. Yusuf Ziya complained about the arbitrary action taken against him and the other deputies in a letter that he wrote to the grand vizier and former president of Parliament, Ahmed Vefik Pasha. He sent a copy of the letter to the *Levant Herald* with a postscript: "As you can see half of the [implicated] including myself are Arabs,"[72] suggesting the action taken had something to do with their ethnic affiliation.

There is no indication that these deputies were regarded as dangerous because it was feared that they would foment ethnic divisiveness among Arabs. The Arab deputies did not express their criticism in Parliament in ethnic or national terms, either individually or as a group, nor did they hint at autonomist aspirations. They did at times voice regional grievances, as did deputies from other regions and provinces. The initiative coming from the Arab contingent to separate Beirut as a new provincial center could have only furthered the fragmentation of the administrative unity of Syria. In any case, Abdülhamid could hardly be accused of an anti-Arab bias. One Arab deputy, 'Abd al-Qadir al-Qudsi, representing the rival faction to the Jabiris in Aleppo, entered the sultan's service after the closure of Parliament and subsequently became his second secretary.[73]

Such regional and local grievances, however, if couched in strong terms, could be perceived as harmful to the integrity of the state. Indeed, such an outburst was probably responsible for the inclusion of 'Abd al-Rahim Badran in the ranks of the banished. In January 1878 Badran began his speech on conditions in Syria by saying that the liberties guaranteed by the constitution were meaningless unless accompanied by equality, which, he claimed, existed only on paper. When he asked rhetorically, "Has anyone from Syria attained in the last six hundred years the office of the grand vizier, *şeyhülislam*, or minister of finance?"[74] he was stopped by the president and accused of encouraging divisiveness.

Abdülhamid prorogued Parliament in order to eliminate political opposition to his rule. It is unlikely that he felt intimidated by the threat of separatism in the Arab provinces. The deputies had proved to be more independent and daring than he was prepared to tolerate, and he took action against the most outspoken. The Arabs among them had posed a threat, not because of any links with a potentially subversive or divisive Arab cause, but because they were articulate in their criticism of government policy at all levels. The fact that the government sent these deputies back to Syria at a time when it knew that there was a movement with separatist tendencies afoot in Beirut[75] also demonstrates that the government regarded their presence in İstanbul to be more troublesome than their presence in Syria.

Parliament, on the whole, functioned in the spirit that the Young Ottomans had envisaged. The deputies were not submissive, as Abdülhamid no doubt had hoped that they would be once he had secured extensive royal prerogatives in the constitution; nor did they use the Chamber as a forum to pursue particularistic or separatist aims. Instead, the deputies concerned themselves with broad issues and expressed opinions on the workings of the state machinery, sharply criticizing the government, and indirectly the sultan. They pressed for legislative rights that the constitution did not accord to them and impeached ministers,[76] in one case forcing the sultan to dismiss the grand vizier, Ahmed Hamdi Pasha.[77]

Russian belligerence and the apparent international isolation of the empire in the aftermath of the crisis of the 1870s were partly responsible for the energy, courage, and patriotism of the deputies. Ironically, it was the war with Russia that offered Abdülhamid the pretext to prorogue the Parliament. Having disposed of it, the sultan was ready to establish his personal rule.

The Hamidian Era: Continuity and Change

Many Muslims were unmoved by the Tanzimat expression of Ottomanism that upheld the political equality of all subjects and robbed them of the psychological crutch that "Muslim superiority" provided. The Young Ottoman opposition did not bear fruits that assured most Muslims. The essence of the Young Ottoman political agenda, justified on Muslim religious grounds, was a constitutional government based on some form of popular representation. While the constitution was eventually achieved, it granted disproportionately high representation to non-Muslims in an attempt to defuse Christian separatism and satisfy the European protectors of the empire's Christians.

Abdülhamid envisaged a different relationship with his subjects, one based on the newly forged aura of the institution of the caliphate rather than on a contractual agreement inspired by Europe. He knew that most Muslim Ottomans were indifferent to a parliamentary regime. He attracted many provincial notables to the capital in order to co-opt them into his centralized rule, and he upheld their economic and sociopolitical interests only in return for their support of his centralizing policy. Meanwhile, he checked the power of the high-level bureaucrats by diffusing and circumscribing their authority and keeping them under the close surveillance of the Palace and the police.

The Ottomanism of the Young Ottomans was a belated ideology that failed to curb or forestall the dismemberment of Ottoman territories. Abdülhamid placed a new emphasis on Islam and his personal religious role as caliph. Yet his Islamism neither negated nor superseded Ottomanism. In Hamidian Islamism as well as in Ottomanism, as it emerged and underwent transformation since the Tanzimat, the focus of loyalty was the Ottoman sultan. Both ideologies stressed the notion of a "fatherland," the geographic expression of which was the territories under the sultan's jurisdiction.

Abdülhamid's Islamism was Ottomanism equipped with ideological embellishment deriving from Islam. It served to justify autocratic rule and contributed to foreign policy objectives. It has been described as a pragmatic policy that availed of Islamic symbols and upheld the Ottoman state's Islamic identity and the Muslim subjects' morale following losses in war.[78] After the Balkan secessions in the 1870s, Muslims constituted a greater percentage of the Ottoman population. The new demographic situation and the subsequent loss of further Muslim-populated Ottoman provinces to imperialism made it politic to emphasize the religious overtones of Ottomanism. Hamidian Islamism was not expansionist, despite what the term (and particularly the expression pan-Islamism, often used interchangeably with Islamism) suggests. It did not entail a novel definition of the fatherland; nor did it jeopardize the legal status and rights that the non-Muslims had gained under the secular Ottomanism of the preceding decades, though clearly Hamidian ideology was exclusionary from a social and psychological point of view with respect to non-Muslims. What makes Islamism politically important was that it gained ascendancy in opposition to the political interests of the European powers that traditionally had abetted Ottoman territorial integrity. Indeed, Islamism was the child of changing international and economic relations in Europe and the position that the Ottoman Empire acquired in the neoimperialist status quo. It had wide domestic implications which were strongly felt in the Arab provinces of the empire.

The ground had already been laid during the Tanzimat for a forward policy in the Arab regions. In the general scheme of provincial reform and reorganization, the Arab provinces had received special attention for several reasons. The government was interested in exercising direct control over the international commercial centers of Aleppo and Damascus and the port cities of the eastern Mediterranean. Ottoman positions in Syria and the Arabian Peninsula needed to be strengthened militarily against possible aggression from Egypt.[79] Moreover, the administration of the provinces of the Fertile Crescent had to be improved to preclude the possibility of European aggression with the pretext of intervening on behalf of any of the non-Muslim communities.

The distance of the Arab provinces from the administrative center of the empire, and their large nomadic populations, posed difficulties in the implementation of the centralizing policies. Therefore, İstanbul sent some of its ablest administrators to the Fertile Crescent as governors.[80] Also during the Tanzimat, the state enhanced its military presence in the Arab provinces. The reorganization of the Ottoman army allotted major army corps to Syria and Baghdad and separate units to Yemen and Libya,[81] though the attempts to recruit local Arabs for the regular armies had only limited success.[82] While the strength of Ottoman military force fluctuated during the Tanzimat, the armies served as a deterrent to local, especially Beduin, insurrection and raiding and assured more efficient tax collection.[83]

The army also helped to bring some of the outlying areas of the Arabian Peninsula under direct Ottoman rule, aided by the extension of the telegraph to Baghdad in 1861.[84] Before Abdülhamid ascended the throne, both al-Hasa in eastern Arabia and the Yemen had been occupied by the Ottoman forces. Sultan Abdülhamid continued the extension of Ottoman authority into Arabia and surpassed his predecessors in expanding communications. The Arab provinces were now designated as first rank and listed ahead of European or Anatolian provinces in official registers, and their governors were granted higher salaries.[85] The sultan built the Hijaz Railway, which connected the holy city of Medina with Damascus, and extended telegraphic communication parallel to the railway, ensuring the organization of the pilgrimage under his close supervision and thus adding to his prestige as leader of Islam.

The flourishing diplomatic connection with Germany, to which the sultan had turned to provide a counterweight to the neoimperialist aggressiveness of Britain and France, induced further attention to the East. The İstanbul-Baghdad railway scheme, prompted by Germany's economic and strategic interests, fit in with Abdülhamid's policy of leading a more active policy near the Persian Gulf, especially now that Britain was acquiring footholds in the area.[86] Germany favored and pressed for an even greater emphasis by the empire on Eastern policy than Abdülhamid envisaged. The head of the German military mission in İstanbul, Colmar von der Goltz, suggested in 1897 that the Ottoman capital should be moved to central Anatolia or possibly even further south so that the government could exercise equal influence "over the two chief components of the Ottoman population."[87] This was a theme that would reemerge after 1908. According to von der Goltz, "a true reconciliation of the Arabs to the Ottoman caliphate was of much greater importance to Turkey than the loss of a piece of Macedonia."[88]

Centers of opposition in Syria, and the accompanying autonomist and revolutionary rhetoric, sensitized the sultan early in his reign to the need to co-opt local Arab leaders to his rule. These opposition groups have received the close attention of several scholars since George Antonius described one of them as the "first organized effort in the Arab national movement."[89] There were at least two secret groups in Syria with alleged or declared separatist aims. First, a society led by Faris Nimr was active between 1875 and 1883. It was composed of young Christians who attempted to rally both Christians and Muslims around an antigovernment and anti-Turkish program, with emphasis on a literary-cultural Arab identity and, in Antonius's words, embodying a new "conception . . . of a politically independent state resting on a truly national basis."[90] Second, an organization of Muslim notables was formed in early 1878 representing distinguished religious, landowning, or commercial families, some with strong links to the Ottoman state.[91] Midhat Pasha's exile as governor in Syria coincided with this period of organizational activity, and his alleged involvement in the subversive agitation made the study of the ferment in Syria more compelling.

Antonius attributed to the first group the authorship of certain revolutionary placards that were distributed in Syria in 1880.[92] Zeine Zeine has convincingly argued that these initiatives remained restricted to a small group and did not constitute the basis of an Arab movement.[93] Jacob Landau's later argument that one such leaflet, dated March 1881 and signed "The Society for the Maintenance of the Rights of the Arab Nation," had Muslim authorship and sought independence for Arabs[94] does not challenge Zeine's conclusion. One of the main grievances expressed by this group was that Arabs were not appointed to high military office. The parallel with the proclamations of 'Urabi, whose revolt in Egypt at this time was motivated by similar professional grievances, is striking. Midhat Pasha was also implicated in the drafting and distribution of the placards.[95] It appears far-fetched that Midhat nurtured ambitions of separating Syria from the empire by declaring himself a semi-independent viceroy similar to the Egyptian khedive. Almost forty years later similar designs were ascribed to Cemal Pasha when he assumed the civil and military control of Syria. It is more likely that Midhat Pasha "regarded Syria as a springboard for restoring his position in İstanbul, not as a power base from which to launch an attack designed to dismember the empire."[96]

As for the second group, its members were primarily concerned about the future of Syria in the event the war with Russia caused the collapse of the Ottoman state. They contacted Arab leaders throughout Syria and resolved to seek independence if faced with the danger of foreign occupation, even though they would continue to recognize the caliph.[97] Their call went unheeded, and the government discovered the group and suppressed its activities. The lenient treatment of the leaders indicates that İstanbul did not feel a threat from the notables' movement. The two societies' activities do not constitute milestones in the evolution of an Arab political movement, but they do point to two of its distinct features as it crystallized later: the articulation of autonomist-separatist agendas in times of imperial crisis and the Syrian focus of Arab political activity.

From the 1850s to 1916 the weakening of the empire due to international complications encouraged some within it to embrace the idea of independence in the hope of mitigating the impact of probable foreign hegemony. As early as 1858, in the aftermath of the Crimean War that led to great suffering and took a toll on the empire's economy, the British consul in Aleppo reported to London regarding the separatist tendencies in that city.[98] Notions of independence and the denunciation of İstanbul's rule were not encountered for the first or last time during Abdülhamid's reign. They failed to develop into ideological movements and to rally popular support.

The political ferment did not extend beyond Syria.[99] The activity of the Christians was further restricted to the coastal areas of the province; even in Damascus they failed to induce Muslim notables to common action.[100] That a few prominent Syrian Arabs entertained the notion of separation from the Ottoman state if it foundered as a result of the Russian War had little to do with a nationalist program. Not surprisingly, when Abdülhamid consolidated his power he was able to conciliate and even co-opt important segments of the Muslim Arab notability.

By emphasizing his role as caliph, Abdülhamid generated support from Arabs, as well as from other Muslims within and outside the Ottoman Empire, at a time when the world of Islam was under Christian imperialist domination. He also won over with money, deference, and benevolent concern many a tribal leader who was out of the Ottoman fold in order to strengthen his position against the same powers. The notables of the more developed Arab regions, however, adhered to the Hamidian regime for reasons that were not entirely of Abdülhamid's making and that had little to do with his Islamist ideology.

Changes in the politics of Syrian notables preceded the Hamidian rule and were due, first, to the emergence of large landholding families after the promulgation of the Ottoman Land Code of 1858 and, second, to the failure of the Muslim leadership to preserve social order in the civil strife of 1860.[101] As the influence of the established religious "ulema families" waned, the secular landowning families acquired posts in the local administration aided by their recently acquired wealth[102] and established similar patronage relations with the local people. Abdülhamid did not reverse the Tanzimat's secularizing policies that had jeopardized the ulema's legal and educational functions. While the more prominent religious families adapted to changing circumstances and managed to retain their land and administrative positions, the diversification of the bureaucracy and the rapidly increasing number of provincial administrative posts[103] enabled the secular landowning families to obtain the new posts and to enhance their influence.[104] In order to keep pace with the bureaucratization and the secular trend, the religious families had to compromise. Like the new landholding families, they sent their sons to the secular schools in İstanbul and increasingly married them into these families. Thus, during Abdülhamid's reign a new coalition of provincial urban leadership emerged which "openly identified with and defended the interests of the Ottoman state."[105] This linkage of the merged Ottomanist leadership to İstanbul was greatly facilitated by Abdülhamid's drastic modernization of communications, which was implemented in the spirit of Tanzimat centralization and with extensive Western participation.

Under Abdülhamid the West continued to be a model. The empire became further integrated into the world political and economic system. Western civilization, it was stressed, was built on borrowings from Islamic civilization, and therefore it was acceptable to borrow from the West.[106] Unlike the Young Ottomans, Abdülhamid exalted medieval Islamic civilization. Most Muslim Ottomans had little trouble identifying with an Arab past. In the 1878 Parliament Abdul Bey, a deputy from Janina, Albania, displayed the self-view so characteristic of most Ottomans at this time when he remarked: "We [Ottomans?] are a *millet* [i.e., community] that has originated from the Arab *millet*. . . .[107] Just as we took civilization from the Greeks, Europe has taken it from us."[108] Identifying with the Arabo-Islamic heritage served to legitimate and reinforce the Ottoman claim to the caliphate, particularly because the Ottoman sultans' adoption of the title had remained tentative, if not controversial.

Nevertheless, Abdülhamid's appropriation of the Arab past was not immune to challenge. Arab intellectuals grew increasingly more conscious of their ancestors' role in the origin of Islam and in early Islamic civilization. Just as they gave credit to the Ottoman rulers for their military prowess, which reunited the Islamic realm, they held them responsible for the empire's subsequent regression and ascribed the decline to their deviation from true Islam. Muhammad ʿAbduh and some of his *salafi* adherents looked to the distant, glorious past of Islam, explored the sources of its early success, and in the process identified precedents for social, economic, and political principles that now rendered Europe strong and superior to Islam.[109] As a one-time comrade of Jamal al-Din al-Afghani, the renowned activist for the political unity of Islam, ʿAbduh's concern for the perpetuity, stability, and independence of the Islamic *umma* (religious community) was paramount; and to that end he was ready to support Abdülhamid, although he found the sultan's claim to the caliphate exceptionable.[110] Abdülhamid's pragmatic motives in emphasizing his role as caliph corresponded with those of the Arab intellectuals in tolerating the very claim.

However, the special importance and consideration that Arabs received as the carriers of the Islamic faith and agents of a great civilization nourished an Arab identity with strong Islamic overtones. ʿAbduh's *salafi* followers gradually instilled political content into this Arab identity.

'Abduh's disciple Rashid Rida outwardly respected the sultan's title as caliph, although, unlike his mentor, he actively opposed Hamidian absolutism. 'Abd al-Rahman al-Kawakibi, another student of 'Abduh, argued that the office of the caliphate be restored to the Arabs.[111] This viewpoint is significant in associating the Arab self-consciousness engendered by *salafi* thought with a political agenda, but it was not one to which most Arab reformists readily subscribed. Nevertheless, an association of Islamic glory with "Arabness" fostered a more powerful Arab ethnic consciousness than did the earlier secular agendas.[112] Arabic as the language of the Quran, bestowed by God specifically on the Arabs, imparted a new potentiality to linguistic self-identification.

Parallel to the currents in the Arab world, the awareness of a Turkish identity was on the rise in İstanbul, also with language playing the principal role. The Turkist current preceded the Hamidian period and was largely exogenous. European linguistic and philological studies that established links between central Asian, Anatolian, and eastern European peoples aroused Ottoman awareness of the Turks outside the empire and restored their pride at a time (in the 1860s and 1870s) when the empire's prestige was rapidly declining.[113] The Young Ottomans favored the simplification of Ottoman Turkish so that it could be a more effective instrument in propagating Ottomanist ideas, but viewed as chauvinism the idea of racial, and certainly political, unity of all Turks.[114]

During the Hamidian period some intellectuals in İstanbul became interested in Turkishness as an ethnic and linguistic expression. The subsumption of Turkist concerns (particularly with regard to Russian expansion in Central Asia) under pan-Islamism reinforced Abdülhamid's anti-imperialist ideology; he therefore tolerated discussions of Turkism until the early years of the twentieth century.[115] But Turkism had no cultural heroes, was outward-looking, and had no perceptible effect on most Turks, who continued to see themselves first and foremost as Muslims, and it had no political appeal to the intellectuals who propagated it. For the Turkish-speaking people of the empire, their language was a weak basis for a broad communality, in part because they, more so than the Arabs, for example, inhabited linguistically heterogeneous regions of the empire. They failed to understand the elite's Ottoman Turkish, much less feel pride in it. While the sultan seems to have encouraged Turkist literary endeavors as a safe substitute to political writing, he grew suspicious of Arabic literary activity. An Arab cultural revival might have contributed to an exclusive ethnic Arab appropriation of medieval Islam and subvert his claim to the caliphate.[116] This may be the reason why

Abdülhamid decided against adopting Arabic as an official state language, which he had contemplated.[117]

Arabist and Turkist currents followed separate lines of development. Arabist identity matured earlier and had stronger appeal.[118] The close association of Arabic language and Islam provided a basis for Arab selfhood, which the *salafi* movement strengthened. Both currents, however, remained insignificant as political agendas. Under Abdülhamid officially sponsored Islamism overshadowed both Arabism and Turkism. For most Muslims the Ottoman sultanate continued to be the focus of political loyalty. While it would take longer for Arabism and Turkism to find political expression, a meaningful synthesis of the two under a redefined Ottomanism (such as the Young Turks would attempt) was prejudiced by the modes of expression of the two trends. For instance, the Arab intellectuals perceived the Turkist attempts to simplify Ottoman by eliminating Arabic grammatical elements as offensive to Arab culture if not to Islam, while the Turkists cannot have ignored some Arabists' singling out of Turkish dynastic rule as the dark period of Islamic history.

Yet few called for the political separation of Arabs and Turks on a national basis. In 1904 Yusuf Akçura, a Turk from the Russian empire, wrote from his exile in İstanbul that pan-Islamism and Ottomanism were not viable political alternatives for the Turkish-speaking peoples of the empire and that Turkism provided the suitable alternative.[119] Nagib Azoury, a Syrian Christian, wrote from Paris in the same year and called for an independent Arab state of Muslims and Christians.[120] Both authors were motivated by a distrust of Islamic and Ottomanist solutions, yet both failed to find an audience for their alternative schemes.

The Young Turk Opposition and the Arabs

It is common practice to describe the liberal opposition *prior* to Abdülhamid's reign as the Young Ottoman movement and to that *during* his rule as the Young Turk movement. These terms, of European origin and sometimes used interchangeably, do not reflect a change in the self-image of the liberal opposition. In the Ottoman context their use becomes misleading on two counts. First, the transition from Young Ottoman to Young Turk implies an ungrounded narrowing of interests toward a more ethnically Turkish emphasis in the liberal currents. Second, it suggests that the ideological content, means of expression, and set of actors in the opposition underwent a distinctive transformation after the 1870s.

During the Hamidian period the different manifestations of political opposition featured an unprecedented ethnic, religious, and geographical diversity. Thus, the Young Turk movement was unmistakably more "Ottoman" than its Young Ottoman antecedent, which was a movement of Turcophone İstanbul officials. As for substantive continuity between the two movements, the set of ideas formulated by the Young Ottomans provided the basis of Young Turk propaganda, notwithstanding a turnover and diversification in the membership. Only gradually did modern currents in European social and political thought, on the one hand, and the broadening of the social base of the opposition, on the other, introduce new elements and emphases to political concepts and ideals first articulated by the Young Ottomans.[121]

For more than a decade following the closing of Parliament in 1878, Abdülhamid encountered little domestic political opposition. The main reason for this was his heavy-handed rule and centralized security apparatus. Once the parliamentary regime failed, hopes faded. Frenzied attempts to topple Abdülhamid with a palace coup were aborted.[122] Liberal ideas, though, did not cease to be passed on. Fugitives in Europe continued the struggle against Abdülhamid. In general, these efforts were individualistic, unorganized, and therefore short-lived.

THE FIRST PHASE (1878–1895)

Though it is customary to view the beginnings of dissent from Hamidian rule as of the mid-1890s, the conspiratorial ventures of that decade and the continuities in the liberal movement can be understood best against the background of political exertions occurring mostly outside the empire in which émigré Arab intellectuals played the major role.

Literary and journalistic activity was intensifying among Syrian intellectuals when Abdülhamid came to power. The sultan's strict press censorship forced many journalists to emigrate to Europe or to Egypt. The historical and cultural links of the Syrian Christian communities with European countries facilitated the exiles' stay in European cities such as London, Paris, and Naples, where they were often backed by friendly governments (which sought to exploit the anti-Hamidian posture of the intellectuals for their own national and imperial interests), individuals, and church groups, but had no coordination amongst themselves.

Only in 1894 Salim Faris, the son of the publisher (Ahmad Faris al-Shidyaq) of an Arabic journal in İstanbul called *Al-jawa'ib* (Current News),[123] brought some coordination to these efforts. He revived in London *Hürriyet*, which had been the principal Young Ottoman publication in Europe.[124] Before then, oppositional activity fit into only the broadest definition of the Young Turk movement, namely, opposition to the Hamidian despotism. In keeping with Young Ottoman ideals, the fundamental demand in this period continued to be a liberal constitutional regime. Hence, the refutation of Abdülhamid's claim to the caliphate, which the sultan used to justify his absolute power, became a focal point in fighting the regime.

Two independent Arabic papers published in Europe carried the name *Al-khilafa* (The Caliphate). One was edited by Louis Sabunji,[125] a Catholic priest, in London and the other by Ibrahim Muwaylihi in Naples. Sabunji dwelled on the idea of an Arab caliphate in *Al-nahla* (The Bee), which he started in Beirut and transferred to London in 1877, as well as in his *Al-khilafa*, founded in 1881. The supporters of Sabunji and his *Al-nahla* included, in addition to his British benefactors and Khedive Ismail (who had harbored rival ambitions to become caliph), Indian and other Muslim leaders of colonies under British rule, suggesting that the British may have tried to undermine the sultan's claim to the office at this early stage. Ibrahim Muwaylihi was an Egyptian and the only prominent Arab Muslim editor in Europe in opposition to Abdülhamid. Muwaylihi published *Al-khilafa* in 1879, in which he denounced the deposition of his patron, Khedive Ismail.[126] He attacked sharply the Ottoman government as well as imperialist Britain and Russia. Both Muwaylihi and Sabunji[127] later reconciled with Abdülhamid and entered his service.

If the Ottoman sultan was unsuitable for the office of the caliph, who met the necessary requirements? Some *salafi* modernists suggested one answer to the question by advancing the idea of an Arab caliph, but refrained from advocating a transfer of allegiance away from the House of Osman lest it undermine the Ottoman state, the only Islamic political entity capable of standing up to Western imperialism. Although Arab Christians had reason to be apprehensive about Islamism, some, such as Sabunji, proposed an Arab caliphate as an alternative to the Hamidian regime.[128]

After the closure of the First Parliament, Khalil Ghanem also joined the journalistic opposition to Abdülhamid in Europe. Though his early career as a journalist is similar to that of the other Arabs in Europe, toward the end of the nineteenth century Ghanem identified with and committed himself to the mainstream of the growing Young Turk movement to a greater extent than any other Arab intellectual or activist. Of the ten opposition deputies banned from İstanbul in 1878, Ghanem was the only one to go to Europe. He settled in Paris and wrote articles criticizing the Ottoman government and urged reforms.[129] He appropriated the expression Young Turkey in his Arabic and French *La Jeune Turquie* (*Turkiya al-fatat*) in Paris, where he wrote as a "democrat interested in [political] reform" in the empire.[130]

Ghanem resisted bribes from Abdülhamid to abandon his struggle,[131] even as the opposition in Europe lost its vigor in the late 1880s. Many individuals were co-opted by the sultan or abandoned the struggle in discouragement, dismayed by the contradiction between the liberal principles of European countries and their imperialist ambitions. While Cairo in British-occupied Egypt increasingly replaced London and Paris as the center of the Arabic press and intellectual activity, Khalil Ghanem continued the struggle in Europe. Indeed, Ghanem was unequaled in his persistence in the liberal cause, and he represented not only the link between the early and later phases of the anti-Hamidian movement but also embodied the liberal Ottoman currents during the entire span of the last quarter of the nineteenth century.[132] The Europe of the 1890s witnessed a new generation of Ottoman liberals and enhanced organizational activity, in both of which Ghanem continued to be a key figure.

THE SECOND PHASE (1895–1908)

A secret political group, formed before 1889 by medical students in İstanbul and named *İttihad-ı Osmani* (Ottoman Union), was the nucleus of the most important opposition to Abdülhamid that consolidated in this second phase. *İttihad-ı Osmani* remained an underground conspiratorial group in İstanbul until it established contacts with liberal-minded officials of the Hamidian regime and engaged in active opposition from Europe under the new name of the Society of Union and Progress (better known as the Committee of Union and Progress [CUP]), with Ahmed Rıza as its leader.

Ahmed Rıza had been the director of education in Bursa.[133] He left that position to go to Paris in 1889, the year when the Ottoman Union in İstanbul was discovered by the government and reprisals against dissidents intensified. He stayed in Europe to take up the liberal cause and kept in touch with the movement in the Ottoman capital. At first, he advocated liberal-constitutional concepts in the same terms as the Young Ottomans, emphasizing the common elements in Islamic political thought and Western liberalism.[134] However, he increasingly adopted the ideas of the French positivists, with whom he associated in Paris. Khalil Ghanem, another adherent of the positivist school of thought,[135] joined Ahmed Rıza in 1895 to found *Meşveret*,[136] the first major organ of Young Turk opposition in Europe. Together with Murad Bey (Mizancı),[137] a Russian-Turkish émigré who had propagated liberal ideas as a teacher in the *Mülkiye* before leaving İstanbul, Ahmed Rıza and Ghanem led the Unionist organization in Europe.

On the eve of the formation of the CUP in Europe, Salim Faris styled himself in his *Hürriyet* (which circulated in Ottoman territories) as the spokesman of an organization he called *Osmanlı Meşrutiyet Fırkası* (or *Parti Constitutionnel en Turquie*). Ahmed Rıza refused to cooperate with Faris, accusing him of pursuing only his own interests,[138] but looked more favorably to another liberal Arab opposition group, the Turco-Syrian Committee, that emerged in Paris immediately before 1895. This committee was led by the Druze emir Amin Arslan, and centered around the newspaper *Kashf al-niqab* (Lifting of the Veil).[139] When the French government closed *Kashf al-niqab* under pressure from Abdülhamid, Khalil Ghanem's *Turkiya al-fatat* served as the committee's organ. In 1896 the Turco-Syrian Committee merged with the Paris-based Union and Progress organization and helped Ahmed Rıza's group establish contacts with the Egyptian-based opposition to Abdülhamid.[140]

Both Faris's *Parti Constitutionnel* and the Turco-Syrian Committee gave primacy to the improvement of conditions in Syria, the internal integration of Syrian society, and the elimination of religious differences. These were explicit expressions of a "Syrianist" current that sought the integration of ethnic and religious groups within Greater Syria around a regional identity within the Ottomanist framework. Abdülhamid's policies undermined this brand of Syrianism by bringing religious differences to the fore and reorganizing Greater Syria's administrative divisions, which resulted in greater fragmentation and ultimately the establishment of Beirut as a separate province in 1888 as well as the carving out of an independent *sancak* (subprovince) of Jerusalem.[141] Certainly, the notion of an integral Syria was not shared by all Syrians, as the demands of Syrian deputies in the direction of Abdülhamid's subsequent policies had revealed in the aforementioned parliamentary debates on the separation of Beirut.

Whereas one of the first and most dedicated proponents of Syrianism, Butrus al-Bustani, did not feel that the success of Syrian integration depended on a constitutional arrangement (and therefore escaped censure),[142] the Turco-Syrian Committee envisioned reforms in Syria within a constitutional framework rather than under Abdülhamid's autocratic rule. Thus the committee's aims were not only compatible with the new movement under Ahmed Rıza's leadership but also reinforced it.[143] The program of the CUP as published in the first issue of *Meşveret* emphasized the principle of reform not for individual provinces or regions but for the empire in its entirety.[144] The Turco-Syrian Committee disappeared before the turn of the century, perhaps because Syrian aspirations for reform were to a large extent fulfilled by Abdülhamid. The province of Syria received preferential treatment from the Palace[145] consistent with Abdülhamid's desire to better integrate the Arab elite into the central administration. Indeed, the special treatment that Abdülhamid accorded to Arab notables and provinces was resented by some, like Mizancı Murad, who denounced the privileges that the government conferred on Arabs as being similar to the capitulations.[146]

The major impetus behind the rejuvenation of the Young Turk movement in the 1890s had been the growth of minority, especially Armenian, nationalism.[147] In 1896, at a meeting of Ottoman liberals held in Paris in order to forge a united front against Abdülhamid, Armenian nationalist demands were denounced, prompting the Armenian delegation to leave the meeting in protest. Mizancı Murad then confronted the Arab participants with the question of whether they harbored intentions of forming an Arab state. Nadra Mutran and Khalil Ghanem renounced any such claims and asserted their firm belief in the necessity of loyalty to the Ottoman state for the sake of Arab interests.[148]

Differences within the movement in Europe had the appearance of personality conflicts at the beginning, but they increasingly crystallized around ideological issues. During the years when the first major wave of exiles was organizing itself in Paris and Geneva, the main point of disagreement emerged as the strategy to be employed in fighting Hamidian despotism. The founders of the Ottoman Union (who joined the ranks of liberals in Europe) and Mizancı Murad were inclined toward the use of violence. As a good positivist, Ahmed Rıza favored a more gradual, nonviolent approach.[149]

A permanent division developed on the issue of administrative organization of the empire. Ahmed Rıza advocated greater political and economic centralization and was opposed by the decentralist camp, which consolidated around Prince Sabahaddin, a nephew of Abdülhamid and the son of the sultan's disgruntled brother-in-law, Mahmud Celaleddin Pasha, who took refuge in Paris in 1899 and engaged in opposition to the sultan. Sabahaddin had Anglo-Saxon proclivities and advocated liberal economic policies in his *Teşebbüs-ü Şahsi ve Adem-i Merkeziyet* (League for Private Initiative and Administrative Decentralization), which became a rival to Ahmed Rıza's CUP.[150] This division plagued the Young Turk movement before 1908 and would provide the central dispute in the more institutionalized political discourse of the second constitutional period.

The Young Turks in Europe held major congresses in Paris in 1902 and 1907 with the aim of reconciling their differences and determining a unified line of action against the Hamidian regime. Arabs participated in both of these conventions but not as a unified interest group. Unlike the Armenians, for example, the Arabs did not constitute a national community identified with a faction. At the 1902 conference Khalil Ghanem acted as the spokesman for the CUP and presided over some sessions.[151] In 1907 the editorial boards of the London- and Cairo-based Turkish-Arabic journals were present.[152] However, no Arab held any leadership positions after Ghanem's death in 1904. There was no pattern to Arab adherence to either the centralist or decentralist agendas.

Abdülhamid's active recruitment of Arabs to his personal service has mistakenly identified Arabs with the regime and have slighted their role in the opposition. At a time when the Palace overshadowed the Sublime Porte (or the ministerial bureaucracy), the sultan's policy did indeed bring many Arabs of conservative leanings to influential positions. Abdülhamid thus drew on a pool of advisers, secretaries, and functionaries who were removed from the bureaucratic power struggles in İstanbul and who harbored personal loyalty to him.[153] The choice of Arab dignitaries with mainstream Sunni and mystical Sufi backgrounds and enjoying religious prestige added to the force of his Islamic policy.[154] Most important, the co-optation of Arab notables into the bureaucracy and palace administration served his policy of centralization.

One of the two principal envoys Abdülhamid sent to Europe to contact the Young Turks and win them over was Najib Malhama, his Lebanese Christian security chief.[155] The choice of Malhama undoubtedly had to do with the large number of Arabs, mostly Christian, among the Young Turks in Europe. To lure the dissenters back, Abdülhamid used the stick (e.g., confiscation of property) and the carrot (e.g., financial incentives) interchangeably.[156] The case of Amin al-Antaki, a Syrian Catholic who did comply with the government's call and return to İstanbul, is illustrative of many Young Turks who were induced to return home or to accept a government post abroad. Given the financial difficulties of living abroad, demoralization due to the disunity of the movement, and emotional and personal reasons, many Young Turks (including such leading figures as Mizancı Murad, Tunalı Hilmi, and Abdullah Cevdet) reached a compromise with Abdülhamid through the constant efforts of his agents in Europe. These men often resisted co-optation, however, and later either returned to the opposition or supported the Young Turk cause covertly. A case in point is al-Antaki, who used the "doors opened to him in the Palace and the Porte" to gather information and reported on his contacts with government officials to the Young Turks in exile through the French post office in İstanbul.[157]

From its inception, the Unionist organization in the capital included Arabs among its membership, as well as Kurds, Albanians, Russian Turks, and members of other ethnic groups. One of the earliest members of the Unionist society was Ahmad Wardani,[158] who was commissioned by the Ottoman Union to establish the first contacts with Ahmed Rıza in Europe and to ask the latter to represent the CUP there. Wardani was later exiled to Tripoli in Libya.[159] In 1900 a Damascene, Mustafa Bey, was sentenced to hard labor for inciting soldiers in İstanbul to revolt against Abdülhamid.[160] The nephew of Shaykh Zafir, one of the prominent Arab religious leaders in Abdülhamid's court, was an army officer who distributed anti-Abdülhamid manifestos.[161] The secret Society of Revolutionary Soldiers, which had pro-Sabahaddin leanings and was founded in the military high school in 1902, also included Arabs.[162] Because Young Turk activity in İstanbul had to be carried out in strict secrecy, little is known about the opposition in the capital and the role of Arabs in it.

Egypt was another center of opposition to Abdülhamid and became a haven to Young Turks because of its central geographical location and its liberal political milieu. Some Syrian intellectuals had left their country in the late 1870s, lured by the liberal atmosphere of Cairo under Khedive Ismail. These authors and journalists were joined by a second wave that came during the early years of British occupation. British rule allowed the proponents of Egyptian nationalism, as well as the supporters of the new khedive Abbas Hilmi, the British, and the French, to write relatively freely and to criticize Ottoman policies, transforming Cairo into the

"Hyde Park Corner of the Middle East." There were intellectuals and politicians in Egypt who were favorably disposed to the Ottoman Empire and saw a greater role for it in Egyptian affairs. Such Ottoman linkages, however, were generally advocated to remove the British yoke, with an eye toward eventual Egyptian independence.[163]

When the Young Turks established a branch in Cairo toward the end of the century, they had most in common with the Muslim Syrian émigrés of Islamic modernist convictions. The Young Turks were aware and suspicious of the khedive's opportunistic policies aimed at strengthening his position vis-à-vis Abdülhamid, but they took advantage of his goodwill whenever possible.[164] Some disaffected members of the khedivial family joined the ranks of the Young Turks for a more active cooperation: Prince Muhammad ʿAli and, most significantly, Saʿid Halim, the future Ottoman grand vizier, worked with Ahmed Rıza's group.[165]

In 1897 the Ottoman Consultative Society (*Jamʿiyat al-shura al-ʿuthmaniyya*) was founded in Cairo by Syrian Muslim Arabs and Young Turks from İstanbul. The architects of the society were Rashid Rida, Rafiq al-ʿAzm, and Saib Bey, a Turkish officer. The organization lasted until 1908. Abdullah Cevdet, a Kurd from Diyarbakır and one of the founders of the Ottoman Union in 1889, was active in the society after he settled in Egypt in 1905.[166] Before coming to Cairo, Cevdet had led the Young Turk faction in Geneva that became a rival to the Ahmed Rıza group. Cevdet, influenced by his reading of ʿAbduh, attempted to dull the cutting edge of Abdülhamid's policies by disputing their Islamic nature.[167]

The Turco-Arab Consultative Society called for Islamic unity embodied in Ottoman unity and under the Ottoman caliph[168] but denounced Hamidian rule together with European imperialism. Its propaganda emanating from Cairo was printed in Arabic and Turkish and distributed widely within the empire;[169] the Arab provinces of the empire in particular could easily be reached from Egypt.[170] As the head of the society's administrative council, Rashid Rida propagated the ideas of the group in his *Al-manar* (Lighthouse), a journal that was widely read in Syria and at this juncture served the interests of the Young Turks. It advocated the integrity of the Ottoman state, called for resistance to imperialism, and condemned Hamidian autocracy. After the 1908 Revolution, the Consultative Society turned into a vocal and influential critic of the centralist Young Turk faction, the CUP.

As differences between the centralist faction of Ahmed Rıza and the decentralists grouped around Sabahaddin became wider, the Young

Turks in Egypt formed another society, the *Cemiyet-i Ahdiye-i Osmaniye* (Ottoman Covenant Society), which attempted to steer a middle course.[171] It promoted the principle of *tevsi'-i mezuniyet* (extension of discretion), which was stipulated in the constitution of 1876, and suggested giving more latitude to administrative officials, though it did not necessarily imply the larger degree of local participation in government that the decentralists wanted.

In the years following the formation of the Ottoman Union, and particularly after the Hamidian police clamped down on the opposition in İstanbul, many Young Turks left the country, while others tried to extend the underground İstanbul organization to the provinces. Exiles from the founding group of the Ottoman Union set up the branches in Europe and Cairo. Inside the empire, revolutionary ideas spread as students with Young Turk leanings graduated from military and professional schools in İstanbul and were appointed to the provinces. Meanwhile, the government exiled cohorts of suspected students, officers, and officials to distant provinces, particularly the Hijaz, Baghdad, Syria, and Tripoli (Libya), where they propagated similar propaganda. The capitals of most of these provinces were headquarters for major army units, among which Young Turk propaganda spread quickly, owing to the influence of sympathetic officers.

The activities of Young Turks elsewhere were followed closely by the population in the Arab provinces. The first (but abortive) attempt of the Young Turks in Europe to convene a congress (in Brindisi in 1899) caused great excitement in these provinces, according to a report of Amin al-Antaki. *Terakki* (Progress), published in Paris by Sabahaddin, was read in Baghdad in 1906.[172] The Muslim youth of Beirut had established contacts with the reformers and students of Damascus.[173] In the North African province of Tripoli, the Young Turks carried out effective propaganda among the military and civilian personnel. When in 1897 the government uncovered yet another revolutionary plot in İstanbul and banished seventy-eight young men (mostly students of professional schools, including at least two Arabs) to Tripoli,[174] many of these managed to escape from their captivity, no doubt with the disguised cooperation of the local authorities.

In the decade between 1895 and 1905 exiles formed at least three revolutionary Young Turk organizations in the Arab provinces.[175] Particularly in Syria, there was interested awareness of Young Turk activities in Europe, Egypt, and İstanbul, and the province became a major center for the CUP. Already in 1895 a government functionary removed to Syria because of his subversive activity, Sharaf al-Din Maghmumi, set up a network of CUP branches with the active support of the officers of the Fifth Army stationed in Damascus and other government functionaries.[176] In 1897 the Committee's organization was elaborate and its following substantial enough in Syria that the European headquarters considered launching an antiregime insurgence there. Before long, however, the inevitable crackdown came and resulted in the arrest and dispersal of the CUP members. Nevertheless, Young Turk activity in Syria remained alive around Damascus as a result of the social dynamics that fostered anti-Hamidian, and therefore constitutionalist, activity, as investigated by David Commins.[177]

The competition of a newly emerging landowning elite in Damascus for posts that traditionally belonged to ulema narrowed the opportunities for the lower ulema and led to an antiestablishment sociopolitical movement nourished by *salafi* modernism. Owing to its emphasis on reason and progress, this movement led by the ulema had particular appeal to the young generation of students attending modern Tanzimat schools. The guiding spirit of this "Islamic reformist" movement was Tahir al-Jaza'iri, who was known for his friendly relations with Midhat Pasha during the latter's governorship in Syria. Abdülhamid was suspicious of al-Jaza'iri's links with the Young Turks and dismissed him from his position as inspector of education.[178]

An important component of the *salafi* ideology was the emphasis it placed on the role of Arabs in Islamic history. The youth of Damascus, while being educated in secular government schools and trained for positions in the Ottoman bureaucracy, also attended outside the classroom the *salafi* circle, where they were exposed to a religious rationalization of modern ideas, institutions, and technology and instilled with an ethnic consciousness. Arabism reinforced their receptivity of modern political and social ideas, which in turn prepared the ground for political identification with the Young Turks, who agitated to reform and change the political system they were trained to serve.

In 1895 three students from Tahir al-Jaza'iri's entourage, Shukri al-'Asali, Salim al-Jaza'iri, 'Abd al-Wahab al-Inkilizi, and an Arab officer in Damascus, As'ad Darwish, formed a political group and established contacts with Young Turk sympathizers in Damascus, including Bedri Bey and the director of education, Hüseyin Avni Bey.[179] One year later these three students and other graduates of the new 'Anbar secondary school in Damascus went to İstanbul for their studies, to be followed in a few years by another cohort.

Social tension existed in the Damascus high school between local students and the sons of upper-level bureaucrats, many of them non-Arab.[180] Once in İstanbul, these tensions transformed themselves into social estrangement with ethnic overtones. In the capital there was general hostility between students from İstanbul and those from the provinces.[181] Like their counterparts from the other provinces, many of the Arab students were from modest backgrounds.[182] They resented the special treatment that the sons of high government officials received in the schools they attended.[183] It was the policy of the Hamidian regime to accord privileged status to the sons of high military and civilian office-holders. The sons of the İstanbul officialdom were favored not only in admissions but also while enrolled. For instance, in the *Harbiye* (Military Academy) there were special classes for these fortunate sons, who not only received better meals and living quarters but also were often awarded promotions while still in school.[184] The fact that the Arab students were separated by a linguistic barrier added to their sense of alienation.

Equally striking to the Syrian students must have been the special treatment that sons of tribal and religious leaders, mostly from the Arab provinces, received in government schools.[185] In 1889 in the *Harbiye*[186] and in 1896 in the *Mülkiye*[187] special classes were opened for sons of Arab *shaykh*s. The privileged students were as a rule less qualified academically, if not intellectually, than the others. Abdülhamid's aim in this policy was not so much to create an aristocratic officialdom as to reward loyal officials and dignitaries and to train the administrative and military cadres to be employed in distant tribal provinces.[188] Nevertheless, the special arrangements in the schools increased the ordinary Arab students' awareness of the socioeconomic discrepancies. The Young Turk opposition found adherents among these students of the higher schools, who also formed cultural organizations in İstanbul to promote their Arab heritage and to provide a support structure for the Arab student community.

Many of these young men were educated in the imperial schools of İstanbul and prepared to take responsible positions in the Ottoman state bureaucracy. The expansion of nonreligious state schools since the Tanzimat and the improvements in communications enabled youths in different parts of the empire to vie for positions in the imperial schools. In provincial centers, the new secondary government schools offered a modern curriculum and preparation for higher education in İstanbul, where they enhanced their proficiency in the Ottoman language and were cast as Ottomans with a future role in the state bureaucracy. These students were taught new subjects like economics and took lessons from foreign teachers. Thus, while the social and geographical base of the Ottoman bureaucracy gradually broadened, modern education trained a generation in tune with new global political and economic trends and sympathetic to liberal ideas.

Conclusion

In 1878 the Ottoman liberal movement was in disarray, having been deprived by Sultan Abdülhamid of constitutional-parliamentary institutions. All oppositional activity concentrated therefore on undermining Abdülhamid's personal rule. With no united front against the autocrat, the movement suffered from a certain ideological impoverishment, disunity, parochialism, and even opportunism. If one can speak of a "vision" of the opposition during Abdülhamid's reign, it consisted of no more than a restoration of constitutional monarchy where the sultan's powers would be held in check. As Abdülhamid tried to consolidate his autocratic regime after 1878 and exploited his attributes as caliph, the logical target of the opposition's attack was his claim to the caliphate.

Christian Arabs contributed more to the resuscitation of the liberal movement that came to be known as the Young Turk movement than they did to the fostering of Arabism. Khalil Ghanem best represents those few among the Christian Arab opposition who adhered to the liberal ideals first articulated (albeit mostly in an Islamic idiom) by Young Ottomans. Ghanem was a Tanzimat bureaucrat who had identified with the Young Ottoman grievances. He was involved in the drafting of the constitution, distinguished himself as an opposition leader in the 1877–78 Parliament, and had been the only deputy in that Parliament to continue actively the struggle after it was closed down. Although a Christian, for a long time his vision of the Ottoman state was a liberal and Islamic one. Only at the end of his career and after a lifetime of opposition to an autocrat who he believed had exploited religion did he become critical of the sultanate as an institution and of Islam as its legitimating ideology.[189]

By the end of the nineteenth century Arab political organizations were primarily interested in the unity of Syria within the Ottoman Empire. Until 1908 Arabs did not constitute a faction in themselves whose interests had to be accorded special consideration in any Young Turk program of action. Unlike the Armenians, and even the predominantly Muslim Albanians, who supported the decentralist movement led by Sabahaddin, the Arabs did not identify clearly with any one of the Young Turk trends. The Young Turk organization in Egypt, which was the branch of the Young Turks in closest contact with the Arab intellectual currents, tried to play an intermediary role between the two Young Turk factions to achieve unity against imperialism.

In the Arab provinces Young Turk ideas were propagated by young officials, officers, and exiles. In the İstanbul schools there were class-based tensions between the sons of the established bureaucratic or notable families and the provincial students of more modest backgrounds. There was little room for open political activity in the capital at the beginning of the century; but in general the younger generation of Arabs remained supportive of Young Turk ideals and of the movement that finally reinstituted the constitutional regime.

2

The Second Constitutional
Experiment, 1908–1909

The Young Turks' struggle bore revolutionary fruit in the summer of 1908, when, on 23 July, Sultan Abdülhamid was forced to reinstate the constitution. Dramatic descriptions of euphoric celebrations that the restoration of constitutional rule occasioned are a compelling prelude to accounts of the second constitutional period. Many Arabs, like many Turks, Greeks, Armenians, and others, rejoiced in the events of July 1908. Yet less than a year and a half after the revolution an "Arab" opposition party had emerged, and growing numbers of Arab critics turned against the Committee of Union and Progress, the paramount Young Turk group.

The manifestations of opposition among Arabs and the unfolding of the tensions in Turkish-Arab relations will be addressed in chapter 3. In an attempt to explore the seeds of the apparent estrangement, customarily ascribed to the CUP's formulation of a Turkish nationalist ideology and implementation of centralizing policies, this chapter will focus on the early phase of the second constitutional era through the closure of the first annual session of Parliament at the end of the summer of 1909. A detailed examination of the CUP's early quest for power and the implications of political change on Arabs and the Arab provinces will demonstrate that the formulation and implementation of policy remained rudimentary and in flux during this period of political transition. The revolution, however, unleashed social and political processes that gave new directions to the conduct of politics in the Ottoman Empire.

The initiative to take up arms to coerce Sultan Abdülhamid to restore the constitution came from the Macedonian branches of the Young Turk organization. The group of constitutionalists in Salonika had been in close contact with the Young Turk leaders in Europe before July 1908 and had cast their conspiratorial group as a branch of the CUP that was being revitalized by Ahmed Rıza in Paris. The decision to resort to the use of force in Macedonia was largely independent of the direction of the expatriate leadership of the CUP. It was influenced by political conditions particular to the European provinces of the empire: the example of Macedonian guerrilla organizations, the prospect of European-imposed and -implemented administrative arrangements, and a heightened sense of the vulnerability of the Ottoman state to secession and annexation in the Balkans.

The 1908 Revolution was the outcome of decades of Young Turk activity in diverse places. When Sultan Abdülhamid conceded the restoration of the constitution, members of the central committee of the CUP in Salonika came to İstanbul to take charge, though Salonika continued to be the Committee's sanctum until the city was lost to Greece in the Balkan War of 1912. The military element in the Macedonian branches of the CUP played the decisive role in the events of July 1908, but the Salonika CUP, like Unionist organizations elsewhere, also had a large civilian membership drawn from the civil service and various professions. After the revolution, these younger cadres, military and civilian, overshadowed the forerunners and ideologues of the Young Turk movement, many of whom sank into oblivion. The politically influential men of the new constitutional regime came not from the ranks of those who fought absolutism and inculcated an entire generation with constitutional ideas but from the fringes of the movement and, in the early years, even from the cadres of the defunct regime.

The public's initial excitement and celebrations were more the result of the submission of a relentless autocrat than the prospects offered by a handful of little-known committeemen based in the provinces. Though the CUP seemed immune to all challenges, it lacked self-confidence and organization. Having operated as a secret body in the capital and the provinces it did not draw on a popular sociopolitical base or avail of a structured and disciplined empire-wide political network. Therefore, it was not prepared to make a bid for exclusive political power,[1] and very soon the general population's rising expectations began to haunt it.

The Committee had a political and social program, and it acted from the first days of the constitutional regime onward like a political party with opinions on matters of public policy. It admitted few newcomers to its inner circles despite its ambition to rally all segments of the pop-

ulation behind it. At the end of August the merger of Prince Sabahaddin's Paris-based League for Private Initiative and Administrative Decentralization with the CUP was announced.[2] Since the Committee
subscribed to a program of centralization, the merger might have been
viewed as a reconciliation of the two principal currents of Young Turk
ideology. In fact, it was an unsuccessful maneuver to neutralize the decentralist faction, which reasserted itself within days by forming a rival
party. The CUP failed to accommodate even the centralist old guard in
exile. Ahmed Rıza was one of the few to be recognized: he was elected
speaker by a CUP-dominated Parliament. Like other prominent Young
Turks of the pre-1908 period, however, he was gradually distanced from
the inner councils of the Committee. The CUP's exclusionism derived
from the social insecurities and administrative inexperience of its members and plagued it in its relations with different political and social
groups, including potential Arab supporters, in the years to come.

In the wake of the revolution the CUP tried to determine the course
of government policy through its influence over the cabinet. In the first
few months censorship was lifted, political prisoners released, the constitutional prerogatives of the sultan curbed, and elections announced.
The CUP rode the wave of enhanced freedoms and unrealistic expectations to popularity. The pressing concern was to preserve the territorial
integrity of the constitutional state. In September 1908, however, came
Austria-Hungary's annexation of Bosnia-Herzegovina and Bulgaria's
declaration of independence. These territorial dismemberments, coming
so soon after the revolution, could be blamed on past policy, and the
CUP managed to channel the reaction to the losses into support through
the effective use of the press, led by the İstanbul daily *Tanin*.

Tanin became the mouthpiece of the CUP under the editorship of
Hüseyin Cahid. Cahid, an İstanbul journalist educated in the *Mülkiye*,
was one of the few individuals admitted into the central committee who
had not been active in the Rumelian branches of the CUP. Since the
Committee maintained strict secrecy in its proceedings, *Tanin* emerged
as the best and often the only source reflecting the views of the CUP.
Damascene deputy Shafiq al-Mu'ayyad's remark that only *Tanin* could
express its opinion without restrictions was not far from the truth.[3]
Tanin's writers did not always follow a strict "party" line, and even Hüseyin Cahid, the Committee's spokesman *par excellence*, at times differed
from what appeared to be the CUP's position. Certainly, there were
divisions within the CUP behind the façade of solidarity and the curtain
of secrecy.

The freedom of the press cut both ways, and soon the Committee's opposition resorted to it with equal force. The politicization of the Ottoman public after 1908 should be appraised as much by the growth and vibrancy of the press as by political activity, elections, and parliamentary proceedings. The press was that component of the expanding public sphere that proved hardest to keep in check. In the first months of the revolution, the absence of strong governmental authority gave free rein to journalistic activity. Just as censorship had become the symbol of Hamidian despotism, the free press became the symbol of the revolution. In the first year, 353 journals and newspapers were published in İstanbul alone, and 200 permits to publish were granted in just the first month of the revolution.[4]

In addition to its direct influence on the government, the CUP also tried to promote its political goals in its capacity as an independent organization. It sponsored cultural activities and undertook community work. The Committee leaders thought that educating the Ottoman people to the benefits of the constitution would strengthen the Committee's political position.[5] Therefore, the Committee organized night classes and opened new private schools that were funded by membership dues and operated, much like the schools for non-Muslims, outside the jurisdiction of the government.[6] One of the stated goals of the program was to *induce* the governments to undertake reform efforts that would supplement the CUP's independent efforts. The distinction between the Committee's and the government's acts became increasingly blurred, as did the distinction between the Union and Progress as a public society and a political party.

The CUP's initial success in achieving its political objectives without constituting itself as a political party had significant consequences. By missing the opportunity to introduce a vigorous and participatory political organization at the critical juncture of 1908, the CUP nourished a calcified nucleus of leadership, consisting predominantly of Turkish speakers and representing a narrow geographical background, which failed to embrace new social elements in the face of growing opposition. Over time, the CUP forfeited its claim to legitimacy, alienated different segments of Ottoman society, and failed to create a coherent base of political support.

Crisis of Authority in the Capital and the Provinces

The Ottoman state experienced a crisis of authority in the aftermath of the revolution that manifested itself on different levels in the capital. The developments in the provinces can be understood only in the light of the transformations in the capital. The CUP's admitted lack of political acumen and social standing necessitated that it rely on statesmen outside the Committee to occupy the top government positions.[7] Its insistence on manipulating the government from outside to conform to its political aims compounded the typical problems associated with legitimacy in revolutionary transfers of power. Not until the spring of 1909 did the Committee create the beginnings of a formal political organ and prepare to take on the responsibility of governing the empire.

The reinstatement of the constitution sparked anew the competition between the Palace and the Porte, which under the autocratic rule of Abdülhamid had been resolved definitively in favor of the former. The revolution left the sultan on his throne but restricted his prerogatives, allowing greater independence to the cabinet. The Committee now became a third contender for the reins of government, particularly through its influence in Parliament after December 1908. The existence of three loci of power, with no defined separation of powers, was at the root of the political instability. Not surprisingly, the first year of the second constitutional period witnessed five changes of government, a counter-revolutionary uprising, and the beginnings of organized opposition.

The Committee showed its determination to exercise its controlling influence over the Palace and the Porte when it orchestrated the downfall of Said Pasha, the first grand vizier of the new era, a mere two weeks after his appointment to the post by Abdülhamid. He was replaced by Kamil Pasha, who, like Said, had served as grand vizier under Abdül-hamid before. On the day of Kamil Pasha's appointment, Hüseyin Cahid wrote in justification of this seasoned statesman's reappointment that one would have to forget the past in view of the shortage of able administrators and confessed that "the old regime did not prepare any of us as men of administration."[8] Kamil Pasha served approximately six months before he became involved in bitter conflict with the CUP and resigned. He was replaced by another "Old Turk," Hüseyin Hilmi Pasha, a diplomat and administrator well known to the Unionists as the former inspector-general of Rumelia.

A second component of the administrative crisis was the tension between civilian officials and army officers. In 1908 officers of the Third Army stationed in Macedonia had played the crucial part in winning over and leading army units to force Abdülhamid to restore the constitution. It was again units from the Third Army, under the command of Mahmud Shawkat Pasha, that suppressed the counterrevolutionary uprising of 13 April 1909, known from the old-style calendar as the "31 March Incident."[9] Shawkat Pasha later exerted considerable influence in government and was appointed minister of war in 1910 and grand vizier in 1913. The issue of the involvement of the military in politics occupied both the councils of the CUP and Parliament.[10]

During the first eighteen months of constitutional rule large numbers of the old regime's functionaries were purged. Unionist pressure forced those who were believed to have had close connections with the Palace — in most cases a precondition for security of tenure before 1908 — to be dismissed, despite the realization that there was a shortage of replacements. Because the ranks of the bureaucracy had been bloated, partly due to Abdülhamid's disposition to distribute sinecures,[11] some lesser bureaucrats could be dispensed with, but at the higher ranks those dismissed needed to be replaced. The cadres with the requisite experience, however, were not there. Administrators were constantly shifted and changed, either because of incompetence or as the result of the frequent shuffling in ministries. A purge took place also in the army. Officers who rose from the ranks through the sultan's patronage (unlike the military members of the CUP, who were graduates of academies) were dismissed by the hundreds.[12] The CUP's determination to purge the bureaucracy of officials with suspected loyalty to Abdülhamid and the scarcity of capable and reliable men to replace them led *Tanin* to plea for the employment of "honest foreign advisors" in the Ottoman government.[13]

In July 1908 Abdülhamid's palace entourage, which included many Arabs and their protégés, was the first to go. Other officials were implicated in having spied for the sultan. Abdülhamid himself, who as sultan-caliph still enjoyed the veneration of the people and who had consented to the reinstatement of the constitution, was spared direct incrimination. The most incisive attacks were directed at one of his closest advisors in the palace, 'Izzat Pasha al-'Abid, who fled abroad in the days following the revolution.[14] Many Arab officials, whose connections with 'Izzat Pasha and other Arab palace functionaries had won them positions in the capital and in the provinces, were removed in the over-haul. Layoffs and new appointments constituted the "driving force of the process of politicization."[15] The attempt by individuals to gain or regain government positions constituted the main arena of political ac-tivity and increasingly underlay ideological rivalries.

The Committee's immediate concern was to consolidate its position in İstanbul, but the reorganization of provincial administration proved to be the greater challenge. Abdülhamid's centralization was premised on patronage and personal ties to local notables, who often received administrative positions with considerable independence. After 1908 the local elites became suspicious of the CUP's designs and feared loss of power.[16] In order to avoid this, the notables attempted to reaffirm their authority vis-à-vis the newly appointed officials.

Consequently, finding qualified administrators to serve in areas where government authority had yet to be asserted proved to be particularly difficult. In the hope of making these administrative jobs more attrac-tive, the CUP declared in September that it would promote the principle of *tevsi'-i mezuniyet* and give wider authority to officials sent to the prov-inces.[17] The measure was also expedient for political reasons because Sabahaddin's decentralist associates announced at this time the forma-tion of the Liberal Party (*Ahrar*) to enter the upcoming elections.[18]

Anticipating the CUP announcement about *tevsi'-i mezuniyet*, Hü-seyin Cahid addressed in the pages of *Tanin* the two main features of the decentralist program, private initiative and decentralized adminis-tration, and endorsed the former while taking issue with the latter.[19] He criticized Sabahaddin's notion of *tevsi'-i mezuniyet*, which he claimed gave the provinces surveillance rights over the central government.[20] No matter how interpreted, *tevsi'-i mezuniyet* was tantamount to affirming one aspect of the administrative practice of the previous regime: select desirable candidates for provincial posts and allow them latitude in ad-ministration.

The CUP was destined to be plagued by the shortage of capable and reliable administrative personnel for several years, particularly in the Arab provinces.[21] The Hamidian administration had indulged the illegal profit-making practices of its appointees to those regions less desirable because of their remoteness or disturbed social conditions.[22] Under the new regime, the local CUP organizations exercised a greater degree of control over the local administration. The confiscation of the rapacious Hijaz governor Ratib Pasha's[23] property and his dismissal just days after the restoration of the constitution, followed by the dismissal of the grand sharif of Mecca, were well-publicized signs that the new regime would look askance at extortion.[24] In January 1909 the minister of the interior lamented in Parliament that officials were reluctant to go to distant provinces, where the authority of the new government had not been established yet. Unqualified and uneducated administrators had to be sent to these areas.[25]

The government had difficulty in making appointments even for the highest positions in provincial administration. For instance, in March 1909 the governorship of the province of the Hijaz in Arabia was offered first to the *müşir* (marshal) of the Fifth Army, Osman Fevzi Pasha,[26] and then to Ferid Pasha,[27] the director of the Infantry Department. Both turned it down. Then the appointment of Kosova governor Hadi Pasha was announced, but never materialized.[28] The governor who was finally appointed, Monastir's military commander Fuad Pasha, arrived in Mecca only in July and stayed at his new post for only a few weeks.[29] The turnover in governorships accelerated in all Arab provinces for several reasons. First, the governors' traditional alliances with local centers of power, often sanctioned independently by the Palace, now gave way to competition with notables for authority and induced frustrated governors to ask for transfers within short periods. Second, because the central government suffered from a shortage of able men, it could not always appoint candidates best suited for the job and, hence, was disposed toward making frequent changes. Third, crises of government in İstanbul and cabinet changes also resulted in dislocations in top-level provincial positions. Finally, many high officials and officers preferred to be in İstanbul at a time when new opportunities for advancement were opening up in the capital and shunned even the more prestigious positions in the provinces.

The news of the restoration of the constitution and the spread of the word of liberty challenged traditional power relationships in the provinces. Consecutive labor strikes affected communications and industry throughout the country.[30] Beirut witnessed strikes in the gas company and the harbor. Workers of the Damascus-Hama railroad struck for wage increases and improved working conditions.[31] Butchers in Damascus and Beirut protested the slaughter tax.[32] In the countryside peasants and tribes engaged in acts of disobedience. In order to restore order a more effective local administration was clearly needed, but, hard-pressed as the regime was to provide the cadres, the traditional political prerogatives of local leaders had to be acknowledged, especially in outlying areas.[33]

In the provinces, as in the capital, there were tensions between the military and civilian functionaries. Stephen Hemsley Longrigg noted about the Iraqi provinces, "A state of feud between the Wali and the General was in each wilaya [*vilayet*, or province] more usual than collaboration, and was curable only when the two posts were combined."[34] Where major army units were stationed, officers often came into conflict with civilian provincial authorities who were relatively more predisposed to ally with local notables. The conflict between the governor of Damascus, Nazım Pasha, and the commander of the Fifth Army, Osman Fevzi Pasha, in the spring of 1909 illustrated the tensions between military and civil authority in that province. Governor Nazım in this case sided with the notables and complained to İstanbul that the commander failed to supply military forces to prevent the Beduin from plundering local crops. Fevzi Pasha, in turn, felt that landowners wanted to exploit the presence of military units on the countryside to augment their authority over the peasants and to enhance their economic and political control by intimidation. He dismissed the Beduin raids as fabrications to induce troops to appear on peasant land and thus to force them to greater obedience.[35]

The CUP's reluctance to take the reins of government because of its inexperience and lack of self-confidence was at the root of the administrative crisis. Its indirect but unremitting interference in the political process introduced a problem of legitimacy. Its policy of availing of the skills and experience of certain statesmen of the old regime by keeping them under surveillance conflicted with its denunciation of all association with the Hamidian era. In İstanbul the CUP failed to displace the old bureaucratic elite. In the provinces it did not succeed in breaking the political power of conservative notables. Centralization continued to be dependent on co-optation, although the exchange mechanisms shifted from the personal framework to a bureaucratic and increasingly partisan one.

The 1908 Revolution and the CUP in the Arab Provinces

The news of the restoration of the constitution was received with caution in the provinces, though the reaction varied from region to region.[36] Provincial authorities in the Arab areas failed to realize the magnitude of the political change, or they believed that the revolution would not succeed. Some deliberately held back the announcement of the political changes in İstanbul.[37] The grand sharif of Mecca, for example, ordered anyone talking about the constitution to be flogged[38] and was further encouraged by Governor Ratib Pasha to try to win over the tribes against the constitution. On the other hand, army officers responded to the news with enthusiasm and energy. They established impromptu local Committees of Union and Progress, often with the participation of government functionaries, and led popular demonstrations in favor of the new regime.

In Greater Syria the response was relatively more enthusiastic in coastal regions[39] compared with the interior, where established landed families viewed the developments in İstanbul with reservations. The CUP in Jerusalem, which consisted predominantly of civilians and also included non-Muslims, established communication with Salonika. Even though the *mutasarrıf* (governor of a subprovince, or *sancak*) of Jerusalem, Ekrem Bey, was unsympathetic to the CUP, he was obliged to announce the reinstatement of the constitution. The prorevolution committee was stronger in Jaffa, where the *kaymakam* (district governor) at once declared his support for the constitution and the CUP.[40] An Iraqi colonel of the Ottoman army established CUP clubs in Iraq and launched the Arabic-Turkish newspaper *Baghdad*.[41] In Mecca the self-appointed local committee released the political prisoners in the town jail. It declared an end to the tax levied on entry into town and all but eliminated the camel tax that had been imposed by Governor Ratib.[42]

The revolution brought into the open social and political divisions throughout the empire. The prorevolution groups represented in individual regions a voice of opposition to the established political and social forces, but there was no common agenda that guided these political bodies. For the most part, the military officers and government officials constituted and led them, but they became rallying points for all disaffected elements, including segments of the indigenous elites. Therefore, the many demonstrations in the Arab provinces and elsewhere should not be viewed merely as public gatherings artificially contrived by officers and officials.[43] These rallies gave an opportunity to the townspeople to vent disaffection with existing conditions, even if one accepts that not many understood the meaning of the constitution. Moreover, the large turnouts can only be explained by the active support that the demonstrations received from local leaders vying for political power. According to reports of the British consul in Baghdad[44] and the French consul in Jidda,[45] the committees in these towns included, in addition to officers of different ranks, a number of notables. The British consul in Jidda reported that several thousand men participated in the demonstrations following the declaration of the constitution and that "crowds of common laborers" marched behind the CUP members to the house of the governor to arrest him.[46]

As in the Hijaz, in the Syrian *sancak* of Nablus the newly formed Committee of Union and Progress challenged established social relationships of the Hamidian period. A group of notables, some of whom held provincial offices, had oppressed the people with heavy taxes, even though these notables obtained *iltizam*s (tax-farm, or right of collection) at low biddings. The complaints of the people pitted the CUP against these notables, who responded with anti-Unionist propaganda. Delegates dispatched by the CUP headquarters persuaded the controversial notables to leave the town. During Nazım Pasha's governorship in Syria, in a move consistent with his favorable relationship with the Damascene notability, he allowed the Nablus notables to return.[47] Indeed, as political exigencies forced the CUP to compromise more and more with landed interests, one of these notables, Tawfiq Hammad, became a deputy from the CUP list in the third term of Parliament.

The restoration of the constitution and the formation of various committees under the name of Union and Progress were accompanied by parallel organizational activity by various social and professional groups. In Damascus, where the CUP was comparatively weak, two clubs, "Freedom" and "Free Ottoman," were formed by October 1908.[48] The names of these two associations reflected developments in İstanbul, specifically the formation there in September of the *Ahrar* party. Also in Damascus the ulema, the physicians, the merchants, and even the shoemakers formed their own separate associations.

The proliferation of local committees of a different ilk alarmed both the CUP headquarters and the Kamil Pasha government. Babanzade İsmail Hakkı, a Unionist and a Kurd from one of Iraq's notable families, criticized in *Tanin* those organizations that sought political power acting under the guise of Committees of Union and Progress.[49] The Committee, İsmail Hakkı reminded readers, had not arrogated to itself executive authority and was convinced of the dangers of doing so anywhere. According to the agent of the Government of India in Baghdad, Kamil Pasha cabled a message stating that "there is a CUP at Constantinople which is doing all it can to assist the new Cabinet, but it does not recognize the various Committees which are said to have formed themselves at provincial towns and which claim to be members of the Central Committee."[50] The grand vizier also announced that attempts by local Young Turk committees to interfere with government would be met with military force. As the CUP had its strongest following in the army units, İstanbul's threat could have had success in curbing only those clubs and committees cropping up—some even under the name Union and Progress—in opposition to the new order.[51]

The CUP Central Committee in Salonika was eager to bring the local prorevolution committees under its direct control. Public announcements to the contrary notwithstanding, the CUP was acting as a government within the government in İstanbul; it also desired to see in the provinces loyal branches that reported to Salonika and exercised influence in local government. The Unionists lacked social standing and were careful not to appear to be functioning as a surrogate government in the provinces.[52] In Jidda they even sent public criers around town to declare that the CUP was nothing more than an advisor to the government.[53] Nevertheless, more often than not, provincial government officials functioned under the control and instruction of the local CUP.[54] The Beiruti notable Salim ʿAli al-Salam testified that all government functions in Beirut were taken over by the president of the local CUP in the days after the revolution.[55]

With the preparations for parliamentary elections under way, the supervision and organization of the local committees assumed particular importance. Left to themselves, the prorevolution bodies faced the danger of being manipulated or losing their zeal and slowly disappearing. In the fall of 1908 the Salonika Central Committee sent delegations to the Arab provinces to reorganize the existing clubs and also establish new ones.[56] Two delegates from Salonika stayed close to six weeks in Syria and tried to influence the elections. They found resistance to the new order on the part of the landlords in Damascus and Aleppo, who feared "the loss of their arbitrary power over their peasants."[57] The delegates reorganized the local CUP and established the principle of strict secrecy in its correspondence with the Central Committee.[58] The CUP successfully implemented in Beirut the boycott of Austrian goods that was called in İstanbul following Vienna's annexation of Bosnia-Herzegovina on 5 October 1908. The boycott created a new opportunity for local business in the production of camel-hair hats to replace the traditional *fez*, the main item of import from Austria.[59] Another CUP delegation, inspecting the Benghazi Committee, criticized the absence among its members of "representatives of the great Arab community"[60] and induced two Arabs to join the Committee, which consisted primarily of Turkish officials. Most Benghazi Arab notables shunned the CUP, which they still considered an unknown quantity, and formed a rival club consisting of twelve members, two from each of the six principal tribes of the *sancak*.

After the initial excitement about the constitution subsided, the usual local political conflicts came back to center stage, and the local committees became targets of attack. Such was the case in Baghdad, where the local CUP was blamed for the "independent attitude" of the town's Jews, who were emboldened by the message of equality.[61] In the fall, the rumors of a new cemetery tax triggered anticonstitutionalist protests in Mecca.[62] The British consul in Jidda, Monahan, viewed the riots as a protest against "the Committee of Union and Progress in Mecca, the new constitutional body, which is meddling in all government affairs," while a French official in Cairo reacted to the same events by reporting on the basis of an article in *Al-mu'ayyad* that "the partisans of the old regime take advantage of this pretext [the cemetery tax] to create agitation against the reforms."[63]

The organizational efforts of the CUP yielded limited results in the parliamentary elections. The Committee candidates were successful in some districts. To assure a Unionist victory in others, however, the Committee included on its slates candidates of the local notability whose sympathy for the new regime was suspect but who commanded patronage and popular following. These maneuvers were used not only in Aleppo, Damascus, and the rest of Arab provinces but also elsewhere in the empire. Therefore, the CUP encountered difficulties in disciplining its group and preventing the growth of opposition when Parliament started its work. Once the Committee reconstituted itself as an open political party, it sent delegations to the Arab provinces to settle disputes, to bring the people together around a party program emphasizing economic issues, and to form new branches of the party.[64]

The 1908 Elections

The 1877–78 parliamentary elections had been held in accordance with the provisional electoral regulations that stipulated the election of deputies by administrative councils in the provinces. A new election law that had been drafted in the same Parliament but never ratified was taken as the basis of the 1908 elections. It stipulated two-stage balloting in which every tax-paying male Ottoman citizen above the age twenty-five was entitled to vote in a primary election to select secondary voters. Secondary voters, each elected by 500 to 750 primary voters, then voted to determine the member(s) of the Chamber in the numbers specified for a particular electoral district, the *sancak*. The law did not make special quota arrangements for the religious or sectarian communities. Each voter was to vote as an Ottoman citizen for deputies representing not a particular community but all Ottomans.[65]

The Young Turks intended to depart from communal politics in favor of "party" politics. Yet in the first elections local prestige and CUP sponsorship proved to be more important than any political program.[66] The CUP hoped to use its popularity and influence to assure the election of supporters from all religious and ethnic groups. The deputies who came to İstanbul in December 1908 were not all Unionists, but many had enjoyed CUP support during the elections, as the Committee's endorsement often attended a candidate's local standing. During the first elections the CUP's program, which had been published toward the end of September 1908,[67] was not made the basis of an election platform. Individual candidates issued personal declarations and ran on individual programs.[68] The CUP drafted lists of endorsed candidates, but such endorsement served more to co-opt the leading candidates than help sympathizers get elected.

The socioeconomic composition of the new Chamber was similar to that of the 1877–78 Parliament, partly because the CUP support tended to coincide with local social prominence and partly because the two-stage balloting favored the election of notables. Even though franchise requirements were liberal in primary voting, patronage-based social and political relationships in the countryside usually resulted in the election of landowners. In the second stage, these electors exercised their choice for a candidate representing their social group. The contingent of secondary electors was also in most cases small enough to be easily manipulated by powerful candidates or government officials.

Article 72 of the constitution stipulated that deputies had to be "from the people" of the province they ran in, but neither the constitution nor the electoral law laid down specific residency requirements. Thus, while officials appointed from İstanbul and coming from outside the province could be elected by virtue of being current inhabitants of that province, individuals living in the capital or elsewhere could also be nominated and elected from provinces where they no longer resided but had family roots. Babanzade İsmail Hakkı defended the right of nonresidents to stand as candidates by writing in the columns of *Tanin* that electing provincial dunces as opposed to enlightened sons in big cities would be insulting Parliament.[69] His *Tanin* associate Hüseyin Cahid displayed similar elitist outlook when he advocated weighted voting for graduates of higher schools, as in England.[70] These attitudes toward representation, certainly not unique to the Ottoman political elite at the time, revealed a conception of government for the people that did not insist on a one-to-one parliamentary representation of different social groups.

The overrepresentation of Turkish deputies in the 1908 Parliament has been cited as indicating a bias in favor of an ethnic Turkish direction.[71] Known cases of the CUP tampering with the electoral process (for instance, in İstanbul, to the detriment of the Greek community[72]) lent credibility to claims of discrimination. The CUP engaged in a limited campaign to have its designated candidates elected but did not as a rule use coercive or illegal methods to assure this. However, there were many irregularities in the electoral process in the provinces, particularly in the Arab districts. In Mecca and Jidda, for instance, primary elections were bypassed, and a group of town notables was designated, presumably by the electoral committees, to serve as secondary voters. In Yemen, deputyships were set aside for the eight principal tribal communities, granting the province more representation than an apportionment based on population estimates would have.[73] In many districts the elected candidates did not actually meet the constitutional requirements for deputyship.

The election in Karak in southern Syria provides examples of a number of the problems encountered in the Arab provinces. The winner in Karak, Shaykh Qadri, chose to defer to the runner-up, Tawfik al-Majali. Parliament rejected the deputyship of al-Majali, because the resignation of a deputy-elect would necessitate new elections; no local or electoral authority had the power to replace Qadri with the candidate who received the second largest number of votes. Al-Majali's deputyship was endorsed after a deputy from Damascus, Shafiq al-Mu'ayyad, pleaded in the Chamber to apply the rules less stringently. He argued that Karak was a new administrative unit with a predominantly Beduin population, and that the actual winner, Qadri, was unqualified to sit in Parliament because he not only did not know Turkish but also was illiterate.[74]

The Arab Parliamentary Contingent
in the First Legislative Year

Parliament opened on 17 December 1908. The event aroused empire-wide interest, and, according to one account, so many people came to İstanbul from the provinces to witness the event that some newly arriving deputies had to be placed in dormitories of boarding schools for lack of vacancies in the capital's hotels.[75] This festive opening in İstanbul was also marked by celebrations in provincial centers that featured speeches and prayers, but only modest public interest. In Jidda the celebration took place in the town hall while the postmaster, "an advanced constitutionalist," had a "wooden triumphal arch" erected near the post office.[76] In Mecca all the dignitaries, including the grand sharif, observed the occasion in the military headquarters.[77] In Medina large numbers of Beduin and their shaykhs also participated. Together with the local Ottoman officials and officers, they listened to a speech by the tahrirat müdürü (director of correspondence) on the formulaic theme of the legitimacy of constitutionalism before religious law (meşrutiyetin meşruiyeti).[78]

On 23 December the Chamber elected a speaker (president). Ahmed Rıza was chosen with an overwhelming majority (205 votes). The two Arab deputies, Nafiʿ of Aleppo (who had the distinction of having served also in the Parliament of 1877–78) and ʿAbd al-Qadir of Medina, finished in distant seventh (nine votes) and ninth place (seven votes), respectively. One of the first items on the newly convened Chamber's agenda was the examination of the records submitted by local electoral committees and the endorsement of the credentials of the successful candidates.

The list of those whose qualifications were in heated contention included several from the Arab provinces: Yusuf Shitwan (Tripoli-Libya), ʿUmar Mansur (Benghazi), Sayyid Talib al-Naqib (Basra), and Shafiq al-Muʾayyad (al-ʿAzm) (Syria). The objections to these deputies were in essence political, but often legal impediments or electoral irregularities were put forward.

Shitwan, a judicial inspector in the previous regime,[79] and al-Muʾayyad, a high-level imperial delegate at the Tobacco Régie in İstanbul,[80] were accused of having spied for Abdülhamid.[81] Al-Muʾayyad was in addition charged with perjury in a personal inheritance case. ʿUmar

Mansur was alleged to have falsified his election papers.[82] As for Talib, the *naqib al-ashraf* [83] of Basra, he was one of those prominent Arab notables whose local standing assured him a spot in the Chamber, although his commitment to the new constitutional regime was suspect.[84] Despite the objections, Mansur, al-Mu'ayyad, and Talib were endorsed after deliberation. In Shitwan's case new elections were ordered on grounds that he secured the deputyship by intimidating certain officials. However, Shitwan was successful also in the reelection. When objections were raised again on the floor in the summer of 1909, Mansur interpreted them as an insult to Shitwan's constituency. Other Arab deputies, including 'Abd al-Hamid al-Zahrawi (Hama), spoke on his behalf.[85] Unlike al-Mu'ayyad and Talib, Shitwan became a CUP loyalist in the years to come, especially after the CUP subscribed to an Islamic political orientation in 1913. Yet another election was repeated in Libya, when the deputy-elect for Fezzan (Tripoli-Libya) decided to return to his business. The Turkish *kaymakam* of the district of Ghat, Cami Bey, won the reelection. On the occasion of his endorsement in the summer of 1909, objections were unsuccessfully raised against him on grounds of administrative malpractice and tax corruption.[86]

No sooner had Parliament opened than many of the Arab deputies joined a society called the Arab-Ottoman Brotherhood (*Al-ikha' al-'arabi al-'uthmani*, or *Uhuvvet-i Arabiyye-i Osmaniye*), which had been formed in İstanbul in September[87] and had welcomed the Arab deputies to the capital with a big reception.[88] *Al-ikha'* served a dual purpose. On the one hand, it constituted an extension of the societies that Arabs, mainly students, had formed in the capital before the revolution in order to promote contacts among the Arabs living there. On the other hand, its founders, who had been officials in the Hamidian regime, hoped to preserve their status "by presenting themselves as the protectors of Arab interests in the empire"[89] and to develop an Arab coalition that would collectively work toward the achievement of Ottoman unity. Shafiq al-Mu'ayyad was one of the founders and served as president; Shitwan was also a member.[90] The close involvement of these two men, both of whom had been incriminated in Parliament, gave to the brotherhood the appearance of an oppositional group. In reality it was a short-lived society in which voices of future rival Arab opinions coexisted. *Al-ikha'* also had branches in the Arab provinces, where its propaganda had a distinctly anti-CUP tone.[91] Just as future supporters of the CUP joined *Al-ikha'*, future opponents such as Rafiq al-'Azm and Rashid Rida denounced the society for its leaders' connections with the old regime. The society was closed after the counterrevolutionary upheaval of April 1909, accused of having had connections in Damascus with the local branch of the *İttihad-ı Muhammedi Cemiyeti* (Muhammadan Union Society), the instigator of the counterrevolution.

Early in the second constitutional period, calls for Arab autonomy and independence came from outside the empire but failed to find enthusiastic reception among the Arabs. In December 1908 a declaration demanding self-government for Syria, written in Paris by an organization calling itself the Syrian Central Committee and signed by Rashid Mutran, circulated within the empire. The author asserted that constitutional government in the Western sense was not possible in the Ottoman Empire and that minority aspirations would inevitably lead to its dissolution. He recommended that the Syrians adopt the principles of the new constitution but apply them in an autonomous Syria. Mutran also suggested to the Western powers that the establishment of an autonomous Syria in the strategic location it occupied would also serve their interests.[92]

Though couched as an appeal for autonomy, the thrust of the manifesto of the Syrian Central Committee represented a reiteration of Syrian separatism that had never found support in Syria, much less among the Arabs in general. Beirut's Christian deputy Sulayman al-Bustani was one of the first to reprehend Mutran.[93] For many Syrians the Syrian Central Committee based in Paris was an unknown entity that represented little beyond the desires of its founders and, like Nagib Azoury's *Ligue de la Patrie Arabe*, did not have a following anywhere.[94] The circular caused widespread anger and sadness in Syria, according to the governor in Damascus,[95] and the British consul in Damascus reported that the proposal to give Syria "partial independence of the Turkish Empire" was received "with disapproval and contempt throughout Syria."[96] Similar denunciation came from a second Arab group in Paris, the Syrian Ottoman Society, led by Shukri Ghanem.[97]

The strong and broad reaction to the Syrian Committee's declaration demonstrated the Ottomanist convictions of different segments of the Arab society. It also evinced the diverse avenues of political expression that had opened under the new regime and to which opponents and proponents of politicized issues would resort in the months and years to come. The matter was discussed in Parliament. The press gave wide coverage to it. Numerous letters and telegrams of protest arrived at the grand vizierate and the presidency of Parliament from the provinces and even from outside the empire.

In Parliament deputies insisted on going on the record with their declarations of support for the Ottoman state, in condemning the circular, and in concurring with the denunciatory letters from Syria.[98] The fear of French designs on Syria added to the consternation. Nafi' al-Jabiri characterized Mutran as a madman and confirmed that all Arab peoples in the entire empire placed their political sentiments under the same banner.[99] Particularly interesting were the comments of a Beiruti deputy;[100] he denounced the references to the Syrian Committee on the floor and in the press as the "Arab Committee." In an effort to disassociate Beirut from the Mutran initiative, he maintained that Mutran's committee pretended to speak for the Arabs in the province of Syria only, thus once again underscoring the localism and diversity in the Arab regions. While all Arab deputies concurred in their criticism of the circular, Muhammad Arslan, deputy from Latakia, pleaded that the condemnation should not be extended to the entire Mutran family; many members of Mutran's own family, he indicated, had been among the first to condemn him.[101] Indeed, Nadra Mutran, one of the founders of *Al-ikha* ' in İstanbul,[102] openly expressed his criticism for brothers Rashid and Nakhla, who professed to be the leaders of the Syrian Committee.[103] Such differences of political outlook between members or branches of the same families were a feature of Arab political life shared by Muslims and Christians.

The Mutran affair suggests that Arab leaders had faith in the Ottomanist vision that the 1908 Revolution promised. Although separatist schemes continued to originate from outside the borders of the Ottoman state, for most Arabs the new constitution and Parliament dispelled any need for a separate existence. Furthermore, even the Syrians did not think in terms of a broader community sharing an alternative political vision. From the vehemence with which Mutran was criticized, it seemed clear that there was faith in Ottoman unity both within and outside Parliament.

The Arab leaders saw no inconsistency between the sentiments expressed on the occasion of the Mutran letter and, within days of that parliamentary debate, undertaking an initiative to form an Arab parliamentary group. This initiative under the leadership of Nafi' was reported in the press.[104] The group counted among its objectives the attainment of proportional representation in Parliament and in state service.[105] Hüseyin Cahid, who had published an article only days earlier in which he contended, on the basis of the Mutran debate, that there was no inclination toward a "politics of nationality" (*milliyet politikası*)[106] in Parliament, came out vehemently against the formation of an "Arab party," interpreting its demands as a desire for independence. The group's formation also coincided with the crisis that led to the vote of no confidence for Kamil Pasha and made the CUP even more sensitive to any potential initiative from an organized opposition. Nafi' had to assuage such reaction by publicly renouncing the pursuit of special Arab interests and declaring the group open to all.

The thrust of Arab opinion in Parliament remained in the direction of unity and uniformity within the imperial framework, not toward particularism. In the first annual session of Parliament, Arab deputies raised concerns pertaining to variant practices in the different provinces, in particular the regional, and seemingly arbitrary, divergence in the kinds of taxes as well as their methods of collection. One of the earliest statements in this regard came from Rajab Efendi, a deputy from Yemen (Hodeida), who argued against the practice of levying an onerous market tax in Yemen instead of the regular Ottoman taxes based on crops, animals, and profits. The deputy stressed that Yemen had no legal distinction from the other provinces and that the market tax hurt Yemen's agriculture and trade.[107] Similarly, 'Abd al-Mahdi Efendi complained about a tax in Karbala that he claimed was not levied anywhere else, as other deputies complained that certain taxes were collected in different proportions, even in neighboring provinces.[108] At the root of the problem lay the government's failure to put tax registers in order. The deputies envisaged a greater role for the government to regularize tax collection.

Demands for special prerogatives deriving from specific concerns of the provinces were also placed on the agenda. A motion to provide for minting coins specific to Yemen was quickly tabled, leaving the rationale for the demand in obscurity.[109] The Aleppine contingent favored a ban on wheat exports from the district of Elbistan, ostensibly on grounds of shortages due to locusts. The minister of the interior, Hüseyin Hilmi Pasha (later grand vizier) addressed the matter during an interpellation. He stressed that provincial governors had no authority to impose such restrictions. Nafi' asked for further empowerment of local authorities and more funding to cope with the problem.[110] Particularly interesting was the discussion of taxes collected in Anatolian provinces earmarked for a medical school in Damascus and an industrial school in Ankara. Some deputies objected to the use of funds collected in their provinces for schools in other provinces. Others countered, arguing that the Damascus and Ankara schools would be open to all and would not be for the benefit of the two provinces only.[111]

There was nothing that distinguished Arab deputies from Turkish deputies in the kinds of issues they raised and the frequency and tone with which they did so. Arab deputies evinced particular interest in issues pertaining to other Arab provinces. This was in part due to the similarity of social, administrative, and economic problems in the broader region, but also to a sense of commonality among these deputies. On the whole, the Arab political orientation reinforced the Unionist conception of a unitary state. The many demands from the Arab provinces pertaining to regional deprivations, administrative irregularities, and security issues presumed the responsibility of the central government and indeed reinforced the role of the center.[112]

The CUP's political program stressed equal rights and obligations for all Ottomans. The new government aimed at systematizing fiscal and administrative practices. Yet the implementation of a reform program embodying these ideals encountered problems in the political turmoil—international complications, financial constraints, and the Committee's ambiguous role in the political process—that marked the initial stage of constitutional rule. During the first of the four months when Parliament held regular sessions its work was devoted mostly to its internal organization. In the second month it was distracted by a showdown between the CUP and Grand Vizier Kamil Pasha, which resulted in the replacement of Kamil by Hüseyin Hilmi Pasha. In April, less than four months after Parliament convened, its work was interrupted by a counterrevolutionary uprising.

The Counterrevolution

The 31 March Incident was an uprising of conservative forces in İstanbul: religious students and functionaries, military cadres with traditional education who faced displacement by younger officers, and loyalists to the old regime. Most likely, it received encouragement from the CUP's decentralist opponents, the *Ahrar* party.[113] In time-honored Ottoman tradition, resistance to change was expressed in a religious idiom. The uprising was led by *İttihad-ı Muhammedi*, which had come to the surface only days before the uprising. It posed a profound challenge to the new regime, and consequently to the CUP, less than nine months after the revolution. The Committee managed to bring the volatile situation in the capital under control only with help from the loyal Third Army units and immediately proceeded to take measures for a more decisive role in government.

According to the responses to a memorandum sent by the restored government to the provinces inquiring about the extent of local agitation, the Incident did not have significant repercussions in the Arab provinces, except in Damascus. The governors reported that there was little reason to fear local uprisings but took the opportunity to ask for troop reinforcements and improvement of the security apparatus.[114] Except for Damascus, there was no link between local elements and the insurgents in İstanbul. However, once the reactionary uprising took place and revealed the vulnerability of the regime, local groups resorted to its slogans to promote specific objectives. In Medina troops took up arms, locked themselves in the Prophet's Mosque, and demanded discharge.[115] In Baghdad an organization called *Mashwar* (Consultation), which had been formed by a member of a local notable family, ʿIsa al-Jamili, with the participation of some officials, surfaced and apparently acquired the support of sections of the army stationed in the city. This group was reported to have been in contact with the tribes of Arabia in an attempt to establish an independent Arab kingdom.[116] Even though *Mashwar* had been known to the government before the Incident, ten days after it the grand vizier urged a thorough investigation lest the reactionary outburst in İstanbul encourage this subversive scheme.

In Damascus a counterrevolutionary upsurge was engineered by conservative notables and the local branch of *İttihad-ı Muhammedi*.[117] The leaders of the Damascus organization included ʿAbd al-Qadir al-ʿAjlani, ʿAbdullah al-Jazaʾiri, Tawfiq al-Qudsi, and Rida ʿAttar. Governor Nazım mentioned that others who "were deceived with the religious propaganda" of this group showed repentance after they found out about the "malevolent intentions" of the leaders.[118] The governor did not elaborate on the true motives of the "reactionaries," which were no doubt the same as those of the parent group and its allies: to undermine the regime by suggesting that the new order threatened religion, an accusation to which the CUP's opposition would resort time and again in the future. The governor feared that the trial of the accused might occasion unruly behavior on the part of segments of the population and that military reinforcements from outside the province would be needed, since the

local reserve forces were suspected of harboring reactionary sympathies.[119]

The events of April 1909 crystallized forces in the Ottoman body
politic that had started to take shape in the aftermath of the 1908 Revolution. An important outcome of the revolt was the deposition of Abdülhamid on charges of complicity in favor of his brother Sultan Mehmed Reşad (r. 1909–18). The Incident pitted the CUP against the
"Liberal" decentralists and compelled the Committee to reappraise its
role in government by defining its political objectives. The successful
suppression of the uprising by the Third Army units under the command of Mahmud Shawkat Pasha enhanced the CUP's stature vis-à-vis
its political opponents, but shook its self-confidence. The Committee
now deemed it imperative to assert itself more directly in the conduct
of state policy and proceeded to take steps that would weaken political
opposition. Mahmud Shawkat Pasha, who commanded considerable
moral authority after the suppression of the uprising, wanted to preserve
the constitutional order, but he did not have faith that the Unionists
could achieve this. The Committee maintained Hüseyin Hilmi Pasha at
the helm of the government instead of appointing a grand vizier from
its own ranks.

Mahmud Shawkat Pasha was the descendant of an Arabic-speaking
family from Baghdad.[120] Like his father, who had served as *mutasarrıf*
in Iraq, he advanced in the service of the Ottoman state, was Ottomanized and dedicated to the survival and integrity of the empire. As the
commander of the forces that had restored order in the capital, Mahmud
Shawkat Pasha enjoyed great prestige. He was appointed inspector-
general of the three European army corps and became a powerful figure
under the martial law regime that was instituted after the counterrevolution was crushed.[121]

Plagued as the CUP was by tensions between its military and civilian
wings, Mahmud Shawkat embodied the enhanced position of the military in Ottoman politics while remaining above and beyond the CUP
and overshadowing it. The best that the CUP could do in the months
following the counterrevolution was to place two of its civilian members, Mehmed Talat and Mehmed Cavid, in the Hüseyin Hilmi cabinet
as the interior and finance ministers, respectively.[122] The suppression of
the counterrevolution did not put the CUP at the helm of the government, but debilitated the opposition and allowed the Committee to
pursue its political objectives more aggressively with two of its most
capable and committed members in key ministerial positions.

Reform and Centralization

Abdülhamid's consent to restore the constitution in July 1908 immediately opened the door for political reform, and the Young Turks quickly forced measures that would prevent the return of autocracy. By imperial decree, the clauses in the 1876 constitution that had made possible the abrogation of that charter were revoked, establishing checks and balances between the legislature and the executive. The grand vizier acquired the right to appoint the cabinet, even though the religious prerogatives of the sultan as caliph were untouched.[123] These early changes lacked a firm legal basis, as Marschall, the German ambassador, observed in September 1908: "Now the Constitution of 1876 includes a number of liberal principles with the rejoinder 'as circumscribed by law.' Thus, Turkey has freedom of press but no Press Law, freedom of association, but no usable Law of Association."[124]

In the months after the revolution a plethora of ethnic-based cultural and political clubs emerged. They were tolerated in the name of freedom of association. Among the newly formed societies were the Greek Political Club (*Rum Siyasi Kulübü*), the Serbian-Ottoman Club (*Sırp-Osmanlı Kulübü*), the Armenian *Dashnak* (Federation), the Bulgarian Club, the Jewish Youth Club (*Musevi Gençler Kulübü*), the Lovers of Anatolia (*Anadolu Muhibleri*), the Albanian *Bashkim* (Union), and the Kurdish Mutual Aid Society (*Kürt Teâvün Kulübü*).[125] The organizational structure and propaganda of some of these bodies soon clashed with the CUP's vision of Ottoman unity. Concerned governors reported to İstanbul about nationalist activity of ethnic clubs. The governor of Trabzon mentioned the Armenian Club's decentralist propaganda in the Black Sea town of Giresun, behind which, according to rumors, the group pursued secret nationalist objectives and was distributing guns.[126] Kosova's governor transmitted a translation of the program of the Serbian Club in Üsküp (Skopje) indicating that the group was assuming the appearance of a general national assembly.[127] Faced with such reports the grand vizier urged the Council of State to draft a law regulating associations and public meetings as early as March 1909.[128] The counterrevolutionary uprising of April 1909 intervened and underscored the urgency of disciplining the activities of associations.

Parliament deliberated on the first legislative acts to define the extent of the freedoms granted by the constitution only in the summer of 1909.

It passed a Press Law on 29 July and a Law of Association on 16 August, both of which were designed to curb the freedoms that had been enjoyed with few restraints before the counterrevolution. Amendments to the 1876 constitution enacted in August 1909 enhanced Parliament's powers to initiate legislation and render cabinet ministers responsible to the legislature individually as well as collectively. Parliament procrastinated in passing other legislation under consideration, such as the Provincial Law, which would have had to address the main points of contention between the CUP and its decentralist opposition. Yet the government did take a conscious interest in the social and material welfare of the provinces, though its efforts were haphazard and rarely backed by legislation.[129]

Like other revolutionaries, the Young Turks accepted education as the pivot of all reform. They were convinced that an increased level of education, both formal and informal, would enhance public consciousness, render the Ottoman people more receptive to constitutional and liberal ideas, and help institute law and order. Unlike the educational policy of Ottoman regimes since the Tanzimat, the Young Turks saw the purpose of education as the enlightenment of all Ottomans rather than the training of administrative and military personnel. The CUP sought to achieve this not only through government sponsored compulsory education but also by mobilizing its resources as a popular society. Among its objectives as a society, the CUP put forth in the resolutions of its first congress in 1908, in addition to private schools and night classes, the recruitment of able instructors (particularly for industrial schools); assistance to chambers of commerce, agriculture, and industry; the publication of practical books and manuals; and sending students to Europe.[130]

The factors that hampered reform in many other areas frustrated also the attempts to build educational institutions. In the first ten months that followed the revolution the Ministry of Education changed hands seven times.[131] The CUP's efforts to establish new schools throughout the country, including many in the Arab provinces, point to the Committee's continuing conviction that progress and unity would follow from increased education. In 1909 the CUP opened a school for 500 students in Damascus in addition to smaller schools and night classes in other Syrian towns,[132] Jerusalem,[133] and somewhat later Medina.[134] The funding for these projects came from donations.

The government observed closely the promotion of provincial newspapers and tried to increase the readership in the provinces.[135] The proliferation and propagation of written material were the most important factors in the politicization of Ottoman society. Political journals introduced the literate to new ideas and initiated debates. Newspapers published selective portions of parliamentary debates. Indeed, the discourse produced by stormy articles and rebuttals made the daily press a more current forum for the discussion of national political issues than the floor of the Chamber. As many newspapers and journals gradually moved to the opposition camp, the CUP found out that manipulating a consensus among deputies in Parliament was easier than bridling the press.

The more backward areas of the Arab provinces received particular and immediate attention in terms of reforms. Two reports, one received from a member of Medina's ulema, ʿAbd al-Rahman Ilyas Pasha, and another from a Najdi notable, Rashid Nasir, illustrate the concern felt for reforms in Arabia.[136] While Rashid Nasir emphasized the need for officials familiar with the local language and customs, Ilyas Pasha listed as the leading difficulties in administration the ignorance of the people, the smuggling of arms on the Red Sea coast, and the arbitrary actions of local officials. Ilyas Pasha's report was studied in İstanbul as the basis of a broader reform scheme not only for the Peninsula but also encompassing the tribal areas of Baghdad, Basra, and Syria. Aware of the difficulty of extending governmental authority in the outlying Arab provinces, the government repeatedly addressed the question of nomadic tribes. The Young Turks believed that a centralized administration could be established only if these tribes could be permanently settled; and they presumed that this could be achieved by providing them the benefits of education. The failure of a school opened in Karak to attract enough students showed that nomads were not enthusiastic about sending their children to school.[137] Ilyas was given a salary to travel in the Peninsula in order to oversee the establishment of schools and to appoint instructors and preachers familiar with the disposition of the tribal elements.[138]

Talat impressed upon the grand vizierate the need to single out the regions where reform would bring timely and tangible results and to tackle the job gradually with the help of a commission of investigation and with a thought-out order of priority. The implementation of drastic reforms within a short period in such a vast and undeveloped region as the Peninsula was considered unrealistic given the government's limited financial and military capabilities. The Ministry of the Interior stressed that the backwardness of these regions did not come about as a result of Ottoman rule, but rather had existed from time immemorial. It could be corrected over time only by the constitutional government.

In the İstanbul papers, articles addressed conditions in the Arab provinces. "If the peasants of Anatolia have been subjected to so many injustices during [Abdülhamid's] administration, how much more must the helpless people of the remote provinces have suffered?" asked *Tanin*, which broached the example of the people of Fezzan, who emigrated to Tunis in fear of physical punishment for their inability to pay their taxes.[139] When writing on conditions in Syria, Hüseyin Cahid indicated that the bitterness (*hiss-i ihtiraz*) that the Syrians felt against the government had to be appreciated. To harp upon the injustices and ill-treatment to which the Anatolians had been subjected, he argued, would not render the grievances of the Syrians less justified.[140] The Committee realized and confronted the problems of outlying provinces, but with a naive conviction that representative government would somehow remedy them, enhance loyalty to the state, and assure territorial consolidation.

The Unionist precondition for reform was the extension of central authority to the widest extent possible and the standardization of administrative and financial practices in the provinces. The Unionists had always subscribed to the centralist trend in the Young Turk movement. They argued that the parliamentary regime would enable fair regional representation in government and thus protect regional interests within the framework of a unified government whose primary aim was the preservation of a united Ottoman state. In September 1908, Hüseyin Cahid wrote, "If our remote provinces that have not yet attained an advanced stage in their political lives were to be administered on the basis of decentralization, and a kind of autonomous administration evolves in these areas . . . the result will be lawlessness."[141] Centralization was viewed as particularly well suited to promote the welfare of the empire's periphery.

In July 1908 those elements in the Arab provinces who had been critical of Hamidian rule for restricting higher administrative and religious positions in the provinces to wealthy ulema-bureaucratic families were ready supporters of the CUP. The Arab opponents of Abdülhamid shared with the Unionists the same social values; they were products of modern professional schools, were exposed to secular European ideas and ideologies, and accepted a representative constitutional order as the prerequisite to strengthen the Ottoman state and to preserve its integrity. They represented families with no particular social prestige, and thus resented the elitism of İstanbul as well as the social esteem and political authority that the traditional leaders enjoyed in the countryside.

As the CUP came to realize that it had to compromise with the conservative notability to ensure its political predominance in Parliament, it gradually alienated its former Arab allies. Arab opinion continued to favor unity under the Islamic Ottoman Empire and was averse to centrifugal influences in the direction of autonomy or separatism. However, toward the end of 1909 an adversarial relationship began to take shape between the Unionists and those Arab leaders who had failed to find immediate rewards under the increasingly more CUP-dominated constitutional regime.

The growing emphasis on education and the proliferation of published material—ushered in by enhanced freedom of expression—highlighted the question of language. The enforcement of the state language, namely, Ottoman Turkish, in all spheres of public life was integral to the Unionist program of centralization. As Armenians and Greeks asked for their respective languages to be accepted as state languages,[142] Arabs, too, became interested in promoting Arabic in an official capacity. The first and most persistent challenge to Young Turk centralization from the Arabs was thus to emerge as the issue of language. The position Arabic would assume in the public sphere in the Arab provinces turned into an increasingly politicized bone of contention between Arabs and Young Turks.

The constitutional requirement for deputies to speak Turkish was only loosely applied in the 1908 Parliament. This averted a political problem but introduced a formidable practical one. Some Arab deputies from less developed regions such as Yemen or Hawran found it impossible to follow the proceedings or make their voices heard.[143] Some complained, in Arabic, that their motions (probably also submitted in Arabic) did not get due attention. Even though Arabic proposals were usually translated into Turkish prior to deliberation,[144] this was not always the case.[145]

Even as the enforcement of the use of Turkish emerged as an important and sensitive issue in the relationship of the central government with the Arabs, the mainstream of Arab politics continued to conform to the broader trends in the empire. The first year of constitutional government did not shake the faith of Muslims in Ottomanism, despite the post-revolution disappointment of expectations and growing criticism of the CUP. Agendas of Arab separatism were repudiated, as the case of Mutran's Syrian Central Committee showed. The Arabs demanded the regulation of administration, the expansion of state education, and the strengthening of the security apparatus: measures that called for an even greater role for the central government in the provinces.

3

The Opposition and the Arabs, 1910–1911

The army's successful suppression of the counterrevolution of April 1909 arrested both the anticonstitutionalist (pro-
Hamidian) and the Liberal (decentralist) opposition to the CUP and
left the Committee, though weakened, as the only viable political group.
As the Committee struggled to consolidate its position, so did its opponents. Its determination to establish itself as the paramount arbiter in
the government of the empire sharpened the differences between the
Committee and the decentralists. By the end of 1911 the opposition dealt
a critical blow to the CUP in a by-election in İstanbul, compelling it to
go to early parliamentary elections.

The division between the centralists and the decentralists did not
crystallize along strict socioeconomic lines. Allegiances remained fluid
and frequently changed depending on perceptions of personal advantage. In general, the centralists drew their support from the lesser Muslim officialdom and lower-middle-class elements who were averse to
European economic domination. Such domination had reinforced political tutelage over the empire and constituted a threat to the integrity
of the Ottoman state, which the centralist Unionists, many of them
members of the civil service and military establishment, were committed
to preserve.[1] Many older bureaucrats and officers who had acquired
wealth or high positions prior to 1908 and sought to maintain their
social and political predominance gravitated toward the opposition. As
the battle lines gradually crystallized, two groups of provincial notables
also identified with the opposition: those who were passed over in the
distribution of favors to the advantage of other contenders and those

whose local predominance was so entrenched as not to be challenged by rivals even when the latter enjoyed government backing. There were also the growing commercial elements; on the one hand they favored the opening up of the Ottoman markets to Europe, and on the other, saw their interests in the loosening of central control over the economy.

The Christian communities also looked favorably on the autonomist thrust of the decentralist platform due to their close links to the European economy, cultural concerns, or ethnic-separatist sentiments. Even though the Armenians and Greeks had largely supported the decentralist Sabahaddin faction prior to the revolution, in the euphoria of July 1908 the Unionists believed that the non-Muslims would be won over to the CUP's Ottomanist platform in the new parliamentary regime. They hoped that religious and ethnic differences would be superseded by a broader Ottoman identity. In the eyes of most Christians, however, Ottoman citizenship based on absolute equality, as preached by the Unionists, would undermine their community privileges, which had expanded since the Tanzimat. Allowing the disintegration of the *millet* as a political entity in favor of a supranational civic Ottomanist identity was also likely to jeopardize Christian economic and cultural interests. Clerical leaders sought modalities of accommodation with the various governments, even as large segments of their communities drifted toward the opposition. The CUP commanded the allegiance of segments of the Christian population only to the extent that it could exploit that population's intracommunal differences.

"Turkification"

The CUP's notion of an Ottomanism that denied political representation on a religious-communal basis, its denunciation of decentralization, and its inflexible attitude toward the demands and organizational initiative of the religious minorities exposed it to charges of "Turkification," a systematic process of depriving non-Turks of their established social, political, and cultural rights. This charge was leveled first by the Committee's European critics. In the mind of European observers of the Ottoman state, the fact that the empire was ruled by a Turkish dynasty rendered Turk, Ottoman, and Muslim synonymous. They therefore regarded the Ottomanism of the Young Turks as Turkification that threatened the empire's Christian population. When a con-

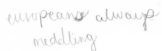
europeans always meddling

temporary European observer wrote that the CUP had a "plan of re-
ducing the various races and regions of the empire to one dead level of
Turkish uniformity,"[2] or when the British ambassador Sir Gerard
Lowther defined Young Turk Ottomanism as "pounding non-Turkish
elements in a Turkish mortar,"[3] their concern was with the empire's non-
Muslims. Lowther viewed Turkification first and foremost as a means
of fighting European tutelage, an "Asianization" of the Ottoman Empire
and its mobilization against Western interests.[4] The Young Turks indeed
believed that the economic interests of the Muslim peoples of the empire, Arabs as well as Turks, had been neglected and thus would have to
be remedied. They would deny, however, that putting the Muslims on
a footing of economic and political equality had to take place at the
expense of the religious or ethnic rights of other groups.

The circumscription of liberties of press and association exposed the
Committee to renewed attacks. Hüseyin Cahid took on the charges leveled against the Young Turks for attempting to Turkify non-Turkish elements. He argued that the charges of Turkification were being advanced
to justify separatist goals. Referring to Turkification he asked, "How
could one be so devoid of political common sense as to believe that what
was not enforced by the sword when there was not even the question
of European intervention will be attempted under the constitutional
regime?"[5] Cahid argued that ethnic and religious differences had to be
superseded to achieve unity and a strong political community, but he
ruled out compromise on two points: the state religion and the state
language. He viewed Islam and Turkish as the cornerstones of the Ottoman state in its six-century-long life and did not see the primacy of
these elements as undermining Ottomanism.

Reference to Turkification, understood as a manifest sociopolitical
program, is ubiquitous in studies of the last Ottoman decade. Even the
more discriminating analyses of Arab politics, society, and ideology during the second constitutional period presuppose Turkification without
adequately questioning the notion. It is accepted to have been a conscious policy conceived in 1908 and systematically implemented, often
as an integral part of a nationalist program. The recent suggestion in
the revisionist historiography of Arab nationalism to view Turkification
as a by-product of Ottoman centralization rather than vice versa represents a useful rethinking of the conventional wisdom, but it leaves the
essence of the notion of Turkification unexplored. Turkification should
be examined as an ideological construct of those opposed to the actions
and policies of Ottoman government as much as a conscious or uncon-

scious element of İstanbul's policies. The question that needs to be asked is what policies of Young Turk regimes, as different from previous practice, gave added privilege to Turkish and Turks? The issue of discrimination against the Arab element in Parliament and in other state offices needs to be addressed because it was voiced by some Arab leaders at the time, not just by later historians and future generations of Arab nationalists when pointing to the roots of Arab nationalism.

The evidence cited most often by Arab critics and contemporary European observers for the deliberate establishment of Turkish domination in the political process comes from the particular composition of the 1908 Parliament. In the absence of numerical data it is difficult to make a statistical evaluation of the results of the Ottoman elections. A general analysis of the results and of the equally erratic census data can be used to determine certain trends and tendencies in 1908. Studies on the composition of the Ottoman Chamber put the number of deputies in the 1908 Parliament within a range from 260 to 288.[6] There is agreement on the approximate number of ethnic Turks (between 142 and 147) and Arabs (60) elected in 1908.[7] Though population estimates for the empire at this time vary widely, it may be assumed that the Arab and Turkish populations were approximately equal.[8] Turkish members of the 1908 Parliament outnumbered the Arabs, however, by a ratio of 2.5 to 1, a proportion far above what reasonable population estimates would warrant. This diagnosis of underrepresentation needs to be evaluated in the historical and demographic context.

An attempt to determine the numbers of Arabs and Turks in the empire during the second constitutional period runs into formidable problems. The absence of accurate census figures at the imperial and provincial levels is one problem. Another has to do with the determination of the proportion of the different Muslim groups within mixed provinces. Ethnic differences had as little meaning for the census takers as for the Muslim populations themselves. What came to be accepted as an objective criterion of nationhood by the critics of the Ottoman regime, language, was not accounted for in the census. Under the assumption of the validity of this criterion, it becomes relatively easy to identify population figures for Arabs (or Arabophone Ottomans), except in the case of the Peninsula, where no census was conducted and estimates were arbitrary and curiously generous. With the exception of the province of Aleppo, where one-third to one-half of the population was non-Arab, and northern Iraq, where sizable Kurdish and Turkic minorities lived, Greater Syria, Iraq, Tripolitania, and the Arabian Peninsula can be assumed to have been preponderantly Arab. The number of Arabs living outside these provinces was negligible. Enumerating the Turks is more problematic because Turcophone Ottomans cohabited several provinces with non-Turkish-speaking Muslim groups (e.g., Kurds, Laz, Pomak). Furthermore, language would be a more tenuous ethnic marker for Turcophone Ottomans, who included segments of Albanian, Slavic, Greek, and Kurdish peoples.

At the time of the elections the African and Asian periphery of the Ottoman state had been incompletely integrated. The goal of the CUP-controlled government to create a politically integrated society notwithstanding, the elections reflected and reproduced existing administrative conditions. Population data needed to determine the number of deputies to which each province was entitled (on the basis of one deputy for every 50,000 male Ottomans) were incomplete. The data of the 1906–07 census, upon which such calculations must have been based, contained no counts, or far lower ones than actual numbers, for many Arab provinces.[9] The Arab *sancak*s where the population was mostly settled and for which population registers were kept received the requisite representation, whereas in nomadic regions populated by Beduins there were wide discrepancies between actual population and stipulated representation. In addition to inherent problems associated with the counting of itinerant populations in remote areas, the nomads consciously avoided the census in fear of state exaction, because the traditional purpose of census registration was taxation and military conscription.[10] Indeed, taxation (more specifically, the payment of a direct tax of any amount) was an eligibility requirement for voters, even though this electoral taxation requirement was not particularly onerous compared with contemporary practices in other countries.

In the Unionist view of Ottomanism, ethnic, religious, and linguistic differences were of no import; to dwell on strict proportional parliamentary representation was wrong and divisive. If the Unionists can be accused of insincerity and idealism on the first score, they may be given the benefit of the doubt on the second. As we have seen, the Unionists did not see Parliament as a microcosm of the Ottoman collectivity, but as a forum where "enlightened sons" of this collectivity would give voice to the interests of the many diverse groups.

The idiom in which the issue of Arab underrepresentation and the breakdown of the composition of the Chamber has been presented in scholarship is shaped by anachronistic categories and subsequent political realities and concerns. Contemporary and later sources provide us with a breakdown of Greek, Armenian, Jewish, Albanian, Arab, and Turkish deputies. Here the Turkish category represents the residual non-Arab and non-Albanian Muslim group. It includes not just Muslim subjects from Slavic Balkans, the Circassians, the Georgians, the Laz, and others, who were not exclusively Turkish-speaking, but also, and more significantly, the sizable population of Kurds, of which only the Ottomanized and educated elements were Turkish-speaking. If, then, all non-Turkish-speaking Muslims are excluded from the Turkish category and the tribal population of the Peninsula is excluded from the population figures for Arabs, the respective parliamentary representation of Arabs and Turks would correspond more closely to the demographic picture.

The acknowledgment of language as the basis of ethnic identity, and of ethnicity as the basis of political identity, is an anachronistic extrapolation from the more recent experiences of Middle Eastern societies and polities. Language became the focal point in the construction of Arab and Turkish identities in the postimperial period and was rallied in the Arab case to counteract political fragmentation imposed by Europe. This did not prevent the flourishing of local territorial political identities responding to the specific realities of individual mandatory arrangements. Ottoman discrimination was invoked in the states that came into existence. Thus, an official Jordanian history points to Ottoman discrimination in the admission to Parliament of only one deputy from Jordan, a political and administrative nonentity in the Ottoman Empire, revealing the force of retrospective reasoning and anachronistic regional-political differentiation.[11]

A more compelling argument for discrimination against Arabs is the election of several Turks from the Arab provinces, between 6 and 11 percent of all delegates from these provinces.[12] (The exact proportion of Turks in the representation of the Arab provinces is not known because of uncertainties about the ethnic affiliation of some Muslim deputies.) This argument assumes that Turks could have been elected only as a result of electoral engineering. Of the four known Turks elected in the Arab provinces in 1908, there is numerical justification in the case of one, Ali Cenani of Aleppo, as Aleppo had a sizable Turkish population. Cenani, judging by his criticism in Parliament of the government for allocating disproportionately large revenues to İstanbul and its surroundings,[13] cannot be considered a CUP yes-man, though he treaded the general Unionist line. A second Turkish deputy, Abdülkadir Cami of Fezzan, won his mandate only in an extraordinary by-election. His candidacy did indeed lead to the objections of one Libyan deputy on grounds that Cami was not of Libyan origin. As an administrator who had served in Libya for many years, however, he was an advocate of local interests. Thus, the election of Turks in Arab provinces, some coming from families assimilated to the local population, does not necessarily reflect a policy of Turkification. The perception or claim that Arabs were subjected to discrimination in the allocation of parliamentary seats is not irrelevant to the development of an Arab collective identity, notwithstanding the argument that such claims reflected little else beyond the bid of Arab notables for greater recognition and power. But relating perceived discrimination or actual underrepresentation to a policy of Turkification remains problematic.

The overbearing attitude of the CUP was an irritant in Turkish-Arab relations and contributed to the politicization of Arabs and to increased alienation between Arab and Turk along ethnic and linguistic lines. In his first rebuttal of accusations of Turkification in August 1909, Hüseyin Cahid wrote with exaggerated frankness:

[The Young Turks] too are attached to their nationality [*milliyet*]. If they had the choice and if this were possible they would lose no time to make Turks out of all nations [*akvam*] within the Ottoman Empire. Had the Young Chinese or the Young Hottentots been in their place they would have desired the same.[14]

Such remarks could hardly have inspired the confidence of non-Turks, but the almost naive juxtaposition of chauvinism against political realities underscores the Unionist commitment to the implementation of policies that would perpetuate the imperial political traditions within a multiethnic and multireligious framework.

In April 1910 Shukri Ghanem, the president of the Paris Syrian Arab Society, wrote an article for *Le Temps* and attacked the Ottoman government for the unjust treatment of its Arab peoples. Just as he had denounced the Mutran circular for seeking autonomy for Syria, he again emphasized that the Arabs did not seek separation. He went on, however, to charge the government with discrimination against the Arabs in the allocation of public office, such as the civil service, army, navy, foreign service, and also Parliament. Once again *Tanin* took on these charges.[15]

Hüseyin Cahid argued against the assumption implicit in the quest for proportional representation that the interests of different ethnic groups were antagonistic to each other. He asserted that setting up quotas would violate the spirit of Ottomanism. Then he refuted the claim that Arabs were underrepresented in Parliament. He reminded Ghanem of the absence of reliable statistics and the difficulty and futility of distinguishing among different ethnic groups. Furthermore, Cahid wrote, a unity of interests was bound to supersede unity based on ethnic consciousness. He argued that if the Arabs were underrepresented in government this was due to their past inclinations or the policies of the previous regimes. "Which senior Arab diplomat can you point to who was denied an ambassadorship?" he asked.[16] In countering the charges of discrimination in public offices and the military, *Tanin* provided the names and ethnic backgrounds of army commanders. Of the top nine positions in the army, two were occupied by Arabs (Mahmud Shawkat Pasha and Commander of the Third Army Hadi Pasha), two by Albanians, two by Circassians, and one each by a Georgian, a Tartar, and a Bosnian. Dismissing Ghanem's incrimination in this manner, but also realizing that at the crux of the issue lay the language question, he emphatically repeated the Unionist position on the state language: "To allow different languages in government would be setting up a Tower of Babel and would lead to decentralization."[17] Yet Ghanem's argument would be repeated by Arab deputies and journalists as the battle lines between the CUP and the decentralists continued to take shape.

The names of some of the ethnic societies that came into existence after the revolution or surfaced after clandestine activity during the Hamidian regime, such as the Kurdish and Circassian mutual aid societies, suggest that ethnic awareness and assertion among the Muslims of the empire were not restricted to Turks, Arabs, and Albanians. In a first step to defuse these organizations after the counterrevolution, the CUP attempted to form an umbrella organization called the Ottoman Allied Committee (*Heyet-i Müttefika-ı Osmaniye*),[18] which included these and other cultural and political societies, including the Liberal Party. A few months later, the new Law of Association banned ethnic-based organizations.

In this first wave of organizational activity, we do not find Arabist or Turkist organizations except *Al-ikha'*, or the Arab-Ottoman Brotherhood. Several months later the Arab Literary Club (*Al-muntada al-adabi*) and the Turkish Society (*Türk Derneği*) came into existence. These literary societies have been ascribed an undue share in the politicization of Arabism and Turkism, because some of the leaders of *Al-muntada* subsequently played a leading role in Arab nationalist activity and were among those executed by Cemal Pasha in 1915–16;[19] and *Türk*

Derneği and its successors had prominent Unionists, including some deputies, as members.

The Turkist societies certainly contributed to the substantiation of the charges of Turkification. In many ways, *Türk Derneği* was the continuation of the Turkist trend (see chapter 1) that had emerged during the Young Ottoman period. Like the Arab literary societies of the nineteenth century, it cast itself as a "scientific" society dedicated to the promotion of the Turkish language. Its language policy was one of simplification rather than purification and did not aim at purging Ottoman Turkish of Arabic and Persian words. The declared objective of the society was to promote Ottoman unity.[20] The existence of Greek and Armenian groups in the empire who communicated in Turkish, even though they wrote it in Greek or Armenian characters, was convincing evidence of the practicality of Turkish as an Ottoman lingua franca.[21]

The Turkish cultural societies gradually rediscovered the elements of an overarching Turkish identity in the same way that the Arabists had begun to rediscover those of a broad Arab identity under the influence of the *salafi*s. Among the Arabs there was relative linguistic homogeneity. Moreover, language and scripture were intertwined to further strengthen the consciousness of Arab group identity among the literate. Ancestry, reinforced by tribal organization and linked to the *salaf*, imparted additional weight to religio-linguistic identification. Arab intellectuals could emphasize an Arab geographic and historical continuity with little straining of the imagination. Nevertheless, the obstacles in translating these elements to a political construct remained formidable. Indeed, the primacy of broader religio-political factors, namely the need to preserve and strengthen the Islamic caliphate, militated against the desirability of such a transformation.

Turkish intellectuals as well applied themselves to the task of imagining the Turkish ethnic community on the basis of the revelations of European Turcology half a century before. One avenue to affirming Turkishness would be to turn to the Central Asian roots of the Turks and to the domain of linguistic cognates. However, geographical contiguity between Anatolian and Central Asian Turks was precarious and historical links between the two groups and common lineage had to be belabored so as not to be confined to the category of myth.

Language and literature became the focus of the activities of the *Genç Kalemler* (Young Pens) society that was founded in 1910 and published a journal of the same name. The *Genç Kalemler* addressed linguistic roots and looked more favorably to the purification of Ottoman Turkish than did the adherents of *Türk Derneği*, but the group did not dwell on organic links with Turks of Central Asia. Their concern with language was less as marker of cultural or political identity and more as a practical vehicle. "The social unit the awakened Turks intended to reconstruct was not the Turkish or Turkic nation, but an Ottoman state."[22] Turkish would need to be taught to all Ottomans so that it would serve as a medium to diffuse progress.

Yet the proponents of stronger links with the "outer Turks" were not absent. They became particularly active in a third Turkist society to be formed in 1911, the *Türk Yurdu* (Turkish Home). Like Christian Arabs (who since the nineteenth century had formulated a linguistic-cultural conception of an Arab nation but were first unheeded and later over-shadowed by Arabists of an Islamic-modernist persuasion), Russian Turks formulated similar constructs of a pan-Turkic commonality (which had equally insignificant appeal). They found, however, an opportunity to renew their activities in İstanbul after 1908. Prominent among them were Yusuf Akçura and Ahmed Agayev [Ağaoğlu]. These immigrants played a more important role in reinforcing the attempts to formulate a Turkish identity than in offering viable political programs.[23]

Yet another Turkist society, *Türk Ocağı* (Turkish Hearth), has been described as the "most durable and important of all organisations with Pan-Turk proclivities."[24] Founded in 1911, the society underwent many transformations and survived through the first decade of the Kemalist period. Most prominent Turkists associated themselves with *Türk Ocağı*, as did some Unionists, including Enver Pasha. As a society, the *Türk Ocağı* focused on Turkist cultural and linguistic activities and concerned itself with political issues perhaps even to a lesser degree than the others. Though it eschewed party politics by statute, some Unionists' association with the society has imparted to it the false appearance of an arm of the CUP.

Problems of practicability or considerations of *raison d'état* inherent in promoting a nationalist policy objective, which a few members of the CUP in Salonika or others more closely related to the state machinery in İstanbul may have harbored, were forbidding. Nevertheless, the CUP's attitude toward the place of Turkish in the Ottoman state and government policies with regard to language were situated at the crux of the Turkification debate. The set of enactments that can be collectively viewed as a "language policy" did not represent a substantial change from the Hamidian regime to the constitutional period. The grievances, then, did not arise from the adoption of novel Turcocentric policies under the new regime, but rather from the failure of the government to adapt its existing policy when confronted with novel demands for greater recognition of languages other than Turkish in the affairs of the state.

The 1876 constitution designated the state language of the Ottoman Empire as Turkish (*Türkçe*). Ottoman Turkish (*lisan-ı Osmani*), a hybrid of Turkish, Arabic, and Persian with Turkish grammar, had historically served this purpose. The designation of the state language as Turkish rather than Ottoman Turkish in 1876 reflects the efforts, if not the decisive input, of the Young Ottomans, who advocated and used a simpler Turkish than the complicated Ottoman. While such designation has ideological and practical implications, none was detailed in the constitution. Neither the particular clause designating the state language nor any other reference to language in the constitution was modified in 1908 or afterward. The constitution stipulated a more rigid definition of ability in Turkish as a requirement for deputies (only to be applied in four years), namely ability to read and, "to the extent possible," write Turkish (Article 68). In 1909 this clause was endorsed as it stood in the original text, and a motion to enforce the stricter requirement effective immediately was defeated.[25]

The CUP's political program in 1908 included the following clauses about the use of Turkish:

The official language of the state will remain as Turkish. All correspondence and official memoranda will be executed in Turkish. (Article 7)

Teaching of the Turkish language is compulsory in elementary schools. For secondary [*idadi*] and higher [*âli*] education, firm guidelines will be adopted on the basis of the Turkish language. (Article 17)[26]

The vague phrasing in Article 17 suggests that Turkish was favored in secondary curriculum as the language of instruction. Neither clause contravened past policy, although past practice was not uniform. The policy as stated in the CUP program and also implemented by the government has been construed as the adoption of Turkish as the language of instruction, which was true only for secondary and higher education, where the local language would also be taught as a subject.

The difference between the teaching of Turkish in elementary education and its adoption as the language of instruction is significant. The overall educational policy of the second constitutional period allowed socialization in the local culture during the formative years through the teaching of the local language. Instruction in Turkish in secondary and higher education aimed at incorporating local groups into the imperial administrative system and at developing an imperial elite. Referring to the post-Tanzimat Ottoman Empire, the authors of a comprehensive study of the education of nondominant ethnic groups in Europe accurately point to the distinction between integration (in this case, Otto-manization aiming to strengthen allegiance to the state framework) and assimilation (ensuring self-identification with the "dominant nation").[27] Curiously, the same authors refer, without explication (and no doubt swayed by the weight of the inaccurate appraisal of Turkification in existing scholarship) to the Young Turks' "expanding assimilation to new elements,"[28] whereas educational policy during the second constitutional period does not depart from the patterns that had existed before. Changes were quantitative (an increase in the number of students and new schools) rather than qualitative (Turkification of the curriculum).

The main substantive change in the implementation of language policy during the second constitutional period came in the domain of law with the requirement to use Turkish in all courts of the empire—a measure that led to discontent, inconvenienced judicial officials and litigants, and threatened the administration of justice. As governor of Syria in 1878, Cevdet Pasha had tried unsuccessfully to implement a similar measure requiring the use of Turkish in courts and administrative councils in Syria.[29] The 1909 requirement was contested even by *Tanin*, not for its principle but for practical reasons.[30] Hüseyin Cahid argued that the time-honored practice of utilizing Arabic in the law courts of Arab provinces should be continued until such time when Turkish spread in these areas. Cahid did declare in unambiguous terms that everyone who wished to be in association with the state had to learn Turkish. According to him, "Turkish ought to be taught also because it is a language of knowledge and civilization."[31] This afterthought, that Turkish is also a language of civilization, reflects literary and cultural Turkist activity that parallels the Arab intellectuals' rediscovery of the civilizational import of Arabic.

The primacy of Turkish in state agencies and secondary education was perceived in different ways by Arabs. Many Arabs accepted the integrative function of Turkish and supported instruction in Turkish. Deputies from Libya lamented the granting of diplomas to students who did not attain proficiency in Turkish. They demanded instruction in Turkish and deplored the fact that there were a hundred times as many

Italian speakers in their provinces as Turkish speakers.[32] All in the Arab provinces favored the appointment of Arabic-speaking local officials. The rationale for this demand was administrative efficiency. The demand was not necessarily for local appointees or native Arabic speakers but merely for officials proficient in Arabic.[33] The *Mülkiye* curriculum had been revised in 1891 to require every student to receive courses in Arabic, Greek, Armenian, or Albanian. The Young Turks continued the same policy.[34] The government favored distributing officials from a particular region throughout the empire, as it also attempted to appoint officials who had gained familiarity with the language of the locality where they were to serve.

While the administrative challenges posed by the language problem were addressed in a centralist idiom, the growth of decentralist opposition to the CUP moved the issue to a different realm. Arab critics increasingly blamed the Unionists for Turkifying the Arabs by imposing the Turkish language and for instituting a selection process that excluded non-Turkish speakers. In Eric Hobsbawm's terms, this was an expression of "linguistic nationalism" and its "battle-lines were manned by professional journalists, schoolteachers, and aspiring subaltern officials."[35] These grievances were closely interlinked with the broader decentralist challenge to the CUP and will be taken up in that context in the next chapter.

Voices that called for greater emphasis on Arabic and the promotion of its instruction in schools came from non-Arabs as well. As the language of religious scriptures, Arabic had a special importance. The Islamist journal *Sırat-ı Müstakim* (The Straight Path), published in Turkish in İstanbul, advocated greater attention to Arabic, particularly compared with French (which was widely taught in schools), and stressed the political and religious benefits that could be derived from a dissemination of Arabic.[36] The association of the Arabic language with Islam was a powerful element in Arabism and a recurrent theme in the Arabist discourse. The Unionists cannot have been unaware of the political value of according greater latitude to Arabic in the public realm. A concession here, however, would have invited similar demands from other linguistic groups and undermined the sense of Ottoman unity transcending communal divisions that the Unionists were trying to forge.[37]

Language as a symbol in the expression of a yet unclearly defined political agenda is implicit in the words of the British consul in Damascus:

The antagonistic sentiment between Arab and Turk has been quietly fomented during the past three or four months now, whether by hasty or somewhat autocratic behaviour on the part of office holders, and by their occasionally contemptuous or discourteous manners towards local notables, or by the over-advanced views of those connected with the "Young Turk" Party who are manifesting themselves (not alone here in Syria I imagine) in a distinct tendency towards xenophoby.

The antagonistic sentiment between Turk and Arab is beginning to permeate downwards to the lower classes; and will soon no longer be confined to the ulama, notables, and grandees, and official circles.

The most sore point of all is the attempt of Young Turks to propagate the use of Turkish in exclusion of Arabic in all official circles. . . .[38]

The rhetoric of supplanting Arabic with Turkish, to which the centralizing policy of İstanbul gave credence, was successfully exploited by those elements dissatisfied with the CUP's role in government. They were menaced by official encroachment on their spheres of influence and underscored the Unionists' break with traditional social and political norms in order to gain political capital in the eyes of the "lower classes." Associating the CUP with a Turkish despotism became a convenient way for those segments of Arab society and individuals whose interests were not served by the regime to attack the Committee government.

Some provincial notables attacked the Young Turk governments not only for their Turkifying but also for alleged anti-Islamic policies. They believed that they could better preserve their social privileges and economic status in a less centralized political organization. In order to achieve this aim they invoked Arab cultural identity and warned of Turkification. With regard to Iraq, Hanna Batatu writes:

[T]he conflicts stirred by the Young Turk Revolution, and which precipitated the movement for Arab autonomy, had a distinct social facet, and were not merely ideological or ethnic conflicts between secularly minded Young Turks and "good" Moslems, or between "Turks" and "Arabs." . . . In other words, it is not only concern for their Arab cultural identity or for the old Islamic beliefs that drove the *sadah* and other Arab landed magnates to seek autonomy.[39]

To those who stressed the CUP's Turkifying policies, the Committee's attitude toward Islam furnished different kinds of handles. Some Christian minority groups and their supporters felt that the 1908 Revolution legitimized Islamic domination because it rejected communal sectarian political prerogatives. The Arab opponents of the CUP, on the other hand, held Turkification also tantamount to the elimination of Islam from public life. Dwelling on the "anti-Islamic" policies of the government and personal impiety of the CUP members became a strategy employed to fight the regime.

Partisans of the CUP who adhered closely to secular principles of personal liberties tended to provoke adverse public opinion, particularly in the provinces. The Aleppines, for example, filed complaints about a newly appointed teacher to the Aleppo *sultani* (high school) who allegedly taught that there is no resurrection.[40] Again in Aleppo, the official handling of the case of an ostensible Muslim prostitute aroused passions. The woman in question, the daughter of a court official in Alexandretta, was seen in unseemly attire, and "even went to the theater as such." The *müftü* took the young woman under his custody and placed her in a hotel room in preparation to send her to her father. The prosecutor, on the other hand, invoking her constitutional freedoms, asked that she be released and—according to the Aleppine deputies who brought the matter to the attention of the Ministry of the Interior—that she even be given the choice of returning to the house of ill-fame. The Ministry of Justice promised to take action against the prosecutor.[41]

In Damascus, it was the newly appointed *müftü*, Sulayman Chukhadar, who drew the ire of a number of town notables, including Saʿid Muʾayyad al-ʿAzm. Chukhadar, who had served as magistrate in a number of Arab and Anatolian towns before his election to Parliament (and who was to serve as minister of justice in Syria in the post-Ottoman period),[42] resigned his parliamentary seat on appointment to Damascus as *müftü*. The petitioners expressed dissatisfaction with what they considered to be his promotion to an undeserved post and went so far as to blame the rebellion in Karak on this appointment. Chukhadar, adding insult to injury, allegedly snubbed esteemed physicians in the government hospital and checked into the British hospital for the treatment of his hernia, "where he spent several nights among nuns."[43]

The surge of complaints about irreligious government officials or their insensitivity to religious sensibilities accompanied a press war between the CUP organs in İstanbul and a number of papers in the Arab provinces. In April 1911, in an attempt to stem further complaints, the Ministry of the Interior wrote to all provinces urging all Muslim officials to observe the Friday prayer diligently and to do so in the principal mosque of the town. The memorandum also mentioned complaints about laxity in prayers and public drinking (or public consumption during the fasting month).[44]

As the accusations in the press increased, some Arab deputies sent telegrams to the Beirut municipality, the Beirut CUP club, and the city's Muslim newspapers offering to mediate in the conflict that "divided Arab and Turk" and to reinforce Islamic union. Dismayed by this initiative, Christian members of the municipality, Christian newspaper owners, and other Christian leaders sent a cable to İstanbul asking the deputies to reconsider their remarks on "Islamic union." "The CUP or the municipality is neither Muslim nor Christian, but Ottoman," the message read. "To call for the unity of one *millet* will damage the existence of the state."[45] The minister of the interior sent his thanks for the patriotic sentiments and played down the initiative of the deputies as their personal opinions.

Parliament: Arabs in Opposition Parties and Issues of Arab Concern

The years 1910–11 were free of external complications for the Ottoman Empire. This allowed the political process embodied in the new constitutional order to take its course in the absence of military upheaval or foreign intrusions. The period witnessed the attempts of the CUP to build confidence and to exert itself more directly and fully in government and, in turn, the formation and growing opposition of rival political groups. Until the end of 1909 the CUP had not confronted an organized opposition. The *Ahrar*'s challenge had become real after the elections in Parliament but had been suppressed after the counterrevolution. In the next two years factions in Parliament, including some from the ranks of the CUP, began to form political parties.

When order was restored after the revolt of April 1909, the Unionists declared the formation of a Union and Progress Party, a political party distinct from the society bearing the same name.[46] Along with the internal regulations of the party, the CUP issued in May 1909 a revised political program.[47] The Unionists hoped that those members of Parliament who were not committed to the CUP and who had supported the opposition before 31 March would opt to identify with the Committee under the rubric of the new party. The intention was not, however, to discipline the Unionist deputies within a rigid political program, which could in turn have encouraged and legitimized opposition. Despite the initiative to move toward a broad-based political organization, the CUP continued to refuse to open up its high-level councils to newcomers, regardless of ethnic background.

Parliament adjourned its first legislative year several days after passing the Law of Association on 16 August 1909. The beginning of the next session witnessed the formation of the new parties. The more prominent of these were the Moderate Liberal Party (*Mutedil Hürriyetperveran*) and the People's (*Ahali*) Party. Arab deputies played a leading role in the Moderate Liberal Party, established in November 1909. This party constituted itself as a conglomeration of national groupings. It might be viewed as a bridge between *Ahrar*, which ceased its activities after being implicated in supporting the counterrevolution, and the oppositional coalition that called itself Liberty and Entente (*Hürriyet ve İtilâf*), which was to be formed at the end of 1911. The dissolution of the Moderate Liberal Party to merge with Liberty and Entente is well documented.[48] Its organizational or ideological links with *Ahrar* are more tenuous. The president of the Moderate Liberal Party, İsmail Kemal Bey, an Albanian deputy from Berat (and one of the former leaders of *Ahrar*), announced that *Ahrar* had merged with the Moderate Liberal Party under a new program,[49] but the merger was repudiated by the general secretary of *Ahrar* in an open letter that announced the dissolution of the *Ahrar*, published two months after the formation of the Moderate Liberal Party. These contradictory statements could have been viewed as a technicality, had it not been for the important substantive differences in the programs of the two parties.

The Moderate Liberal Party formally placed a number of Arab deputies in the ranks of opposition to the CUP, whereas *Ahrar*'s Arab sympathizers had not played a role in the organization of that party. In fact, Arab deputies dominated the new party, which also included Albanian, Christian, and a few Turkish deputies. As Albanian parliamentary deputies became identified with the Albanian nationalist movement and party president İsmail Kemal left to join the movement, the Moderate Liberal Party turned into an "Arab party," though no Arab held its presidency. Nafiʿ served as vice-president, while ʿAbd al-Mahdi (Karbala) and Shafiq al-Muʾayyad (Damascus) were founding members. The tenor of the Moderate Liberal program[50] contrasted sharply with the particular action of its founder and first president. The program was fervently Ottomanist, with references to the Ottoman "nation" (*millet*) and "national" sovereignty (Article 1), and explicitly castigated decentralism as the principle that constituted the prelude to—"God forbid"—the disintegration of Ottoman possessions (Article 2). This language cannot be dismissed as political prudence, because the program begins with quotations from Western scholars of politics (one being from Johann Bluntschli) about the virtues of opposition in a democracy, thus leaving no doubts about the intentions of the founders.

The Arab membership of the Moderate Liberal Party showed great diversity in terms of political outlook during its two-year existence. It was joined on the one hand by supporters of the CUP such as Yusuf Shitwan and Sulayman al-Bustani and on the other by opponents like Shukri al-ʿAsali and Sayyid Talib, who formed one of the two branches of the party in Basra. Several of the Arab members were from landed families and were less interested in administrative decentralization than protection of property at a time when uprisings were breaking out in the tribal regions. Article 11 of the program sought the implementation of measures to prevent the Beduin from plundering settled areas.[51] The party provided a legitimate organizational framework under which Arab deputies could meet after the closure of the Arab-Ottoman Brotherhood and the prohibition by the Law of Association of ethnic-based societies. Baptized in the controversial surroundings of the Lynch concession (see pages 100–102), several members of the party emerged as the most prominent segment of parliamentary opposition to the CUP. The party program included clauses that reflected the interests of Arabists. It stipulated the protection of the language and literature of all Ottoman populations from extinction and expressed the Islamist modernist view of extending support to religious education consonant with modern science (Article 13). Yet, as a whole, the Moderate Liberal program fell short of offering a true alternative to that of the CUP, nor did the party have a cohesive membership.

The People's Party, which included several Arab members, shared these traits and similarly failed to constitute an ideological alternative to the CUP. This party, however, was more representative in its composition of the liberal trend in İstanbul. In January 1910, when one of its most vocal members, Rıza Nur (deputy from Sinop), was arrested for alleged conspiracy against the government,[52] the Moderate Liberals and People's Party jointly petitioned for a parliamentary investigation of the government's action. The petition, signed by fifteen deputies, carried the signatures of Arab deputies Shafiq al-Muʾayyad (Damascus), Dawud Yusfani and Muhammad ʿAli Fazil (Musul), and ʿAbd al-Hamid al-Zahrawi (Hama), Saʿid al-Husayni (Jerusalem), and Rushdi al-Shamʿa.[53]

The new parties were indicative of a general dissatisfaction with the

CUP, even though they did not offer a meaningful opposition. A fair appraisal of the condition of political parties in the empire was provided by a prominent opponent of the CUP, Lütfi Fikri (deputy from Dersim), in a speech he wrote in July 1910 for delivery in Salonika. Lütfi Fikri described the CUP contingent in Parliament as a conglomerate lending support to the cabinet under the appearance of a political party.[54] He maintained that it was also unclear how the recently constituted parties differed from each other and that the three fundamental political currents (the conservative, the moderate, and the left) had yet to crystallize in the Ottoman Empire.[55] Such differentiation was to occur within the CUP in 1911 temporarily with its splintering into a right (*Hizb-i Cedid*) and a left (*Hizb-i Terakki*) wing.[56]

The various parties and factions that came into being in 1910 and 1911 did not have the ideological or organizational strength to oust the CUP. Their importance lay in impressing on the CUP that it was in need of ideological consolidation. They also demonstrated that an opposition would be capable of asserting itself under a formal party organization in the constitutional regime. Indeed, the various groups that emerged in opposition to the CUP joined forces at the end of 1911 to form the Liberty and Entente Party, which successfully challenged the CUP's monopoly of political power.

The oppositional party activity in 1910 and 1911 exposed the estrangement of an important group of Arab deputies from the ranks of the CUP. While the convergence of several Arab deputies as the largest single contingent responsible for the formation of the Moderate Liberal Party, and the key role they then played in it, may be construed as an effort by Arabs to assert themselves politically as a national group, there was no ideological basis to this mobilization that would substantiate an Arab political movement. On the whole, Arab deputies remained divided in lending support to the CUP. In March 1911 a vote was taken on a motion by Lütfi Fikri challenging Grand Vizier İbrahim Hakkı Pasha on a cabinet decision that called for an extension of martial law in İstanbul. Of 38 nonabstaining Arab deputies, 19 voted in support of the government and 19 against it in a total tally of 112 to 62 in favor of the cabinet decision.[57] Clearly, many deputies were shifting to the opposition, but the Arab contingent remained politically divided. Of the Arab deputies whose political inclinations can be identified at this juncture, Sabine Prätor classifies 33 Arab deputies as supporting the CUP and 25 as having joined the opposition.[58]

During the 1909–10 and 1910–11 annual parliamentary sessions three issues of imperial significance concerned the Arab provinces directly: the Lynch concession, Zionist settlement, and the war with Italy over Libya. In deliberations on all three issues Arab deputies, both from the ranks of the CUP and those who identified with the opposition, participated extensively, as the questions bore upon their constituencies directly or indirectly. More than to the consolidation of discernible Arab collective interests, these issues pointed to the continued diversity of opinion among Arabs. The beginning of the creation of an Arab party group during the first crisis was undercut by the later growth of ideological polarization.

THE LYNCH CONCESSION

The government's plan to offer a commercial concession to a foreign enterprise in Iraq triggered a political crisis that pitted Iraqi and a number of other Arab deputies against the government and culminated in the resignation of Grand Vizier Hüseyin Hilmi Pasha. A British navigation company, Lynch Brothers, had operated on the Tigris since 1839.[59] More than a commercial venture, the Lynch Company signified Britain's interests in this critical region between its Egyptian and Indian possessions. Toward the end of 1909 the Ottoman government considered the proposed merger of the Ottoman Hamidiye Company (also operating on the Tigris) with Lynch, which would have given the latter a long-term monopoly over river transportation. The Unionists for the most part favored the merger in the hope of receiving a much-needed loan from the British government in return for the concession.[60] Some Arab deputies interpreted this as a lack of governmental concern for the empire's Arab territories. They opposed the expansion of British influence in the area, which would not only undermine local trade but also expose the region further to the Anglo-German rivalry in that part of the empire.[61]

Hüseyin Hilmi Pasha pressed for the endorsement of the merger. Earlier in his career Hüseyin Hilmi had served as *mutasarrif* in Karak and in Nablus. In 1898 he had been sent to Yemen to undertake reforms and establish government authority. He did not distinguish himself and was removed from that post in 1902. Immediately following this inglorious service he was appointed inspector of Rumelia. The Arabic *Al-khilafa* (London) had expressed astonishment about his new appointment and written that Hüseyin Hilmi Pasha's governorship in Yemen was clearly responsible for the worsening of the situation in that troubled province.[62] The perception of disservice in the Arab provinces may have reinforced Arab opposition to him.

Hilmi Pasha was only implementing the Committee's decision. The CUP's material need for loans and the psychological need for the political support of the liberal European powers were such that it was willing to recognize the British monopoly in the two rivers, which already existed de facto, in return for closer relations. The Committee failed to predict the reaction of local elements, whose economic and political interests the concession jeopardized. By acting in the face of local demands the government not only allowed a political issue to manifest itself as a national one but also set a precedent for Britain to aggravate such differences in an ethnically divisive direction. The concession was opposed by Iraqi deputies, Unionist and non-Unionist alike, including *Tanin*'s Babanzade İsmail Hakkı. All but four Arab deputies abstained in the vote of confidence that the Chamber granted Hüseyin Hilmi Pasha.[63] Despite the vote in his favor, the grand vizier resigned his post. Mahmud Shawkat Pasha, an Iraqi himself and like many officers not a friend of Britain, most likely threw his weight for Hüseyin Hilmi's resignation following the vote.

There was a growing need in the CUP for a grand vizier who was better versed in foreign affairs and someone who could accommodate the will of the Committee and the quest of the army, led by Mahmud Shawkat Pasha, for a greater share of political power. The choice fell on İbrahim Hakkı Pasha, who was serving as ambassador in Rome. Having received his education in the *Mülkiye* and served in several diplomatic and administrative posts, he offered wide experience and promise to deal with pressing issues confronting the government such as the search for loans, the related Lynch question, and insurgency in different parts of the empire. İbrahim Hakkı had worked on commissions that regulated commercial and diplomatic relations with foreign countries before serving in Young Turk cabinets as minister of education and later minister of the interior.[64] In his new cabinet he appointed Mahmud Shawkat as the minister of war. İbrahim Hakkı's first task was to reverse his predecessor's decision in the Lynch affair.

The crisis over the Lynch concession lasted only two weeks, and when it ended the initiative for merger was scrapped. The crisis revealed much about the state of imperial politics. It pointed to the CUP's ineptitude in formulating policy and judging local reaction. It thus demonstrated that the CUP's control over both the central and provincial government was incomplete. The Lynch affair was the first time that a local issue was vigorously pressed against the will of the government in the Chamber. There was remarkable unity against the measure in Iraq. The landlords, the merchants, the tribes, Christians, Jews, Arabs, Kurds, Turks, and also the local Committees of Union and Progress all opposed the measure.[65] The Lynch affair gave the fledgling decentralists the opportunity to assert themselves. Future parliamentary leaders of the opposition, such as Lütfi Fikri and Rıza Nur, jumped on the bandwagon. Finally, the Lynch affair revealed that other modes of participatory politics could transcend Parliament. This would not be the first time that a CUP-led vote of confidence failed to forestall a political crisis in the face of extra-parliamentary pressures. Local rallies and a petition campaign backed by Iraqi as well as overlapping contingents of Arab and decentralist deputies ultimately obstructed the concession. İstanbul had no choice but respond to pressures from the widening public realm. Interestingly, the Arab deputies would not display similar unanimity in Parliament again. The Lynch crisis developed immediately before the crystallization of parliamentary opposition. Though it partly explains the propensity of the Arabs to join the Moderate Liberals, once ideological divisions between the centralists and the decentralists started to take shape, future political divisions followed those lines.

JEWISH SETTLEMENT

The second parliamentary showdown between the CUP and its opposition occurred in the spring of 1911. The decentralist opposition launched a frontal attack against the CUP-controlled government by bringing to the agenda the sensitive issue of Zionist settlement, which closely concerned segments of the Arab constituency. The budget discussions, in the context of which the Zionist issue was broached, became also the forum in which Turkish-Arab tensions, concurrently unleashed in the press, were voiced.

At the end of 1910 an article by the owner of the İstanbul daily *Al-'arab*, Ubeydullah (deputy for the Anatolian province of Aydın), used language offensive to the Arabs while discussing the rebellion in Asir. Immediately picked up by the increasingly vocal opposition press, this particular article reverberated widely in the Arab provinces. Sharif Husayn, who was waging the war in Asir against Idrisi, expressed his concerns about the article, and the government had to send assurances that Ubeydullah was properly advised.[66] The opposition press in Beirut and Damascus made the article the launching pad of a systematic antigovernment campaign in an anti-Turkish idiom. The first outburst appeared in ʿAbd al-Ghani al-ʿUraysi's *Al-mufid* in Beirut in the form of an anti-Turkish poem. Alarmed by the divisive language, the Ministry of the Interior communicated to the provinces that similar publications should be prevented. It also dispatched to Beirut an official, who spoke Arabic and was expected to render useful service in ending the dispute.[67] As the Damascus governor Galib Bey reported after five months of this press campaign, some papers had taken it upon themselves to promote the "separation of elements" (i.e., Arab and Turk) by sowing discord and little could be done with the existing press law to suppress such action.[68]

Other factors contributed to making an assault against the government particularly opportune in the first months of 1911. The winter had been a particularly severe one, especially in northern Syria, causing much suffering and inducing the tribes to raid villages and towns.[69] More relevant to the issue of Jewish settlements, reports from Jerusalem and Beirut had raised alarm about some families selling land to Jewish immigrants, on which large-scale construction was rumored to be taking place.[70]

In the spring of 1911 the deliberations on the budget provided the opposition with an opportunity to embark on a multifaceted attack on the CUP government. On 25 February ʿAbd al-Hamid al-Zahrawi[71] took the floor to denounce salary increases endorsed in Parliament for some high officials. He dwelled on a proposed increase for the salary of the secretary of the Chamber of Notables and pointed to the wide discrepancy in pay between the highest and lower officials. He concluded that a certain lower-level secretary in the same Chamber, "from the Arab nation that has no representatives in the offices of government," was being paid less than his colleagues.[72] This was the first assertion in Parliament that Arabs were underrepresented and underprivileged in state offices, indeed in Parliament itself. During the budget talks the ultimate concern was with finances and these intimations of alleged discrimination were not addressed.

Two sessions later, opposition deputies Lütfi Fikri and İsmail Hakkı (Gümülcine) accused the Unionist government of operating under the influence of Zionists in concluding certain loan agreements and favoring Jews with alleged links to Zionism when granting economic concessions.[73] İsmail Hakkı referred to Zionism as an appalling malady in the internal politics of the state and went on to describe the goals of Zionism as the establishment of a state extending from Palestine to Mesopotamia through a systematic increase of the number of Jews in those regions.[74]

The opposition's charges were taken up on the one hand by the Jewish deputies,[75] and on the other by Minister of the Interior Talat and
Grand Vizier İbrahim Hakkı Pasha. The Jewish deputies rejected the
claim that there was an attempt to establish a Jewish government and
disavowed any links between Ottoman Jewry and the Zionists. The ministers disclaimed the alleged links of the implicated Ottoman Jews with
Zionism. The Arab deputies remained passive during the discussion.
The brief interjections by two deputies, 'Abd al-Rahman al-Yusuf (Damascus) and Ruhi al-Khalidi (Jerusalem), served to discredit the arguments of the opposition deputies. But when Ubeydullah, the deputy
from Aydın, who had been tainted by his derogatory remarks about
Arabs in his *Al-'arab*, accused the opposition of being motivated by
spite, four Arab deputies—Zahrawi, Khalid al-Barazi (Hama), 'Abd al-
Mahdi (Karbala), and Rida al-Sulh (Beirut)—rallied to the opposition's
support and threatened to leave the floor unless Ubeydullah retracted
his words. "We will leave," al-Sulh declared, "so that you can go ahead
and insult the Arabs now."

On the whole, during this first debate about Zionism, the division
of the Arab deputies between the government and the opposition remained the rule. Nevertheless, the parliamentary debate highlighted the
Zionist issue, and more attention was paid to it in the Arab provinces
in its wake. Palestinian Arabs sent telegrams to Parliament asking for a
halt to Jewish immigration. The press took a keener interest in the issue.[76] For the first time a work written by an Arab, Najib Nassar, on
Zionism appeared in Haifa warning of the dangers of Jewish immigration and urging the people to assume greater responsibility to stop the
Zionist tide. This increase in public awareness of Zionism led the Arab
deputies to take a clear position in the question of Zionist immigration
and land purchase. Shukri al-'Asali, who had carried out an anti-Zionist
campaign as *kaymakam* of Nazareth and was elected to Parliament in the
Damascus by-election as these debates were taking place in İstanbul,
joined al-Sulh and al-Khalidi in this effort.[77]

In May 1911 the Arab deputies brought the issue of Zionism to the
Chamber during the deliberations on the budget of the Ministry of the
Interior. On 16 May Ruhi al-Khalidi took the floor expressing his wish
to hear the government's position on an "internal issue," namely Zionism, before the budget negotiations started.[78] He addressed how the
Jews had settled in Palestine and acquired property despite legal prohibitions and maintained that this had been possible because of the officials' corruption. He proceeded with an extended lecture on Zionism.

Even though such a lengthy discourse was out of place in the context of the budget talks, his account was heard with interest. The floor, betraying its ignorance on the subject, urged al-Khalidi on as he talked about the difference between Zionism and Semitism, the different origins of Jews, the formation of the first colonies by Russian Jews in Jaffa, Herzl's and Mendelsohn's theories, and so on. He also read various telegrams from Ottoman Jewish leaders and societies denouncing Zionism. He cited biblical verses that depicted Palestine as the Jewish promised land, drawing criticism from the Jewish deputies.[79]

Khalidi was followed by Saʿid al-Husayni, who dwelled on Jewish land purchases in Jerusalem and urged the government to take more effective measures against Jewish land acquisition. When it was Shukri al-ʿAsali's turn, he proceeded with the same kind of historical introduction to Zionism as al-Khalidi's. Claiming to speak on the basis of his firsthand experience and investigations, he asserted that three-fourths of Tiberias and one-fourth of Haifa had been acquired by Jews. He accused the government of indifference and of yielding even strategic sites to them. Talat responded that Jews were entitled to buy property anywhere in the empire except in the Hijaz.[80]

The speeches of the Arab deputies did not create the desired alarm. An Albanian deputy, Hafız İbrahim (İpek), raised objections about procedure and complained that the deputies should not be allowed to make speeches on whatever matter crossed their minds. He said that the question of the Jews was neither novel nor as alarming as presented. He scoffed at the notion that "one hundred thousand Jews who have come to Jerusalem will conquer Syria and Iraq." According to Hafız İbrahim, the Jews were taking over not territories but the economy, as they had done even in Britain, and added that all of Salonika's trade was in their hands. Dismissing Rida al-Sulh's attempts to remind him that the Salonika Jews were not foreigners, he pointed to the fact that the trade of Beirut was also in the hands of foreigners. Instead of resenting the foreigners, he concluded, the Ottomans should try to reach their standards.

The discussion on Zionism came to an abrupt halt and the Chamber proceeded to other matters. The next day, apparently swayed by the representatives of the Zionist movement in İstanbul,[81] the Bulgarian deputy Dimitri Vlahof took the floor to speak about the potential economic benefits of Jewish immigration.[82] His statements, at times factually incorrect, met with the protests of Arab deputies. Yet the Arabs were not able to pursue the issue further and apply pressures on the government. The deliberations on Zionism dissipated amidst the broader issue of the budget negotiations.

The unanimity that the Arab deputies had displayed in the Lynch affair was missing during the debates on Zionism, when the battle lines between the centralists and the decentralists were drawn more sharply. Decentralist Arab deputies strengthened the opposition's assault through periodic outbursts. No sooner had al-ʿAsali entered Parliament than he took up the theme of discrimination that had been broached by al-Zahrawi in more militant terms. He decried Arab underrepresentation in state offices, disagreed with the proposition that there was a shortage of properly trained Arabs, and maintained that being Arab was the main reason for rejection when applying for a government post. He demanded legal regulations to ensure the appointment of Arabs to official posts.[83]

These proceedings in Parliament should be viewed against the background of the articulation of the decentralist agenda in an Arabist idiom outside of Parliament. The press articles in Beiruti and, to a lesser extent, Damascene papers advanced similar demands for upholding Arab interests. Accusations and counteraccusations between the Unionist and the Arabist press started in November 1910 and continued through the entire duration of the parliamentary debates on the budget, Arab discrimination, and Zionism. This period also witnessed a renewed effort to constitute an Arab caucus in Parliament. A meeting was held in the home of Sayyid Talib, one of the decentralist leaders in Parliament and later outside it, with the participation of the majority of Arab deputies.[84] Presumably, one initiative that came out of this organizational activity was a letter that was secretly relayed to Sharif Husayn of Mecca imploring him to assume the leadership of an anti-Turkish Arab movement.

The deputy governor in Beirut communicated to İstanbul in April his apprehensions about the growing rancor in the press. He impressed on the government that "up to now such national conflict would have been unimaginable here." He also reported on a meeting he arranged with the owners of local newspapers. The journalists blamed the CUP for the animosity and stated that they were simply responding to the accusations of Turkish papers. The deputy governor expressed concern about foreigners seizing the opportunity to create further division. He urged the Ottoman navy to visit Beirut "to confirm bonds."[85] The Ministry of the Interior replied that a delegation would be sent at the end of the parliamentary session. The despatch of this delegation would have to wait until the election campaign of the following year.

LIBYAN WAR

Italy's declaration of war against the Ottoman government in September 1911 broke the quiet on the international front, jolting the Ottoman government and public opinion. Arab deputies and the opposition accused the cabinet of neglect both in its appraisal of Italian foreign policy and in securing the defense of the Libyan provinces. İstanbul had recalled the Tripoli commander İbrahim Pasha and moved troops and ammunition from Libya for use against the Yemen rebellion.[86] The government came under particularly heavy attack from the Libyan deputies. Foreign invasion of provinces where Ottoman sovereignty had never been disputed and the population was exclusively Muslim had a profound psychological effect on the government and the people of the empire.

İstanbul's concern with domestic political issues and provincial unrest rendered Libya vulnerable to attack from Italy, which had been waiting for the opportune moment to join the colonial scramble. Despite Italy's apparent military superiority and tactical advantages, the Ottoman government fought Italian aggression with all resources that were available. The most promising and best-trained officers, including Enver and Mustafa Kemal (later Atatürk), were sent to Libya. Since Italian naval superiority hampered the mobilization of troops in the Mediterranean and the Egyptian administration did not allow troop movements through Egypt, Libyan militias and tribal forces played the leading role in the fight against the Italians. İstanbul engaged in a sustained effort to preclude Italian annexation, but it failed as a result of a more ominous threat from the Balkan countries in the fall of 1912.

The argument that the Unionist government attached little importance to the Arab provinces and hence dismissed Libya too easily is not convincing. A corollary of this view holds that the Italian War was an eye-opener for Arabs who after 1911 concluded that a government dominated by Turks would sooner or later dispense with the Arab regions of the empire; thus were the Arabs driven to autonomist, if not separatist, programs. A more plausible argument maintains that the Italian War showed that the Ottoman Empire could no longer realistically defend itself against even the weaker European states, and that at a time of growing tensions between European coalitions an isolated Ottoman Empire would either perish or diminish. Therefore, some Arabs came to the conclusion that independence from İstanbul might spare them this grim eventuality.[87]

The Italian crisis had a unifying effect at the beginning. The unwarranted aggression galvanized Muslim Ottoman public opinion and rallied Muslims to the defense of the caliphate. The *Revue du Monde Musulman* reported that the Arabs were the first ones to forget their hatred of the Turks and that the CUP was actually able to profit from the war to maintain its position of power at a time of mounting opposition within Parliament and outside.[88] The expression of support from around the empire was overwhelming.[89] From Iraqi and Syrian tribes (including the Rwala *shaykh* who was reported to command 20,000 cavalry) to a retired brigadier in Aleppo, from Kurdish leader Seyyid Abdülkadir to Algerian and Tunisian immigrants in Syria, thousands of Ottomans volunteered to actively join the fight. In Baghdad large crowds gathered in front of the town hall while leading religious scholars pledged material support by forming commissions to recruit volunteers and to raise funds. There were donation drives in Acre and Tripoli (Syria). Progovernment Druze chief Shakib Arslan's patriotic appeals echoed in the poetic rhetoric on Islamic bonds among the people of Kirkuk in Kurdish Iraq. A telegram of support and sympathy from Baghdad decried the "unseemly attack at a time when all were striving in the path of civilization irrespective of nationality [*cins*] or religion."

İstanbul tried to subdue this initial outburst of enthusiasm, commending the patriotic sentiments while at the same time conveying the impression that the situation was under control. The antigovernment criticism in Parliament seemed out of touch with the sentiments pouring into the capital. In general, the opposition's momentum dissipated in the face of the national emergency. Popular Ottomanist sentiments aroused by the war convinced the CUP to prevail upon Grand Vizier Said Pasha, who had replaced İbrahim Hakkı at the outbreak of war, to maneuver for early elections.

Unrest in the Arab Provinces

In 1910 and 1911, despite a respite from international complications, domestic insurgency was on the rise in the empire's outlying areas for a variety of reasons: the government's unmistakable intent to establish direct authority throughout the empire in contrast to its insufficient administrative, financial, and military resources; the general disillusionment with the new regime's inability to bring about fundamental social change; and misinterpretation of the now widely preached concept of "liberty." The radical political transformation in the Balkans kindled nationalist sentiments that bore the greatest responsibility for the uprisings in Albania and Crete in the first half of 1910. In the Arab East, rebellions were stimulated by the local chiefs' fear of the extension of central authority.

The major centers of trouble in 1910 and 1911 were in Syria and the Arabian Peninsula. Uprisings broke out in mountain strongholds, areas where nomadic tribes lived, and regions furthest removed from the reach of the central government. Local warfare and insurrections were not new in these regions, but in 1910 and 1911 several erupted simultaneously. In southern Syria and the Hijaz the railway connecting Damascus and Medina, in operation since the fall of 1908, altered relations among local political factions and between them and the government. In these two years İstanbul had to deal with disturbances in Hawran and East Jordan, Asir, Najd, and Yemen.

The insurgencies were isolated and fomented by local leaders in reaction to increased central controls that came in the form of census registration, taxation, and the railway. These autonomist uprisings were quite different from the Balkan rebellions in substance and rhetoric, despite the tendency of histories oriented on future nation-states to interpret them as nationalist uprisings or reactions to the CUP's racialist policies.[90] The general state of anarchy in these regions placed a major burden on the financial and military resources of the government. It also sustained the army's predominant role established in April 1909.

The Hawran–East Jordan region was the scene of successive uprisings in 1910 and 1911. The Druze had long enjoyed autonomy in the mountain districts of Hawran. Their sporadic local revolts had been brought under control at the end of 1909.[91] In the summer of 1910 they raided the settled areas. İstanbul sent forces under the command of Faruq Sami Pasha, a high-ranking Arab general, a member of the Senate, and former minister of the gendarmery, to quell the rising.[92] The dispatch of an Arab commander was meant to counter the rhetoric on the "Turkishness" of the government that accompanied these movements and counterbalance the use of predominantly Turkish troops.[93] Sami Pasha next turned his attention to the uprising in Transjordan, where the Beduin between Amman and Maan were in arms, with the help of the Druze.[94] The apparent reason for the uprising was the nonpayment to the tribes of their traditional subsidies for the protection of the roads and the pilgrims. The Beduin destroyed a station on the Hijaz Railway,[95] as the new railway made the region easier to access and led to complacency and procrastination in the payment of subsidies. More important, the railway was the symbol of central control in the region. The disturbances in Hawran and East Jordan resulted in the dismissal of Syria's governor, İsmail Fazıl, allegedly for his failure to pay the tribes the usual protection money.[96] The governor denied the charges and contended that the real reason behind the uprising was the attempts to register the Beduin for purposes of a census.[97] Following Sami Pasha's Hawran expedition there was greater attention on the part of the government to improving conditions in the region. New roads and schools were built, such that the American consul could report that "a new and brighter day seems to be dawning in the trans-Jordan country."[98] However, rebels were severely punished, and in the spring of 1911 several Druze chiefs were executed. Similarly, many Beduin were court-martialed and their leaders hanged.[99] Yet, the government's resumption of payments to certain tribes showed that complete control was not established.[100]

There were pockets of unrest in Asir, in Eastern Najd under the control of the Saʿud family, and in Yemen under the domination of the rebellious Imam Yahya. The regime was aware that a more active policy had to be pursued in the Arabian Peninsula in order to bring the area under central control, even though Ibn Rashid of Najd and Sharif Husayn of Mecca were loyal to the government. In 1910 İstanbul enhanced its military presence and strengthened the administration in northern Hijaz (see chapter 5). To implement İstanbul's policies in the interior of the Peninsula, the government relied on the Sharif of Mecca. Sharif Husayn conducted a successful expedition against Ibn Saʿud, who sought to extend his sphere of influence from Riyadh westward.[101] The first major threat to government authority and to the Sharif's position in the Hijaz, however, came in 1911 from Idrisi of Asir. Encouraged by the apparent helplessness of the government against Imam Yahya of Yemen, assisted militarily by Italy, and espousing a messianic religious message, Idrisi led the tribes of Asir to rebellion. Combined sharifian and Ottoman military forces confronted the rebels and were able, after initial setbacks[102] and several months of fighting, to subjugate them.

Further south, in Yemen, Imam Yahya enjoyed the allegiance of the Shiite population as the Zaydi imam and successfully challenged central authority. At the end of 1910 Yahya blocked the Hodeida-Sana road and declared a holy war against the Ottomans.[103] The government resolved to send a major force under Ahmed İzzet Pasha,[104] who set out from İstanbul in February 1911.[105] The government forces failed to overcome

Yahya. In October 1911 an agreement had to be signed which not only gave a measure of autonomy and financial concessions to Yahya in exchange for ending his revolt and declaring loyalty to the sultan, but also allowed him to apply Zaydi legal practices free of government judicial controls.[106] Such an arrangement further augmented Yahya's religious-political prestige and power in Yemen, but established long-lasting quiet in the region.

In Yemen and Asir traditional leaders aimed at carving out spheres of influence to resist the centralizing measures of the government. The Syrian uprisings were triggered by the implementation of a government policy that appeared to threaten the local leaders' established privileges. Nevertheless, the British consul in Jidda reported at the height of disturbances in the Peninsula that "coffee house politicians of Jidda talk about Yemen and Asir rebellions as being a great nationalist Arab movement."[107] European observers tended to either see "hidden nationalist movements"[108] of the Balkan kind in these revolts or purposefully misinterpret them as nationalist uprisings. *Tanin* criticized in July 1910 the outlandish suggestion of the European press that the Ottoman Arabs were ready to join forces with the rebels of Albania in order to rid themselves of the Turkish yoke.[109]

More significantly for the empire (and not least because of its implications for intra-Muslim, and hence Arab-Turkish, relations) the government confronted in Albania for the first time a nationalist movement in which its Muslim subjects were involved. In 1910 and 1911 major army units had to be dispatched to suppress a series of uprisings and disarm the people. Despite religious, regional, and socioeconomic differences, the people of Albania, in the midst of Balkan nation-states that had recently separated from the empire, had developed a national consciousness nourished by a literary revival and fostered by the Albanian intelligentsia. Schemes of an independent Albanian identity to be constituted on the basis of common language had been discussed in Great Power councils since the end of the nineteenth century.[110] The Albanians elicited many concessions from İstanbul in the realms of taxation, education, and administration, and they secured a degree of autonomy that barely fell short of national independence by the end of 1911. For most observers, it was easy to extrapolate from the Albanian situation that other Muslim groups in the empire harbored similar political ambitions and were engaging in a struggle to attain them. The example of and association with their Albanian counterparts must have in fact influenced the Arab deputies in İstanbul. Yet during these years Arab leaders both in İstanbul and Syria saw the uprisings in different Arab regions for exactly what they were, namely the pursuit of local autonomy. In the spring of 1911 the execution of Beduins brought from Karak to Damascus met with the general approval of Arab notables.

Several months after the suppression of the Syrian revolts, al-ʿAsali criticized the government for not fulfilling its promises of reform in the tribal areas of Syria. He argued that the resentment against the government could be eliminated by extending an amnesty to all those imprisoned during the suppression of the revolts.[111] This proposal was opposed even by *Al-mufid*, the leading Arabist-decentralist paper in Beirut, which saw such a measure as contrary to administrative wisdom. The *Al-mufid* author who wrote under a pseudonym attacked the local notables for inciting the people to revolt and drew on the example of the British suppression of the Boers to argue that reforms would have to be fully enacted before the prison doors can be opened.[112]

In 1910 and 1911 the Ottoman government pursued an especially vigorous policy of fighting revolts in the Arab provinces. The disturbances had been chronic in many areas and kept under control with difficulty. In the absence of diversions abroad, İstanbul exerted its energies to settle local insurgencies and remove obstacles to administrative centralization. The regime perceived no imminent threats from nationalist movements as had been the case in Albania, but was increasingly concerned about foreign machinations and penetration in the outlying areas through cooperation with local leaders. İstanbul was specifically suspicious of British designs around the Persian Gulf,[113] Italian interference in the Red Sea, and provocations by the government of Egypt.[114]

In May 1911 Sultan Reşad embarked on a trip to the European provinces for a display of state authority in the region.[115] He led the Friday prayer on June 16 on the plains of Kosova, where his ancestors had routed the Serbs in 1389. The government took the occasion of his return to stage a festive display of Ottomanist solidarity, which was meant not only to be a gesture of reconciliation but also to impress on the elements of the growing Arab opposition the aura of imperial pomp in the capital. Stressing that it was important that they witness Ottoman might and benevolence, the Ministry of the Interior asked the Syria province that the Beduin *shaykh*s and Druze chiefs, as well as "the young men belonging to the press," accompany the *mutasarrıf* of Hawran to İstanbul to take part in the reception ceremony of the sultan.[116]

Conclusion

A student of Arab nationalism writes: "[The Young Turks] favored a secular state, and one based on Turkish rather than Ottoman nationalism. . . . After the Young Turk revolt the Turks came to see themselves as a master race and sought to impose a Turkish imprint on the minority peoples."[117] Such widely accepted generalizations offer an inaccurate appraisal of Young Turk policies and obscure the political and social realities of the day. Even in a recent and very significant contribution to the new thinking on the linkages of a segment of the Arab elite to the Ottoman center it is not unusual to encounter the persisting generalizations: "The Young Turks, whose regime followed the 1908 coup in Anatolia, accelerated the education program while implementing their policy of Turkification of the non-Turkish population via schools."[118] The statement suggests the existence of one distinct "Young Turk regime" associated with predominantly Turkish Anatolia (the Balkans would have been more accurately singled out as the region where the Young Turks organized and the revolution broke out) and bent on utilizing education first and foremost as indoctrination in the implementation of a deliberate Turkification program. Indeed, any campaign aimed at Turkification would have had to include Turks as well, if Turkification meant more than teaching the language, as those who spoke Turkish hardly perceived themselves as an ethnic community.

In the new game of politics introduced by the parliamentary regime, opposition to government came to be expressed in an anti-Turkish idiom by different sectors of the Arab population. The "establishment" came to be defined as Turkish, regardless of the fact that many Arabs were part of it or supported it. Yet the CUP's Arab critics were not motivated by an Arab nationalist ideology in accusing the CUP of Turkification, just as the CUP itself had not conceived of Turkish nationalism as a politically viable alternative to Ottomanism.

The question of Turkification was an extension of the centralization-decentralization debate and became an issue when Hamidian autocracy crumbled and the social groups dominating the revolutionary government prepared to establish a centralized government buttressed by a national economy. Although the decentralists submitted to the CUP in 1908, they became visible again as many deputies of the new Parliament came to support their program. The decentralists continued to favor diminished state control in the provinces and cut across all religious and ethnic groups. Those Arabs who found the centralizing policies of the CUP unpalatable for political, socioeconomic, or cultural reasons increasingly identified with the decentralist camp and found in the charges of Turkification a weapon to fight Unionist centralization and to produce a shift in the pro-CUP Arab public opinion. The Unionists soon saw that their version of Ottomanism, which presumed the ascendancy of a monolithic CUP, could not be made acceptable to all Ottomans merely by making constitutional and parliamentary principles an integral part of the Ottomanist package. The direction the Committee took was toward accommodating those "elements" (*anasır*) that did not harbor a political allegiance other than to the Ottoman state. During the 1910 convention of the CUP, Talat, as the minister of the interior, acknowledged that securing the allegiance of the non-Muslims to the Ottoman state had not been possible.[119] A consequence of this admission would be the future policy of according greater emphasis to Islam.[120]

The loss of Libya influenced the CUP's redefinition of Ottomanism in a direction that gave primacy to the Muslims of the empire. İbrahim Hakkı Pasha expressed concern about "relinquishing an Arab province to a Christian power" and appearing to neglect "the interests of other races of the empire."[121] But İbrahim Hakkı and other Unionists were more concerned about the general effect of the annexation of Tripoli and Benghazi on the CUP's centralization policy. They were sensitive not just to the Arab reaction but to that of all Ottomans. The Arab press exploited the Ottoman loss of Libya in order to weaken the CUP in the Arab provinces. In turn, when Italy decided to bomb eastern Mediterranean ports with the purpose of forcing the Ottoman government to yield in Libya, the CUP reinforced its position by availing of emergency measures and also by harnessing pro-unity sentiments arising from the immediate foreign threat. The most important outcome of the loss of Libya was that it highlighted the failure of Unionist policies of centralization, the justification for which had been the preservation of the empire's territorial integrity.

By 1911 the CUP-backed government in İstanbul encountered vigorous organized opposition, in which many Arabs participated both inside and outside Parliament. Even though Arabist propaganda imparted strength to the decentralist agenda, the following contemporary appraisal of Arab nationalism and Turkish-Arab relations by the German consul in Beirut has a ring of truth about it: "A general Arab Question exists only in the heads of philologically-minded Orient-politicians who are charmed by the idea of a future Arabic empire because of their sympathies towards the Arabic language and poetry. . . . The racial antipathy that the Arab feels towards the Turk has only as much political importance as do the various Arab uprisings, namely none."[122]

4

The Decentralist Challenge and a New "Arab Policy," 1912–1913

The opposition to the Committee of Union and Progress coalesced at the end of 1911 around the newly organized Liberty and Entente (*Hürriyet ve İtilâf*) Party. In the first true two-party general elections held in the spring of 1912, the CUP engineered a dubious victory that failed to confer legitimacy to it. Removed from government through extraparliamentary pressures, it was unable to return to power until it carried out a violent coup d'état in January 1913. By then Ottoman losses in the Balkan Wars had transformed the multiethnic and multireligious empire to a Turco-Arab core. The demands of Arab reformist groups induced the CUP to devise a policy that would defuse autonomist tendencies in the Arab provinces by accommodating decentralist demands. Meanwhile, the changed political and demographic circumstances further necessitated a redefinition of Ottomanist ideology by placing a greater emphasis on Islam as a binding force. At the end of 1913 the Unionist government launched an intensive Islamic propaganda effort embellished with anti-imperialist rhetoric. This strategy also complemented the evolving "Arab policy."

The 1912 Elections

The Entente Party's by-election victory in İstanbul in December 1911 was a warning that the CUP, if it failed to check the opposition at this early stage, might eventually have to relinquish power.

Thus the Committee decided to prevail upon the sultan to dissolve Parliament and go to new elections. It hoped that its superior empire-wide organization would secure in early elections a Unionist majority more loyal than the contingent in office. On 2 January 1912, Sultan Reşad complied.

In the spring of 1912 the political climate was very different from that of the 1908 campaign. Having lost the İstanbul by-election on the second ballot by a vote of 197 to 196, the CUP could leave nothing to chance in the approaching general elections and had to undertake a multifaceted campaign to win. The 1912 election is known as the "big-stick" election because of the manipulation, intimidation, and violence that it entailed. This designation, however, obscures the effort that went into the planning and conduct of the campaign and the rigorous contestation and popular mobilization it involved.[1]

The CUP first secured with a tactical move the replacement of Grand Vizier İbrahim Hakkı Pasha by Said Pasha. An experienced statesman who had served as grand vizier under Abdülhamid eight times, Said was hardly a Unionist, and commanded wide respect despite his versatility, described as chameleonlike by one critic.[2] As soon as Said Pasha came to office, the CUP engineered the predictable government crisis that enabled the sultan to dissolve Parliament, decree new elections, and reappoint Said as grand vizier. In order to facilitate the dissolution of the Chamber less circuitously, the CUP also tried to maneuver a constitutional amendment that, had it not been successfully blocked by the Entente, would have restored the arbitrary powers of the sultan over Parliament. The CUP's plan to eliminate the constitutional immunity of Parliament and to manipulate it through its influence over the weak sultan was an act of desperation. The Committee had vigorously fought, and successfully annulled in 1908, a clause in the 1876 constitution that had recognized such powers in the sultan, who had abused them by shutting down Parliament for thirty years in 1877.

After the speedy dissolution of Parliament, the government applied itself to the task of obstructing the organization of the new party in the provinces. In 1912 the CUP enjoyed the significant advantage of having Unionist branches throughout the empire. To be sure, in many areas, including the Arab provinces, the CUP clubs had dwindled. There was, however, a critical nucleus of pro-Unionist functionaries in the provinces who owed their jobs to the Committee and frustrated the Entente's efforts. The scarcity of local branches impaired the capability of the Entente for spreading effective propaganda and close supervision of the conduct of elections. Perhaps more important, the Entente's low profile disheartened potential supporters among local leaders when it was time to endorse one of the contesting parties.

The CUP appointed declared Unionists as civil and religious functionaries and mayors to create an effective counterweight to Ententist propaganda. The Entente sounded out political opinion in the Arab provinces and was not encouraged. A need for change was felt by segments of the Arab notability, but many were hesitant to openly declare themselves for the new party.[3] The CUP exploited its control over the administrative apparatus to redefine provincial electoral districts in order to ensure the success of its candidates.[4] Meanwhile, the government modified existing laws to restrict freedom of association and speech and took special measures to close the traditional channels for recruiting support to the opposition.[5] For instance, the discussion of political subjects in mosques was banned as a result of reports that religious functionaries, who would not be expected to "distinguish good from bad" in political issues, were preaching on matters of elections and politics.[6] There was also an attempt to manipulate the tribal vote. According to the British consul in Baghdad, the government obstructed the registration of tribal groups who lived outside of towns and villages, apparently in order to curtail the power of their *shaykh*s, some of whom had formally requested the enfranchisement of their tribes.[7] Open support for the Entente put at risk political standing and ambitions, particularly in view of the determined efforts and machinations of the CUP to maintain its power.[8] Many candidates leaning toward the Entente quickly switched allegiance.

There was, however, more to the 1912 elections than manipulation, forceful tactics, and fraud. Both parties engaged in effective campaigns. The CUP did not simply react to the Entente challenge, but rather initiated major campaign drives in Rumelia and Syria. Some of the Arab cities were the scenes of heated political rallies. In February 1912 both the CUP and the Entente organized campaign tours in Syria.[9] The CUP had been urged by governors to undertake a propaganda campaign in Syria even before the elections were called. It deemed an aggressive campaign in the Syria and Beirut provinces crucial for several reasons. First, though many Syrian Arab leaders had taken sides with oppositional factions and some had even assumed leadership positions in them, public opinion in the Arab provinces continued to be divided between the two parties.[10] The Committee leaders felt a special effort would secure a Unionist edge. Second, the government was concerned about the possible effects on the Arabs of deteriorating fortunes in the Libyan War and the impending capitulation to Italy. Finally, the damaging campaign in the Arab press about CUP-engineered "Turkification" had to be defused before the elections.

In general, the decentralist program had wider appeal in the incompletely integrated outlying provinces, in ethnically homogenous regions (where increasingly articulate elites held that decentralization would better preserve a distinctive cultural ethos), and among non-Muslims constituting majority communities in their regions (whom decentralization would bring closer to self-determination). Thus, Arabs, Kurds, Albanians, Armenians, and Greeks were susceptible if not always responsive to decentralist propaganda. In advocating decentralized administration, the Entente reinforced particularism by appealing to parochial sentiments. This gave a new lease to Arabist propaganda.

In the two major urban centers of Beirut and Damascus the former allies of the CUP, deriving from the aspiring middle-class elements with modern schooling and *salafi* leanings, united around an Arabist platform and expressed full support for the opposition through the two leading Syrian papers, *Al-mufid* (Beirut) and *Al-muqtabas* (Damascus).[11] Many notables, particularly outside these cities, felt little pressure or reason to respond to the call of the Arabists. The CUP's compromise with the landed interests prevailed, though the Committee had not fully co-opted them.[12] Some notables gravitated toward the Liberals in pursuit of further political and economic gain, but the base of the opposition's power was not the countryside.

Beirut, a business center where the interreligious commercial middle class was the ascendant if not the dominant social group, extended strong support to the decentralist Entente. Beirut's mercantile links were not so much with other areas of the Ottoman Empire as with Europe. The Beiruti merchants, whose prosperity depended on the local economy, favored a decentralized regime that would free the province from central administrative checks.[13] The convergence in Beirut of Arabist intellectuals and an autonomous commercial middle class provided fertile ground for the growth of a local autonomist current, which in turn rendered active support to the decentralist Entente Party. The CUP enforced a rearrangement of electoral districts in the Beirut *vilayet* in order to break up the city's support for the opposition.[14]

The experience of neighboring Mount Lebanon made the Beiruti intellectuals and other upper-middle-class elements particularly disposed toward autonomy. An autonomous regime had been set up in Mount

Lebanon in 1860, and by 1912 the area had achieved political and social structures that made it a viable entity largely independent of İstanbul.[15] While Beirut was administratively separate from Mount Lebanon, its economy was linked to that of the mountain and there was a large population movement between the two areas. The example of Mount Lebanon, with its financial autonomy, lower taxes, and military exemption, did not escape the Beirutis.

The relative strength of commercial middle-class elements was less in other Arab towns. Furthermore, unlike the notables of Beirut, those "from Damascus, Aleppo, and Jerusalem held public appointments at the highest levels, and Iraqis from Musul and Baghdad joined the Ottoman army in large numbers and sometimes rose to high ranks."[16] Because of traditional opportunities in state service for the urban elite of these towns, Ottomanism maintained its political moment while also nourishing its rival, Arabism, within the dynamics of intra-elite competition. The CUP was still relatively strong in these towns, especially after it evinced its determination to remain at the helm of the government.

Both in the election campaign of 1912 and later in trying to harness the reform movement, the CUP seems to have exerted a special effort to appeal to and manipulate the urban lower strata. In Beirut the Committee had links with local chiefs of guild workers and the unemployed who could create mobs. Some of these headmen engaged in illicit activities. The leader of pier and customs workers in Beirut, Ahmad Sharqawi, was an unavoidable intermediary between stevedores and shipping agents. He was an agitator with close relations to the CUP and had also been instrumental in carrying out the 1908 boycott of Austrian goods.[17] In 1912 local bosses like Baydun of the Basta district and Sharqawi came to be important factors in city politics.[18] In addition, the Sunni notable families of Beirut who remained loyal to the CUP acted as intermediaries between the urban poor and the state and dispensed patronage much like the commercial and landowning notables who controlled the countryside.[19]

The electoral race in the spring of 1912 was tight. The Entente ran an anti-Unionist campaign without pressing substantive issues. It banked on arousing latent ethnic and religious prejudices. For instance, consistent with the polemical arguments it brought to the Chamber the previous year, the Entente blamed in a campaign publication the impending loss of Libya on a CUP-Zionist plot.[20] Fearful of losing more of its Arab support, the CUP countered such propaganda with Ottomanist-Islamic rhetoric. Sharif Ja'far, cousin of Grand Sharif Husayn and a member of the Senate, was chosen to lead this propaganda effort and Unionist rallies in Syria.

On the whole, the CUP's election calculations were accurate, but its fears regarding Libya proved to be unfounded. Instead of fueling the opposition, defeats in Libya helped the CUP muster support. The war came home to coastal Syria in the midst of the election campaign in February, when Italian battleships bombarded Beirut to force the government to make concessions in North Africa.[21] The CUP used the panic caused by the sight of the enemy effectively to stress the importance of unity against European aggression. In the interior, where such threats were still not perceived, the Unionists orchestrated meetings in which Italian aggression in North Africa was denounced and the appropriate lessons in favor of unity were imparted to urban crowds.[22]

In most localities the conduct of officials during the election was high-handed. Haqqi al-'Azm, an Arab decentralist opponent of the CUP, published a booklet after the elections in which he cited numerous different breaches of law by the Unionists during the elections.[23] Much of the violence, intimidation, and fraud was perpetrated by local officials, who acted on their own behalf keen on preserving their jobs. At times, the government actually tried to curb their measures.[24] Even though the CUP actively lured Entente supporters to its own camp, it did not approve of candidates converting at the last moment.[25]

On 26 March 1912 Ambassador Lowther summed up his impressions of the upcoming elections as follows:

[T]he opinion is general that the Committee will prove victorious. As they are the only party of any strength it is recognized that their success is desirable in the interests of the country. . . . Should they be defeated a fresh impetus will be given to the disruptive forces and perhaps fresh encouragement to its neighbors without, as in any case an opposition majority could only be a very small one.[26]

Lowther was mindful of the tactics that the CUP was using and the foreign complications that served its objectives. His prognosis might have been less favorable to the CUP had he based it on the Arab provinces alone. The fact remains that while the CUP employed unacceptable pressures and was aided by foreign aggression and martial law justified by the war, the mandate it received reflected a political reality that was not in its entirety forged by the Committee.

Compared with the 1908 Parliament, the 1912 Parliament showed an increase in representation of the Arab provinces (from 23 percent to 27 percent of the Chamber).[27] The more noticeable change, however, was in the body's political turnover and ethnic composition. Only about one-fifth of the Arab contingent from 1908 was reelected. Furthermore, the ratio of Turks elected in the Arab provinces in 1912 more than doubled its 1908 size to somewhere between 14 and 22 percent. Yet more significant was the increase in 1912 of known Unionists in the contingent representing the Arab provinces (67 percent as opposed to 39 percent in 1908).[28] Since state functionaries generally constituted a reservoir of Unionists, the CUP put up and supported the candidacy of such functionaries, among whom Turks were highly represented relative to other occupational and social categories. There was a 12-point increase in the percentage of functionaries compared to other professions between 1908 and 1912, from 23.5 percent to 35.5 percent.[29]

The excess of coercive measures that the Unionists employed to win a majority tarnished the elections. The short mandate of this assembly ended in July 1912 with intervention from the army and a compromise government favorable to the Ententists. Ultimately, the CUP strategy backfired: the size of its continued majority in Parliament proved to be a source of weakness rather than strength.

The CUP's Broken Fortunes and Arabs

By going to early elections the CUP had hoped to secure a parliamentary majority for another four years, yet it was only able to hold on to power for several weeks. The election campaign exposed the Unionists' weaknesses, and, although the elections resulted in a CUP majority, the gross imbalance in its favor in the new Parliament was not only a sign of the Committee's inequitable electoral conduct but also betrayed a lack of self-confidence, thus exposing it to a challenge from the army. Once again a faction of army officers, who called themselves *Halaskâran* (Saviors), intervened in the political process by asking the Said Pasha government to step down.[30] Disenchanted with the Committee, Said Pasha resigned despite a vote of confidence in his favor, clearing the way for the "Great Cabinet" of Gazi Ahmed Muhtar Pasha, elder statesman and general, which also included two other former grand viziers, Kamil and Hüseyin Hilmi. The new government dislodged the CUP and gave new hope to the Ententists.

The period from July 1912, when the Gazi Ahmed Muhtar cabinet took over, to January 1913, when the CUP made a forceful comeback, was replete with political changes both domestic and external. Ahmed Muhtar Pasha dissolved Parliament in August and prepared for new elections. In October the Balkan countries opened hostilities against the empire, forcing the government to conclude a peace settlement with Italy and to cancel the elections. At the end of October Kamil Pasha came to the grand vizierate, a post he held until the Unionist coup of January 1913.

The Great Cabinet resolved to break Unionist influence in the provinces. Many in administrative positions were replaced, and orders went to the provinces enjoining all functionaries, clerks, and teachers to refrain from getting involved in party politics.[31] Ahmed Muhtar Pasha did not intend, however, to weaken the CUP until it could not survive. Despite its Ententist sympathies, this cabinet functioned in the spirit of a compromise government that remained above party politics. A Unionist Arab deputy and the vice-president of the disbanded Chamber, Muhammad Fawzi Pasha (al-'Azm) of Damascus, served in the cabinet as minister of religious foundations.[32]

When Kamil Pasha resumed the grand vizierate, however, he attempted to eradicate the CUP. The CUP clubs in the provinces were searched and their records sent to İstanbul.[33] This also induced defections from the party. Leading Unionists escaped abroad[34] as the government moved to court-martial them.[35]

In the second half of 1912 political activity and intrigue intensified in the Arab provinces as a result of several factors: the renewed—but ultimately aborted—hope that new elections offered; uncertainty regarding the future of the Ottoman state in view of foreign threats; diminished central authority and administrative control in the provinces; and the intensification of foreign machinations.

ARAB DISSIDENCE AND THE
EGYPTIAN FACTOR

In July 1912 the Ottoman authorities in Cairo reported the printing and distribution of pamphlets in Egypt critical of the CUP and "inciting the entire Arab nation to rise with the pen and the sword."[36] Soon after, there were reports from Syria regarding the arrest of spies of Algerian origin sent to Syria to provoke traitorous activities. The governor suspected European instigation and reiterated the need for an investigation in Egypt. Moreover, he advised the suppression of Arabist newspapers in Syria.[37] These developments preceded the formation of the Ottoman Administrative Decentralization Party (*Hizb al-lamarkaziyya al-idariyya al-'uthmani*) at the end of 1912, with the approval, if not encouragement, of the British administration and with links to Syria.[38]

Already in occupation of Egypt and systematically acquiring footholds along the eastern fringes of the Arabian Peninsula, Britain was hardly disinterested in the Arab lands in between. European consuls in these regions reported frequently before 1912 on alleged activities of British agents among the Arabs and warned of British motives to occupy these areas. But London's policies vis-à-vis the Arab East were shaped in general by its traditional interests in the region, namely the maintenance of its trade, the security of routes to India, and the continuation of its control over Egypt. As long as these interests were not threatened by either a strengthened Ottoman government or by the intervention of other powers, occupation was not desirable for diplomatic, political, and military reasons. In addition, Britain had to be more sensitive than before to French ambitions in Syria following the naval agreement concluded between the two powers in 1912.[39]

In the summer of 1912, in view of the unstable political situation inside the empire and threats to it from outside, the British government reappraised its role in the Arab provinces and explored the option of occupation. Lowther sent a confidential query to the consulates regarding conditions pertaining to mobilization of local resources in Syria. Detailed reports responding to the query arrived from Damascus, Jerusalem, Aleppo, and Beirut and were relayed in London to the War Office. Consul Fontana (Aleppo) wrote in his report: "I have been informed by more than one Englishman in touch with the tribal sheikhs of upper Mesopotamia that these chiefs of tribes ask when the English are coming to occupy 'Jezireh' [Mesopotamia], declaring that they will help them to conquer the country."[40]

The British administration in Egypt sought to exploit to its advantage the opposition movement in the Arab regions and the weakness of the Ottoman government. Syrian intellectuals residing in Cairo, having fled repressive Ottoman policies and found a safe haven under British administration, had little sympathy toward the Ottoman government. Egyptian nationalists, on the other hand, still looked to İstanbul in their anticolonialist struggle and were uninterested in the Arab political movement in Syria.[41] The British, who all too vividly remembered the

Egyptian nationalists' declaration of anti-British sentiments during celebrations of the revolution in July 1908, condoned, if not encouraged,
the anti-Ottoman attitude of the Syrians in Egypt. Anti-Ottomanism,
even if it came with its potentially subversive corollary of demand for
Arab unity, suited the British, because it weakened the ostensible case
of Egyptian nationalists, who dwelled on the ties of Egypt to the Ottoman caliphate.

There were tensions between Syrians in Egypt, who tried to weaken
the links with İstanbul by appealing to a common Arab identity, and
followers of the Egyptian nationalist Mustafa Kamil, who professed allegiance to the empire.[42] Ironically, the rhetoric of both Egyptian nationalists and Syrian Arabists reflected political expediency rather than
an accurate and genuine expression of objectives. In both cases the stated
aims did not conform to political realities. Egyptian nationalists were
actually committed to the idea of "Egypt for the Egyptians," which was
incompatible with Ottoman suzerainty. As for the Syrians, they were all
too uncertain about the political basis upon which the Arab unity they
advocated could be achieved. By assisting the pro-British Syrian movement Britain hoped to enhance its own stature in Syria. It also proceeded
to strengthen its position in Cairo by abrogating the post of Ottoman
high commissioner in Egypt.[43]

The outbreak of the Balkan War shook the empire in October 1912.
As the already precarious political, economic, and diplomatic situation
further deteriorated, British and French interest in the Arab provinces
intensified. In November 1912 Edhem Pasha, the governor of Beirut,
warned İstanbul of two disintegrative political currents in the province,
one that desired the unification of Beirut and Mount Lebanon under a
French protectorate and a second that sought the annexation of Syria
to Egypt under British auspices. A third group advocated reforms and
tevsi'-i mezuniyet (extension of authority) in order to countervail the first
two tendencies. The governor pointed to the widely held view in Beirut
that those countries that separated from the Ottoman Empire had advanced more rapidly. Warning that this conviction could strengthen the
pro-French and pro-British currents and lead to foreign occupation he
concluded by urging substantive and urgent reforms.[44]

It is debatable to what extent the governor's representation of Beirut's political inclinations conformed to reality. Convinced as he was of
the need for the execution of reforms to appease the population, he tried
to impress its urgency on the government by depicting the fulfillment
of demands for reform as the only solution that would maintain Beirut

and possibly other provinces within the Ottoman Empire. Certainly, many reformists, at this stage consisting mostly of Muslims, favored the maintenance of ties to the Ottoman state and sought to improve conditions in their province and thus to forestall foreign encroachments.

THE REFORM MOVEMENT IN THE ARAB PROVINCES

The demands of the reformists led to the formation of the reform societies in Beirut and later in other Arab cities. İstanbul advised the governor of Beirut that the general council of the provinces should meet and discuss measures for reform until such time as Parliament met and the deputies gave expression to the needs of their constituencies.[45] Such vague encouragement for reform proposals did little to excite the proponents of change at a time when the outbreak of the Balkan War and swift Ottoman defeats shook the confidence of Arabs in the capability of the Ottoman state to survive the military, economic, and political crisis aggravated by the war or to protect its Arab-populated provinces against external threats. Advances by the armies of the Balkan states toward the capital created the fear that the seat of the caliphate might fall.[46]

Rumors circulated at this juncture, probably spawned and propagated by Rashid Rida and the British in Egypt (see chapter 6), that there was an agreement among Arab leaders (the khedive, ʿIzzat Pasha, Sharif Husayn, Shaykh Sanussi, and Ibn Rashid were some names that circulated) to overthrow the government in İstanbul and establish an Arab caliphate. Further rumors about an antigovernment alliance between Arabs and Kurds in the North[47] were an attempt to append to an exaggerated Arab nationalist movement an invented Kurdish one.

Expectation of higher taxes, forced loans, and requisitions due to the war effort in the Balkans troubled the Arab population. The American consular agent in Haifa wrote that the Arabs there "say if Turkey has given up the Tripolitana, European Turkey will also surely be given up; and now they ask themselves who will pay for the support of the sultan, Pashas, Valis and the whole government, and they have come to the conclusion that the Arabs will have to pay the greater part."[48] These fears were justified: the government sent commissions to Damascus and Beirut to assess property taxes. The Beirut commission concluded that Beirut's tax revenues should amount to 430,000 liras instead of the 110,000 previously appraised. Agitated by the prospect of heavier taxes, the people of Damascus obstructed the work of the commission. In Beirut the governor was asked by the townspeople to disband the commission and cancel all its work.[49]

The expectation that the Arab provinces would have to sustain the financial burden of the war effort coupled with the distinct possibility of an Ottoman collapse strengthened the pro-British tendency among the Syrians as well as the British interest in Syria. A British report from Jaffa reflected the mood in the town:

[T]he effect of the recent Turkish defeats upon the population of Jaffa has been to increase greatly the unpopularity of the Turkish government, and one hears from all sides the opinion that the Turkish regime is doomed, and the best thing that could happen for this part of the world would be an extension of the Egyptian frontier to its boundary at Acre. There has always been loose talk in this sense . . . but just now many Muslim notables are freely expressing the idea. These persons are afraid that the severing of a large part of the Empire will throw a much greater burden of taxation on the provinces which remain, and they hope equally that the value of their property will be increased, as site values have gone up so much in Egypt.[50]

If Britain displayed reserve in abetting pro-British propaganda out of consideration for its ally France, attempts by France to enhance its influence in Syria only contributed to the growth of pro-British sentiments. The pro-British and pro-French factions were divided roughly on religious lines. While Lebanese Maronites looked favorably to French intervention, Britain appealed primarily to Muslim notables. A delegation of Arab notables visited the British consul in Beirut and expressed concern about French propaganda.[51] Both British and other European diplomatic agents in Syria reported on the strength of agitation for a British protectorate, even annexation.[52] On 12 December Mallet advised Ambassador Lowther that no encouragement should be given by His Majesty's consuls "to the idea that Syria might come under British rule, as it is neither practicable nor desirable that His Majesty's government should entertain such an extension of territorial responsibility."[53]

The consuls exaggerated the local enthusiasm for foreign intervention in Syria, but clearly there was a propensity on the part of some local notables to seek such an intervention in view of an anticipated Ottoman collapse. Since the 1908 Revolution decentralist proclivities had gained strength in the Arab provinces. Yet at the end of 1912 it became apparent that the Liberal government of Kamil Pasha, too, was failing to implement the administrative overhaul that would have expanded the prerog-

atives of local government. As the empire seemed to totter toward collapse, with defeats on the war front and economic and political
difficulties internally, disaffected elements in the Arab provinces entertained Great Power intervention in search of a political formula that
would secure a measure of autonomy under foreign supervision.[54]

At this juncture some Arab leaders revived the notion of the Arab
caliphate as the only feasible Arab political arrangement.[55] Social and
political norms as well as economic conditions showed a broad variety
in the Arab provinces. Like Ottomanism, the notion of the Arab caliphate offered the framework for an umbrella ideology that would accommodate particular interests and regional, linguistic, and socioeconomic
diversity in the Arab-populated lands. Yet the idea widened the religious
division between Muslims and Christians. As a fairly clear split along
religious lines already existed between the pro-English (Muslim) and
pro-French (Christian) factions, the notion of an Arab caliphate enhanced Britain's position in predominantly Muslim Syria.[56] The prop-
agandists for an Arab caliphate included 'Izzat al-'Abid, an Anglophile
now living in Egypt.[57] The khedive of Egypt, 'Abbas Hilmi, emerged
as a logical and eager candidate for caliph.

The British consul in Beirut argued that the pro-British current was
waning because of the restraint in responding to local requests for intervention.[58] With the pro-British Kamil at the helm of the Ottoman
government now, the British authorities may have been less keen about
generating provincial dissent. There were other important factors that
effected the political climate in Beirut and the other Arab provinces,
namely the changing circumstances of the Balkan War and İstanbul's
renewed initiatives to encourage reform proposals for these provinces.
On 16 December 1912 peace negotiations between the Ottoman Empire
and the Balkan states began at the London Conference. The war-weary
Balkan states were willing to sit at the conference table and halt their
advance. Despite some territorial losses, the Ottoman government had
managed to arrest a vital threat to its integrity. Whereas only weeks
before the fall of İstanbul seemed imminent, the Ottoman delegation
was now bargaining in London to regain Edirne, a city of strategic and
historical importance and the empire's former capital, now under Bulgarian siege.[59]

The Kamil Pasha government formally consented to the drafting of
reform proposals by local leaders in the Arab provinces. On 25 December
Governor Edhem reported from Beirut that the royal decree issued to
the provincial council calling for negotiations toward reform was re-

ceived with great joy. The governor commented that public opinion, which had been divided between various foreign and Ottomanist currents only a month ago, was now united in loyalty, with a firm belief that the provinces would attain reforms and progress.[60] In addition to the official commission that was appointed to draft the preliminary reform proposals, Christian and Muslim notables held occasional meetings to exchange opinions on reforms and formed the Beirut Reform Committee. The governor summoned the general council of the province to a meeting at the beginning of January to discuss the draft proposals. Preliminary proposals formulated in the general council included acceptance of Arabic as the official language in the Arab provinces and the appointment of foreign advisors in government offices.[61] On 1 January 1913 the minister of the interior advised the provinces of Syria and Aleppo as well to proceed with the preparation of reform proposals.[62]

The Beirut Reform Committee was composed of an equal number of Muslims and Christians. Kamil Pasha allowed this self-appointed committee to supplant the official commission, for the voluntary cooperation of different religious communities was a welcome development and an indication of their willingness to live together and abandon the desire to seek foreign intervention. Muslim and Christian members of the Beirut committee shared the same economic interests and cooperated closely, as the two presidents Muhammad Bayhum (Muslim) and Yusuf Sursuq (Christian) mediated between the Ottoman government and the reformists.[63]

In Damascus the reform project was worked out by the provincial general council. The fundamental points in both the Beirut and Damascus proposals bore a striking similarity: appointment of provincial functionaries from the local population, permission to use Arabic in government offices, local and shorter military service. In fact, the Damascus proposal went further in expressing localist demands.[64] Clauses pertaining to the appointment of judges locally and the use of Arabic in court proceedings were, for instance, explicitly laid out by the Damascene general council. In addition, Damascus asked for financial subsidies to fund public works, agricultural development, and educational institutions. Yet the Damascus program did not contemplate a loosening of ties with the central government. The Beirut Reform Committee, on the other hand, made specific stipulations regarding the separation of provincial prerogatives and imperial ones in such a way as to restrict the latter to foreign and military affairs, customs, and communications.[65] The Beirut Committee attempted to regulate the relations of the governor with a reorganized provincial council and to define and separate their respective powers in favor of the provincial council. Beirut also stipulated the employment of foreign advisors. These demands were most probably inspired by the example of autonomous Mount Lebanon.

The CUP Comeback

THE SUPPRESSION OF THE REFORM MOVEMENT

The Ottoman defeat in the Balkan War had been so swift and so massive that by December 1912 Grand Vizier Kamil Pasha had asked for the cease-fire that led to the London Conference. As these negotiations continued, the CUP leaders, in an apparent attempt to prevent Kamil from surrendering besieged Edirne to Bulgaria, stormed the Sublime Porte on 23 January 1913, ousted the cabinet at gunpoint, and took over the government. The fall of Salonika, where the CUP was headquartered, had constituted a psychological blow to the Unionists. The impending loss of Edirne motivated the violent intervention. The Unionists were also alarmed about the reprisals against the CUP by Kamil Pasha, the Committee's political archenemy since his ouster in 1909. Whatever the reasons for the raid at the Sublime Porte (or the *Bab-ı Âli baskını*), it restored the Committee to power for the next five years, until the end of World War I.

The reform committees in Beirut and Damascus issued their projects only a few days after the coup and the formation of a Unionist government under Mahmud Shawkat Pasha. The CUP takeover had significant implications for the reform movement and the general course of events in Syria. Though opposed in principle to the extension of local autonomy to the provinces, the CUP seemed inclined to reconcile with the decentralists. It made overtures to include Sabahaddin in the new government.[66] Having witnessed the ferment in Syria and the failure of the policy of centralization to retain regions affected by autonomist sentiment in the Balkans, the new Shawkat Pasha government set up a committee to study Arab demands.[67] The government was inclined neither to concede the prerogatives that the Beirut Reform Committee demanded for the provincial council nor to accept a medley of reform proposals from the empire's various provinces. Instead, it promulgated the long-deliberated Provincial Law in March 1913, which included decentralizing measures. But the reformists, and especially those of Beirut, adamantly opposed compromising their demands, which they thought they were so close to obtaining, and stepped up their campaign in Syria and Cairo. The Egyptian press featured articles about annexation as others contemplated an "Arab government" as the alternative to the implementation of reforms.[68]

In the spring of 1913, though now back in charge, the CUP was not yet strong enough politically to assert itself in the reform question. Edirne could not be secured at the London Conference or in the aftermath of resumed warfare. The government came to feel the burden of defeats and extended warfare more fully. Removed from the scene of hostilities, the Arab provinces had been at first affected relatively little by the war, though, of course, they had to contribute to the war effort with recruits, which inevitably led to economic and social dislocation. In February both Damascus and Aleppo were the scene of popular demonstrations. In Damascus the price of bread increased by close to 30 percent in two weeks, triggering street riots.[69] In Aleppo a demonstration of women protesting the increase in bread prices in front of the governor's palace had to be dispersed by the police.[70] There was a similar increase in the price of meat in Aleppo arising from the requisitioning of the province's meat supply for the army. The government managed to take some effective measures to control shortages and prices. In Damascus the export of cereals was banned and speculation prohibited.

The Austrian consul in Damascus wrote that the Damascenes had been led to think that Britain was responsible for fomenting unrest in pursuit of its own political ambitions, namely setting up a caliphate under British protectorate with the grand sharif of Mecca as caliph.[71] The rumor of a British-sharifian alliance circulated in Syria as early as 1913 and was unpopular with the Damascenes. In February the CUP-led government in İstanbul appointed an Arab, ʿArif al-Mardini, as governor of Damascus, a tactical maneuver designed to appease the opposition there. The ability of the Unionist government to restore order and create a favorable public opinion in Damascus, at a time when sacrifices were being solicited for the war effort, represented a political success.

In Aleppo the burden of contributions for the war, borne primarily by the notables, was particularly heavy. The authorities considered raising a forced loan but resorted instead to requisitioning necessities such as meat, oil, and wheat from the notables. According to the Austrian consul, former leaders of the Entente Party (possibly some of the wealthiest individuals in town) suffered most from requisitions.[72] This may help to explain why Anglophile sentiments lingered in Aleppo longer than in Beirut and Damascus.[73]

Shortly after the Unionist takeover, Hazım Pasha, who had been ousted by the Liberal government in favor of Edhem, returned to Beirut as governor. Unionist policies aggravated the estrangement between Beirutis and the government. Hazım applied stricter controls on the press and closed two papers in Beirut. The rumor of a forced loan to be imposed on property holders never materialized, but the reformers' suspicion of the government grew.[74] Hazım Pasha refused to act on the Beirut reform proposal.[75] The Provincial Law was designed to render various local demands obsolete by stipulating for limited decentralizing measures such as local administration of tax revenues in the provinces. Declaring the Provincial Law inadequate and angered by Hazım's reticence to address the reforms they had proposed, the reformers undertook antigovernment protests. The Beiruti notable Salim ʿAli al-Salam, who had served as vice-president of the Beirut commercial court and president of the municipal council, quit his position in the provincial administrative council.[76] Shukri al-ʿAsali declined the governorship of Latakia that was conferred on him in an attempt to secure his compliance with the new provincial regulations.[77]

Hazım's decision to close the society of the reformists (Reform Club) in Beirut at the beginning of April triggered even stronger reactions. The government was threatened by the unity of purpose that the Beiruti leaders displayed over the reform question and viewed their demands tantamount to provincial autonomy. According to the American vice-consul in Beirut, İstanbul's decision to dissolve the Reform Club came after the latter opened negotiations with the reformists in Damascus.[78] The reformists had extended their propaganda outside Beirut in order to increase the pressure for reforms on the government. The reform idea also found a response in Mesopotamia, particularly in Basra under the leadership of Sayyid Talib.[79]

İstanbul anticipated the reaction that the decision to suppress the Reform Club would elicit in the provinces. The official journal of the Damascus province, *Suriye*, prepared the ground for the closure by publishing a polemical article about the reform movement. It urged a complacent attitude and advised the people to leave important issues concerning the province to their representatives in Parliament (which had not been in session for nine months).[80] But the events in Beirut had a considerable impact on Damascus. Local papers sharply criticized the government and denounced the Provincial Law as a meager concession.

Having misjudged the intensity of public reaction against the suppression of the local reform movement, İstanbul sought to remedy the situation in two ways. First, it mobilized the large sectors of the population who were either indifferent or opposed to the reform movement. Second, it took some urgent measures to impress upon the population that it was serious in effecting change consistent with local demands. In its efforts to mobilize the lower strata of Beirut's townspeople in response to the protestations of the reformists,[81] however, the government did not have the success it had had during the election campaign of the previous year. Some notables who preferred to remain in the government fold did send telegrams condemning the reformist agitation, but the counterpropaganda was not very effective. İstanbul also sent agents to Syria to try to bolster the government position there, only to encounter the accusation that it was trying to create sectarian discord and to break up the remarkable unity that the Beirutis had displayed to promote their common interests.

One of the agents sent to Syria was 'Abd al-'Aziz Jawish. Jawish was an Egyptian nationalist agitator who had fled from Cairo to İstanbul in 1912. When the Ottoman authorities had refused to extradite him, Egypt's Consul General Lord Kitchener had asked the British Embassy in İstanbul to keep a close watch over Jawish's activities, expressing the fear that he might influence Egyptian students in the Ottoman capital.[82] Attempts to extradite Jawish constituted a diplomatic issue that had also been taken up in the CUP Congress, which decided that the surrender of a refugee in the seat of the caliphate would be unacceptable. In reporting on the proceedings of the CUP Congress, Lowther had written that the CUP, now out of power, was trying to make a *cheval de bataille* out of Jawish in order to appeal to "nationalistic elements" in the country.[83] The CUP was in fact invoking Islamic symbols, which had proven increasingly more effective in Ottomanist propaganda against imperialist ambitions.

In the aftermath of the suppression of the Reform Club, the British intensified their propaganda emanating from Egypt. The ouster of the pro-British Kamil added a further strain to relations between İstanbul and London.[84] The CUP's dispatch of Jawish to Syria led to British consternation and the resumption of all-out subversive propaganda against the Unionist government. An article published in the *Egyptian Gazette* of 22 April 1913, and couched in language that differed noticeably from that of even the most bitter discourse on the reform question, was aimed specifically at instigating racial hatred between Arabs and Turks. After denouncing Jawish's mission, the article went on:

The struggle is between Semitic Mohammedan and Turk Mohammedan. . . . Race is the fundamental fact. And the Turk physically differs from the Arab somewhat as a drayhorse differs from a Derby winner. Greater still is the difference intellectually and spiritually, between the slow, placid, steady, autocratic, materialistic, unspeculative, unaesthetic Turk, and the quick-witted, restless, democratic, political, romantic, artistic, versatile Arab.

The article, which referred to England as the "regenerator of Egypt," read both as a blueprint of the schemes taking definite shape in the minds of British authorities in Egypt at this time and an exhortation to the Arabs:

[T]he old renown of Ottoman arms has gone down before Bulgarians, Greeks, and Servians, and the Arab is watching and waiting for his opportunity. On the occupation and protection of Mecca rests the sole claim of the Sultan to be Khalif; that is the loss by him of Mecca implies the loss of his right to command the temporal obedience of Mohammedans.

The author also mentioned that "the Hedjaz Railway would be torn up," that "Egypt would break the last link of nominal dependence upon Turkey that still exists," and predicted the "contraction of the Turkish Empire to its possessions in Asia Minor, Armenia, Upper Mesopotamia."[85] Another article predicted discord between Arabs and Turks in the aftermath of the Balkan War as a result of the decline in the military power of İstanbul[86] and "the rise of an independent Grand Sharif at Mecca with the consent of the dominant naval power [Britain] in the Red Sea."[87]

The sharp change in the tone of British propaganda emanating from Egypt did not escape the attention of the Austrian consul in Beirut, who reported that the Egyptian propaganda was taking a more tangible form which is no longer concealed under the "harmless expression 'decentralization.' " In this context, Pinter mentioned flyers distributed in Beirut, which were anonymous but probably authored by those sympathetic to French interests in the region, who worried that Britain would take undue advantage of the government's embarrassment in the reform question. These flyers urged Beirutis not to pay taxes, to close all businesses, schools, mosques, and to go to the "free Lebanon" until conditions changed.[88]

THE DECENTRALIST CHALLENGE

COMPROMISE

The sequence of events that led to the dissolution of the reform movement convinced the government of the need to respond to demands in the Arab provinces. Concessions in the realm of language had the widest appeal and greatest symbolic weight. The language question was the issue that had received the greatest attention from all reform groups. The demand for the local use of Arabic also happened to be the least disagreeable to the CUP, whose principal aim was to defuse the more radical demands voiced by the Beirut Reform Committee, specifically the strengthening of the provincial council vis-à-vis the governor and the employment of foreign advisors.

A decree issued in April 1913 sanctioned the use of Arabic in law courts and as the main medium of instruction in schools (except the higher *sultaniye* schools, which existed in some provincial centers) and provided for the drafting of petitions and official communications in Arabic.[89] Lowther described the new decree as the adoption by the CUP of the opposition's policy of decentralization. The new language policy, and especially its immediate implementation, came as a surprise and produced the desired effect. In Damascus, court officials who did not know Arabic were replaced. Implementation of Arabic in schools, however, had to wait because textbooks could not be rewritten overnight.[90]

The Ministry of the Interior received petitions from district officials, some written in Arabic, requesting the replacement of certain non-Arabic-speaking functionaries.[91] The provinces saw an opportunity in the new language policy to remove unpopular or politically undesirable local officials. The Damascus governor ʿArif, for instance, asked that the chief judge of the province, Hurşid, be replaced by the former deputy for Acre, Asʿad Bey (al-Shuqayri), because of the former's unfamiliarity with Arabic. The Ministry rejected the request and argued that Hurşid was not only competent in his job but also in Arabic.[92]

With the exception of Beirut and Basra, where Talib now sought to enhance his position by means of the reform society that he established, the CUP government was able to restore its authority in the Arab provinces. This should be considered a political success for the CUP, especially in light of its failures on the military and diplomatic front. When the First Balkan War came to a conclusion in May 1913, the CUP had not been able to regain Edirne and, thus, had forfeited the justification for the coup of January 1913.

The government did intend to go beyond palliative measures in order to satisfy Arab demands and to establish effective administration in the Arab provinces. With further losses of land in the Balkan wars, the Arab provinces came to constitute a greater percentage of the empire in terms of population, territory, and economic potential. The reform movement brought home the fact that the Arab peoples could no longer be regarded merely as other Muslims within the Ottomanist framework that downplayed economic, ethnic, and regional differences. The government would have to consider the demands by different social strata in diverse Arab regions lest these groups turn to separatist programs and create the conditions that the Ottoman government had found impossible to curb in its former European possessions.

In view of the territorial losses incurred in Europe, the relocation of the Ottoman capital away from the proximity of enemy lines came on the agenda. From a more central location the influence of the sultan-caliph could be projected more effectively into the Arab provinces. An article by Marshal von der Goltz in the *Neue Freie Presse* on 18 May 1913 started the debate on the transfer of the capital.[93] Von der Goltz contemplated an Austro-Hungarian model for the Ottoman Empire and viewed Aleppo, with its central location and multiethnic population, as an appropriate choice for the imperial center.

The proposition attracted much interest. The French ambassador in İstanbul, Boppe, commented that the measure could be used by the Young Turks to win over Arabs to a stronger Ottomanist position, and added that it would be easier to administer the empire from its middle than from the periphery.[94] Boppe's German counterpart, Wangenheim, also contemplated the pros and cons of the issue. He indicated that, on the one hand, the luxury of life in İstanbul had a demoralizing and corrupting influence on government officials; but, on the other hand, having served as the seat of the government for centuries and occupying a coveted strategic location, İstanbul's abandonment as capital could have serious domestic and international implications. In fact, the German ambassador maintained that displacing the seat of the caliphate would further encourage the agitation for the establishment of an Arab caliphate.[95]

Wangenheim also mentioned that Grand Vizier Mahmud Shawkat Pasha was partial to relocation. As a general, Mahmud Shawkat was mindful of the strategic vulnerability of İstanbul. As an Ottomanist Arab he probably also thought that the transfer of the capital to Aleppo would help remedy the estrangement of segments of the Arab elite from the government. In the Ottoman press other suggestions were put forward.

Ahmed Ferid [Tek], former deputy from the western Anatolian town of Kütahya, proposed Kayseri in south-central Anatolia as the best choice. He argued against a shift further south, because such a move might again peripheralize the capital, should the Arabs strive for autonomy. He also justifiably criticized the notion of a biracial Turco-Arab empire on the Austria-Hungary model. According to Ahmed Ferid, Austria-Galicia-Bohemia-Carinthia provided a more appropriate analogy than Austria-Hungary. The Ottoman Empire's Arab lands did not constitute a single unit, and social and political circumstances differed from one region to the other.[96]

In the end the Unionist position prevailed. The CUP's power base had always been in Rumelia. For psychological and political reasons the CUP did not favor the proposed relocation of the Ottoman capital. In fact, all public reference to the subject was prohibited, bringing an end to the debate once and for all. Mahmud Shawkat Pasha's assassination in June 1913 resulted in the abandonment of the idea. Nevertheless, even if the Unionists objected to moving the capital, they were increasingly convinced of the need to satisfy demands voiced in the Arab districts and inclined to give further thought to the "Austria-Hungary model" in order to preclude potential separatism. Indeed, in preparation for the next elections, the Ministry of the Interior instructed Hüseyin Hilmi Pasha, now ambassador in Vienna, to investigate the Austro-Hungarian electoral law.[97]

The reform movement did not disappear with the closing of the Beirut Reform Committee, the ensuing protests of the townspeople, or the resignations of new Arab appointees. A group of Syrians residing in Paris took the initiative to revitalize the movement. Eight Muslim and Christian Syrians wrote a circular that denounced Unionist policies, called for the unification of all Syrians around the principle of decentralization, and invited delegations to a general Arab conference in Paris where the following four main issues would be discussed: the national existence of Arabs and their opposition to foreign occupation; the rights of Arabs in the Ottoman Empire; the necessity of reforms on the basis of decentralization; immigration to and emigration from Syria.[98]

The call from Paris found receptive ears in Beirut, but not in the interior. In Damascus, Medina, and even Aleppo, the conservatism of the notables prevailed. Some Damascenes protested a congress in Paris by establishing the "True" Reform Party.[99] In Aleppo, according to the Austrian consul, the town's poorer merchants and craftsmen were sympathetic to the movement, yet too weak and timid to call for reforms.

The idea was popular with the town's sizable Christian population, which was also relatively better educated and more Europeanized. Any initiative on their part in favor of reforms, however, would have appeared as schismatic and invited repression.[100] Indeed, the strong representation of Christians in the Arab Congress, coupled with the fact that it was held in the capital of a European state that was hardly disinterested in Syria, undermined its credibility.

The Congress met in Paris between 18 and 24 June 1913. The majority of delegates consisted of Syrians, many living outside the Ottoman Empire. ʿAbd al-Hamid al-Zahrawi presided over the sessions. The largest contingents were from Beirut, the Decentralization Party in Cairo, and the Syrian Arab community in France. The proceedings revolved around the idea of reform within the Ottoman Empire, with no mention of any separatist aims.[101] It came out, however, that Christian members of the Beirut delegation (Dr. Ayyub Thabit and Khalil Zainiyyah) had held prior private meetings with French officials in Beirut.[102] When Beirut's Muslim members found out about these links, they felt compromised and decided to settle the questions of reform directly with the Ottoman government. Eager to co-opt the Arab leaders in Paris, the CUP had sent a delegation under the leadership of Midhat Şükrü, a CUP Central Committee member, to carry out negotiations,[103] in which a Christian CUP loyalist, Sulayman Bustani, also participated.[104] Midhat Şükrü signed an agreement with the members of the Arab Congress granting many of the latter's demands: enforcement of Arabic in provincial government and in schools at all levels; employment of foreign experts in provincial administration; local military service; and specified quotas of Arabs as governors, *mutasarrıf*s, and senators.[105]

While the agreement between Arab leaders and the Ottoman government fulfilled some of the demands of the decentralists, its overall effect was to moderate the decentralization movement. During the organizational stages of the Congress it had become evident that the commitment to decentralization did not supplant integrationist political and social forces among the Arabs outside of Beirut. In Paris, the pro-Europe separatist component of the reform movement was exposed to the dismay of the majority of Ottoman participants. The Muslim members of the Beirut delegation to the Arab Congress (Salim ʿAli al-Salam, Ahmad Mukhtar Bayhum, Ahmad Tabbara) visited İstanbul on their return, and at a special audience with Sultan Reşad declared their loyalty to the Ottoman state and caliphate.[106]

In the meantime, Mahmud Shawkat Pasha's assassination was used by the CUP to crush the Liberal opponents in İstanbul. Prominent Liberals held responsible for plotting the grand vizier's murder were rounded up and court-martialed, and 350 were exiled to Sinop in the central Black Sea region. The execution of twelve opponents of the CUP in İstanbul, now under Cemal Pasha's military governorship, coincided with the closing day of the Arab Congress. The executions eliminated the Liberal opposition in the capital and foreshadowed similar drastic measures (including trumped-up charges, summary executions, and deportations) that Cemal would employ against the Arab decentralists as governor of Syria and commander of the Fourth Army in Syria during the war.[107] The purge of the leaders of the opposition was a clear sign that politics as usual would be curtailed. In the absence of party politics, Arabism lost much of its meaning.

The Ottoman state had greater relative success in the Second Balkan War, which ended with the recapture of Edirne by the Ottoman army in July 1913. The second half of 1913 saw a respite from military engagements and a reevaluation of the country's internal condition. Warfare had impoverished the economy and hurt the commercial elements,[108] weakening (quite apart from the reprisals) the Liberal opposition to the CUP in the Arab districts and elsewhere in the empire. Progovernment groups in the provinces became more vocal in their support of İstanbul and rejection of the decentralists.[109]

The appointment of Saʿid Halim Pasha, a statesman with Arab affinities, as grand vizier upon the death of Mahmud Shawkat Pasha in June 1913 signified the new outlook in İstanbul vis-à-vis the Arab element in the empire. Saʿid Halim was the son of a disaffected member of the khedivial family, Halim Pasha, who settled in İstanbul in 1870, when Saʿid was seven years old.[110] The language spoken at home may have been Turkish, though Saʿid Halim was proficient in several Middle Eastern and European languages. He studied political science in Switzerland and preferred French as his pen language in drafting his Islamist-modernist essays later on. Upon his return to İstanbul, he was made a member of the Council of State in 1888. His association with the CUP led to his ouster from the capital. He spent his exile in Egypt and Europe, primarily in Cairo, where he was commissioned by the CUP to promote Unionist propaganda among Arabs. He returned to İstanbul after the revolution, was appointed to the Senate, and rose in the ranks of the CUP to join the Said Pasha cabinet as the president of the Council of State and to be named secretary general in the Committee's 1912 Congress. He was serving as foreign minister in the Mahmud Shawkat cabinet at the time of the assassination of the grand vizier. Despite Sultan Reşad's alleged reservations,[111] he was pushed by the CUP to replace Mahmud Shawkat.

The CUP appointed more and more of its partisans to posts in the provinces, and a greater proportion of the new appointees were Arabs. One result of this policy was that party and ideological differences supplanted ethnic and regional ones. For instance, in Acre Liberal notables raised objections about the replacement of a Turkish Liberal *mutasarrif* by an Arab Unionist. At this time, none of the four *mutasarrifs* in the Beirut *vilayet* were Turkish: three were Arab, and the fourth was a Kurd.[112]

The agreement that the Arab Congress concluded with the government signified a separation of the reformists from those decentralists who viewed foreign involvement as a necessary condition of decentralization. While not all Beiruti Muslim reformists were co-opted to Unionism, the reform movement petered out in Syria following the Congress. Important Arab notables such as Muhammad Fawzi Pasha al-ʿAzm, ʿAbd al-Rahman al-Yusuf, Shakib Arslan, and Shaykh Asʿad al-Shuqayri declared their opposition to the Arab Congress and contended that it was not representative of the Arab provinces.[113] The government attempted to co-opt other Arab notables, primarily Damascenes, who opposed the reform movement.[114] It recalled the four Unionist deputies from Damascus for consultations. In İstanbul the government formed commissions, in which Arab officials took part, in order to supervise the implementation of reforms, apparently in particular the enforcement of Arabic language policies.[115] Many of the reforms actually implemented fell short of expectations.[116] Now that the Balkan quandary was settled and domestic opposition stifled, the CUP procrastinated on reform issues in the Arab provinces, envisaging more fundamental, empire-wide reforms.

Meanwhile, France intensified its missionary activity in Syria and established closer links with the disaffected elements, while Britain shifted its attention to the Persian Gulf.[117] It was partly due to this enhanced British presence near the Persian Gulf that the reform movement in Iraq gained in force. On 9 June 1913 the progovernment Baghdad paper *Al-zuhur* pointed out the growing British influence in the region and held Britain responsible for the unrest in Najd.[118] In Baghdad the general provincial council convened in November, and its delegates voiced the demand that Iraq should belong to the Iraqis.[119] In Basra Sayyid Talib, head of the Basra Reform Committee, provoked protests against the

Ottoman government, which he then "quelled" in a crafty demonstration of his local power and prestige.[120]

In the Fifth CUP Congress that met in September 1913 economic issues predominated. (With Salonika lost in the Balkan Wars, the 1913 Congress was the first to be held in İstanbul.) The only explicit endorsement of policies that had been enacted in the spring was instruction in local languages. The first item of the Congress's political program was an administrative clause that called for the time-honored precept of *tevsi'-i mezuniyet*, or the extension of the administrative prerogatives of local officials.[121] This was hailed by the French ambassador Bompard somewhat inaccurately as a "striking conversion of Young Turks to the ideas of administrative decentralization."[122]

Most noticeable in the new program was an explicit denunciation of the capitulations that perpetuated the economic bondage of the empire to Europe. The idea long current in İstanbul that the economic concessions enjoyed by European countries in Ottoman territories caused the economic decline of the empire spread also in the provinces. In November the Austrian consul reported from Aleppo:

Differences between Turks and Arabs have lost their intensity noticeably. The number of adherents of the Young Turk Party is on the increase. The view is expressed more and more loudly that the Europeans are aiming at the destruction of Turkey, and thus that of the Muslim world-view, and at the economic exploitation of its people.[123]

Conclusion: Islamist Reinterpretation of Ottomanism

As a result of the events of the years 1912 and 1913, Islam gained further in importance in the Ottoman body politic and in the thinking of the Young Turks. Many factors were responsible for the ideological reorientation. The most obvious was the shrinkage of the physical boundaries of the empire to yield a numerical predominance of Muslims. This contraction was also proof that the secular Ottomanism espoused in 1908 had not worked well as an ideology to ensure the allegiance of the empire's diverse communities to İstanbul. Not only had the mere fact of dismemberment of Ottoman territories reduced the scope of an Ottomanist ideology, but the government's failure to maintain territorial integrity had caused ethnic and religious groups still within the geographic boundaries of the empire to question the efficacy of Ottomanist policies. Finally, the blows to the Ottoman Empire in Libya and in the Balkans, coming from Christian Europe, provoked Islamic sensibilities.

In its efforts to bring the reformist movement under control, the government found it expedient to depict the movement as generated by the complicity of Christian Syrians with Christian European powers. The *Egyptian Gazette* reported that an Arabic pamphlet titled *Al-haq ya'alu* (Truth [or God] Will Triumph), published in the capital under the direction of Jawish, circulated in Syria and aimed "to stir up Moslem fanaticism by stigmatizing all the Christians of Turkey as secret agents of Europe and the betrayers of the Moslem fatherland."[124] The *Gazette*'s hyperbole notwithstanding, İstanbul attempted to blunt the vitality of a broad-based sociopolitical movement that was gaining momentum. In Beirut, where the social forces desiring reform were stronger than in other Arab regions, this tactic had limited results, despite deliberate propaganda. But after a number of Christian reformists established close, secret links with European countries, especially France, in order to promote separatist aims, the Unionist government managed to discredit the reform movement by depicting it as a Christian conspiracy.

Even as the decentralist movement was disparaged because of its contrariety to Muslim unity, the need to address the decentralist grievances was recognized. Celal Nuri [İleri], a Turkish modernist author, who, like many others, was attracted to political Islamism in 1913, wrote a book titled *İttihad-ı İslam* (Union of Islam). The book denounced imperialist Europe for creating discord between Arabs and Turks and urged decentralizing measures in the Arab provinces that would "foster . . . a special relation between Turks and Arabs within a Muslim union."[125]

At the end of 1913 the Unionist government promoted Islam as the main pillar of its ideology. Arabs wishing to see the continuation of the Islamic empire under the Ottoman caliph embraced the idea. The best example of the expanded propaganda effort was a detailed report drafted in December 1913 by the leading Arab proponents of the Islamic idea, including Jawish and Shakib Arslan, "who was admitted to the inner circles [of the Young Turks] in 1913."[126] The report was written following the celebrations in Medina that marked the groundbreaking for an Islamic university.[127] It touched on improvements necessary for the Hijaz, because the holy places were to serve as the locus of Islamic propaganda among both the Ottomans and Muslims elsewhere.[128] Much of the propaganda effort in the Arab provinces was carried out by a government intelligence unit that around this time came to be called *Teşkilat-ı Mahsusa* (Special Organization).[129]

As the year 1913 came to an end, Ottoman participation in the impending international hostilities may have seemed far-fetched. But it was a short step to the mobilization of Islam for the Ottoman war effort, once the world war broke out. Sa'id Halim Pasha, a prominent Unionist statesman with multiple cultural identities, an ardent Islamist modernist intellectual, and a member of the Egyptian royal house with a Turco-Arab upbringing, embodied the new outlook in İstanbul and led the Ottoman government as grand vizier for the next four years.

5

A Case Study in Centralization: The Hijaz under Young Turk Rule, 1908–1914

The preceding chapters situated Arab political trends against the broader Ottoman imperial background. The province of the Hijaz is taken up here to illustrate the dynamics between the center and an Arab region during the second constitutional period. The Hijaz does not stand out as the obvious choice for a case study of the policies of the Ottoman government in its Arab regions. It was peripheral geographically and relatively stagnant from the point of view of its social, political, economic, and intellectual processes. Most studies of Arab lands during the Ottoman period focus on the province of Syria, mainly Damascus, Beirut, and Mount Lebanon. While the rest of Greater Syria and Mesopotamia have also received some attention, the study of the Peninsula in general and the Hijaz in particular, in the context of Ottoman political, social, or economic trends, constitutes a relatively recent departure.[1]

Yet several considerations make the study of the Hijaz in the second constitutional period particularly compelling. The career as grand sharif (or emir) of Husayn ibn ʿAli, the leader of the Arab Revolt of 1916, started with the 1908 Revolution and continued unbroken until 1916. As emir of Mecca, Husayn was the most prominent local notable in the Arab provinces, and İstanbul's relations with him illustrate the manner in which the governments of the second constitutional period obliged local notables in the direction of their centralizing policies while cooperating and compromising with them.

Furthermore, because the Hijaz did not constitute the framework or contain the nucleus of a future nation-state, prospective questions that throw light on Ottoman policy are relatively less encumbered by concerns pertinent to the states that were subsequently formed.[2] The Hijaz is a poor laboratory for an examination of the growth of nationalist thought, because the social conditions that enhanced the appeal of Arabism elsewhere did not mature in its remote and economically backward towns during this time. Nevertheless, it was a movement in this province and under the leadership of Sharif Husayn that gave the impetus to an Arab nationalist program incorporating the beginnings of popular appeal and a secessionist thrust. Thus, the choice of the Hijaz, on the one hand, extricates us from the tendency to study a certain Ottoman province as the prenational history of a later nation-state. On the other hand, it allows us to appraise the backdrop to an event, the Arab Revolt, that has come to be appropriated as the single most important milestone in the coming of age of Arab nationalism.

Finally, the study of the Hijaz, which contains the holiest places of Islam and became a center of Islamist-Ottoman propaganda after 1913, is also interesting from the point of view of the increasing emphasis placed on religion in Ottomanist ideology.

The Young Turk Revolution and the Hijaz

Ottoman authority was established in the Hijaz when the emir of Mecca, the head of the sharifs representing the Prophet's family of Hashim, declared his allegiance to Sultan Selim I upon the latter's conquest of Syria and Egypt in 1516–17. In the early centuries of Ottoman rule the holy cities of Mecca and Medina were under the jurisdiction of the governors of Egypt, but the effective rulers were the Hashemite grand sharifs. The *emirülhac* (*amir al-haj*), a Syrian grandee and later the governor of the province of Damascus, also exercised authority over the region as the chief official in charge of the pilgrimage caravan. In the aftermath of the Tanzimat provincial reorganization, the Hijaz was designated as a distinct province governed by a governor sent from İstanbul. Tension was endemic between the governor and the emir in the administration of the province, and central authority remained precarious. Rival claims of two Hashemite families, the 'Awn and the Zayd, further complicated the political conflict in the Hijaz.[3] The city dwellers of the Hijaz were privileged by virtue of inhabiting the holy places; they did not pay taxes or send their sons to the army.[4] Its large tribal population enjoyed the customary independence of nomads while extracting large sums of money both from the pilgrims and from the government for protecting, aiding, and often for merely not harassing the pilgrim caravans.

For a province that was traditionally oblivious to even the profoundest of events in the capital, the revolution triggered exceptional reverberations. More changes came about in the Hijaz in the first few months following July 1908 than in any other Arab province. While these were felt most strongly by the small political elite in the cities, they also affected directly or indirectly the lives of the Beduin who had long been living in isolation from the mainstream of events in the capital.

The news of the revolution was kept from the inhabitants of the Hijaz for several days by Governor Ratib Pasha and the Grand Sharif 'Ali Pasha. However, when the new government in İstanbul dismissed the governor and had him brought from his summer quarters in Taif to Jidda, crowds stormed his residence on 21 August.[5] He was arrested and his property confiscated, and was then imprisoned by a group of military officers.[6] Meanwhile, the top government functionary in Medina, *Muhafiz* Osman Pasha, was dismissed and temporarily replaced by *Müşir* Abdullah Pasha for opposing the reestablishment of the constitution and casting some officers into prison.[7] These changes in the highest civil administrative posts were soon followed by the deposition of the Grand Sharif 'Ali, rumors that his uncle, Sharif 'Abd al-Ilah, would succeed him, and finally Husayn's appointment.

The overhaul in the top offices in the province upset the equilibrium of interests that had been maintained between the officeholders and the tribal leaders, merchants, and other local notables. The breakdown of local authority and renewed competition for political power compounded the volatile political situation. Since İstanbul had asserted its authority in the province in the mid–nineteenth century, the duality of power between the grand sharif and the governor had been a constant irritant in the administration there. It was occasionally mitigated by a personal understanding between the two leaders that often rested on a reconciliation of their personal material interests, as had been the case in the latter half of Abdülhamid's rule. Starting in the fall of 1908, new actors struggled for a new balance of power under the increasingly vigilant eye of a central government that desired to carry out structural changes aimed at incorporating the provinces into the emerging centralized constitutional system.

During these critical months the completion and official opening on

1 September 1908[8] of the Hijaz Railway's Damascus-Medina line contributed to the disarray in the Hijaz. The railway posed two dangers to the Hijazi notables. It allowed the government to maintain a closer watch on the local exercise of power through enhanced communications. It also threatened commercial interests that rested on the caravan trade and pilgrim traffic. Moreover, the extension of the railway to Medina signified the more ominous prospect of the line's continuation further to Mecca and Jidda through regions of even greater commercial significance. The tribes rose in armed opposition.

Some Hijazi towns witnessed instances of flagrant renunciation of the established order consistent with the revolutionary mood of the day. In Mecca prisoners both in the government jail and held by the grand sharif were released. In a symbolic act of defiance, Grand Sharif 'Ali was forced to publicly proclaim, while he was still in office, his legal equality to a slave, a Beduin, and an enlisted man. Chanting crowds abused the governor.[9] According to the acting British consul, members of the Committee of Union and Progress led the demonstration. In Taif members of such a self-proclaimed Committee publicly declared the constitution and led large crowds to the tomb of Midhat Pasha, the architect of the Ottoman constitution who had been executed in 1883 while in exile in Taif. In Jidda the crowd arrested the secretary of the governor and a close associate, who was a prominent merchant in the town.

In the Hijaz, as in other Arab provinces, officers and officials who were sympathetic to the principles of the constitution formed the committees and rallied dissatisfied local elements to augment their strength. There is no evidence of any overt or secret organizational activity in the Hijaz in favor of a constitution immediately prior to the revolution. The spontaneously constituted committees took it upon themselves to give direction to government affairs in the province. Their insistence on the implementation of reforms was an uphill battle in the deeply conservative Hijaz and was to be resisted by the new grand sharif, who strove to restore the traditional prerogatives of the office.

The Grand Sharifate of Husayn Ibn 'Ali

CIRCUMSTANCES OF HUSAYN'S APPOINTMENT

In light of Husayn Ibn 'Ali's role in the Arab Revolt, there has been a great deal of retrospective speculation about the conditions of his fateful appointment to the emirate of Mecca. While some (including Shakib Arslan) have argued that his appointment was a decision of the Unionists,[10] others have maintained that Abdülhamid appointed Sharif Husayn in the face of opposition from the CUP.[11] It has also been argued that Husayn was the candidate favored by the British, who exerted influence through the Anglophile grand vizier, Kamil Pasha,[12] as well as the British ambassador.[13]

One candidate for the post of grand sharif was Sharif 'Ali Haydar, who represented the Zayd family, rivals to the 'Awn, of which Husayn was a scion.[14] Between 1908 and 1916 Haydar stayed in İstanbul and maintained friendly relations with the Unionist leaders as a member of the Chamber of Notables (Senate). It was in the interest of the Unionist-dominated governments to cultivate good relations with Husayn's rival in order to intimidate the latter into cooperation. Yet even though 'Ali Haydar was upheld in this alternate role and was in fact appointed grand sharif after the revolt, it is doubtful that he was a strong candidate, or the main rival to Sharif Husayn at the time of the latter's appointment.

When Sharif 'Ali (also of the 'Awn family) was deposed in October 1908 his uncle 'Abd al-Ilah emerged as his legitimate successor. 'Abd al-Ilah had been bypassed in 1905 in favor of 'Ali, a younger sharif of the 'Awn family.[15] He now seemed to be the obvious choice to replace his nephew, who had not been accorded formal investiture as grand sharif until three months before the revolution,[16] had now fallen in disfavor for his equivocal endorsement of the constitutional order, and defied the new governor Kazım Pasha's[17] request to come from Taif to Mecca.[18] On 26 October *Tanin* reported the designation of 'Abd al-Ilah in İstanbul as grand sharif. However, he died before he set out for Mecca.

The death of the emir-designate vexed the government, because it feared the escalation of lawlessness among the Beduin tribes, who were all too ready to take advantage of the political turmoil and to oppose the recent completion of the Damascus-Medina stretch of the Hijaz Railway. The Grand Vizierate informed Governor Kazım Pasha that the İstanbul papers had incorrectly announced the appointment of 'Abd al-Ilah Pasha as grand sharif and urged him to deny the rumor, should it spread in the Hijaz, because the Pasha had died unexpectedly.[19]

The circumstances made it imperative to appoint a grand sharif in the shortest time possible. Even though the official decree of Husayn's appointment bears the date of 24 November 1908, an earlier decree dated 12 November refers to him as emir of Mecca.[20] The decree of appointment lacks the usual enclosures that accompany this kind of document. Thus it falls in the category of *re'sen* (direct) *irade*s, which were decrees issued by the sultan without the benefit of recommendations and counsel of the cabinet. It can be deduced, therefore, that the appointment of Sharif Husayn did not come as a result of competition among various parties (the CUP, the sultan, the grand vizier, the British Embassy, Sharif Haydar) but rather represented the reasonable and not especially controversial choice by Sultan Abdülhamid. Indeed, it is questionable whether the CUP was a real factor at this early stage in determining the decisions pertaining to prominent provincial posts. Furthermore, because of the political ferment in the Hijaz, the sultan had to act under pressure, which did not allow for drawn-out negotiations. Husayn, having received an Ottoman training and served in the Council of State, possessed the necessary qualifications for the grand sharifate, for which he had made a first bid in 1905. In 1908 he was, after the death of 'Abd al-Ilah, the rightful heir of the 'Awns. Finally, given the precarious political conditions, the government was not inclined to undertake as drastic an action as the transfer of the grand sharifate to the Zayd family, the competitor for the honor.

HUSAYN IN MECCA: QUEST FOR AUTHORITY

Upon the finalization of the appointment to the grand sharifate in mid-November, İstanbul advised Husayn to proceed to Mecca swiftly and designated his brother Nasir ibn 'Ali, who already resided in Mecca, as acting grand sharif until his arrival.[21] The new emir arrived in Jidda on 3 December 1908 in pilgrim garb to find a less than enthusiastic popular reception.[22] In an address to tribal *shaykh*s he announced that he could secure with one telegraph enough troops to turn the entire Hijaz upside down.[23] Indeed, İstanbul expected him to quell tribal unrest and to pacify the caravan routes in order to ensure the orderly progress of the starting pilgrimage season.

Husayn's first few months in Mecca set the tone of his term as grand sharif. Relatively discredited and weakened as the grand sharif's office was in the fall of 1908, Husayn did his utmost to reestablish his authority. He could enhance his power with respect to the tribes and rival emirs in other parts of the Peninsula only to the extent that he could demonstrate İstanbul's support for him. Conversely, he could maintain a certain amount of freedom of action only to the extent that he could convince İstanbul of his unchallenged local power. Therefore, his aim was not so much to discredit central authority but to prove to the state authorities that he was a capable and reliable ally. On the one hand he tried to elevate his political position and the status of the office of the grand sharif, and on the other, he fulfilled the assignments given to him by the central government.

At the time of Husayn's arrival, the Beduins were in revolt near Medina because pilgrims were being transported for the first time from Syria on the recently extended railway, threatening the Beduin livelihood based on the camel business. The new *muhafiz* of Medina, Basri Pasha, who was appointed to his post only days before Sharif Husayn,[24] wrote to İstanbul asking for the grand sharif's intercession and his counsel to the Beduins in arms.[25] Husayn sent an emissary to Medina "equipped with the necessary advice," which the sharif thought would elicit the desired end, but he also urged serious negotiations between the Beduins and the government for a comprehensive settlement.[26] To complement his services, the sharif also asked İstanbul to send uninscribed medals to be awarded to various *shaykh*s, as he saw fit.[27] The grand vizierate complied with the request, merely asking that the names of the conferees be submitted subsequently. As this specific case of the appeasement of a tribal group shows, both the sharif and the government found it necessary to allow the other's local prestige to grow in order to achieve their respective objectives.

Husayn's first opportunity to demonstrate his influence over the tribes of the Hijaz came at the end of the pilgrimage season in January 1909, when the officially appointed leader of the pilgrimage caravan, ʿAbd al-Rahman al-Yusuf, resigned his post to protest the inadequacy of military protection supplied for safe passage through regions of Beduin unrest on the return journey.[28] Husayn nominated his brother Nasir, who had served as acting sharif during Husayn's journey from İstanbul, to lead the caravan from Mecca to Damascus, accompanied by his son ʿAbdullah. Nasir and ʿAbdullah executed the mission, dutifully keeping the Ministry of the Interior informed of their precise movements.[29] The safe return of the caravan to Medina, and from there by railway to Damascus, enhanced Sharif Husayn's standing both in the eyes of the government and the tribes.

In his later memoirs, ʿAbdullah interpreted the safe passage of the caravan under the auspices of the grand sharif—when the official entrusted with the duty refrained from making the journey—as a political victory that gained Husayn the upper hand in the Hijaz vis-à-vis the government early in his term.[30] This interpretation has prevailed without critical examination, and the historical significance of the post of *emi-rülhac* has lent credibility to it. Indeed, when the direct authority of İstanbul did not extend beyond Damascus, the command of the caravan by a prominent representative of the central government had signified the assertion of central authority in the tribal areas of the Hijaz.[31] In the eighteenth and nineteenth centuries, the governors of Damascus them-selves had fulfilled this important task. With the Hijaz Railway making Medina an Ottoman outpost further south, however, the symbolic im-portance of the *emirülhac* diminished. The grand vizier considered elim-inating the office altogether confronted with ʿAbd al-Rahman's non-compliance.[32]

In fact, the government deliberately sought to enhance the prestige of its newly arrived agent in Mecca and hence gave approval to the transfer of the command of the pilgrimage to members of Sharif Hu-sayn's family.[33] The sharif did not so much seek a tour de force to em-barrass the government as to establish himself locally as its trusted agent. From Husayn's viewpoint, the completion of the task by Nasir would establish the emirate's authority in northern Hijaz, and would coinci-dentally remove a potential rival from Mecca, while he tried to assert his power there as a newcomer. Thus, Sharif Husayn asked İstanbul in February 1909 for a precise definition of his prerogatives as emir.[34] In the same letter he asked the grand vizier that his brother be invited to İstanbul and appointed to the newly constituted Chamber of Notables. Husayn had an interest in having members of his family in high office in İstanbul so that they could maintain contacts with Ottoman states-men, follow up political developments, and report to him. (For this purpose he later chose his sons.) But he also wanted to remove Nasir from the Hijaz. Nasir's senate membership did not take effect immedi-ately.[35] He did not go to İstanbul until July 1909[36] and was subsequently admitted to Parliament as senator.[37] Similarly, Husayn insisted on the removal of the former grand sharif, ʿAli, who was ailing and repeatedly postponing his departure.[38]

Sharif Husayn arrived in the Hijaz too late to influence the elections to Parliament. The 1908 elections were highly irregular in the Hijaz, and there was the semblance of official electoral process only in the towns of Mecca, Medina, and Jidda, each of which elected one deputy. On 4 November, almost one month before Husayn arrived in the Hijaz, Gov-ernor Kazım Pasha reported to the Ministry of the Interior that ʿAbdullah Saraj (Mecca), Qasim Zaynal (Jidda), and Sayyid ʿAbd al-Qadir (Medina) had been elected as deputies for the province.[39] Both

'Abd al-Qadir and Saraj, who was the Hanafi *müftü* of Mecca,[40] represented the Hijazi religious notability, but no member of the sharifian families was elected. In Jidda the town notables elected Zaynal, the well-educated son of a wealthy Persian (naturalized Ottoman) shipping agent, "for reasons connected with their own local trade."[41] Zaynal's business was in decline, and he ventured into a public career, which had started with a prior experiment with journalism in Egypt.[42]

British Consul Monahan described the conduct of the Jidda election as follows:

About two months ago the local government invited the inhabitants of Jidda to register themselves as voters but there was no response as the inhabitants thought it might mean enrolment for military service. Then the three headmen (sheikhs) of the three wards of the town were charged to choose 600 notables, 200 from each ward. These notables chose a body of 25 and the 25 finally voted about four weeks ago, the largest number of votes, eight, being obtained by one Kasim Zeinal. Little or no public interest was taken in the election.[43]

The consul also added that the eight electors who voted in Zaynal's favor were either his relatives or in close business contact with him.

While 'Abd al-Qadir[44] and Zaynal[45] took their seats in Parliament, neither Saraj nor any other representative from Mecca went to İstanbul.[46] Therefore, the Mecca election had to be repeated one year later, in February 1910. By this time Sharif Husayn had managed to assert his authority in Mecca. Taking advantage of the general lack of interest in Parliament among the Meccan notables, he managed to have his son 'Abdullah elected as deputy in an election where a few hundred notables chose among twenty-four candidates.[47]

The local Committees of Union and Progress that had been organized in August 1908 carried on their activities in the Hijaz, often all too ready to frustrate the sharif's schemes to dominate the politics of the three major towns. Two newspapers were established in Mecca after the Revolution, *Hijaz* and *Shams al-haqiqa* (Sun of Truth). The first was the official Turkish/Arabic weekly, which promoted İstanbul's policies and featured "articles in praise of Islam and freedom, and, in one of its earlier numbers, a seemingly rather fanciful lucubration about the Prophet and the Arab race being the originators of parliaments."[48] The second paper, *Shams al-haqiqa*, was the local Unionist paper and had separate Turkish and Arabic issues differing in content. The Turkish numbers contained criticism of the sharif's conduct of policy. *Shams al-*

haqiqa's readers were the relatively better-educated and more cosmopolitan elite of Mecca, and its objective was to counteract the sharif's domination of urban politics.[49]

Shams al-haqiqa emerged in the spring of 1909 as the organ of the sharif's political opponents, apparently Unionists.[50] Husayn was incensed by an article that reported his mission against the Mutayr tribe as a failure. He protested to the grand vizier, specifically accusing three reporters (two of whom worked in the financial administration of the province) of disturbing with inflammatory articles the peace and order that he was struggling to establish.[51] In these letters Husayn did not fail to make references to the honorable life he had led despite the injustice and oppression of Sultan Abdülhamid (just deposed by the Unionists), thus ingratiating himself to the new leadership, but also suggesting that he would insist on demands that he perceived were necessary to secure his honor and prestige.[52] He blamed Governor Fuad Pasha, who had replaced Kazım a few months before, for allowing the paper to be printed in the government printing house and for procrastinating in taking action against the two officials Hasan Makki and 'Abdullah Qasim and their accomplice Nuri Daghistani, a merchant.[53] Sharif Husayn urged the government earnestly to expel these three men in the interests of the "nation and the state."

In the summer of 1909 the CUP had started to assert itself in imperial administration, with Talat and Cavid now in key cabinet posts. The sharif's complaint about the financial officials involved with the *Shams al-haqiqa* and the governor's alleged permissive attitude to their wrongdoing was directed to Talat and Cavid's ministries, the Interior and the Finance, both of which declined to take action on the sharif's request for the removal of these officials. The grand vizier independently informed the sharif that the third person, Nuri Daghistani, was not a government official and that no action could be taken against him unless he were found guilty of some crime by a court.[54] Talat enjoined the governor to find out from the sharif the circumstances that would justify a dismissal or transfer of the two officials—an initiative interpreted by the sharif as a sign of distrust.[55] In a similar manner, Cavid maintained that there were no sound grounds upon which his ministry could take action for a transfer, and that such a transfer would in any case be contrary to the principle of *tevsi'-i mezuniyet*, which stipulated that the appointment and dismissal of such officials be carried out by the provincial government.[56]

During the course of this correspondence in October 1909, the gov-

ernment replaced Governor Fuad Pasha with Şevket Pasha, governor of
Baghdad and commander of the Sixth Army, in view of the differences
of opinion between Fuad and the sharif.[57] However, the change in the
top administrative position of the province did not satisfy Sharif Husayn, who continued to push for the transfer of Makki and Qasim.
Makki was still in Mecca during the February 1910 by-election and was
nominated as a candidate. He received the fourth-largest number of
votes in a race that took place among two dozen candidates for two
positions.[58] The Ministry of Finance finally transferred Makki and Qasim
from Mecca in March 1910—with promotions.[59]

Even though the local branches of the CUP continued to be a factor
in local politics, the influence of the Unionists steadily diminished in
the Hijaz, reflecting the CUP's declining fortunes in İstanbul. On the
eve of the 1912 elections the new Liberty and Entente branch in Mecca
had entirely overshadowed the local CUP.[60] Sharif Husayn's attitude
toward the Entente remained as equivocal as his attitude toward the
CUP. In the elections he promoted his sons, while the two Hijazi incumbents who had sided with the Entente lost their seats. In general,
Husayn's endeavors to preserve the emirate's power and prestige required that he continue to cooperate with the central government.

Extension of Ottoman Influence in the Hijaz

REFORM

Efforts to introduce reform had only limited success in
the Hijaz. There were few demands for change from the inhabitants,
who were rarely receptive to reforms conceived in İstanbul. Sharif Husayn resisted innovations that might limit his local authority. Even before he arrived in the Hijaz, when the CUP enjoyed much popularity,
an attempt by the Committee to impose a tax to be used for sanitary
improvement had led to an uprising and a confrontation between the
troops and the townspeople, who opposed paying taxes in any form.[61]
Newly instituted municipalities were severely handicapped in their ability to improve public works or general hygiene for financial reasons.[62]
There were nonetheless some advances, particularly in sanitation. In
Mecca postpilgrimage cleaning efforts improved.[63] In Jidda *Mutasarrıf*
Sadık undertook urban reforms, including the regulation of the water
supply.[64] Finally, consistent with the high priority that the government

placed on education, new government schools were opened in the towns of the Hijaz in which "much time [was] given to the literary and official Turkish language and the literary Arabic." Monahan did not find the available education satisfactory. "But very few parents or pupils wish to seek a better elsewhere," he added, "and, indeed, I am not sure that there is any much better to be had in Muslim boys' schools anywhere else in the Turkish Empire."[65]

Legal reform proved to be more difficult to implement in the Hijaz. In February 1910 the Ministry of Justice proposed a reorganization of the courts in the Hijazi cities and appealed to the Ministry of Finance for the allocation of the necessary funds.[66] In contrast, Talat, as the new minister of the interior, recommended that in order to bring the nomadic tribes into the government fold it would be appropriate to apply only the *şeriat* law in the region and to select the judges from local ulema.[67] The Hijazi deputies 'Abdullah, 'Abd al-Qadir, and Hasan al-Shaybi stressed to the grand vizier that the presence of any courts other than the *şeriat* courts would be unacceptable in the holy cities inhabited solely by Muslims.[68] Thus, it was decided to place the courts of Mecca and Medina under the auspices of the office of the *şeyhülislam* by removing them from the jurisdiction of the Ministry of Justice. The actual reorganization took place only in 1912.

Perhaps no other issue illustrates the difficulty of executing reforms in the Hijaz and the necessity for compromise better than slavery. There the question of slaves posed an embarrassing problem to the government. Slavery, of course, was anathema to the principles of equality and freedom that the new regime espoused. Although it had been legally abolished during the Tanzimat, the trade in and use of slaves had not stopped in the Hijaz.[69] Yet the government feared that forced manumission would provoke the tribal chiefs to rebellion. Slaves often fled to take refuge in foreign consulates in Jidda, which insisted on their being freed. The grand vizierate advised that official manumission papers should be granted to any slave who managed to seek asylum in the consulates. It also recommended, however, that the authorities should act according to the particular circumstances of each case, while urging slaveholders to treat their African slaves humanely so as not to force them to seek the intercession of foreign consuls.[70]

The manumission of slaves taking asylum in consulates meant that their owners, for the most part Beduin chiefs, would have to be compensated by the grand sharif to keep them at peace. The sharif complained that given the frequency of such cases these payments went beyond his means. He conveniently argued that, since in five or ten years there would no longer be any slaves due to the prohibitions against importing them, ownership of the current slaves be tolerated until that time.[71] The Ministry of Finance, consulted by the grand vizierate in an attempt to find an alternate source of funding for manumission payments, held that effective control of the long Red Sea coast was impossible, and payment of manumission fees would in fact encourage trading in slaves and constitute a major strain on the budget.[72] The final recommendation of İstanbul to the grand sharif was the meaningless suggestion that those slave owners with a grievance should take their case to court.

As the issue of slavery also demonstrates, the grand sharif, due to his traditional status in the eyes of the tribes and his recognized prerogatives in Beduin and pilgrimage affairs, was an indispensable intermediary in the conduct of policy in this remote province of great religio-political importance. İstanbul's aim was to channel the sharif's local standing and energy to its own ends while assuring him that his ambitions could best be served by being responsive to the requirements of the central government. Such a relationship with the sharif did not entail a compromise of İstanbul's centralizing policies.

THE RAILWAY PROJECTS

The Hijaz Railway was conceived by Abdülhamid as one of the pillars of the Ottoman policy of centralization, and certainly perceived as such by the Young Turks. The completion of the line to Medina coincided with the Young Turk Revolution and facilitated the efforts to extend central authority into the Arabian Peninsula. An extension of the railway, from Medina to Mecca and eventually to Yemen, remained an issue about which there was much deliberation, but no concrete results were achieved. This failure has generally been regarded as a frustration of Young Turk efforts to bring the Hijaz under central control.

Even though the strategic value of the extension to Mecca was appreciated in İstanbul, the government actually subordinated the continuation of the railway to other centralizing measures in the Hijaz. The difficulties of ensuring the security of the railway in tribal areas, where friendly tribal *shaykh*s could turn against the government overnight in order to further their particular aims, was apparent to the policy makers. They were all too familiar with the tribal unrest that the Damascus-Medina line triggered in southern Syria and northern Hijaz. Thus İstanbul opted for making full use of the advantages that the Hijaz Railway provided for its centralizing policy by strengthening its position in Medina, whence it could exert close control over the rest of the province and the neighboring regions. Instead of extending the railway, the Ottoman government chose to rely on the grand sharif in Mecca as a proxy to preserve its interests and to further its aims in Arabia. The government also had an interest in improving communications in the Peninsula for purposes of trade and the pilgrimage. İstanbul gravitated toward promoting the Red Sea routes and building shorter railway lines from the coast to the interior, specifically between Jidda and Mecca, Yanbu and Medina, and Hodeida and Sana, instead of constructing the costly Medina-Mecca line.

The scheme of building several shorter lines gave primacy to economic considerations over strategic ones. *Tanin* wrote in favor of a branch to Aqaba (which would circumvent the British-controlled Suez Canal for commercial transport) from the Damascus-Medina main line with additional short lines between the Red Sea ports and the towns of the interior, rather than extension of the line from Medina to Mecca.[73] Christian deputies in Parliament urged that the railway in the Hijaz not be seen as serving religious objectives only but that economic considerations should also be taken into account.[74] On the local level, too, a railway connecting the busiest commercial port of the Hijaz with Mecca was favorably received by the Hijazi merchants. The deputy for Jidda, Qasim Zaynal, declared his support for the Jidda-Mecca line.[75]

The project of building coastal lines implied a shift of the major commercial and pilgrimage routes to the Red Sea. It offered practical advantages (in terms of speed and elimination of camel transport) and economic ones, once Ottoman ships started regular traffic along the coast. This shift would, however, constitute a strategic liability as well, as the Italian blockade of Ottoman ports along the Red Sea brought home during the Italian War.[76] Nevertheless, the most significant of the links between the Red Sea and the interior, the Jidda-Mecca line, received more official attention than the Medina-Mecca extension. Because of its anticipated profitability for carrying seaborne pilgrimage groups to and from Jidda (most arriving from the Indian Ocean), this line could have generated funds needed for the longer and costly Medina-Mecca stretch. In Parliament, the minister for the Hijaz Railway, Zihni Pasha, declared that he gave priority to the Jidda-Mecca line.[77]

Governor Kamil Bey arrived in the Hijaz in June 1910 and announced that construction on the Jidda-Mecca railway, along with the related improvements of the landing facilities in the Jidda harbor, would soon begin.[78] The director of the Railway Department of the Ministry of Public Works confirmed that the construction of the line had been decided upon and that experts were being dispatched.[79] Indeed, by March 1911 ten engineers had arrived to join the three already in Jidda there to proceed with the survey work.[80] Sharif Husayn reported in mid-March that one-third of the survey work had been completed.[81] He was advised by the grand vizierate to arrange for the protection of the construction.[82]

The sharif's ambivalence toward the construction of the Jidda-Mecca line continued. Even though he had joined the governor in 1909 in urging the construction of a railway between these two cities,[83] he resorted to obstructionism as more definite steps were taken. In 1911 he requested the postponement of the construction until his return from the Asir campaign and also suggested a formal investigation of how the livelihood of the tribes that were engaged in camel transport between the two cities would be secured.[84] The French consul in Jidda interpreted the sharif's preparations in January 1912 for an expedition against Ibn Sa'ud as a strategy to further delay construction.[85]

If the Jidda-Mecca line was never built, factors other than the sharif's obstructions were instrumental. Military strategists placed their weight on the extension of the Hijaz Railway from Medina to Mecca instead. As the minister of war, Mahmud Shawkat Pasha argued for maximizing the military benefits derived from the Hijaz Railway by extending it further south into Yemen. He pointed to the problems posed by the Italian War in the defense of the Red Sea coast and maintained that the degree of naval preparedness that would enable effective defense of the coast would be too costly. In contrast, he maintained, the railway could be extended from Medina to Yemen for the price of one dreadnought.[86] Mahmud Shawkat Pasha also dwelled on the difficulties involved in the supply of construction materials near Jidda as a result of the Italian hostilities. He urged the grand vizier to shelve the plans for the Jidda-Mecca line until the conclusion of the war.[87] Among the shorter lines envisaged, only one, the Hodeida-Sana line, progressed. A French company started construction in 1911, despite Yemeni objections to the foreign concession, but the work was halted with the outbreak of the world war.[88]

MEDINA: AN OTTOMAN OUTPOST IN
THE HIJAZ

The most significant measure that the Young Turk governments took to enhance central authority in the province was the modification of the administrative status of the *sancak* of Medina, Islam's second holy city. Much more so than Mecca, Medina remained outside the reach of Western diplomats and intelligence, and hence scholars. The new importance it acquired during the Young Turk period has therefore been overlooked.

The Young Turk governments viewed Medina as a base from which they hoped to implement policy not only in the Hijaz itself but also in the entire Arabian periphery. Even though Medina lay in a gray zone between Damascus in the north and Jidda and Mecca in the south, and had political and economic links to both regions, Ottoman governments had long recognized the strategic importance of the city and its crucial role in the organization and safe conduct of the pilgrimage. As its administrative designation, *muhafizlik* (wardship), suggests, Medina had been a strategic outpost under the governorship of a military commander.

Medina, situated at a central position in the Arabian Peninsula where the distance between the Red Sea and the Persian Gulf is shortest, has been described as the "gateway to Central Arabia."[89] It was built on terrain relatively easy to defend, supports some agriculture, and has abundant water compared with the rest of the Hijaz.[90] It was located at major crossroads for trade and especially for the transportation of pilgrims to and from Mecca. The town was historically a literary and cultural center commensurate with its religious importance as the Prophet's burial place. The added significance that the city acquired during the Young Turk period was primarily a result of the construction of the Damascus-Medina line of the Hijaz Railway, which made the town easily accessible from Damascus.

The Ottoman government saw in Medina's improved communications the opportunity to project its power further south in Arabia without necessarily extending the railway to Mecca or Yemen. The physical features, strategic location, and refurbished communications of Medina made it an excellent military outpost. Medina also offered the geopolitical advantages of keeping a check on Ibn Sa'ud of the Najd and the growing influence of Britain along the Eastern coast of Arabia.[91]

At a time when the rivalries of the European powers in the broader region intensified and Ottoman suspicions of European intentions grew, Medina's isolated location beyond the reach of European intelligence was an added advantage to the Young Turk governments. This isolation is evident in the reports of the Jidda and Damascus consulates, from which news of Medina was conspicuously absent. British consular reports, the best informed in the region, often expressed frustration stemming from a dearth of information from Medina. The Foreign Office encouraged its consulate in Damascus to collect any information on matters pertaining to Medina, while the Jidda consulate's extensive reports, primarily on Jidda but also on Mecca typically ended with a postscript stating, "As to Medina I have no information."[92]

In the summer of 1910 the Ottoman government changed the administrative status of Medina from *sancak* of the Hijaz *vilayet* to "independent *sancak*."[93] The designation *muhafizlik* was retained. That the separation was implemented with an eye toward extending direct central control over the Hijaz did not escape Sharif Husayn, who immediately cabled the grand vizierate to inquire about the implications of the latest decision on the traditional prerogatives of the grand sharif. The Ottoman government took the opportunity to remind the sharif that his sphere of influence comprised the pilgrimage and Beduin affairs, as had been previously established, and that in these two domains his prerogatives would extend to the newly constituted *muhafizlik*.[94] Despite this reassurance, however, the grand sharif had no legally defined prerogatives,[95] and the strengthening of central control in Medina threatened his regional power and standing.

The administrative separation of Medina from the rest of the Hijaz signified its integration into the mainstream of Ottoman policies. The CUP sent inspectors to Medina, and *Tanin* maintained a correspondent in the city. The CUP club in Medina had many members from the local townspeople as well as from the *shaykh*s of Beduin tribes in the area.[96] During the pilgrimage, the CUP organized public lectures on topics such as the unity of Muslims.[97] The Ottoman government took a much greater interest in implementing reforms in Medina than in any other part of the Hijaz. The Medina CUP built schools in the city. In 1909 İstanbul acted on the aforementioned reform plan of an *'alim* of Medina, 'Abd al-Rahman Ilyas, which was drafted to improve conditions in Arabia.[98] Two years later *Muhafiz* 'Ali Rida Pasha (al-Rikabi) submitted a program specifically concerned with Medina, proposing reforms ranging from encouraging the sedentarization of the Beduins to the surveillance of the Red Sea coast in order to prevent the smuggling of arms and slaves. The *Muhafiz* was invited to İstanbul to discuss his reform scheme. The reform proposal called for soliciting the cooperation of the population (by declaring a general amnesty and implementing the conversion of the Medina court of appeal into a *şeriat* court), encouraging the settlement of tribes by promoting agriculture and servicing of the railway, bringing about improvements in municipal facilities, and encouraging education.[99] Even though some of the measures proposed by the *Muhafiz* were found unnecessary (e.g., the founding of an agricultural bank)[100] or their implementation financially unfeasible (e.g., the establishment of an industrial school),[101] the improvement of conditions in Medina received high priority in İstanbul. Many of 'Ali Rida's proposals were carefully studied by the ministries, which made provisions in the budget for the following year.[102]

The extension of the railway to Medina and the modification of the town's administrative status became the centerpieces of the Young Turk policy of centralization in Arabia. İstanbul thus exerted its influence in the Hijaz by tempering and directing Sharif Husayn's ambitions. With the imposition of the coercive elements of the "Ottoman order"[103] on Medina, the government was able to exert more influence than ever in the Peninsula dominated by tribal and religious leaders. The government's penetration did not signify incorporation, though the economic integration of the region was contemplated, as evidenced by the coastal railway schemes.

Sharif Husayn's Campaigns

Once the Ottoman government strengthened its position in northern Hijaz, it collaborated with the sharif in campaigns aimed at bringing under control centers of unrest further south. Rather than overextending itself in the Peninsula, İstanbul chose to avail itself of the resources that the sharif could summon up and to assist him militarily, if and when needed. Husayn sought to extend his sphere of influence through these campaigns. His interests were best served by cooperation with the government.

The major local tribal potentates and several lesser ones in the Peninsula were all interested in expanding their spheres of influence. Ibn Rashid of Hail (in northern Najd) had been in alliance with the government since the turn of the century against Ibn Sa'ud, his powerful rival in the Najd. The enhancement of the government presence in nearby Medina put an effective check on any expansionist ambitions of Ibn Rashid and assured his loyalty. Another local power holder, Imam Yahya of Yemen, was far removed from the reach of the others. İstanbul found it necessary to make a separate peace with the imam in 1911, which granted him autonomy and also removed him from the power struggles to the north. The newest competitor near the Hijaz was Muhammad al-Idrisi. Like Ibn Sa'ud and Yahya before him, Idrisi gathered a following by propagating his own particular religious message. Thus, Ibn Sa'ud and Idrisi came to be the principal rivals of Sharif Husayn in his efforts to maintain his authority among the tribes of the Hijaz and to extend it to neighboring areas.

The sharif first set out to consolidate his position vis-à-vis Ibn Sa'ud. In March 1909 a confrontation between the forces of Ibn Rashid and Ibn Sa'ud near Medina ended in the latter's defeat.[104] During the conflict one of the largest tribes of eastern Hijaz, 'Utayba, submitted to Ibn Sa'ud. At the end of the hostilities the 'Utayba chiefs wanted to re-establish a connection with the Hijaz. In view of the weakness of the Sa'udis, whose leader *Shams al-haqiqa* claimed to have been killed during the fighting with Ibn Rashid,[105] Sharif Husayn convinced the government to accept the pleas of the 'Utayba chiefs, who argued that the 'Utayba could constitute a buffer at the Najd border against any attacks on the railway.[106] The grand sharif also sent an expedition against another important tribe, Mutayr, under the leadership of his two sons 'Abdullah and 'Ali.[107]

In the spring of 1910 Sharif Husayn prepared for another display of force, this time against Ibn Sa'ud. The sharif was prompted to some extent by the fear of a joint action by Ibn Sa'ud and the newly ascendant Idrisi against the grand sharifate. In April Sharif Husayn informed İstanbul of his decision to send deputies to Najd to collect the religious *zekat* tax that had not been paid for more than thirty years.[108] He demanded from Ibn Sa'ud the taxes for the Qasim region and invited the people of Qasim to pay allegiance to the grand sharifate. At the end of July Husayn designated his son 'Abdullah as his deputy and left his summer residence in Taif with his three other sons, Faysal, Zayd, and 'Ali, and a Beduin force of 4,000 for an "investigative" expedition.[109] He contacted both the governor and the commander of the Hijaz forces for military assistance, but İstanbul was reluctant to see a major showdown in Najd and did not comply with the request.[110]

One of the objectives of Sharif Husayn's hastily prepared expedition against Ibn Saʿud was to show his rivals that, despite the recent separation of Medina from the Hijaz, he retained his following among the tribes as the strongest local chief in the region. He also hoped to receive military assistance from the government and thus lead his enemies to believe that he could count on the capital's full support. It seems that İstanbul chose to curb his ambition. Husayn's renewed request for aid after he engaged in hostilities with Ibn Saʿud's forces, taking prisoner in the process Saʿd ibn ʿAbd al-Rahman, the brother of Emir ʿAbd al-ʿAziz al-Saʿud, was also denied.[111]

The sharif signed a pact with Ibn Saʿud. According to the terms relayed to İstanbul by ʿAbdullah, it stipulated that Ibn Saʿud would refrain from collecting the *zekat* among the ʿUtayba, that the *shaykh* of Qasim would be elected by its inhabitants, and that the latter would pay an annual tax to the province of the Hijaz.[112] While Sharif Husayn attempted to present his expedition as a victory for himself and the government, the *muhafiz* of Medina, ʿAli Rida Pasha, reported that the grand sharif had to withdraw from Qasim because he was running out of supplies and Ibn Saʿud was preparing to attack him from his rear. According to the *muhafiz*, the sharif had to return shorn of glory, pretending that the gifts he had received along the way were really booty.[113] The absence of any change in the relations of Ibn Saʿud and the sharif, as well as Saʿud's subsequent noncompliance with the terms of the pact, support the view that the sharif's "victory" in 1910 was a hollow one.[114] In 1911 Ibn Saʿud restored the taxes on the ʿUtayba. "It has been rumored," Ambassador Lowther wrote to Sir Edward Grey in his report for the last quarter of 1911, "that the Grand Shereef contemplated another expedition against Bin Saʿud, the success of his former expedition in 1910 being considered very doubtful."[115] Husayn was mostly on the defensive vis-à-vis his rival in Najd during the rest of his term.

Only a few months after Husayn arrived in Mecca as emir, Idrisi of Asir declared himself *mehdi* (messiah) in Sabya and invited all Muslims to join in a jihad (holy war) against the Ottoman government. As the governor of Yemen sent a copy of the declarations that Idrisi distributed among the tribes and urged the government to take effective measures to secure his arrest,[116] Sharif Husayn dispatched an emissary to Asir to investigate the situation.[117] Husayn maintained that it was the shortage of civil and military functionaries in this region that allowed the uprising and urged that central authority be strengthened in the region by sending additional officials.[118] This would be an unusual request for a local notable who did not have a symbiotic power relationship with the central authority.

İstanbul sought to establish a relationship with Idrisi similar to the one it had with Sharif Husayn. Indeed, in March 1910 the sharif alleged that a secret agreement concluded between the government and Idrisi was prompting Idrisi to renewed attacks.[119] Grand Vizier İbrahim Hakkı Pasha assured the sharif that Idrisi had no official capacity or prerogatives and that the government was merely trying to deal with him in friendly ways.[120] In November 1910 Husayn expressed his indignation regarding the İstanbul paper *Al-ʿarab*,[121] which published articles of a nature, he claimed, that would dissipate all measures previously taken against Idrisi. He described the articles as depreciative of Arabs and nothing less than open and official encouragement to the tribes to join forces with Idrisi.[122]

Idrisi's insurrection was not perceived in the capital to be as serious a threat as Sharif Husayn's alarm suggested. Despite İstanbul's conciliatory stance toward the rebel chief, however, later reports from not only the grand sharif but also from other civil and military authorities in the region (the command of the Seventh Army,[123] the *mutasarrıf*s of Asir[124] and Jidda,[125] and the Hijaz governor[126]) led the government to reappraise the situation. These reports mentioned that Idrisi was bringing many tribes under his influence and was planning an attack on Mecca during the pilgrimage season. This would threaten more than the sharif's regional influence and could also invite foreign intervention, since colonial subjects of European powers like Britain and France would be in Mecca in the pilgrimage season.

Idrisi blockaded Abha at the end of 1910, cutting the communications of the Ottoman garrison in the town.[127] As İstanbul authorized Husayn to undertake a campaign against Idrisi, the sharif asked for his son ʿAbdullah to be granted a leave from Parliament to come to Mecca.[128] Meanwhile, İzzet Pasha was sent to the Hijaz with reinforcements to join the sharif and his sons in the military campaign against Asir.[129] On his way to battle, the sharif met with tribal chiefs in the Qunfidha region, who rendered their submission to him.[130] However, on the battleground Idrisi managed to repulse the forces loyal to the government.[131] Further setbacks followed;[132] any victories the sharif's forces had were modest.[133] In spite of the lack of any apparent success in his expedition against Idrisi, the government sent Sharif Husayn decorations in August 1911.[134]

In the spring of 1912 Idrisi renewed his attacks in cooperation with Italian forces. Italy, at war with the Ottoman government in Tripolita-

nia, was applying naval pressure in the Red Sea. The skirmishes continued into the summer with no decisive confrontations between the rebels
and the sharifian and Ottoman forces led by Sharif Faysal and Hadi
Pasha.[135] Despite Husayn's objections, resistance to Idrisi was relaxed as
the conclusion of peace with Italy seemed near.[136] In October, on the
eve of the agreement with Italy, Husayn urged the grand vizier vehemently that Idrisi should not be a beneficiary of the peace agreement.
İstanbul, however, replied that a pardon had been extended to Idrisi and
that he was expected to submit to the government.[137]

Both Idrisi and Ibn Saʿud remained irritants to the sharif in his quest
for predominance in Arabia. The government discouraged Husayn from
decisive showdowns with these two leaders. İstanbul's aim was not to
establish direct control over the Peninsula once and for all, but rather
to maintain a position of strength vis-à-vis the different local power
holders. This policy denied the sharif the greater eminence that he hoped
to attain in the Peninsula by virtue of his loyalty to the government.
However, no alternative was left to Sharif Husayn other than to continue to play the role designated for him in the capital.

Sharif Husayn's Struggle to Maintain His Authority

The separation of Medina from the province of the Hijaz
and the imminent danger of railway construction to Mecca forced Sharif
Husayn to engage in acts that would show the central government that
he was an indispensable representative of the government in the region.
He systematically challenged, and at times harassed, other high officials,
particularly the governor of the Hijaz and the *muhafiz* of Medina.

Conflict between governor and grand sharif was endemic in the administration of the Hijaz. Provincial notables challenged the governors'
authority elsewhere in the empire (as did, for example, Sayyid Talib in
Basra), but in the Hijaz the grand sharif's authority, based on his ped-
igree and services in the holy places, had acquired historical legitimacy.
Although the Young Turk governments recognized the sharif's authority
in any explicit way in affairs pertaining to the Beduin and the pilgrimage
only (after searching for royal decrees that may have defined the grand

sharif's prerogatives more precisely), there was little else to be regulated in the Hijaz.

Much has been said about the inimical relationship between the sharif and the governors in the Hijaz. Against the immediate background of the second half of the Hamidian period, when there was a durable and corrupt alliance between Governor Ahmed Ratib Pasha and grand sharifs Muttalib and ʿAli, the tensions between Husayn and the governors and the high turnover of governors during the Young Turk period appear striking. Whether these feuds were in fact politically significant enough to frustrate the government's policies in the Hijaz is doubtful.

Some of the difficulties of making appointments in remote provinces (such as the shortage of qualified candidates, the vicissitudes of the new political order, the reluctance of appointees to serve in harsh geographical and climatic conditions in remote regions) were pointed out in chapter 2. These factors resulted in frequent replacements of governors and other high officials. It is true that in the Hijaz the governor felt overshadowed by the grand sharif, which made the governorship of the province an even less desirable and more difficult post. Sharif Husayn repeatedly sent reports to İstanbul about the lack of experience of the governors.[138] He sometimes complained that, even though a governor's good intentions and integrity were incontestable, the incumbent was ignorant of local conditions and customs. He went so far as to hold the governors' inexperience responsible for the delay of measures he in fact had an interest in obstructing. Whenever the sharif heard that İstanbul was contemplating a change of governors he applied pressure to have his personal candidates appointed. It would not be correct, however, to ascribe the constant resignations of the governors chiefly to Sharif Husayn's efforts to oust them or to view the turnover simply as an indication of his inimical relationship with İstanbul or of the independent power he attained in the Hijaz.

The most noted confrontation between a governor and the grand sharif occurred in the fall of 1911. Earlier that year İstanbul sent Hazım Bey, a Unionist and an able administrator, as governor to the Hijaz.[139] A strong governor was needed during the troubles in Asir and the sharif's absence on his campaign against Idrisi. Upon his return from Asir, Husayn claimed to have been insulted to see Hazım in the reception party together with sharifs from the rival Zayd clan.[140] Prominent among the latter was Sharif Muhammad Nasir, a descendant of the brother of Grand Sharif ʿAbd al-Muttalib of the Zayd, who had maintained good relations with the CUP.[141] Husayn's insistence that Nasir should be dismissed from the party angered the governor, who refused afterwards to pay a courtesy visit to Sharif Husayn. Husayn turned to the grand vizier, who applied pressure on Hazım to pay the requested visit. Hazım complied, and soon after left Taif for his new post as governor in Beirut. Sharif Husayn's ability to prevail upon the government to have a governor of Hazım Bey's stature removed suggests that he was able to establish a degree of independence in the Hijaz. However, a more intricate combination of factors was generally responsible for the transfer of a governor. Hazım's transfer, for instance, may have had more to do with the need for his services to deal with the growing agitation in Beirut than with the appeasement of Sharif Husayn.

The sharif had little positive influence on the appointment of governors. His attempts to secure permanent appointments for military commander and acting governor 'Abdullah Pasha in 1910[142] and Münir Pasha in 1913 were not successful.[143] Nor was the sharif able to influence the decisions for minor provincial posts. His appeals in this regard were frequently declined.[144] In December 1912, in a telegram to Grand Vizier Kamil Pasha, he protested the retention of an official in Jidda by the Ministry of Finance contrary to his advice. He claimed that four officials, including the controversial one, who were all Unionists, added to the Jiddans' existing resentment of the Committee, which derived from the unfavorable results of the Balkan War. Even though the Unionists were neither in power nor influential at this time, the effect of Husayn's pleas was the replacement of a single official only.[145]

An especially acrimonious antagonism existed between the *muhafiz* of Medina, 'Ali Rida Pasha, and Sharif Husayn as a result of the new status of the *muhafizlik* and the implications for the grand sharifate. If Sharif Husayn had some degree of success in maintaining his political preponderance in Mecca, he was generally frustrated in his dealings with the *muhafiz*s of Medina. Traditionally, the grand sharifs maintained deputies in the towns of the Hijaz to perform duties related to the pilgrimage and matters of the Beduin. In the spring of 1910 a crisis broke out between *Muhafiz* 'Ali Rida Pasha and the grand sharif's deputy in Medina, Sharif Shahat. The *muhafiz* claimed that Shahat had helped a convict—exiled to Medina for his involvement in the counterrevolutionary uprising of April 1909—escape to Egypt and that subsequently Shahat himself had fled to Mecca. 'Ali Rida asked the minister of the interior to have Sharif Husayn dismiss Shahat and to entrust the Medina government with the conduct of the affairs traditionally pertaining to the sharifate's representative in Medina.[146]

Prior to the July 1910 decision of the government to separate Medina from the Hijaz, *Muhafiz* ʿAli Rida Pasha complained that both the emirate and the directorate of the Hijaz Railway were acting in Medina like governments within a government and indicated that their arbitrary acts caused excitement and confusion among the tribes. For example, the grand sharif deducted from the government subsidy earmarked for a tribe an amount that the pilgrimage caravan officials had traditionally given its *shaykh*s as a gift. He also asked for the arrest of some tribal chiefs. The *shaykh*s, in turn, wrote to the *muhafiz* threatening to blow up the railway. The *muhafiz* concluded that the government in Medina could not tolerate the implementation of heedless policies, much less take responsibility for them.[147] In response, Husayn allied himself with Governor Kamil and asked for the replacement of ʿAli Rida Pasha, but without success.[148]

The grand sharif took liberties in his recognized domain of relations with the tribes to promote his local agendas. As the complaints of the *muhafiz* reveal, one of Husayn's tactics to maintain broad local authority and to prevent İstanbul from taking measures to increase direct central control in the Hijaz to the detriment of his own authority was to encourage dissension among the tribes in the Medina area.[149] The campaign against Ibn Saʿud, which the sharif undertook without any military assistance from the government, was another maneuver designed to serve as a display of his power both to the tribes in the region and to İstanbul. Nevertheless, Husayn's correspondence with the grand vizier during the Najd campaign included elaborate references to the resolute and long-standing obedience of the sharifs of his family to the Ottoman caliph since the days of Sultan Selim. He presented his latest campaign as an attempt to protect the rights and interests of the state and the caliphate not only in the Hijaz (which, Husayn added, boasted orderly and stable government compared with the other provinces) but also in the entire Arabian Peninsula.[150]

Whatever his success in asserting his will vis-à-vis the governors in the Hijaz, the grand sharif failed to abort İstanbul's decision regarding Medina. Tension between the *muhafizlık* and the emirate became chronic. Toward the end of 1911 Sharif Husayn displayed an independent attitude in Mecca. He was frustrated by his apparent loss of control over northern Hijaz but emboldened by the removal of Governor Hazım in the fall of 1911. At this juncture his dismissal in favor of Sharif Haydar seems to have been considered in İstanbul, but was opposed by Mahmud Shawkat Pasha, then minister of war.[151] The British consul, also irritated by the recent attitude of the sharif, pointed to the influential support of the minister of war that the sharif enjoyed.[152] In reality, Mahmud Shawkat Pasha had friendly relations with Sharif Haydar and disagreed with Husayn on the extension of the Hijaz Railway. His opposition to any plans for Husayn's removal can be explained by his fear of altering the status quo in the Hijaz during hostilities with Italy in the Red Sea.

During the period of the CUP's political troubles, from the spring of 1912 to the summer of 1913, the sharif enjoyed relative freedom of action. The 1912 elections were held in the Hijaz with little regard for established procedures, and the sharif was allowed to secure the election of his second son, Faysal, as deputy from Jidda, in addition to ʿAbdullah, who was reelected for Mecca.[153] The successful completion of the sharif's second Asir campaign, due not so much to military victories but to the cessation of Italian support to Idrisi, added to his prestige in the Hijaz.[154] Yet the sharif's attempts to increase his civil and military authority in this opportune period did not bring substantial results. Following Governor Hazım's departure, Husayn reacted to the reports that İsmail Fazıl Pasha, former governor of Syria, was under consideration for the position. Citing the ineptitude of İsmail Fazıl, he proposed two local functionaries, over whom he probably enjoyed some influence, Münir Pasha (commander of forces in the Hijaz) and Ziver Bey (the şeyhülharam, or keeper of the Prophet's tomb), as his candidates.[155] The Ministry of the Interior appointed Halil Pasha, Governor of Kosova, instead. Then, advancing Halil's unfamiliarity with the local language and customs, the ministry rescinded the appointment in favor of Mustafa Zihni Pasha (Babanzade), a Baghdadi Kurd and governor of Janina.[156] Not surprisingly the relationship between the sharif and Mustafa Zihni Pasha was adversarial from the beginning. When Zihni Pasha was transferred later in 1912, Sharif Husayn not only renewed his request for the appointment of Münir but also asked that the positions of military commander and governor be united in his candidate. The Gazi Ahmed Muhtar government, which by this time had displaced the Unionists, reminded Husayn that it was established practice to appoint governors from the civil list (even though arrangements along the lines of the sharif's request were not uncommon in certain provinces). He was also informed that the new appointee, Reşid Pasha, was due to arrive in Mecca shortly.[157] It seems that Reşid Pasha never went to the Hijaz and that Münir served as acting governor for the next few months.

The year 1912 was exceptional in terms of the sharif's relations with the British. As early as January 1912 the French consul in Jidda reported a trip 'Abdullah took to Cairo with the purpose of seeking the khedive's support.[158] The first contact between 'Abdullah and the British authorities, the precursor of negotiations that opened the door to a British-sharifian alliance in 1916, may have occurred on this occasion.

But it is also at this juncture that the sharif's endeavor to assert his authority resulted in a clash with the British authorities. The sharif reorganized the appointment procedure of pilgrim guides to maximize his profits and undermine the British Consulate's control over Indian pilgrims.[159] He also proceeded to take over the supervision of the water condenser that insured Jidda's water supply from the official Hijaz Commission of Health. A transfer of control to the sharif, the consul claimed, would risk the lives of pilgrims, among them 30,000 British subjects.[160] In the summer of 1912 Jidda's telegraphic communication with the outside world was interrupted for an extended period and could not be restored because of the Italian presence in the Red Sea. During this period, the Beduin attacked military barracks in Jidda and shot at the British Consulate to protest the emancipation of certain slaves. The consul maintained that the sharif gave his implicit consent to these acts of aggression "to impress the local authorities with his power, [and to show them] how entirely at his mercy they are." The consul recommended that British subjects be discouraged from performing the pilgrimage in order to deal the sharif a financial blow and to show him that "he is not entirely beyond the reach of the Powers." He wrote, "[T]he fear of a repetition of the lesson would mitigate more than half of the evils and eliminate more than half the difficulties with which we have to contend, and this, moreover, without wounding the pride and damaging the financial interests of the central government which derives no profit from the Haj."[161] That the British authorities were contemplating in the summer of 1912 action intended to damage the grand sharif's finances and religious prestige suggests that any contacts with the British in Egypt earlier in the year were inconsequential.

The return of the CUP to power in January 1913 heralded a tightening of central control. The sharif's reaction was predictable. In two letters sent to İstanbul in April 1913, following the promulgation of the Provincial Law, he revisited some of the difficulties that arose because of the separation of Medina from Mecca, particularly the ambiguity that ensued in the responsibilities of the grand sharifate with respect to the pilgrims and Beduins.[162] He accused the *muhafiz* of injustice, ineptitude, and unlawful acts. In a detailed memorandum the *muhafiz* denied all the accusations.[163] A few weeks later Husayn requested once again the appointment of Münir Pasha as titular governor. The previous government had already designated Nedim Pasha, the Governor of Bitlis, for the post and the sharif was informed of the new appointment.[164] However, the CUP government reversed that decision, apparently before Nedim Pasha went to the Hijaz, and commissioned Vehib Bey for the post.

Starting in 1914 the reorientation of İstanbul's imperial policy toward an Ottomanism with greater emphasis on Islam and the crystallization of international factors that ultimately precipitated the world war were conducive to a more fundamental change in the established relationship of the grand sharifate to the capital. In the months preceding the war the sharif was irked by officially sponsored aggressive Islamic propaganda, which had the potential of robbing him of his moral force in Arabia, where he had posed as the protector of Islamic traditions and practices. Although his political fortunes were tied to that of the government, he opposed further centralization and deemed reform as contrary to religion. İstanbul's espousal of an Islamic ideology not only threatened to overshadow his religious standing but also directed the government's attention to the holy places as bases for propaganda.

In the meantime, the growing international tensions prompted Britain to renew contacts with the sharif regarding a prospective alliance against the Ottoman government. Sharif 'Abdullah, apprehensive about the subjugation of the Hijaz to stricter central controls and the removal of his father over disagreements with the new governor Vehib, responded positively to British overtures in Cairo and sounded out British willingness to aid his father in the event of deteriorating relations with İstanbul. These contacts were resumed after the outbreak of the war. The story of British-Hashemite relations is too well-known to be related here.[165] The next chapter will examine the Ottoman flank of the balancing act that the sharif was forced to play after the outbreak of war.

Conclusion

Centralization as conceived and implemented by the Young Turks had two objectives: to establish control over the economic and human resources of the empire and to keep in check fissiparous trends in the periphery. The introduction of standard administrative, fiscal, and educational procedures was considered necessary to implement centralization. The destruction of local loci of power was a desirable but not necessary condition for exerting central authority. The Young Turks found it more convenient to come to terms with local power holders in such a way as to allow them to implement İstanbul's political objectives and to reward them for doing so.

The economic potential of the Hijaz was too insignificant and its privileged status too entrenched for religious reasons for the Young Turks to extend direct centralized rule over the province. But for strategic and religious reasons, factors which acquired growing importance for İstanbul, the Hijaz had to be kept under central control. The Young Turk governments fulfilled this objective by using Sharif Husayn, the most influential notable of the Hijaz, if not of the whole Peninsula, as a proxy. They ensured his cooperation by increasing their military capability within easy reach of the sharif's sphere of influence.

The sharif played the role assigned to him willingly, because he in turn could use it to promote his position vis-à-vis perennial rivals in the region and maneuver for enhanced local power and prerogatives. He made bids for greater support from İstanbul and also launched his own local initiatives independently of the government. In so doing, he often came into conflict with government officials at different levels. Ultimately, İstanbul's appraisal of the degree to which its objectives were being served determined to whose satisfaction such conflicts were resolved.

In 1914 imperial and international political circumstances led Sharif Husayn to pursue opportunities other than those emanating from a close identification with İstanbul that would enhance his personal power and prestige. Aided by the Ottoman government's fateful entanglement in the hostilities of the World War, this pursuit culminated in a revolt in the Hijaz in June 1916 that weakened Ottoman resistance to Allied incursions and raised hopes for independence and nationhood among the Arabs of the empire. Insofar as the collapse of Ottoman power was the strongest factor in the growth of political Arab nationalism, Sharif Husayn was one of its heroes for having led the revolt that facilitated the British invasion of Syria and Palestine.

The history of the Hijaz under the Young Turks has been written with the kind of patent biased romanticization exemplified in the words of one author: "[In] 1908 there succeeded to the office of Grand Sharif of Mecca a Hashemite of spiky temperament, by no means obsequious to Turkish dignities, and crotchetily conscious of Arab rights."[166] More recent scholarship, especially the pioneering revisionist work of Ernest Dawn, has shown that the contribution of Sharif Husayn and of the Hijaz to Arab nationalism has to be evaluated more critically. However, Husayn's success in maintaining his traditional rights and promoting his personal power and prestige at the expense of İstanbul's authority in the Hijaz has been generally acknowledged. A closer examination reveals that during the greater portion of Sharif Husayn's emirate in the Hijaz not only were the prerogatives of the grand sharif considerably proscribed—particularly in northern Hijaz—by an extension of direct central control, but also that the Young Turk governments successfully steered Sharif Husayn to conduct those policies that advanced the interests of the imperial center.

6

The War Years, 1914–1918

The six turbulent years that followed the 1908 Revolution revealed to the Committee of Union and Progress that its role in the revolution did not confer upon it an indefinite moral and political influence. The fluctuations in the Committee's political fortunes taught its leaders how to contend with different political factions. By 1913 the CUP grew confident enough to engineer a coup and take the reins of government. Within one year it went to elections in order to legitimize its grip on political power. The elections took place during the winter of 1913–14 and in some localities continued into the spring.

There was no organized opposition to the CUP during the elections. The campaign and balloting occurred against the background of the new emphasis on Islamic unity, reflected in publications such as *İslam Mecmuası* (Islamic Journal), founded by the CUP in February 1914. Intellectuals with pan-Turkist tendencies, such as Tekin Alp (alibi Moise Cohen) and Ziya Gökalp, now wrote for *İslam Mecmuası*.[1] Islamism, an inclusionary ideology, implicitly legitimated single-party rule. Elections were meant to elicit further endorsement.

The Elections of 1914 and the Eclipse of the Reform Movement

From its position of strength, the CUP pursued a co-optive strategy vis-à-vis Arabs with leanings toward the Liberal camp.

It compromised with the Arabist and decentralist trends, the two overlapping pro-Liberal platforms of the preceding years. In many districts it stood by to watch Unionists lose their bid for reelection. In Aleppo the head of the local CUP ran as a candidate but lost.[2] In some districts the government withdrew its support from Unionists and manipulated the electoral process in favor of the Liberals. In Acre, for instance, the authorities detained secondary electors who were largely favorable to Shaykh As'ad al-Shuqayri, a pro-Unionist deputy since 1908,[3] in order to grant newcomer 'Abd al-Fattah al-Sa'adi a victory. The CUP had apparently promised al-Shuqayri's ouster to 'Abd al-Hamid al-Zahrawi, who as religious scholar from the Prophet's lineage, former Arabist journalist, president of the Arab Congress, and now senator (see page 176) embodied the compromise with the Arabists.[4] In Nablus Amin 'Abd al-Hadi[5] and Tawfiq Hammad ousted incumbent Haydar Tuqan amid accusations of manipulation of electoral districts and obstruction of the vote in favor of the challengers,[6] as Nablus sent two deputies to Parliament for the first time.[7] In 'Amara (Iraq) Unionist incumbent Munir's candidacy was not supported—and in fact was sabotaged, according to the candidate—possibly as a concession to Sayyid Talib.[8]

In Beirut the CUP created an Islamist organization to neutralize Arabist loyalties.[9] Here and in Damascus the deputies-elect were compromise candidates, and all but one in each district were newcomers. Basra, another center of the reform movement, elected nearly twice the number of deputies it had in the previous two elections, all with decentralist leanings, though they did not belong to the Entente.[10] In general, the CUP manipulated the electoral process to privilege candidates from the notable class, who commanded the esteem of the population, yet would be less inclined to engage in active opposition than the Arabist Liberals.[11]

The increase in numerical and proportional representation of the Arab provinces in Parliament continued from the 1912 elections to the 1914 elections and was significantly larger than the increase between 1908 and 1912. With the loss of the Balkan provinces (which contained no Arab populations) since 1912, the proportion of Arab deputies to the total number predictably increased (from 24 percent to 32 percent). In absolute terms, too, the contingent from the Arab provinces registered an increase of sixteen (or 25 percent of its size in 1912). This proportional and numerical increase is particularly striking, however, given that the Arab contingent lost ten deputies because of the loss of Libya to Italy. The representation of the Arab provinces that remained within the empire increased by some 30 percent from 1912 to 1914. The number of Turks representing Arab provinces did not change significantly in this period in absolute terms, and diminished by about 5 percent in proportion to the total representation from the Arab provinces.[12]

The dramatic increase in the size of Arab representation in the 1914 elections illustrated only one facet of the CUP's policy of accommodation with the Arabs. Even prior to the elections,[13] and apparently to strengthen the CUP position at the polls, several senators were selected for the Chamber of Notables from the Arab provinces: Yusuf Sursuq (a Greek Orthodox Christian from Beirut), 'Abd al-Hamid al-Zahrawi (Hama), and Muhammad Bayhum (Beirut), all three former opponents of the CUP; and Ahmad al-Kakhia (Aleppo), 'Abd al-Rahman al-Yusuf (*emirülhac* in 1908 and Unionist deputy after 1909), Muhi al-Din al-Kaylani (Baghdad), and Sulayman al-Baruni (Tripoli-Libya).[14] Senate membership carried considerable symbolic, though little practical, weight. The appointments more than doubled the number of Arab senators to twelve,[15] even though the number of new appointments fell short of the demands that the Arab Congress had expressed.[16] His appointment subjected al-Zahrawi to the accusation of treason by "certain Arab circles,"[17] presumably former associates in the reform movement.

The new Parliament elected as its deputy president the Damascene deputy Amir 'Ali 'Abd al-Qadir al-Jaza'iri, a newcomer.[18] The cabinet included Sulayman al-Bustani as minister of commerce and agriculture. Two leading reformists, Shukri al-'Asali and 'Abd al-Wahhab al-Inkilizi, were among the six new Arab appointees (out of a total of twenty-four) as provincial civil inspectors.[19] Their appointment to Damascus was vetoed by the governor of Syria, and therefore al-Inkilizi was reassigned to Bursa and al-'Asali to Aleppo,[20] despite similar objections from the governor of Aleppo.[21]

Al-Zahrawi, al-'Asali, and al-Inkilizi were among the Arab leaders whom Cemal Pasha sent to the gallows in 1916. The executions made the three men later into heroes of Arab nationalism; and viewed as such, the motives and circumstances of their reconciliation with İstanbul in 1914 has posed a problem. Their acceptance of government jobs substantiates Ernest Dawn's point that recognition and official position induced Arab leaders to an Ottomanist stance. But would these men or other reformists have accepted government positions earlier as readily? Al-'Asali's rejection of the governorship of Latakia in 1913 seems to suggest otherwise.

One explanation for their acceptance of official positions is their conviction that reforms promised by the government could only be achieved if the reformists accepted an active role in government. Samir Seikaly regards this as an apologetic explanation and writes, "It is probably [sic] that al-'Asali's return to government service was facilitated by the expectation of immediate economic relief and the receipt of a regular salary."[22] Rashid Khalidi's appraisal of the decision as "temporary apostasy" and "momentary opportunism"[23] sounds less charitable, but implies that the co-optation was an ephemeral one that did not derail these leaders from their Arabist convictions. Seikaly argues that al-'Asali "was committed to the continuation of the empire of [sic] a political entity in which all races would be equal and in which Arabs and Turks, bound by the links of a re-created Ottomanism, would jointly cooperate in its government."[24] Ahmed Tarabein advances a similar argument for al-Zahrawi, whose "being an Arab nationalist was not incompatible with being committed to Ottomanism."[25] These authors represent the prevalent view that İstanbul's commitment to an Ottomanist reconciliation, in which men like al-'Asali and al-Zahrawi placed their sincere hopes, was illusory and deceptive.

While the Arabist agenda negotiated in Paris may not have been addressed in its entirety, İstanbul's concessions to Arab demands, made within the logic of a new Turco-Arab fusion buttressed by an Islamist official outlook, deserve a closer look. The CUP adopted in 1914 a noticeably lenient attitude toward its former Arab opponents. Muhammad Kurd 'Ali, the convicted Arabist editor of *Al-muqtabas*, received a pardon.[26] The Ministry of the Interior solicited the *müftü*s of Damascus[27] and Aleppo[28] for positions in the office of the *şeyhülislam* in İstanbul. 'Izzat Pasha, the infamous second secretary of Abdülhamid who had fled İstanbul in disgrace in 1908, was allowed to return in order to take care of matters related to his land interests in Damascus. In return, he made donations to government-sponsored Islamist organizations.[29] There were also new official initiatives designed to reach agreements with those tribal leaders who maintained an adversarial posture.

The government proceeded with diverse reforms in the Arab provinces. Talat Bey, restored as the minister of the interior, showed particular concern to drumming up popular support by fulfilling some of the promises the CUP had made to the Arab Congress leaders, even though the publication that contained the minutes of the Congress (along with the text of congratulatory telegrams sent to it) was banned.[30] Together with Cemal Pasha, Talat met with Arab leaders to discuss the demands for reform.[31] As a result of these initiatives, the requirement that officials

appointed to the Arab provinces have knowledge of Arabic was enforced. The functionaries had to take an Arabic language examination
in İstanbul before they could proceed to their provincial posts. Furthermore, more and more provincial officials appointed from outside
were replaced by locals. New regulations allowed documents to be
drafted in Arabic (in addition to Ottoman and French) in Ottoman
consulates, a measure aimed at assuaging the expatriate Arabists outside
the empire.[32] The application of the new policies was erratic. Particularly
in the province of Aleppo, which contained mixed populations of Turks
and Arabs, the clauses of the provincial law pertaining to local language
caused confusion and even chaos.[33]

By 1914 questions that pertained to ethnic differences became indis-
cernible in the public sphere as political activity tapered. From its position of power, the CUP had gone on to crush the Liberals with executions and deportations. The opposition gradually lost ground until
the government's emergency powers, assumed on grounds of wartime
security during the Balkan Wars, silenced it altogether and forced its
leadership into exile, where the Liberals lost contact with what had remained of their Arab proponents.[34] As the political alliance of the Liberals with ethnic (including Arab) and religious groups foundered in the
face of reprisals against the Liberals and the disappearance of party contestation, new manifestations of an "Arab opposition" were to emerge
elsewhere.

Two secret Arab organizations, *Al-jam'iyya al-'arabiyya al-fatat* (The
Young Arab Society) and *Al-'ahd* (Covenant) included in their ranks
members with revolutionary or separatist proclivities.[35] Arab organizations and committees had existed since 1908, but they were primarily
cultural organizations (not unlike the Turkist groups) that had only weak
popular roots and vague political programs. *Al-fatat* was founded in
Paris in 1909 and soon found adherents in Syria. While the organization
remained secret, it maintained contacts with the reform movement and
included Arabists such as 'Abd al-Ghani al-'Uraysi as members. *Al-'ahd*
was a successor of *Al-fatat*'s counterpart in the army, *Al-qahtaniyya*.
Founded in October 1913 in İstanbul by 'Aziz 'Ali al-Misri, *Al-'ahd* may
have grown to include more than half of nearly 500 Arab officers in
İstanbul. It also had branches in Baghdad and Musul.[36]

The activation of Arabism among the officers of the Ottoman army
had to do with a purge that Enver Pasha implemented upon being promoted to general and minister of war in the 1914 cabinet.[37] No sooner
had he taken office than he sent some 300 officers to retirement.[38] Arab

military officers benefited neither from the political compromise the CUP had struck earlier with the Arab political leadership or from Enver's reorganization of the officer corps. In Damascus, for instance, ninety officers were retired. The positions of most were eliminated, while a few Arab officers were replaced by Turks.[39] Enver's reorganization was accompanied by measures that reflected the official Islamic reorientation and were aimed at curtailing dissidence, such as stricter enforcement of religious observance in the barracks.[40]

In 1914 the government initiated a systematic policy to cultivate the Arab provincial press. The role that the press had played in politics had become evident in the preceding years. Several papers in the Syrian provinces received subsidies from İstanbul; some entered the government's service. This, to some extent, reflected the rising Islamist-Ottomanist feeling among the Arab public. It also pointed to the malleability of an influential segment of the Arab intellectual elite. Already in January, the Beiruti papers *Ray al-'am, Ababil,* and *Al-balagh* received subsidies from İstanbul,[41] as the criticism of the government shifted to Arabist journals abroad.

In Basra Sayyid Talib's posture offers a remarkable indication of how Arab leaders appraised changes in domestic and international political conditions and of the implications of these developments for local and personal interests. Talib was not only a local notable with extensive influence over town, country, and tribes but also a deputy in Parliament, elected to represent Basra for a third time in the 1914 elections. As the leader of the reform movement in Basra, however, he had been in strong opposition to the government in 1913 and had come to dominate the administration of Basra "condemn[ing] the official government authorities to an absolute and shameful inactivity."[42]

A new set of circumstances in 1914 induced Talib to come to an understanding with İstanbul. Despite his effective leadership and the propaganda campaign emanating from Cairo, the reform movement had failed to produce unity in Iraq, in part due to religious (sectarian) and tribal differences. Arab officers in the region who looked to the reformist agenda with favor were in contact with Talib.[43] As part of Enver's reform in the army, therefore, officers stationed in Basra and al-Hillah, to the south of Baghdad, were either replaced or brought under closer supervision, while the number of troops stationed in the region was increased.[44] With the dissipation of the reform movement in Iraq, Talib sought to further his personal aspirations through different venues.

Prior to announcing his reconciliation with İstanbul, Talib sounded out British representatives in search of support for "the cause of Arab decentralization." Describing him as a "slippery customer," the Foreign Office denied assistance. In a printed declaration, Talib then pronounced his differences with İstanbul settled and pledged to promote Ottoman unity.[45] İstanbul proceeded to consolidate its position in the region by replacing, in the spring of 1914, the acting governor and commander İzzeddin Pasha, held responsible for the deterioration of government authority in the province, with Sulayman Shafiq Pasha. The new governor immediately embarked upon elaborate urban projects characteristic of attempts to solidify the authority of the central government.[46] Talib engaged in public manifestations of his support for the government. He conducted a campaign in Basra for donations to the Ottoman navy in addition to his personal generous contributions. He agreed to preside over a commission to bring about a settlement with Ibn Saʿud in al-Hasa district.[47] However, he never submitted to central authority and asserted his local stature by periodically engaging in demonstrations of force to settle local strife.[48]

In Arabia İstanbul favored improving relations with the other tribal notables in order to reduce Ibn Saʿud, suspected of seeking an alliance with Britain, to submission.[49] Ibn Rashid was further reinforced against Ibn Saʿud,[50] inducing the latter to seek to negotiate with the government through the mediation of Sayyid Talib.[51] Especially after the outbreak of war in Europe, the government renewed its efforts to befriend Arab tribal *shaykh*s, in competition with Britain, which aspired to expand its sphere of influence beyond the eastern fringes of the Peninsula. When it appeared that Ibn Saʿud was entering into closer relations with İstanbul,[52] Ambassador Mallet convinced London to seek "friendly relations" with Ibn Saʿud.[53] Cognizant of the need for the military support of the Najdi tribes in any war effort, İstanbul attempted the reconciliation of Ibn Rashid with Ibn Saʿud and formed a commission to achieve this.[54]

The French consul in Damascus remarked in March 1914 that the reentry of Enver's troops into Edirne the previous year, the executions in İstanbul, and the promise of reforms established the prestige of the caliph, the authority of the CUP administration, and the loyalty of the separatists.[55] Two months later the German ambassador reported to Berlin that the Arab movement had been dormant because of the concessions over the last year, adding that the leadership that could put it back in motion was missing.[56] On the whole, with the consolidation of the CUP government after the elections, dissidence among Arabs was either resolved, shelved, or went underground or abroad. Against this background, in the Hijaz relations between Sharif Husayn and the central government took a new turn.

The Hijaz on the Eve of War

On 15 January 1914 İstanbul appointed Vehib Pasha to the dual post of governor and commander of the forces in the Hijaz.[57] While the Unionists valued the services of Sharif Husayn in restoring relative order to the region and in furthering government influence in Arabia, the appointment of a high-ranking general to the combined post signified the intention of İstanbul to strengthen its direct authority in the Hijaz. This decision was motivated, on the one hand, by the revival of rumors of an alliance of Arabian tribal chiefs under an Arab caliph, and, on the other hand, by the intensifying competition between the Ottoman and British governments for the allegiance of local Arabian potentates.

The notion of an "Arab caliphate" had persisted not as a well-conceived program, which it never had become, but as an expression of defiance to the Ottoman government in view of its political instability and foreign complications. Rumors of a meeting of Arab leaders to discuss the issue of the Arab caliphate, that had circulated as early as the end of 1912, became rife at the beginning of 1914.[58] The scheme, which never came to fruition, had to do with the activities of a secret organization called *Al-jami'a al-'arabiyya* (Arab League) established by Rashid Rida in Cairo with the aim of creating "a union between the Arabian Peninsula and the Arab provinces of the Ottoman Empire."[59] Rida corresponded with Ibn Sa'ud and sent a representative, 'Izzat al-Jundi, to Imam Yahya and Idrisi.

The idea of an Arab caliphate and a conference among Arab chiefs (none of whom would wish to be left out of such a scheme) may have been encouraged by the British, who, in view of the impending German presence in the Persian Gulf by way of the Baghdad Railway, had intensified their efforts to bring Arabian chiefs to the British fold.[60] This British desire was best exemplified by the pressure that London exerted on the Ottoman government in 1913 to conclude an agreement that would extend British influence in Kuwait, Qatar, and Bahrain.[61] There were also renewed contacts between Sharif 'Abdullah and the British authorities in Egypt at the beginning of 1914.[62] According to Tauber,

Rashid Rida presented ʿAbdullah during the latter's stay in Cairo with a "programme for a pact among the rulers of the Arabian Peninsula" and proposed Sharif Husayn as the president of the council of the pact at meetings to be held in Mecca.[63]

In reference to Sharif Husayn's alleged contacts with the principal chiefs of Arabia, the French consul ascribed the strain between İstanbul and the emirate to the sharif's unsuccessful bid to have a third son, ʿAli, elected deputy in the 1914 elections. Medina, where Sharif ʿAli was alleged to have stood as candidate, was by 1914 under the irreversible direct control of İstanbul. The consul attributed the Ottoman government's more energetic policy in the Hijaz to Husayn's contacts with British agents in Egypt and suggested that a possible replacement of Husayn with Haydar was under consideration in İstanbul.[64]

Having resolved the reformist agitation in the Fertile Crescent, İstanbul could now turn to Arabia. Escalating neoimperialist rivalries around the Peninsula and the logic of centralist and Islamist policies warranted the new attention to the holy cities and beyond. The intention was not to revamp the established power relations, but rather to preserve them. The government's decision to appoint Vehib to his dual role was not meant to supersede the grand sharif's power but to remind him of the limits of his authority, though Vehib himself took a different view of the situation in the province of the Hijaz.

Upon his arrival in Mecca in January, Vehib set out to address the irregularities in the government of the Hijaz. At the same time, the sharif demonstrated his local authority by inciting tribes to insubordination. One of Vehib's first acts was to deprive the sharif's personal Beduin guards of the arms previously given to them by the government, prompting Husayn to issue a diatribe against the new governor. Judging by Husayn's communications with İstanbul, Vehib interfered in the illegal practice of slave owning[65] by trying to draft black slaves to the army[66] and censored postal communication between the Hijaz and the outside.[67] Husayn argued that the governor would obliterate his own efforts to maintain the peace and security in the province. He enumerated his many services to the government.[68] At the Ministry of the Interior Talat dismissed Husayn's remarks as impressionistic, emotional, and devoid of any specific and concrete grievances.[69] However, aware of the sharif's son's connections with the British, İstanbul wanted to preempt an agreement between Sharif Husayn and Britain.[70]

In March 1914 Vehib, doubtless upon the urging of İstanbul, drafted with the sharif a joint letter recommending the continuation of the status quo in the Hijaz. Grand Vizier Saʿid Halim's reply affirmed the status quo: the Medina-Mecca railway idea was abandoned; there would be no conscription in the Hijaz; and religious law would be in full effect in the courts, except in cases involving foreigners.[71] The British agent described the terms endorsed by the government as "compliance with all of Sharif Husayn's requests except the recall of the vali."[72] While a formal official pledge on these matters was symbolically significant for the sharif, it had little practical value. İstanbul had been at best ambivalent about any extension of the railway; conscription had been attempted by Vehib but already abandoned in the face of Beduin resistance; and the concession to religious law in the holy places had a political rationale from local, imperial, and international viewpoints.

Indeed, to the governor, the understanding with the sharif was as much a formal delimitation of prerogatives as a concession. It was followed by Vehib's unrelenting attack on misgovernment, arbitrary practices, and self-assumed privileges in the Hijaz. From April to August 1914 Vehib dispatched a string of reports to İstanbul to justify his conviction that the administration of the province should be revamped and the sharif be replaced. İstanbul closely monitored Vehib's reports, but consistently urged conciliation and the maintenance of the status quo.

The governor persistently and eloquently related to İstanbul what he perceived as the deliberate attempts of the sharif to diminish state authority by arrogating privileges to himself, by assuming ceremonial trappings, and by dispensing with patronage and justice to the discredit of government authority. According to the governor, the grand sharif used the military police assigned to the emirate for his personal affairs. Always eager to exploit state authority for his personal benefit, he made these soldiers collect the taxes that went to his own account. The governor saw a more insidious motive beyond this practice: by employing uniformed men for the much feared and hated task of tax collection, the sharif ensured popular hatred of state authority while filling his own pocket. Vehib recommended that either these men be stripped of their uniforms or taken away from the sharif.[73] He also pointed to Husayn's practice of registering large tracts of state land in his own name and dispensing some of it to others, contrary to all established laws and practices.[74]

Further, the governor attacked the sharif's ceremonial suite of attendants, who received government salaries even though they provided no worthwhile services.[75] Similarly, he regarded the emirate's jails (upon which the sharif had independent jurisdiction) with their arbitrary practices and wretched conditions as serving no other purpose than embarrassing the government, and in particular called for the demolition of the prison in Taif.[76] Vehib lamented the desolate condition of the tomb of Midhat Pasha in the same town and asked for the transfer of Midhat's tomb to İstanbul alongside the graves of the heroes of the revolution.[77]

The governor and the grand sharif disagreed over priorities and jurisdiction. Vehib took issue with the sharif's demand to accord top priority in construction projects to those related to the pilgrimage.[78] He wanted to reimpose the controversial sanitation tax, to which Husayn would consent only if the proceeds entered the emirate's treasury.[79] The governor accused Sharif Husayn of spreading slanderous rumors in order to have certain government officials removed in favor of his own men[80] and of inciting rebellious acts against government forces.[81]

İstanbul continued to respond to Vehib's reports by urging conciliation, advising that on matters such as the sharif's usurpation of state lands measures would be taken at the suitable time.[82] The Ministry of the Interior prevented Vehib from provoking the sharif when, for instance, it denied Vehib permission to make an investigative tour up the coast and returning along the eastern route through tribal regions where Husayn's authority was paramount.[83] The governor, however, continued to argue against the government's conciliatory policies, insisting that they would fail. Finally, in July 1914 he advised "for the sake of Ottomanism" that Sharif Husayn should be dismissed and replaced by his frail predecessor, 'Ali, for Husayn desired the downfall of the state.[84] Vehib urged that Husayn's two sons serving in Parliament should not be allowed to leave the capital. Both Vehib and the authorities in İstanbul were certainly aware of Sharif 'Abdullah's contacts in Cairo, if not their precise nature.[85] As İstanbul once again exhorted Vehib to get along with the sharif,[86] Vehib concluded that either he should be transferred to another post or Sharif Husayn be dismissed, as friendly relations with the sharif were no longer possible.[87] He added that he was convinced that Sharif Husayn would not forego the smallest opportunity to cooperate with the enemy should there be a hostile attack against the Red Sea coast.[88]

The Arab Provinces and the
Early Period of the War

Even though the Ottoman Empire did not formally enter the war until the beginning of November 1914, it had signed a secret treaty with Germany in August. This important decision was taken by a small group of Committee leaders and signified the beginning of the monopolization of political power by a narrow circle within the CUP. The CUP general assembly was dissolved following the outbreak of the war, enhancing the concentration of power in the hands of a small number of Committee leaders who constituted what amounted to a shadow cabinet.[89] The actual cabinet, itself dominated by the Committee, endorsed decisions that originated in the CUP Central Committee, which replaced legislative acts normally deliberated upon in Parliament. One result of this decision-making process was the considerable narrowing of the scope for the exercise of political influence by Arabs who had been given positions in Parliament and other high offices.

The impending entry of the empire into the war triggered a number of developments. In October the British administration in Egypt sounded out Sharif ʿAbdullah about his father's willingness to render support to the British, in case Turkey entered the war on the side of the Central Powers.[90] Some Arab leaders once again turned to the British and the French authorities contemplating a separate peace. The Decentralization Party in Cairo resolved to initiate a revolt against the government and received French and British pledges for assistance. Between the outbreak of war in Europe and Ottoman entry into it, members of the Decentralization Party (including Iskandar ʿAmmun and ʿAbd al-Ghani al-ʿUraysi) received the promise of "20,000 rifles, three warships to cover the rebels, and French officers to direct the action" as other members, Rashid Rida and Rafiq al-ʿAzm, negotiated conditions for cooperation with the British authorities and received 1,000 Egyptian pounds to send emissaries to the Ottoman Arab provinces to incite the revolt.[91] Pro-British leaders in Beirut broached to the British consul their desire for the extension of Egyptian rule to Syria. They separately drafted a petition addressed to Khedive Abbas II urging him to take on the leadership of an Arab government as a British dependency.[92]

Most Ottoman statesmen had desired a wartime alliance with the Western European powers. "Innumerable snubs"[93] by Britain and

France, however, forced the Ottoman government, which feared isolation, into an alliance with the Central Powers. With the conclusion of this alliance, geostrategic considerations left the Arab provinces most vulnerable to British naval incursions. Once Russia formally declared war on the Ottoman Empire at the beginning of November, Britain quickly proceeded to a two-pronged attack against Ottoman positions in the Arab districts to the north of the Red Sea and in the Persian Gulf.

In the tempest of the war, Britain was less interested in lasting political arrangements than in revolts that would tie down and undermine Ottoman military forces. Moreover, it intended to circumscribe rather than expand the role of the khedive. Thus, to the disappointment of the Decentralization Party, the British authorities refrained from a commitment to secure the independence of Arab areas outside of the Peninsula, and thus frustrated the initiative of the Decentralization Party.[94]

Gerald Fitzmaurice, formerly dragoman at Britain's İstanbul embassy, recommended reviving the Arab movement with British "prodding" from Kuwait or Baghdad, or with French provocation from coastal Syria. In Greater Syria support for Britain was uncertain. Baghdad, on the other hand, "since the majority Shia here have never been reconciled [to Ottoman rule]," offered opportunities.[95] As for the Hijaz, on the eve of the Ottoman entry into the war, it seemed to British authorities in Cairo "almost certain that the Sharif of Mecca [had] now definitively thrown in his lot with Turkey [as] part of a general pan-Islamic movement."[96] Fitzmaurice, too, argued that the Hijaz should be left outside the sphere of British activity.

Thus, no sooner had the Ottoman Empire entered the war than did the British establish contacts with ʿAziz ʿAli al-Misri in the hopes of inciting a rebellion within the disaffected Arab nucleus of the Ottoman army in Mesopotamia.[97] ʿAziz ʿAli, of Circassian ancestry and Egyptian background, had been a prominent officer in the Ottoman army until he fell out with Enver Pasha, with whom he had had a long-standing rivalry.[98] Like Enver and Mustafa Kemal (another officer with whom Enver had personal rivalries), ʿAziz ʿAli had distinguished himself in the Libyan War. Known as an Ottomanist partial to a federal Turco-Arab arrangement, ʿAli was a cultural Arab who, like Saʿid Halim and Mahmud Shawkat, had non-Arab ancestry. Unlike these two, however, he involved himself with secret Arab societies while continuing to perform distinguished service in the Ottoman army. Even as a cofounder of *Al-qahtaniyya* in 1909 and founder of *Al-ʿahd* in 1913, ʿAziz ʿAli remained an Ottomanist, as Majid Khadduri's revisionist study of his life and ca-

reer demonstrates. Because of his differences with Enver and the Ottoman government, he left İstanbul for his native Cairo in the spring of
1914. In August 1914 he had an audience with a British official in Cairo,
to whom he broached the idea of an Arab state under British tutelage.[99]
The British authorities, who did not entertain such a notion in August,
would reestablish contact with ʿAziz ʿAli after the Ottomans entered the
war. Torn between his conflicting loyalties and possessing an unrealistic
view of his influence among Arab leaders, ʿAziz ʿAli was not prepared
to be a pawn of the British and ultimately proved to be ill-suited for the
role that the British expected him to play in inciting Arabs to a rebellion.

In Basra Sayyid Talib renewed his bid for cooperation with Britain
when he perceived that the Ottoman government would enter the war
on the side of Germany. He wished to be recognized as the local ruler
(emir) of Basra under British protection, but he could obtain only eva-
sive answers to his plea, having apparently turned down prior overtures
for cooperation.[100] After the British forces occupied Basra in November,
London saw no need to come to an agreement with Talib, whose reli-
ability had remained suspect.

Upon entering the war, the Ottoman government took two measures
with significant implications for the Arab provinces. First, on 11 November the sultan-caliph declared a jihad against the Triple Entente. Second,
as the British forces occupied Basra, Cemal Pasha was sent to Damascus
as governor of Syria and commander of the Fourth Army while continuing to hold his portfolio as minister of the navy.

In order to secure allegiance to the state, the government continued
to resort to religious propaganda on the one hand and time-honored
tactics of enticement and alliances on the other. The call for jihad was
the culmination of the Islamic propaganda carried out by the Ottoman
government since 1913. In appraising the effectiveness of the jihad, later
historians have subscribed to the Entente's counterpropaganda aimed at
invalidating it: the call could not have had legitimacy, when the sultan
himself was in alliance with Christian powers. It has also been argued
that the Muslim subjects of the Entente powers did not incur the obli-
gation, or possess the ability, to engage in jihad by virtue of being in
subjugation.[101] It is clear, however, that the jihad was not meant to pit
the Muslims of the world against the Christian European powers, but
rather to achieve more limited aims consistent with and supported by
the ideological and political circumstances preceding it. It was, first of
all, designed to increase domestic support for the government's war effort, and, second, to provide an obstacle to the Entente's mobilization

campaign. As later events proved, both of these goals were achieved to a large extent.[102]

The holy places in the Hijaz became a center of propaganda by virtue of being reference points to which all Muslims could relate. Sharif Husayn's blessing in Mecca for the holy war would have been significant for its success. Yet the officially sponsored Islamist campaign also impinged on the traditional functions of the grand sharif, from which accrued his power and prestige. Thus, Husayn found himself under pressure to endorse and promote the jihad from the moment it was declared, but he refused to commit himself.

The few contacts that Husayn had with the British, and the few positive signals that he had received regarding cooperation, did not persuade him to throw in his lot with Britain. In contrast, cooperation with İstanbul had been proven useful in fulfilling his personal ambitions in the Hijaz. The initiation of the hostilities coincided with the pilgrimage season and cut the number of pilgrims by half compared to the previous year.[103] (The fact that Britain discouraged its Muslim subjects from traveling to Mecca was an important factor in this decline.) The region's economy, so dependent on the pilgrimage, suffered. The possibility that an İstanbul-sponsored call for jihad might find fertile ground in Arabia under these circumstances and steal the show from Husayn, if he failed to endorse it, deepened his apprehension.

Nevertheless, Husayn's adoption of the jihad would have presented equally problematic prospects. The call was intended to create trouble for Britain among the Muslim populations in the colonies. Ottoman entry into the war had rendered the Hijaz particularly vulnerable to British aggression. Britain blockaded the Red Sea ports, leading to food shortages. It then prepared to land supplies in those ports, posing to the populations as the saviors.[104] The endorsement of the jihad would have ruled out any maneuvers to mitigate British reprisals against the Hijaz. Even worse for the sharif, the Red Sea coast was the most exposed region of imperial territories, while Ottoman commitment and ability to defend it was precarious. Finally, an alliance with the British might have offered new and enhanced opportunities to Husayn for aggrandizing his power in Arabia.

Thus, the declaration of jihad further complicated the careful balancing act that the sharif had been practicing all along in order to maintain his political position and power within the broader interests of the Ottoman state. While his energy was now primarily directed toward buying time, the sharif also tried to blunt the cutting edge of the new factor of jihad. He made a special effort to display to the faithful that İstanbul had no monopoly over commanding religious sensibilities. He declared a war on *bid'a* (innovation), a concept frowned upon in orthodox Islam, even expressing disapproval of trappings of contemporary urban life, from European-style women's shoes to the telephone and automobile,[105] all the while resorting to delaying tactics that would enable him to sit on the fence and to use noncommitment to his advantage. In December 1914 he told a British agent that "because of his position in the world of Islam and present political situation in the Hidjaz he could not break with the Turks immediately and that he was awaiting a colorable pretext."[106] Even German envoys, who must have been cognizant of these contacts, concluded that the sharif appeared to have been won over by Britain. His signals to Britain, indeed his later negotiations, comprised only one side of the waiting game that he played.

Sharif Husayn continued to be in contact with İstanbul as well as with Cemal Pasha after the latter took office as commander of the Fourth Army in Damascus in December 1914 and prepared for the first of the two ill-fated expeditions against the Suez Canal. Cemal wanted to mobilize the army units in the Hijaz for the canal expedition and insisted on this despite Talat's reservations. Any troop movements that would remove Vehib, governor as well as commander of forces in the Hijaz, from Mecca was welcome to Husayn. To encourage the participation of the Hijazi army units in the war, the sharif also expressed his own willingness to contribute a Beduin force to the expedition. Cemal actively sought the sharif's participation in command of his Beduin forces. This would not only have given a shot in the arm to the Egyptian campaign, but also it would have been tantamount to Husayn's endorsement of the jihad. Cemal had organized the expedition as a contrived manifestation of Ottoman-Islamic unity, with the participation of separate units of 200 to 300 troops each from the Druze (led by Shakib Arslan), the Kurds (led by senator 'Abd al-Rahman al-Yusuf), the Circassians, Libyan resistance fighters, and Bulgarian Muslims in a military force named *Halaskâr Mısır Ordu-yu İslamiyesi* (The Savior Islamic Army of Egypt).[107] The sharif subsequently bowed out, though he continued to uphold his pledge to dispatch units under the command of his son 'Ali.

The denouement of the rift between the sharif and the government, we are told, followed from events during the joint movement of Vehib's forces and 'Ali's contingent from Mecca to Medina. One of 'Ali's men reportedly discovered documents that spilled from a case belonging to

a member of Vehib's escort. The documents revealed plans between Vehib and İstanbul "to depose Husayn and his family and to end the special
position of the Hijaz."[108] When the disclosure was communicated to
Husayn, he lost all hope of conciliation with İstanbul and not only
ordered ʿAli to stay put in Medina but also charged his other son, Faysal,
to travel to the capital, ostensibly in order to make representations about
the revelations but in fact to contact nationalists in Syria.[109] While in
Syria, Faysal also served as the conduit between his father and Cemal.
If this chance incident in fact occurred, it is unlikely that the documents
obtained by ʿAli's men would have constituted such apocalyptical revelations, as the sharif no doubt knew full well the governor's feelings
about his emirate. If the cache containing communications with İstanbul
provided unmistakable proof for such, it may also have well contained
some evidence of the constant temperance and amicable relations that
İstanbul had urged to Vehib.

Following Ottoman defeat in the Sinai, the Entente powers engaged
in deliberations to determine the political future of the Ottoman territories after the expected collapse of the Ottoman state. The Constantinople Agreement concluded in April 1915, based on diplomatic correspondence by Russia, Britain, and France, called for the establishment
of independent Arab rule in Arabia.[110] This agreement provided the basis
for the secret correspondence that took place between the British high
commissioner in Egypt, Sir Henry McMahon, and Sharif Husayn between July 1915 and January 1916. Deceptive and controversial as the
terms offered to Sharif Husayn were, the McMahon-Husayn exchange
resulted in an alliance of the sharif and Britain against the Ottoman
government.

The Sharif Husayn–İstanbul Correspondence

It is customary to start the historical account of twentieth-
century, or "contemporary," Middle East with three seminal, yet out of
the ordinary, covenants: the agreement between Sharif Husayn and Mc-
Mahon, which pledged a large independent Arab entity to the Hashemite family; the Sykes-Picot Treaty of May 1916, which contravened
the first pledge and partitioned the Arab Middle East between Britain
and France; and the Balfour Declaration of November 1917, which
promised a Jewish national homeland in Palestine and spawned the
Arab-Zionist conflict. In the midst of the historical narratives that focus

on these agreements and their consequences, and, indeed, even on their precedents, Ottoman history tends to vanish.

At least the first of these agreements came as a result of a drawn-out correspondence in the second half of 1915, the backdrop to which was an even more protracted exchange between Sharif Husayn and Ottoman authorities that has been overlooked. An analysis of the correspondence between Sharif Husayn and İstanbul will posit the Ottoman government as well as Sharif Husayn as actors who sought out their options and best interests, and not as merely passive victims of Great Power intrigue.

The underlying tenor of the contacts between the sharif and İstanbul was suspicion, as the two sides engaged in a standoff. The interchange of telegrams and letters, however, revealed more than hollow pleasantry, cautious standstill, or guile. Both sides explored options in the midst of which novel policy initiatives took shape.

During the critical month of February 1915—as Cemal moved to the Suez, hostilities started in Gallipoli, and emergency measures forced the adjournment of Parliament[111]—Husayn assured Enver Pasha, now deputy commander-in-chief, that he would protect the rights of the caliphate in the holy places, as long as attacks on his position and person were not tolerated.[112] At this juncture, the bulk of the Ottoman forces in the Hijaz had been moved to the Suez. More important, their commander, Vehib, was recalled, soon to take command of the Third Army on the Eastern front. Even as Cemal Pasha urged İstanbul for the appointment of a farsighted and strong new governor in the Hijaz,[113] the implications of Vehib's transfer did not escape either side.

Events during the spring of 1915 did little to alleviate the sharif's dilemma about his stance vis-à-vis İstanbul. With Vehib and a large portion of the forces that had been under his command having left in different directions, Husayn was more exposed to the British presence in the Red Sea. Whether he chose to cooperate with the British or not, it made sense for him to augment his personal forces. He proceeded to order the levying of armed Beduin from designated tribes.[114]

Meanwhile, the British confined their naval activity and attacks to the northern coast near Medina and al-Wejh.[115] The *muhafiz* of Medina sent a unit of soldiers mounted on camels against the British, pleading to İstanbul at the same time for timely payment of stipends and sufficient food for the men and the animals. Cemal Pasha decided to transfer by train up to ten carloads of food from Damascus to Medina in order to preclude dangerous shortages in the Hijaz, the links of the province via the sea having been cut.[116] Considering that Syria was afflicted by similar food shortages (soon to become a full-fledged famine), the dispatch of food from Damascus pointed to the importance Cemal attached to keeping the enemy pressure off of the Hijaz and thus maintaining Sharif Husayn in the Ottoman camp.

At the end of May Sharif Faysal visited Cemal Pasha at the army headquarters before returning from Syria to the Hijaz. He declared his family's readiness to shed its blood for the Ottoman caliphate and promised to come back with a force of Beduin fighters in two months.[117] Six weeks later, on 10 July, Sharif Husayn gave similar assurances. In reference to the jihad, he stated that he had not attempted to relieve himself of service to the holy war, but urged that his actions in the Hijaz demanded caution and prudence.[118] He requested arms and money from the government. At exactly the same time, on 14 July, he commenced the infamous correspondence with McMahon.[119]

Enver thanked Sharif Husayn for his determination to achieve unity of purpose and wrote, "So long as all Muslims act as one body against the enemy, divine victory will always be with us." He added that 5,000 liras had been dispatched and the requested arms were being prepared.[120] A few days later Enver Pasha wrote a letter to Sharif Husayn on the matter of organizing an Islamic society (*Cemiyet-i İslamiye*), presumably to advance Islamic propaganda in Arabia.[121] Sharif Husayn's response to this letter reveals more than a passing interest in the initiative. Cautious because of his relations with the British, he proposed the formation of either a highly secret committee of six or the use of the cover provided by a benevolent society that would operate under the name of *Cemiyet-i Umumiye* (Public Society). Enver asked Husayn to proceed with the second option, as long as the true objective of the society would remain secret.[122]

Syria under Cemal Pasha's Governorship

Cemal Pasha's appointment to Syria came with full powers in military and civilian affairs. A provisional law granted him emergency powers in May 1915, such that all cabinet decrees that pertained to Syria became subject to his approval.[123] His draconian rule following the defeat in February 1915 at the Suez Canal,[124] coupled with the wartime exigencies and natural disasters that afflicted the region during these years, alienated the population from the Ottoman government.

In the spring of 1915, Cemal instituted a reign of terror in Syria against Arab opponents. After the severance of relations with France, Ottoman authorities had occupied the French consulates in Beirut and Damascus and confiscated documents that revealed evidence about subversive activities of these opponents. Cemal's clampdown was based on information deriving from these documents as well as from others belonging to the Decentralization Party, which had been turned over to the Ottoman authorities by a former member, Muhammad al-Shanti.[125] Historians such as George Antonius and Sulayman Mousa have argued that the crackdown on the Arabists was motivated by Cemal's humiliation in the Egyptian campaign. "Failing in his attempt," Mousa writes, "he returned to Damascus and began to seek a pretext for his failure. It dawned upon him that his best chance lay in levelling accusations against Arab political and cultural leaders."[126] The public hanging of a Francophile Maronite priest for treason was followed by trials at the military court in 'Aleyh (Âliye Divan-ı Harb-i Örfisi). Eleven Beiruti leaders, ten of them Muslims, were executed on 21 August 1915 in the town square.[127]

The massive reign of terror was consistent with the measures Cemal had taken in his previous emergency posts in Baghdad and Istanbul. Cemal applied himself to reprisals against local leaders and former opponents as soon as he arrived in Syria by utilizing incriminating evidence that had been obtained from the French records and the papers of the Decentralization Party. Though most of the evidence pertained to activities prior to the reconciliation with the Arab leaders, the reprisals had little to do with the humiliation at Suez. Before the Egyptian expedition, and a few weeks after he arrived in Damascus, Cemal reported to the Ministry of the Interior that the vice-president of the council of inspectors, 'Abd al-Wahhab al-Inkilizi, had been determined to be a member of a society aiming at the establishment of an Arab state. Cemal asked that al-Inkilizi should be sent to Syria for trial and denied contact with anyone. At the same time, he had Shukri al-'Asali, inspector in Aleppo, arrested and sent to Damascus.[128] Both men were executed in a second round of hangings in May 1916.

A second component of the terror involved deportations. Under Cemal's orders numerous Syrian families (5,000, according to one contemporary account[129]) were deported to Anatolia. One of the earlier and better-known deportees was Nakhla Mutran, whose brother, Rashid Mutran, had created much commotion with the autonomist manifesto disseminated from Paris in 1909. The confiscated documents revealed that he had approached the French authorities in 1913 with a plan for the territorial expansion of the *mutasarrıflık* of Mount Lebanon under French auspices. While being deported, he was killed under suspicious circumstances.[130] Most deportees had not been politically active or influential. Many had done no more than sign pro-French petitions during the reform movement.[131]

Cemal's was more than an overreaction to sensational revelations, most of them now obsolete and not of a nature to justify retroactive legal action. The reprisals constituted yet another phase of his persecution of the CUP's opponents. But the revelations also convinced Cemal that a nationalist movement in Syria was a real, if not an imminent, threat, notwithstanding his characterization of the matter as "one of treachery, not nationality."[132] He did his utmost to destroy it by eliminating potential supporters, thereby leaving the movement without direction and causing such dislocations in Syrian society as to eliminate the chance for success of any future movement.

Cemal's actions in Syria were comparable in nature, if not in extent, to those policies pursued with respect to the Armenians in Eastern Anatolia. Both emanated from a fear that a nationalist uprising would come into being with encouragement from enemy powers. The threat was more perceived than real. The relocation of Arabs, only a fraction compared to that of Armenians, took place in relatively more humane circumstances.[133] But the dislocation of a large group of well-to-do Syrians put an added strain on social and economic life in wartime Syria. The psychological effect of these deportations was perhaps more significant, giving reason to the Syrians to believe that they might share a fate similar to that of the Armenians.[134] As the Armenians were resettled among them, their own people were forced out of their country.

Cemal implemented measures contrary to the promises made to the Arabs about the local employment of Arab civilian and military personnel and about giving wider scope to the Arabic language. He removed Arab troops to distant theaters of war. In the spring of 1916 Cemal proceeded to enforce widespread use of Turkish in public life as an extrapolation of a new law promulgated in March 1916 that required all companies to use Turkish in their correspondence and documents.[135] Turkish came back as the language of instruction in the Damascus *sultaniye* (high school),[136] suggesting that Arabic had been made the language of instruction in this school earlier. As the Austrian envoy in Beirut enumerated the practical and psychological problems associated with the imposition of Turkish in new spheres, the German consul urged Cemal Pasha to adopt a more constructive policy with respect to the Arabs, the ultimate purpose being the creation of a *Kulturstaat* on the Austro-Hungarian model.[137]

Cemal's independent attitude in Syria triggered a flurry of diplomatic exchanges between the Entente countries toward the end of 1915. This pertained to rumors about a possible coup by Cemal against the İstanbul government, with an eye to establishing himself as the ruler of Anatolia and Syria. The correspondence was about whether, how, and under what conditions this alleged scheme should be abetted, but the matter was dropped at the beginning of 1916.

If one subscribes to the often held view that real political power rested in the CUP in the hands of a "triumvirate" composed of Talat, Enver, and Cemal, one will find it easier to ascribe individual conspiratorial designs to them. It seems, however, that during the war years the policies that the three men pursued in their ministerial capacity were to a large extent determined by the collective will of several Unionist strongmen, many of them behind the scenes. There were factions within the broader CUP leadership, as there were differences between Talat, Enver, and Cemal. If a certain faction or individual vied for greater power, the others imposed checks such that there was hardly ever a basis for independent action, even with outside assistance.[138] Therefore, it is doubtful that Cemal Pasha actually considered a coup as a realistic option, even though it may have appeared as a possibility to the Entente and its sympathizers.

Against the background of the energetic diplomatic exchange in the Entente camp regarding the idea of cooperation with him, Cemal undertook, together with Enver and the *müftü*s of some of the chief Arab towns, a much-celebrated trip to Medina. By all accounts, the visit to Prophet Muhammad's tomb was a cathartic spiritual experience for the two men, especially Enver, who was overwhelmed by emotion and burst into tears by the grave.[139] First and foremost, however, it was part of a broader effort to strengthen the government's position in the Arab districts. Dismayed by the drastic decrease in the number of pilgrims since the beginning of the war, and attempting to keep the war outside their territory, the tribes of northern Hijaz had obstructed the passage of fresh troops and the new governor, Galib Pasha, south of Medina.[140] In Beirut the execution of the eleven leaders in August 1915 had caused panic and animosity toward the government. In the Damascus province problems associated with the food supply were causing serious shortages and demonstrations.[141]

The two leaders' trip to Medina was followed by attempts to strengthen the government's position through military reinforcements and propaganda. The Arabic language newspaper *Al-sharq* was initiated as the mouthpiece of government propaganda. On 6 May 1916 Cemal Pasha decided to employ further terror to enhance government authority, and the second group of Arab leaders, including well-known personalities of the Reform Movement who had later made their peace with the government and had accepted positions in İstanbul and elsewhere, was tried in the spring of 1916. In addition to al-Inkilizi and al-'Asali, the twenty-one leaders sentenced to death in May also included 'Abd al-Hamid al-Zahrawi, Shafiq al-Mu'ayyad, and 'Abd al-Ghani al-'Uraysi.[142] The executions signified in the eyes of the Syrians the government's resolve to revoke whatever concessions that it had agreed to give to the Arabs. Cemal's actions may have expedited the revolt in the Hijaz.

The Arab Uprising and İstanbul's Response

In early June 1916 Sharif Husayn and his sons rose in arms and attacked Ottoman positions in Mecca. Husayn issued a justificatory declaration on 27 June 1916, in which he cited his past services to the government, including campaigns against other Arab chiefs; condemned secular legal reforms; decried the CUP's curtailment of the sultan's rights; and denounced the executions in Syria.[143] The reaction of the Ottoman government to the events in the Hijaz was guarded and low-key. No mention of the revolt was allowed to appear in the press until a whole month after the uprising.[144] Whether or not İstanbul knew about the exact scope of the alliance between Sharif Husayn and Britain, the government continued to harbor the hope of undermining Husayn's position and containing the uprising with minimum damage.

In view of the sharif's repeated military successes, however, İstanbul engaged in an intensive propaganda effort in the Arab districts to discredit him. Sharif Haydar, whom the government proclaimed the new and legitimate emir, took office in Medina in August and issued his first counterproclamation that denounced Sharif Husayn.[145]

The outbreak of Husayn's revolt had serious implications both from the domestic point of view and for the progress of the war. The İstanbul government's reaction was to concentrate its propaganda effort in the Arab districts while elsewhere depicting the revolt as just another Beduin uprising. Alarm about the revolt would have been detrimental to morale on the war fronts. The Ottoman government also failed to provide its allies with full information about the progress of events,[146] even though prior to the revolt there had been an initiative to establish a propaganda center in Arabia by the Germans.[147] Germany was able to help little, if at all, in the military operations in this sacred terrain. The active involvement of a Christian power on the side of the government in the Hijaz would have done more harm than good. Sharif Haydar's proclamations reinvoked the call for jihad. They asserted that Husayn acted out of disloyalty and found the courage to challenge the caliph only because he had made common cause with Britain, a strong European power which, unlike Germany, wanted to grab the holy places, as it had Egypt and Zanzibar. Haydar's manifestos were meant for the broader Arab and Muslim public.

The government authorities in Damascus called the leading ulema to a meeting and enjoined them to pass judgment on Sharif Husayn's actions in the form of a formal religious decree (*fetva*), which posed the question, "What befits a person who has been heaped with the goodwill of the Caliph and who has been elevated to the highest of honors, when that person betrays the Caliph by joining the latter's enemy?" The answer was, "Deposition and death." Thus was the death sentence passed upon Husayn by the Arab ulema.[148] At the end of September the *müftü*s of the Syrian and Palestinian towns jointly signed another *fetva* urging opposition to Sharif Husayn.[149] Most Arabs outside of the Hijaz remained ambivalent, if not hostile, to the revolt. Cemal's violence shortly before and after the outbreak of the revolt deterred Syrians sympathetic to the sharif from rising against the government.[150] When in Tripoli (Syria) a faction emerged in open support of Husayn's revolt, several of its members were executed, as the local CUP delegate procured a decree from the local ulema in justification of Husayn's execution.[151]

The systematic campaign in Damascus to counteract the Hijaz uprising contrasted with the silence in İstanbul, where the sultan's opening speech to the reconvened Parliament in November 1916 and the customary reply of the deputies condemned Husayn's disloyalty with merely a few words.[152] In Damascus any sympathies for the uprising had to be defused. The German consul reported during the early stages of the Hijaz revolt that, even though Husayn was viewed as a traitor by the local population, many seemed to be happy that a representative of the Arabs was challenging Turkish authority.[153] The town was also the main meeting place of pilgrims before their journey to the Hijaz. Damascus rather than İstanbul was, therefore, made the center for press propaganda and the government's organ *Al-sharq* was printed there.[154]

While the motives of Sharif Husayn were to strengthen his power in the Hijaz and aggrandize it at the expense of other potentates in the Peninsula,[155] his rhetoric was anti-Turkish and increasingly stressed Arab unity and independence. In November Husayn declared himself "King of the Arab countries." Regardless of whether independence was a political goal shared by most Arabs, it did not escape the Ottoman government that the expression of these goals could become subversive, particularly in conjunction with British war propaganda. Britain, though, was the first to take issue with the new title because of its commitments to France and, as it became painfully clear to the Arabs after the war, its political designs in the region.

Cemal's execution of Arab leaders (both those who had entered into a compromise with the government and those who remained defiant of the regime) radicalized the Arab officers in the Ottoman army, who emerged as the main group seeking to further nationalist objectives. Many defected to Sharif Husayn's side and offered important assistance to the Anglo-sharifian effort. Yet, not only did Arab officers remain divided into progovernment and pro-independence groups but also some of those who did side with Sharif Husayn, including ʿAziz ʿAli, were not willing to exert their efforts for an eventual separation from the Ottoman state. ʿAziz ʿAli joined Husayn's camp briefly, but defected when faced with the prospect of attacking Ottoman positions in Medina.[156]

Government propaganda was aimed at preventing the revolt from spreading beyond the Peninsula, but the news of Husayn's victories won him supporters to the north. Three prominent Arab leaders residing in Egypt (and previously condemned to death by the ʿAleyh court), ʿIzzat Pasha al-ʿAbid, Rafiq al-ʿAzm, and Rashid Rida, went to the Hijaz to perform the pilgrimage and to show solidarity with Husayn. Some pro-British decentralist opponents of the CUP who had been forced to leave the empire to settle in Europe also declared their support for Sharif Husayn.[157] French authorities in Algeria, Morocco, and Tunisia sent delegations of Arab notables to Mecca.[158]

Following Husayn's assumption of the title of king of the Hijaz in the fall of 1916, the court martial in Damascus brought to trial Syrian leaders suspected of collusion with Husayn. Charges were also brought against the sons of Husayn, the Nasib and Fawzi al-Bakri brothers (who had hosted Sharif Faysal during his stay in Damascus but left the town at the outbreak of the revolt), Tawfiq Halabi (editor of the Damascus paper *Al-ra'y*), Faris Khury (the Christian deputy from Damascus, a lawyer and formerly dragoman of the British Consulate), and two Arab brigadier generals previously pensioned off, Shukri Pasha al-Ayyubi and 'Abd al-Hamid Pasha (al-Qaltaqji). The preacher of the Umayyad Mosque, Shaykh 'Abd al-Qadir Kiwan, was also implicated. Kiwan and Shukri Pasha al-Ayyubi were sentenced to death. The same verdict was passed in absentia on many of the others, including Faysal, 'Abdullah, and the Bakri brothers.[159]

After the outbreak of the revolt there was a renewed interest in conciliation with the Arabs both in İstanbul and also in Damascus. The continuation of hostilities in the Hijaz gave the Syrians a respite from the iron rule of Cemal.[160] But hardship continued in Syria, particularly in the provisioning of food. The harvest was poor, the war further disrupted production, the army requisitioned some of the crop, and, most important, Britain and France blockaded the Syrian coast to prevent imports.[161] Cemal's attempts to control the food production met with failure. Arab notables, who were given concessions to buy the harvest for the government using devalued banknotes, confronted resistance and failed in their endeavor.[162] Food products remained out of the reach of most people due to transportation problems arising from the requisitioning or ruination of draft animals and the shortage of coal.[163] The shortages and ensuing starvation were not so much the result of confiscation and government requisitioning of available crops as of speculation, transportation difficulties, and lack of organizational skills and infrastructural resources necessary for distribution.[164] Similar problems afflicted other regions of the empire. According to French reports, in İzmir and environs, which were situated in perhaps the richest plain of the Asiatic Ottoman lands, some 200 persons lost their lives daily.[165] Between 1913 and 1919 close to 90 percent of all oxen in the country perished.[166] Human loss and suffering was heaviest in Syria because of the unrelenting blockade of the coast by the Entente.

In Damascus the expenditures that Cemal devoted to public works, urban improvements, and preservation of historical works[167] contrasted with the prevalent famine and squandered matériel, money, and expertise that could have been used in the war effort.[168] These measures may be seen as part of the government's broader attempt to assert Ottoman central authority and to improve the infrastructure and public institutions in the Arab cities.[169] Cemal had imposing avenues built in Jaffa and Damascus. He had pursued similar schemes during his governorship in Baghdad in 1912, when he had commissioned a team of German engineers to implement construction projects including the widening and paving of streets.[170] But there was, of course, an element of self-aggrandizement in these projects. Particularly in Syria, Cemal cultivated the sycophancy of his entourage and had compiled laudatory poetry.

In the spring of 1917 the new Ottoman government under Talat adopted an unmistakable policy of rapprochement and conciliation toward the Arabs. The regime was convinced, reported the German Embassy to Berlin, that the retention of the Arab territories was imperative if the Ottoman Empire was to remain a "great power," but whether Cemal could be entrusted with such a policy in Syria was doubtful. Rumors were rife that Cemal was preparing to leave the governorship of Syria.[171] In December he tendered his resignation and returned to his ministry.

War, Politics, and Ideology

A cabinet change occurred in İstanbul during the second month of 1917. Sa'id Halim, who had already relinquished his foreign ministry portfolio in October 1915, resigned his post as grand vizier. He was replaced by Talat Pasha, the first Turkish Unionist insider to occupy the office of the grand vizier.

Sa'id Halim, a Unionist since the days preceding the 1908 Revolution, had been the Committee's choice for the grand vizierate in 1913, not only because his princely background would impart weight and credibility to the Young Turk regime at home and abroad, but also because he embodied what had come to be the predominant ideological direction of the Ottoman state on the eve of the war. A political outcast from the khedivial family, he represented the opposition to imperial designs in Muslim territories. He had been born in Egypt and brought up and educated in Cairo and İstanbul, and thus was a Young Turk eminently suited to lead the Turco-Arab state that the Ottoman Empire had come to be. Finally, as a strong adherent of Islamic traditions and values in a modernist framework, he represented the greater emphasis placed on Islam in the political ideology of the Ottoman state. Sa'id

Halim has been viewed as merely a puppet of the Committee of Union and Progress. That he could be manipulated by the Committee is not inaccurate. It is more appropriate, however, to compare him to personalities such as Said Pasha and Mahmud Shawkat Pasha, who were brought to power to achieve certain goals that the Committee could not attain by relying on its mainstream cadres. Saʿid Halim Pasha was an influential thinker and author of Islamic modernist ideas. He was maintained in office, allegedly according to Talat, "in deference to public opinion."[172]

As the war progressed Saʿid Halim's influence waned. He was believed to have given Sharif Husayn the benefit of the doubt for too long for the sake of Islamic unity and thus of jeopardizing this unity. The spread of the Arab Revolt diminished his usefulness as a leader. Indeed, his resignation from the Ministry of Foreign Affairs as early as the end of 1915 had cut him off from decisions determining the conduct of war and reduced his power.[173]

Talat's grand vizierate did not signify a break with the policies that had taken shape after the Balkan Wars. It is possible to view his appointment as the culmination of the CUP's consolidation of power. However, his tenure belied the widespread view that the further reinforcement of the CUP's position would be synonymous with greater Turkish domination of the body politic, an enhanced dependence on Germany, and an increased authoritarianism. Talat emerged as a compromise candidate, but not necessarily a second-rate one, from a group of strong political personalities, including Enver and Cemal. In his capacity as the minister of the interior, Talat had been most influential in the conduct of policy and had been described in 1914 by the German consul in Haifa as the "most pro-Arab of a multiheaded Young Turk hierarchy."[174]

The choice of Talat represented a strengthening of that faction within the CUP that favored a certain independence from Germany.[175] Consideration for the grand vizierate had also been given to Halil [Menteşe], who had taken over the Ministry of Foreign Affairs from Saʿid Halim Pasha. He was known for his pro-German views and was supported by the German embassy. In the new cabinet Halil, Enver, and Midhat Şükrü were strongly pro-German, while Cavid, Ahmed Nesimi, and Talat were more moderate in their views. As the United States ambassador Elkus reported, however, "apparent divergence of views [did] not prevent these two parties from working harmoniously in the same cabinet under the orders of the [CUP]."[176] One of Talat's early pronouncements emphasizing the constitutional rights of all Ottomans was interpreted by

Elkus as "a prelude to disavowing some of the responsibility for the treatment of Armenians, Arabs, etc."[177] Cavid accepted the position of finance minister in the new cabinet on condition that changes were to be effected in "the policy hitherto followed with respect to the non-Turkish races."[178]

The reshuffling in İstanbul and international developments accompanied a more favorable phase in İstanbul's relations with the Arab provinces in the last year and a half of the war, in spite of the weakening of the Islamist agenda after the replacement of Sa'id Halim.[179] The withdrawal of Russia from the war and the conclusion of peace on the eastern front raised the hopes of Ottomanists, both Arab and Turkish. The Ottoman government made fresh overtures to Sharif Husayn as Russian revelations of the terms of the Sykes-Picot Treaty offered new possibilities. Even as the British and sharifian armies pushed north and Ottoman positions in and near major Arab towns fell like dominoes, Sharif Faysal negotiated with Cemal Pasha and Mustafa Kemal, the victorious commander of Ottoman forces in Gallipoli, now serving as commander of the Seventh Army in Syria.[180]

The End of the Empire and Turkish-Arab Relations

With the occupation of Damascus and the rest of Syria by the Anglo-Arab forces in October 1918 and the Ottoman surrender at the Mudros cease-fire at the end of that month, it became clear that the İstanbul government had lost its hold on the Arab provinces. What was less certain was the future of the Arab regions. Ottoman armies withdrew, exposing differences among former allied powers, among the various Arab factions, as well as between the Arabs and Britain and France.

In İstanbul the Talat Pasha government resigned on 8 October. The new cabinet under Ahmed İzzet Pasha pledged to settle the question of the Arab provinces in accordance with the "national will" of the Arabs. The proposal to maintain these provinces within the empire by granting internal autonomy was received by the Arab deputies with cheers. Turkish and Arab deputies referred to the religious bonds that united the two groups.[181] British proposals for a cease-fire in October 1918 suggested the establishment of autonomous Arab governments under the sultan's sovereignty.[182]

Awareness of the difficulties that hindered the realization of Arab sovereignty was conducive in Syria to a predisposition in favor of an alliance with the Turks against European ambitions. Ottoman subjects in Europe considered initiatives for Turco-Arab cooperation. Ottomanist Arabs like Shakib Arslan pointed to the need for political unity under the Ottoman dynasty in view of the foreign menace and urged all parties to forget past differences and to seek a reunion with wide autonomy for Arabs and Kurds in line with Wilsonian principles.[183]

In May 1919 the Greeks landed troops in Anatolia, triggering an active defense movement to the Allied occupation organized by Mustafa Kemal. In the early stages of this resistance the territorial objectives of the Kemalist movement were not clearly defined, and the general goal was to free as much of the former Ottoman possessions as possible from foreign occupation. Any active resistance in Syria against the French was seen as an asset to the struggle in Anatolia.

In the fall of 1919 there were preparations for a joint Arab-Turkish resistance against the French in northern Syria as a result of the coalescing of various irregular troops throughout the region.[184] Resentment over the withdrawal of British forces to make way for a French takeover strengthened in both Damascus and Aleppo the inclination toward an alliance with the Anatolian resistance. The Nationalist government set up in Damascus during the peace talks established links with the Turkish resistance movement.[185] Negotiations between Anatolians and Syrians took place for joint action and the setting up of a binational state, even though Faysal remained ambivalent about this initiative.[186] The American consul in Beirut reported that the British authorities fear "that the Arabs may consider the British and Americans have failed them, and not being willing to accept French sphere of influence, may consequently decide to accept preferred support of Mustafa Kamel [sic], which might bring about a serious pan-Islam movement."[187]

While the idea of cooperating with the Anatolian resistance found more and more proponents in Damascus and Aleppo because of fear of French occupation, the impending carving up of Greater Syria and the granting of a "national home" to the Zionists produced the same kind of response in Palestine. The Supreme Committee of Palestinian Assemblies wrote to the American representative in Jerusalem:

Turkey which was supposed to be the greatest enemy working for the dismemberment of the Arab nation, a weak people, did not prove to be so
tyrannical as to sentence us to this slow death. How then could our friends
the Allies who acknowledge that the Arabs contributed to their victory in
the Near East allow such a sentence to be passed on us?

If we rose up against Turkey it was only for asserting our rights and had
we only foreseen that our alliance was to lead to this partition of our country
and to this colonization thereof we would not have declared our animosity
to the Turks.[188]

At the end of 1919 the Anatolian resistance to Allied occupation had
not crystallized as a Turkish nationalist movement, even though the two
congresses held by resistance groups in eastern Anatolia had prepared
the groundwork of the National Pact (*Misak-ı Milli*). The National Pact
has come to be recognized as the manifesto of the Turkish nationalist
movement since its formal adoption by the Ottoman Parliament in February 1920 (and thus triggering its dissolution the next month) and by
the newly established Grand National Assembly of Turkey in 1921. The
first clause of the Pact as enunciated in Parliament referred to the right
of self-determination of Arabs of Ottoman territories under foreign occupation. It did not posit a clear articulation of a Turkish homeland,[189]
thus leaving the door open for the expression of the Arab will in favor
of cooperation with the Anatolian movement.[190] It was hardly a coin-
cidence that Celal Nuri's *İttihad-ı İslam*, that had been published in 1913
to urge Turco-Arab unity against European imperialism, was translated
into Arabic in 1920, under the title of *Ittihad al-muslimin* (Unity of
Muslims).[191] Particularly after the French occupation of Syria, the Iraqi
nationalists, too, became favorably disposed toward collaboration with
the Anatolians.[192]

Cooperation with Arabs was consistent with the anti-imperialist
objectives of the Anatolian movement. Yet in view of an increasingly
bitter conflict about the fate of Syria and Iraq in international forums,
embroiling European, Arab, and Zionist delegations in a host of conflicting claims, the Kemalists extricated themselves from these con-
troversies over Arab-populated territories. Instead, they devoted their
energies to Anatolia, laying the foundations of a Turkish nation-state.
As late as the end of 1922 some Palestinian Arab leaders appealed to
the Kemalists to seek a Turkish mandate under which they could
achieve self-determination.[193] The frustration of Arab expectations of
independence led to feelings of nostalgia for the empire or hopes for
a more active cooperation with the Turks against imperialism. How-

ever, the emergent nationalist leadership in the Turkish regions heeded *Realpolitik* and devoted its attention to delivering Anatolia. It prepared to renounce irredentist ambitions and to work out the necessary arrangements with the imperialist powers to achieve the limited aim.

The Arab Revolt had an impact on İstanbul in two opposing ways. On the one hand, it led to the belief that it was futile to struggle to preserve the multinational empire. On the other, it prompted the adoption of modern propaganda methods consistent with traditional religious values to prevent the revolt from spreading. The attacks and counterattacks between the sharif and the government were intended to appeal to the religious sensibilities of the Ottomans and all other Muslims. While the defeats in the war and the Arab Revolt may have strengthened the Turkist position, the government, even after the cabinet change of 1917, sought to reverse the disintegrationist trends by stressing an Islamist-Ottomanist outlook in public life. It is significant, for instance, that Yusuf Akçura, the prominent ideologue of the Turkist movement, lost his job during the university reform of 1916. If Turkish irredentism had its appeal to Committee leaders such as Enver, others, like Talat, were ambivalent. Still others, such as Cavid, opposed it and believed that efforts should be made to retain the Arab provinces rather than dissipate energy in Turkic Russia.[194] Yet, the ultimate defeat in the war and the severe terms of the armistice sealed the fate of the Ottoman Empire and of Ottomanism.

Conclusion

From the first half of the nineteenth century, when the spread of nationalism in the Balkans and the apparent weakness of the Ottoman state vis-à-vis imperialist Europe strengthened disintegrationist movements in the empire, Ottomanism evolved as a supranationalist ideology designed to arrest these trends by creating state patriotism and allegiance to the ruler who embodied the state. A constantly redefined Ottomanism accommodated the many changes in the political fortunes of the empire until its final partitioning at the end of World War I.

Ottomanism as conceived during the Tanzimat promoted an identity based on territory; predicated upon the political equality of subjects regardless of religious affiliation and reinforced by a sense of loyalty to the House of Osman. Political equality had little appeal to the Muslim subjects who felt their psychological superiority within the Ottoman polity compromised. Thus, the secularizing Tanzimat policies in fact contributed to an overarching Muslim collective identity and reduced the likelihood of the politicization of ethnicity among the Muslims, who confronted Christian Europe and nationalist movements of Ottoman Christians.

The literary-political quest of the Young Ottomans for a constitutional representative regime culminated in the declaration of the 1876 constitution and the institution of Parliament. Parliament signified recognition of regional interests and of the political power of ascendant social groups in the provinces. While such power was forcefully asserted against the Palace and the Porte, a basis for a communality deriving from a common ethnic background did not emerge among the different Muslim groups in Parliament. Arab deputies were concerned with issues pertaining to either their local constituencies or to the empire at large.

Sultan Abdülhamid perceived the threat to his prerogatives latent in the constitutional regime and aborted the first Parliament. His Islamic policy shifted the emphasis in Ottomanism toward a reorientation of exclusive political allegiance to the sultan-caliph. Arabism and Turkism as protonationalist currents grew during the long reign of Sultan Abdülhamid on a literary and cultural level. The main thrust of political activity under Abdülhamid focused on the reinstitution of the constitution. Many Arabs, both Christian and Muslim, played a prominent role in the opposition movement. The constitutionalist groups in Europe as well as the younger generation of disaffected students in the capital included in their ranks Arabs who were ideologically opposed to the Hamidian regime. As the constitutional movement matured during Abdülhamid's long reign, two distinct and rival political currents evolved among the constitutionalists: the centralist and decentralist. Arab and Turkish constitutionalists remained divided between these two currents, while the decentralist platform had a manifest appeal to the remaining Christian communities for cultural and economic reasons.

Evidence of isolated instances of subversive activity and occasional manifestos point to sporadic attempts to politicize Arab and, to a lesser extent, Turkish national consciousness in the second half of the nineteenth century. Arabist initiatives came mostly, though not exclusively, from Christians, many residing in Europe. Turkism had its strongest proponents within the ranks of Russian-Turkish immigrant intellectuals in İstanbul, who envisaged for Turkism a more universal range of influence than was the concern of the Turks of the Ottoman Empire. The sympathetic response to these political currents remained limited.

The view that Turkish nationalism engendered Arab nationalism has been long adopted by historians explicitly or implicitly, just as George Antonius's presupposition about the early-nineteenth-century origins of Arab nationalism had not been questioned for many years. Non-Turkish opponents of the Committee of Union and Progress construed the Unionist policy of centralization as a methodical policy of Turkification. The Unionists' eventual commitment to centralization was unmistakable. They viewed administrative centralization as a prerequisite to achieve the Ottomanist ideal, which assumed a new meaning under the constitutional order introduced in 1908. The Election Law was revised to exclude the requirement of proportional representation from different religious groups and aimed at replacing communal politics with party politics. This ideal of a secular and centralized civic Ottoman collectivity proved to be undesirable for Christian communities, not necessarily because it was found unworkable, but because it challenged the rights and privileges they had acquired as distinct communities. Charges of Turkification as an agenda to homogenize Ottoman peoples became the focal point of the decentralist propaganda of all non-Turkish opponents of the CUP. Such charges on the part of Arabs were based, first, on the enforcement of Ottoman Turkish in postelementary education, courts, and administrative offices and, second, on the relative scarcity of Arabs among the holders of higher state offices.

The uniform enforcement of Ottoman throughout the empire was viewed in İstanbul as a prerequisite for effective centralization. Benedict Anderson draws a distinction between the two different uses of a state language. It can be an administrative language, "a language used by and for officialdoms for their inner convenience [with no] idea of systematically imposing the language on the . . . various subject populations," or it can be a tool employed by rulers "confronted with the rise of hostile popular linguistic-nationalisms."[1] The Unionist policies did not jeopardize the use of Arabic in the press, in primary education, or in matters pertaining to religion. The use of Ottoman in state institutions had a pragmatic goal consistent with the centralist agenda, which was supported by large sections of the Arabs. Furthermore, Ottoman had always served as the state language, and its use in administration or secondary education did not constitute a new departure.

The second matter that caused resentment (and rendered to interpretation as a main facet of Turkification) was the low proportion of Arabs among incumbents of high office. The Young Turk policies were perceived as discriminatory partly because the Unionist purge of the Hamidian cadres from important positions had resulted in the dismissal of many Arabs, the influential ones from the palace coterie of Abdülhamid. Historical patterns of recruitment, in fact, point to low Arab representation in the highest ranks of the İstanbul bureaucracy. Setting aside the aberration of the Hamidian regime, which departed from bureaucratic norms in the recruitment of a palace administration, the Young Turk period compared more favorably to past patterns with respect to the recruitment of Arabs. A comparison of the 1877–78 and 1908 Parliaments does not show a relative decline in the size of Arab representation.[2] Unless the same prejudices can be ascribed to Abdülhamid or the statesmen of his regime, the reasons for underrepresentation should be sought in institutional and structural rather than ideological factors.

The Young Turk regimes responded to the various demands voiced by Arabs for a larger representation in state offices and a wider use of Arabic in the Arab provinces. Measures such as a stricter and more uniform enforcement of Ottoman Turkish in courts were repealed in view of local opposition and their impracticability. In 1913 and 1914 İstanbul took several steps in the direction of the fulfillment of the demands of the Arab Congress and the reform societies, including demands pertaining to the language question.

The leadership of the CUP consisted almost exclusively of Turkish speakers. Unsophisticated about questions of nationality, the Unionists betrayed Turkish chauvinism, particularly by their refusal to broaden the geographical, ethnic, and religious base of their core organization. However, they upheld the imperial polity and multiethnic agendas rather than implement a Turkish nationalist program in the conduct of state affairs. In fact, Turkish nationalist activity continued to be restricted to the cultural-literary domain. The CUP as a political party subscribed to Ottomanist and Islamist political ideals. Like Arabs, Turks (including Unionist Turks) carried multiple layers of identities. Some Unionists were attracted to Turkism, but cultural identities and allegiances did not correspond to political agendas.

Though the CUP initially attempted to dismantle the network of alliances that the Hamidian regime had forged in the countryside, political expediency gradually forced the Unionists to compromise with established landed and commercial interests, especially in those parts of the empire where the Committee's organization was rudimentary and the semifeudal relationships were strong between urban notables and peasants or tribes. Thus, the CUP alienated some components of the constitutional opposition that had shared its social values and political goals. Furthermore, the decentralist trend reasserted itself and commanded wide appeal as the CUP's popularity, which had derived from its role in the restoration of the constitution, diminished and as unrealistic expectations were disappointed. The Liberal-decentralist opposition was also joined by some notables who were excluded either by personal choice or by regional competitors from a symbiotic relationship with the Committee. Arab exponents of decentralization utilized the rhetoric of Turkification to discredit the Unionist governments. What one revisionist reexamination of nineteenth-century Russification (in this case, that of the Baltic provinces) concludes is also true for the

Ottoman Empire: Turkification, like Russification, can "no longer serve as a generic designation of a constant governmental policy: it has been used in too many contexts as a term of political agitation and to articulate certain fears."[3]

The CUP remained the most important political group in the Ottoman Empire during the second constitutional period. Yet, different factors prevented the Committee from completely imposing its will in the government of the empire: the political inexperience of its leadership, the predominance of older politicians, the influence of European governments, strong political opposition, economic difficulties and dependency, international complications, an imperfect organizational structure as a political party, and, last but not least, differences of opinion among a diffuse leadership. Only for a brief interlude from mid-1913 to the outbreak of the world war in 1914 was the Committee able to overcome some of these handicaps. This period also witnessed a renewed emphasis on Islam as the ideological basis of the Ottoman Empire, which now consisted predominantly of Muslim peoples.

Secular Ottomanism failed to live up to the expectations of Young Turks. Its weakness was revealed and its relevance diminished as an ideology as separatist movements and dismemberment in Europe continued. In view of the fact that Arabs and Turks constituted the large majority of the empire in the aftermath of the Balkan Wars and that religion continued to be the primary focus of allegiance for the Muslim masses, Ottomanism underwent a final redefinition to stress Islam as its main underpinning.

Thus, the Unionists came to rely on religion in their quest for centralization and social harmony much as their nemesis Abdülhamid had. Both the sultan and the CUP reacted to the failure of a secular experiment in arresting disintegration by turning to the powerful symbols and vocabulary of Islam. Islam's "egalitarian doctrine" and "its scripturalist, orderly, restrained theology made it compatible with the requirements both of centralising regimes and of developmental programmes."[4] Compared with Hamidian Islamism, Young Turk Islamism had a better chance to serve as a unifying ideology given the new political and demographic circumstances that made the empire much less of a religious patchwork. The official emphasis on Islam defused the political overtones and divisive potential of Arabism and Turkism.[5]

Discussions of Arab or Turkish nationalism in the prewar period are for the most part ambiguous with regard to the political framework within which the professed nationalist ideologies were to find expression. References to Turkish nationalism in the Young Turk period evoke the image of a political project that would unite all the Turks, if not all the so-called Turanian peoples. The Arab provinces would then be either forsaken or Turkified. References to Arab nationalism, in turn, bring to mind a political movement encompassing all Arab populated areas of the empire, whereas it would be more appropriate to refer to "Syrianism" rather than Arab nationalism in the period before the world war. Both the decentralists in the major towns of Syria and the Arab voices calling (mostly from Europe or Egypt) for a political existence independent of İstanbul thought in terms of Syria when espousing Arab group consciousness as a political idiom. The ambivalence about Sharif Husayn's revolt revealed the preponderance of localist (and Ottomanist) attitudes in Syria.

The predominant sentiment among the Arabs of the Ottoman Empire in the Young Turk period favored allegiance to the Ottoman sultan and remaining as an integral part of the Islamic empire, even though demands for decentralization within this framework were voiced more and more loudly. Notions of Arab independence that had been current but not popular since the second half of the nineteenth century gained strength at times of unsuccessful foreign entanglements of the Ottoman government because of a desire to mitigate the impact of probable foreign hegemony following a breakdown of the Ottoman state. As early as 1878, when Russian armies came within miles of İstanbul, several groups—Christian and Muslim—in Syria called for Syrian independence. Similarly, in 1912 Ottoman involvement in wars against a coalition of powerful Balkan states fueled the propensity for independence in Beirut, Damascus, and Basra. Such stirrings frequently received European backing. Finally, during World War I Sharif Husayn's conviction that rendering support to the Ottoman government against the British would result in the political demise of his dynastic family and the encouragement he received from segments of a disintegrated Arab elite in the rest of the empire initiated the Arab Revolt. This showdown in a side theater, with active British support, contributed to the separation of the Arab regions from the empire and, under the new geopolitical realities of foreign occupation, prepared the ground for the rise of particularistic nationalist movements in Anatolia and the Fertile Crescent.

Notes

Introduction

1. From Albert Hourani's foreword to Rashid Ismail Khalidi, *British Policy towards Syria and Palestine, 1906–1914* (London: Ithaca Press, 1980), ii.

2. See Ulrich W. Haarmann, "Ideology and History, Identity and Alterity: The Arab Image of the Turk from the 'Abbasids to Modern Egypt," *IJMES* 20 (1988): 175–96. Representative of a segment of modern Turkish opinion on Arabs is İlhan Arsel's *Arap Milliyetçiliği ve Türkler* (İstanbul: İnkılap, 1987).

3. The Ottoman surrender to the Entente powers and the resignation of the wartime government in October 1918 is generally regarded as the end of the constitutional period. The ouster of the Ottoman dynasty in November 1922 or the declaration of the Turkish Republic in October 1923 constitute equally valid end points.

4. Much of the correspondence and minutes of the Committee of Union and Progress, the paramount political organization in this period, is in these categories.

5. Karl Deutsch, *Nationalism and Its Alternatives* (New York: Alfred A. Knopf, 1969), 50.

6. Cyril E. Black and L. Carl Brown, *Modernization in the Middle East: The Ottoman Empire and Its Afro-Asian Successors* (Princeton, N.J.: Darwin Press, 1992), 160.

7. For instance, Ömer Kürkçüoğlu's *Osmanlı Devleti'ne Karşı Arap Bağımsızlık Hareketi* (Ankara: Ankara Üniversitesi Siyasal Bilgiler Fakültesi, 1982) relies predominantly on British archival documents in examining Turkish-Arab relations. Zekeriya Kurşun's more recent book on the topic constitutes a fresh departure in its use of Arabic published materials and Ottoman newspapers. *Yol Ayırımında Türk-Arap İlişkileri* (İstanbul: İrfan, 1992).

8. The Ottomans conquered Syria and Egypt in 1517–18 and had to abandon all Arab provinces in 1917–18.

9. Frank Füredi discusses this problem with respect to Western countries. *Mythical Past, Elusive Future: History and Society in an Anxious Age* (London: Pluto Press, 1992), 4–7.

10. George Antonius, *The Arab Awakening: The Story of the Arab National Movement* (New York: Paragon, 1979). First published in 1938.

11. Zeine Zeine, *The Emergence of Arab Nationalism*, 3d ed. (New York: Caravan, 1973). First published in 1958.

12. Ibid., 132.

13. Albert Hourani, *Arabic Thought in the Liberal Age, 1798–1939* (London: Oxford University Press, 1970). Also, "*The Arab Awakening:* Forty Years After," in his *The Emergence of the Modern Middle East* (Berkeley and Los Angeles: University of California Press, 1981), 193–215.

14. A. L. Tibawi, *A Modern History of Syria* (London: Macmillan, 1969).

15. "The Ottoman Background of the Modern Middle East," in Hourani, *The Emergence of the Modern Middle East*, 8–11.

16. "Ottoman Reform and the Politics of Notables," in Hourani, *The Emergence of the Modern Middle East*, 62.

17. ʿAbd al-ʿAziz Duri, *The Historical Formation of the Arab Nation* (London: Croom Helm, 1987).

18. Ibid., 215.

19. Ernest Dawn's collected essays were published as *From Ottomanism to Arabism* (Urbana, Ill.: University of Illinois Press, 1973).

20. Ibid., 148–79. First published in *Middle East Journal* 16 (1962): 145–168.

21. For a more nuanced and concise articulation of these points three decades later, see Ernest Dawn's "The Origins of Arab Nationalism," in *The Origins of Arab Nationalism*, ed. Khalidi et al. (New York: Columbia University Press, 1991).

22. Rashid Khalidi, "Social Forces in the Rise of the Arab Movement in Syria," in *From Nationalism to Revolutionary Islam*, ed. Said A. Arjomand (Albany: SUNY Press, 1984), 69ff. Also by Khalidi, "Arab Nationalism in Syria: The Formative Years, 1908–1914," in *Nationalism in a Non-National State*, ed. W. Haddad and W. Ochsenwald (Columbus, Ohio: Ohio State University Press, 1977); "Ottomanism and Arabism in Syria before 1914: A Reassessment," in *Origins of Arab Nationalism*, ed. Khalidi et al.; and "The Press as a Source for Modern Arab Political History: ʿAbd al-Ghani al-ʿUraysi and *al-Mufid*," *Arab Studies Quarterly* 3 (1981). This last article occurs in slightly modified form also in *Intellectual Life in the Arab East, 1890–1939*, ed. Marwan R. Buheiry (Beirut: American University of Beirut Press, 1981).

23. See, for instance, William L. Cleveland, *The Making of an Arab Nationalist: Ottomanism and Arabism in the Life and Thought of Satiʿ al-Husri* (Princeton, N.J.: Princeton University Press, 1971); Philip Khoury, *Urban Notables and Arab Nationalism: The Politics of Damascus, 1860–1920* (Cambridge: Cambridge University Press, 1983); and Mary Wilson, *King Abdullah, Britain, and the Making of Jordan* (Cambridge: Cambridge University Press, 1987).

24. Thus, in a recent reassessment of the scholarship on the topic, Mahmoud

Haddad sees early Arab political nationalism as the outcome of (1) "opposition to Turkish nationalism and Pan-Turkism," (2) "the Turcocentric Ottomanism of the CUP" (i.e., Young Turk centralization), and (3) prospects of European control of Arab areas. In an attempt to reconcile the different viewpoints on the genesis of Arab nationalism, Haddad urges distinguishing among cultural, social, and political dimensions of Arabism. "The Rise of Arab Nationalism Reconsidered," *IJMES* 26 (1994): 213.

25. Rifa't 'Ali Abou-el-Haj, *Formation of the Modern State: The Ottoman Empire, Sixteenth to Eighteenth Centuries* (Albany: State University of New York Press, 1991), 63–64.

26. Ibid., 69.

27. Şerif Mardin, "Center-Periphery Relations: A Key to Turkish Politics?" in *Post-Traditional Societies*, ed. S. N. Eisenstadt (New York: Norton, 1972), 175.

28. Eric Hobsbawm, *Nations and Nationalism since 1780* (Cambridge: Cambridge University Press, 1990), 73–74.

29. Ibid., 86–87.

30. Eugene Weber, *Peasants into Frenchmen: The Modernization of Rural France, 1870–1914* (Stanford, Calif.: Stanford University Press, 1976). Weber describes France close to a century after the 1789 Revolution as "an entity formed by conquest and by political and administrative decisions formulated in (or near) Paris" (p. 485) and the French nation "not as a given reality but as a work-in-progress, a model of something at once to be built and to be treated for political reasons as already in existence" (p. 493).

31. Hobsbawm, 93.

32. Ernest Gellner, *Nations and Nationalism* (Oxford: Basil Blackwell, 1983), 1.

33. John Breuilly, *Nationalism and the State* (Manchester: Manchester University Press, 1982), 11.

34. See, for instance, Hroch's "From National Movement to the Fully-Formed Nation," *New Left Review* 198 (1993): 6–7.

35. Hobsbawm, 12.

36. Edward Shils, *Center and Periphery: Essays in Macrosociology* (Chicago: The University of Chicago Press, 1975), 11.

37. Even though Abdülhamid was not deposed until 1909, the 1908 Revolution marks the end of Hamidian period.

38. Bassam Tibi describes the revolt as "the backwards-oriented utopia of an Arab Caliphate coexisting with the aspirations of a modern nation building." *Arab Nationalism: A Critical Enquiry*, 2d ed. (New York: St. Martin's Press, 1990), 21.

Chapter 1.   Arabs and Arab Provinces in the Evolution of the Young Turk Movement

1. P. M. Holt, *Egypt and Fertile Crescent, 1516–1922: A Political History* (Ithaca, N.Y.: Cornell University Press, 1966), 67.

2. Hourani, "Ottoman Reform," 47–50.

3. The word *Tanzimat* has come to denote a vaguely delimited period in Ottoman history characterized by these changes, generally accepted to span from 1839 to 1876.

4. Halil İnalcık, "The Application of the Tanzimat and its Social Effects," *Archivum Ottomanicum* 5 (1973): 127.

5. Ibid., 110.

6. As regional autonomies were eliminated, the Tanzimat leaders intended to prevent the newly appointed governors from acquiring excessive powers and setting down roots in the provinces. See Moshe Ma'oz, "The Impact of Modernization on Syrian Politics and Society during the Early Tanzimat Period," in William R. Polk and Richard L. Chambers, *Beginnings of Modernization in the Middle East: The Nineteenth Century* (Chicago: University of Chicago Press, 1968), 335–42.

7. Joseph S. Szyliowicz, "Changes in the Recruitment Patterns and Career Lines of Ottoman Provincial Administrators during the Nineteenth Century," in *Studies on Palestine during the Ottoman Period*, ed. Moshe Ma'oz (Jerusalem: Magnes Press, 1975), 264–65.

8. Bernard Lewis, *The Emergence of Modern Turkey* (London: Oxford University Press, 1961), 375.

9. Âli Pasha, the strongest of Tanzimat statesmen and long-time grand vizier (prime minister), was the son of a shopkeeper in İstanbul. As a child he attended the local religious school but was unable to complete it because he had to take a job to support the family as a scribe. Meanwhile, he learned some French from a Greek physician. His familiarity with French and his diligence at his job helped him to attract the attention of his superiors and to enter the Translation Bureau. İbrahim Alaettin Gövsa, *Türk Meşhurları Ansiklopedisi* (Ankara: Yedigün Neşriyat, n.d.), 34; *İnönü Ansiklopedisi* (Ankara: Maarif Matbaası, 1948), 2:92; Abdurrahman Şeref, *Tarih Musahebeleri* (İstanbul: Matbaa-ı Âmire, 1923), 88.

10. Stanford J. Shaw, "Some Aspects of the Aims and Achievements of the Nineteenth-Century Ottoman Reformers," in Polk and Chambers, 37.

11. İsmail Hami Danişmend, *İzahlı Osmanlı Tarihi Kronolojisi* (İstanbul: Türkiye Yayınevi, 1961), 4:528. İlber Ortaylı argues that the Turkish element started to become ascendant in the administration in the eighteenth century. See *İmparatorluğun En Uzun Yüzyılı* (İstanbul: Hil, 1987), 58.

12. Zeine, *Arab Nationalism*, 9.

13. Hourani, "Ottoman Background," 10; Sir Hamilton Gibb and Harold Bowen, *Islamic Society and the West* (London: Oxford University Press, 1963), (pt. 2): 83, 100.

14. See Butrus Abu Manneh, "The Islamic Roots of the Gülhane Rescript," *Die Welt des Islams* 34 (1994). One *âlim* who kept pace with the transformation of the Ottoman institutions was the father of Sati' al-Husri, famous as the ideologue of twentieth-century pan-Arabism. Muhammad Hilal al-Husri, a native of Aleppo, was a graduate of al-Azhar and served for several years as *kadı* (judge) in Aleppo. He later passed the necessary examinations to serve in the new courts and was appointed to various posts in Arab as well as Anatolian provinces. In

Husri's home, in keeping with the tradition of Ottoman bureaucrats, the language spoken was Ottoman. See Cleveland, *Sati ʿ al-Husri*, 12–15.

15. Confronted with the problem of distinguishing Arabs from Turks in her study of the Arab graduates of the *Mülkiye* (Civil Service School), Corinne Blake used "self-definition," i.e., in which country an individual (or if already deceased, his family) chose to live after World War I. "Training Arab-Ottoman Bureaucrats: Syrian Graduates of the *Mülkiye Mektebi*, 1890–1920," (Ph.D. diss., Princeton University, 1991), 291.

16. Afaf Lutfi al-Sayyid Marsot, *A Short History of Modern Egypt* (Cambridge: Cambridge University Press, 1985), 53.

17. Engin Akarlı, "The Problems of External Pressures, Power Struggles, and Budgetary Deficits in Ottoman Politics under Abdulhamid II, 1876–1909: Origins and Solutions" (Ph.D. diss., Princeton University, 1976), 20–21.

18. Land grants for service in the cavalry and administration. According to Norman Itzkowitz, in the fourteenth century "most of the high ranking positions in the state were concentrated" in the hands of *tımar* holders. See Norman Itzkowitz, *Ottoman Empire and Islamic Tradition* (Chicago: University of Chicago Press, 1972), 15.

19. The second Ottoman method of elite formation, based on the levy of boys from newly conquered Christian territories (*devşirme*), did not apply to the Arab areas.

20. Roderic Davison, *Reform in the Ottoman Empire, 1856–1876* (Princeton, N.J.: Princeton University Press, 1963), 228–30.

21. Alexander Schölch, "Ein Palästinischer Repräsentant der Tanzimat-Periode: Yusuf Diyaʾaddin al-Halidi (1842–1906)," *Der Islam* 57 (1980): 311–21.

22. His father was an officer in Muhammad ʿAli's service. At sixteen Raşid went to Paris for his studies and subsequently found employment in the Translation Bureau in İstanbul. See Max L. Gross, "Ottoman Rule in the Province of Damascus, 1860–1909" (Ph.D. diss., Georgetown University, 1979), 119–25.

23. Schölch, 314.

24. Zirikli, Khayr al-Din, *Al-aʿlam: qamus tarajim li ashhar al-rijal wa al-nisaʾ min al-ʿarab wa al-mustaʾribin wa al-mustashriqin* (Cairo, 1954–1959), 2:362.

25. Filip de Tarazi, *Tarikh al-sihafa al-ʿarabiyya* (Beirut: Al-Matbaʿa al-Adabiyya, 1913), 2:269.

26. Şerif Mardin, *The Genesis of Young Ottoman Thought* (Princeton, N.J.: Princeton University Press, 1962), 105, 115, 134.

27. Hourani, *Arabic Thought*, 67.

28. Ibid., 149–92.

29. Antonius, 47–54.

30. Hourani, *Arabic Thought*, 101. Butrus Abu Manneh convincingly argues that Bustani was an Arabist culturally but a committed Ottomanist politically. "The Christians Between Ottomanism and Syrian Nationalism: The Ideas of Butrus al-Bustani," *IJMES* 11 (1980): 293–97.

31. Tibawi, 11; Tibi, 104.

32. Hourani, "Ottoman Reform," 61.

33. Mumtaz Ayoub Fargo, "Arab-Turkish Relations from the Emergence of Arab Nationalism to the Arab Revolt, 1848–1916" (Ph.D. diss., University of Utah, 1969), 86. The Tanzimat governments made special provisions for schools

opened in the Arab provinces. In 1867 the literary Arabic that was taught to all students in the teacher's school in İstanbul (founded in 1847) was deemed insufficient for the purposes of instructors going to the Arab provinces. As an experiment, the Ministry of Education proposed to send ten students to Aleppo and Damascus to gain practice in colloquial Arabic. The Council of State recommended instead that ten Arab students be recruited from Syria to attend the school. Further, the council suggested that conversational Arabic be offered in the teacher's school, to be taught by Hamid al-ʿAlusi of Baghdad, who was presently at the *Mülkiye.* Osman Ergin, *Türk Maarif Tarihi* (İstanbul: Eser, 1977), 2:573.

34. Enver Ziya Karal, *Osmanlı Tarihi* (Ankara: Türk Tarih Kurumu Basımevi, 1962), 8:497.

35. Niyazi Berkes, *The Development of Secularism in Turkey* (Montreal: McGill University, 1964), 221; Lewis, 339.

36. See I. E. Petrosyan, "On the Motive Forces of the Reformist and Constitutionalist Movement in the Ottoman Empire," in Jean-Louis Bacqué-Grammont and Paul Dumont, eds., *Economie et sociétés dans l'empire ottoman* (Paris: CNRS, 1983), 13–24.

37. Robert Devereux, *The First Ottoman Constitutional Period* (Baltimore: The Johns Hopkins Press, 1963), 123. Devereux's book is the most comprehensive existing account of the 1877–78 Parliament.

38. Ibid., 124; see also Hasan Kayalı, "Elections and the Electoral Process in the Ottoman Empire, 1877–1919," *IJMES* 27 (1995): 266–71.

39. The parliamentary records as they were made public in the official government paper, *Takvim-i Vekai*, were not only edited but also censored. They were collected in Hakkı Tarık Us, ed., *Meclis-i Mebusan, 1293–1877*, 2 vols. (İstanbul: Vakit, 1940 and 1954).

40. According to Kemal Karpat, the debates "provided a unique insight into the philosophical-ideological orientation of the Empire's newest social group, the middle class." "The Ottoman Parliament of 1877 and Its Social Significance," in *Actes du 1er congrès des études balkaniques et sud-est européennes* (Sofia, 1969), 247.

41. Parliament was composed of a Chamber of Deputies (*meclis-i mebusan*) and a Senate, or Chamber of Notables (*meclis-i ayan*).

42. One hundred and nineteen in the first session; 113 in the second.

43. Devereux, 140–41. These statistics are based on the 1877 *salname* (official yearbook).

44. These disparities can be explained by the degree of politicization in the various provinces. In determining the size of contingents, İstanbul seems to have taken into consideration the interest evinced for constitutional government in (or on behalf of) the various provinces as well. This is particularly obvious in the case of the European provinces, most of which were highly overrepresented.

45. ʿAbd al-Rahim Badran, an Arab deputy from Syria, mentions in a speech that he is originally from the ethnically mixed Diyarbakır; but he is an Arab. There is no indication that any of the deputies from the two areas with Arab "minority" populations, Adana and Diyarbakır, were of Arab descent.

46. Manuk Karaja of Aleppo was Armenian.

47. Henceforth, the word *Chamber* will refer to the Chamber of Deputies, the elected lower house.

48. In the selection of the one candidate to which the independent *sancak* of Jerusalem was entitled, for instance, Ziya al-Khalidi's rival was a member from the other prestigious family of the town, the Husaynis, known for their conservatism. Schölch, 315.

49. He expressed his objection to the clause in the internal regulations stipulating that the presidents of the arbitrarily divided groups in Parliament be the oldest member in each group. He went on to suggest that group membership should be functional rather than arbitrary, and that each deputy should be active in a group in line with his professional qualifications.

50. Us, 1:26. I/3 (first term, third sitting), 23 March 1877.

51. Ibid., 1:37. I/5, 25 March 1877.

52. Ibid., 2:349. II/25, 8 February 1878.

53. Devereux, 182.

54. Us, 2:24–25. "Preliminary meeting," 17 December 1877. (The second session started officially on 31 December 1877.)

55. Ibid., 2:68. II/4, 3 January 1878.

56. Ibid., 2:184. II/14, 23 January 1878; Devereux, 215.

57. Us, 2:187. II/14, 22 January 1878.

58. Ibid., 2:30–31. II/1, 31 December 1877.

59. Ibid., 2:86. II/5, 5 January 1878.

60. Ibid., 1:29. I/3, 23 March 1877.

61. During the deliberations on the draft of a press law, he proposed to replace the stipulation of one to three years' imprisonment for press items prejudicial to the sultan's rights and privileges with three to fifteen years'. Ibid., 1:236. I/28, 12 May 1877.

62. Ibid., 2:209. II/16, 24 January 1878.

63. For instance, in denouncing the declaration of war by Russia (Ibid., 1:173–84. I/21 and I/22, 25–26 April 1877); on elections for administrative councils (1:72. I/10, 1 April 1877); on the government policy in regard to printing presses (1:201. I/24, 7 May 1877); on tax reform (2:235–36. II/18, 28 January 1878).

64. Tibawi, 150.

65. Particularly Ahmad and 'Abdullah in the first session. See Us, 1:117. I/15, 16 April 1877; 1:178. I/21, 25 April 1877; 1:201. I/24, 7 May 1877; 1:275. I/34, 22 May 1877; 1:318. I/41, 31 May 1877.

66. Ibid., 1:390. I/54, 21 June 1877.

67. Ibid., 1:344. I/46, 9 June 1877; 1:380. I/51, 16 June 1877.

68. Ibid., 1:363. I/49, 13 June 1877.

69. Most deputies represented landowning families and must have been concerned about issues of security pertaining to their social class. Ibid., 2:112. II/8, 10 January 1878.

70. Ibid., 2:132. II/9, 12 January 1878; 2:252. II/19, 29 January 1878; 2:266. II/20, 30 January 1878; 2:410. II/24, 6 February 1878. For an account of the development of Beirut in this period, see Leila T. Fawaz, *Merchants and Migrants in Nineteenth-Century Beirut* (Cambridge, Mass.: Harvard University Press, 1983).

71. Devereux, 247; Us, 2:410.

72. Us, 2:411. One of the five, Manuk Karaja, an Armenian Christian, was not an Arab, though he probably was Arabophone.

73. Butrus Abu Manneh, "Sultan Abdulhamid II and Shaikh Abulhuda al-Sayyadi," *Middle Eastern Studies* 15 (1979): 137.

74. Us, 2:222–23. II/17, 26 January 1878.

75. Fritz Steppat, "Eine Bewegung unter den Notabeln Syriens, 1877–78," *Zeitschrift der Deutschen Morgenländischen Gesellschaft*, supplementa I, 17 (1969): 634. (See p. 33.)

76. Tarık Zafer Tunaya, *Türkiye'nin Siyasi Hayatında Batılılaşma Hareketleri* (İstanbul: Yedigün, 1960), 45.

77. Devereux, 240; Mümtaz Soysal, *100 Soruda Anayasa'nın Anlamı* (İstanbul: Gerçek, 1969), 28.

78. S. Tufan Buzpınar, "Abdulhamid II, Islam and the Arabs: The Cases of Syria and the Hijaz (1878–1882)" (Ph.D. diss., University of Manchester, 1991), 314–15.

79. Moshe Ma'oz, *Ottoman Reform in Syria and Palestine, 1840–1861* (Oxford: Clarendon Press, 1968), 35.

80. Fuad Pasha, one of the Tanzimat's three leading statesmen, together with Mustafa Reşid Pasha (whose protégé he was) and Âli Pasha, served as governor of Syria after the civil war of 1860 in Mount Lebanon and Damascus. (See Gross, 31.) Cevdet Pasha, historian, jurist, and reformer, was entrusted with the application of the 1864 Provincial Law in the newly created province of Aleppo. In 1869 Midhat Pasha was sent to Iraq with the same purpose. *Serasker* and Minister of the Navy Namık Pasha, Grand Vizier Kıbrıslı Mehmed Emin Pasha, Grand Vizier Mehmed Kamil Pasha, and Foreign Minister Mehmed Reşid Pasha, the friend of the Khalidi family, had careers during the Tanzimat period as governors in the provinces of Greater Syria. (See Stanford J. Shaw and Ezel Kural Shaw, *History of the Ottoman Empire and Modern Turkey*, vol. 2, *Reform, Revolution, and Republic: The Rise of Modern Turkey, 1808–1975* [Cambridge: Cambridge University Press, 1977], 64–66, 164, 506; Ma'oz, "Impact of Modernization," 355; Tibawi, 139.)

81. Shaw and Shaw, 85; Ma'oz, *Ottoman Reform*, 45–57.

82. Ma'oz, *Ottoman Reform*, 81–86.

83. Ma'oz, "Impact of Modernization," 343.

84. Holt, 253.

85. Karal, 331.

86. Britain concluded agreements with the Sultan of Oman in 1891 and the *shaykh* of Kuwait in 1899, supported in Najd 'Abd al-Rahman ibn al-Sa'ud against the İstanbul-backed Rashidi family, and established friendly relations with the Zaydi *imam* of Yemen. (See Yusuf Hikmet Bayur, *Türk İnkılabı Tarihi* [Ankara: Türk Tarih Kurumu, 1983], 1:133–36, 147–49). For an extensive account of the British presence in the Persian Gulf, see Briton Cooper Busch, *Britain and the Persian Gulf* (Berkeley and Los Angeles: University of California Press, 1967). As Feroz Ahmad argues, the informal British agreement with Shaykh Mubarak of Kuwait was not recognized internationally. See "A Note on the

International Status of Kuwait before November 1914," *IJMES* 24 (1992): 181–85.

87. Colmar Freiherrn von der Goltz, "Stärke und Schwäche des türkischen Reiches," *Deutsche Rundschau*, 93 (1897), 114–16; Antonius, 78.

88. Von der Goltz, 109.

89. Antonius, 79. See, for instance, Shimon Shamir, "Midhat Pasha and Anti-Turkish Agitation in Syria," *Middle Eastern Studies* 10 (1974).

90. Antonius, 86. See also Zeine, *Arab Nationalism*, 52; Steppat, 637–40.

91. Zeine, *Arab Nationalism*, 54.

92. Tibawi disagrees with Antonius's claim that these placards were written and distributed by the Christians and that they had a revolutionary aim. (Tibawi, 166).

93. Zeine, *Arab Nationalism*, 53.

94. Jacob M. Landau, "An Arab Anti-Turk Handbill, 1881," *Turcica* 9 (1977): 215–27.

95. John Dickson's dispatch to the Foreign Office, quoted in Zeine, *Arab Nationalism*, 58.

96. Shamir, 124.

97. Zeine, *Arab Nationalism*, 54.

98. Tibawi, 159, quotes PRO. FO 78/1389. J. Skene to P. Alison (31 July 1858); also Zeine, *Arab Nationalism*, 59. The consul mentioned that "[t]he Mussulman population of northern Syria hope for a separation from the Ottoman Empire and the formation of a new Arabian state under the sovereignty of the sharif of Mecca."

99. The handbill examined by Landau had made its way to European consulates in Algeria, Khartoum, and Baghdad. As Landau surmises, this did not signify a widespread movement but an attempt to recruit [Europe's] support.

100. Zeine, *Arab Nationalism*, 53.

101. Khoury, 23–30.

102. Ibid., 47.

103. Karal, 332.

104. Butrus Abu Manneh, "The Rise of the Sanjak of Jerusalem in the Late Nineteenth Century," in *The Palestinians and the Middle East Conflict*, ed. Gabriel Ben-Dor (Ramat Gan, 1978), 26.

105. Khoury, 51.

106. Berkes, 263; Buzpınar, 31–32.

107. "Arap milletinden neşet etmiş bir milletiz."

108. Us, 2:210. II/16, 24 January 1878.

109. Hourani, *Arabic Thought*, 139.

110. Ibid., 269.

111. Sylvia G. Haim, ed., *Arab Nationalism: An Anthology* (Berkeley and Los Angeles: University of California Press, 1964), 27; Tibawi, 184; Hourani, *Arabic Thought*, 272.

112. Dawn, *Ottomanism*, 135–41.

113. Berkes, 314–15; David Kushner, *The Rise of Turkish Nationalism, 1876–1908* (London: Frank Cass, 1977), 27–30.

114. A. D. Jeltyakov [Zheltiakov], *Türkiye'nin Sosyo-Politik ve Kültürel Hayatında Basın (1729–1908 Yılları)* (İstanbul [?]: Hürriyet, n.d.), 70–71.

115. Ercümend Kuran, "The Impact of Nationalism on the Turkish Elite in the Nineteenth Century," in Polk and Chambers, 114.

116. Abu Manneh, "Sayyadi," 148. Most literary activity occurred in Egypt and was carried out by Syrian immigrants who fled censorship.

117. Karal, 543; Shaw and Shaw, 260.

118. In 1900 the Turcologist Necib Asım wrote, "We must . . . turn first, like the Arabs, the French, and all European nations, to our own 'mother tongue.' " Kushner, 44.

119. Yusuf Akçura, *Üç Tarz-ı Siyaset* (İstanbul: Matbaa-ı Kader, 1327 [1911]) (first published in 1904 in the newspaper *Türk* in serialized form); Berkes, 322; E. Kuran, 116.

120. Hourani, *Arabic Thought*, 278–79.

121. However, the expressions Young Ottoman and Young Turk are used here too, as well as in established scholarship, to refer to the two distinct periods of the opposition movement. See also Karal, 511, for a discussion on the use of these terms and Karl Blind, "The Prorogued Turkish Parliament," *North American Review* 175 (1902): 42.

122. One such attempt took the life of its principal perpetrator, Ali Suavi, who had been one of the leading Young Ottomans. See Mardin, *Genesis*, 360–84. Another member of the early circle, Ali Şefkati, barely saved his life after a second aborted attempt and fled to Geneva. Ahmed Bedevi Kuran, *İnkılap Tarihimiz ve Jön Türkler* (İstanbul: Tan, 1945), 18–23.

123. On the pan-Islamic thrust of this journal, see Jacob M. Landau, *The Politics of Pan-Islam* (Oxford: Clarendon Press, 1994), 60–62.

124. M. Şükrü Hanioğlu, *The Young Turks in Opposition* (New York: Oxford University Press, 1995), 41–42. This is a revised translation of Hanioğlu's *Osmanlı İttihad ve Terakki Cemiyeti ve Jön Türklük, 1889–1902* (İstanbul: İletişim, 1986). The author also discusses Arabs in the liberal movement in his "The Young Turks and the Arabs before the Revolution of 1908," in Khalidi et al., 31–49. See also A. B. Kuran, *Jön Türkler*, 24.

125. Caesar Farah, "Censorship and Freedom of Expression in Syria and Egypt," in *Nationalism in a Non-National State*, ed. William Haddad and William Ochsenwald (Columbus: Ohio State University Press, 1977), 161.

126. Tarazi, 2:264.

127. Farah, 161; Zirikli, 6:115.

128. Tarazi, 2:250–53; Hourani, *Arabic Thought*, 269. For a retrospective accusation of these intellectuals, who explicitly or implicitly upheld Arab-Islamic ideas, for having exploited national feeling to further their personal interests, see Muhammad Jamil Bayhum, *Qawafil al-'urubba wa mawakibuha khilal al-'usur* (Beirut: Matba'a Kashaf, 1950), (pt. 2): 19. Sabunji also published a journal called *Al-ittihad al-'arabi* (Arab Unity).

129. Tarazi, 2:270–71.

130. Şerif Mardin, *Jön Türklerin Siyasi Fikirleri, 1895–1908* (Ankara, 1964), 17; Karl Blind, "Young Turkey," *Fortnightly Review* 66 (1896): 835.

131. Mardin mentions, however, that Ghanem was in charge of the French

bulletin *La France Internationale*, which was published in France with funding from Abdülhamid (*Jön Türklerin*, 17).

132. Hourani, *Arabic Thought*, 264.

133. See his memoirs, *Ahmed Rıza Bey'in Anıları* (İstanbul: Arba, 1988), 10. Ahmed Rıza was the leader of the procentralization faction of the Young Turks. His ideological influence in the 1908 Revolution was paramount, but after 1908 he was phased out of positions of power in the government and in the CUP.

134. Berkes, 307; Karal, 527.

135. E. E. Ramsaur, *The Young Turks: Prelude to the Revolution of 1908* (Princeton, N.J.: Princeton University Press, 1957), 24, 37, 52.

136. Kuran, *Jön Türkler*, 29; Erik Jan Zürcher, *The Unionist Factor: The Role of the Committee of Union and Progress in the Turkish National Movement* (Leiden: E. J. Brill, 1984), 16.

137. Mehmed Murad Bey was better known as Mizancı Murad because he edited a paper called *Mizan* (Balance).

138. In 1897 Faris capitulated to Hamidian enticement to accept the concession for the water supply of the city of Beirut and abandoned opposition temporarily. See Hanioğlu, *Young Turks in Opposition*, 43–44.

139. Mardin, *Jön Türklerin*, 18; Hanioğlu, *Young Turks in Opposition*, 45–46.

140. Hanioğlu, *İttihad ve Terakki*, 105–8.

141. Abu Manneh, "Sayyadi," 145–46.

142. Abu Manneh, "Christians," 299.

143. Rıza refrained from a closer cooperation with Faris, possibly because he viewed the latter's *Parti Constitutionnel* to be too Syria-centered to further the broader aims of the Union and Progress Society.

144. Sina Akşin, *100 Soruda Jön Türkler ve İttihat ve Terakki* (İstanbul: Gerçek, 1980), 28.

145. Hans Kohn, *Western Civilization in the Near East* (New York: Columbia University Press, 1936), 264; Elie Kedourie, "The Impact of the Young Turk Revolution on the Arabic-Speaking Provinces of the Ottoman Empire," in *Arabic Political Memoirs and Other Studies*, by E. Kedourie (London: Frank Cass, 1974), 125–26.

146. Mardin, *Jön Türklerin*, 91.

147. Ibid., 18–20.

148. Ghanem said: "We Arabs know that if [the Franks (*al-afranj*)] enter our country, in a couple of years our territories will be in their hands; and they will rule it [*yatasarrafuna*] as they wish. As for Turks, they believe in our religion and are acquainted with our customs. In their four centuries [*ajyal*] of rule they did not take an inch of our property to their possession. They left to the inhabitants their land, their property, their industry, and their commerce. The Arabs have benefitted from the trade of the Turks and from our uninterrupted bond. Would it be right for us to replace them with someone else? . . . It is only those who want to curry favor with the ruler who accuse the Muslims with the [wish to] establish an Arab state and the Christians with conspiring with the foreigners. . . . The Arab intellectuals and notables have no wish for their *umma* to live other than within the domain of Ottoman interests." *Al-mu'tamar al-'arabi al-awwal* (Cairo: al-Matba'a al-Salafiyya, 1913), 61; Bayhum, 19.

149. Karal, 517.

150. Ramsaur, 81–90; Lewis, 201.

151. Blind, "Turkish Parliament," 42; Ramsaur, 68.

152. Ramsaur, 125.

153. These included the aforementioned Tunisian reformer Khayr al-Din Pasha (grand vizier) and al-Qudsi (second secretary) as well as 'Izzat al-'Abid (later second secretary), Abulhuda al-Sayyadi (Aleppine Sufi propagandist), Muhammad Zafir (Tunisian Islamic propagandist), and Najib Malhama. See Karal, 544–45; Landau, *Pan-Islam*, 70–71; and Engin Akarlı, "Abdülhamid II's Attempt to Integrate Arabs into the Ottoman System," in *Palestine in the Late Ottoman Period: Political, Social, and Economic Transformation*, ed. David Kushner (Jerusalem: Yad Izhak Ben-Zvi, 1986), 77–78.

154. The sultan employed Christian Arabs in his service (rather than members of the less-trusted Christian groups) to demonstrate that he did not forsake the empire's non-Muslim population.

155. İbrahim Temo, *İttihad ve Terakki Cemiyetinin Teşekkülü ve Hidemat-ı Vataniye ve İnkilab-ı Milliye Dair Hatıratım* (Mecidiye, 1939), 151. The brother of Najib, Salim, was minister of the mines. See Akarlı, "Abdülhamid II's Attempt," 78.

156. Those whose property had been confiscated because of their refusal to abandon their damaging antigovernment publications and to return to the empire included the names of Salim Sarkis and Najib Hindi, a Chaldean from Syria. (A. B. Kuran, *Jön Türkler*, 148.) Others like Faris, Sabunji, and Muwaylihi were rewarded with government posts and economic concessions for leaving the ranks of the opposition. See also M. Şükrü Hanioğlu, *Doktor Abdullah Cevdet ve Dönemi* (İstanbul: Üçdal, n.d. [1982]), 210.

157. Ibid., 210.

158. Tarık Zafer Tunaya, *Türkiye'de Siyasi Partiler, 1859–1952* (İstanbul, 1952), 109; Temo, 45; Kuran, *Jön Türkler*, 31. According to Kuran, he was known as "Arap Ahmedi" in İstanbul.

159. Ahmed Bedevi Kuran, *İnkılap Tarihimiz ve İttihat ve Terakki* (İstanbul: Tan, 1948), 160.

160. Ibid., 62.

161. Temo, 51.

162. This group survived a crackdown by the Hamidian police in 1907. In 1909, when they graduated from the War Academy soon after the abortive counterrevolution in April (see chapter 2), they were arrested for their sympathies for Prince Sabahaddin. Several of them escaped from İstanbul to go to Morocco and accepted duties as officers in the Moroccan army. Of ten officers whose names are cited, three were from Arab provinces: Ramzi and Hilmi from Damascus and Mahmud Nadim from Tripoli. See Kuran, *Jön Türkler*, 221–31, 282–85.

163. Hourani, *Arabic Thought*, 205.

164. See Mardin, *Jön Türklerin*, 59–65; A. B. Kuran, *İttihat ve Terakki*, 158, on fluctuations in the khedivial policy vis-à-vis the Young Turks. The Prince Sabahaddin group contacted the khedive in 1902 to seek his assistance for an

attempt to dethrone Abdülhamid. 'Abbas Hilmi received the plan favorably, but it did not materialize for other reasons. See Kuran, *Jön Türkler*, 160.

165. Rıza, 19; Kuran, *İttihat ve Terakki*, 136–37, 204–5, 215–17; M. Hanefi Bostan, *Said Halim Paşa* (İstanbul: İrfan Yayınevi, 1992), 21–26.

166. Zeine, *Arab Nationalism*, 50–51; Hanioğlu, *Abdullah Cevdet*, 54.

167. Hanioğlu, *Abdullah Cevdet*, 134–42.

168. Wajih Kawtharani, *Al-ittijahat al-ijtima'iyya al-siyasiyya fi jabal lubnan wa al-mashraq al-'arabi, 1860–1920* (Beirut: Ma'had al-Inma' al-'Arabi, 1978), 163.

169. Zeine, *Arab Nationalism*, 50–51.

170. A. B. Kuran, *İttihat ve Terakki*, 216.

171. Akşin, 53.

172. A. B. Kuran, *İttihat ve Terakki*, 131, 186.

173. Kawtharani, 152; Mustafa al-Shihabi, *Muhadarat fi al-isti'mar* (Cairo: Matba'a Nahda, 1957), 37.

174. For an account of this deportation, see Ali Fahri, *Emel Yolunda* (İstanbul: Müşterek el Menfaa Osmanlı Şirketi Matbaası, 1328 [1910]).

175. Zürcher, 19, cites the following organizations: Medeniyet-i İslamiye Cemiyeti of Rodoslu Süleyman in Syria, the Arabian Revolutionary Committee of Kuşçubaşı Eşref in the Hijaz, and Vatan Cemiyeti of Mustafa (Cantekin) in Damascus. See also Kuran, *Jön Türkler*, 32.

176. Hanioğlu, "Young Turks and Arabs," 38. Maghmumi became one of the key figures in the early Unionist movement in Europe. See also Hanioğlu, *Young Turks in Opposition*, 106–9.

177. See David Commins, "Religious Reformers and Arabists in Damascus, 1885–1914," *IJMES*, 18 (1986): 405–25, and *Islamic Reform: Politics and Change in Late Ottoman Syria* (New York: Oxford University Press, 1990).

178. Commins, "Religious Reformers," 410; Mustafa al-Shihabi, *Muhadarat 'an al-qawmiyya al-'arabiyya* (Cairo [?]: al-Jami'a al-'Arabiyya, 1959), 50.

179. Al-Shihabi, *Muhadarat fi al-isti'mar* (Cairo, 1957), 2:36; Commins, *Islamic Reform*, 93. Bedri Bey, a teacher at the military school, was appointed governor of Monastir after the 1908 Revolution. See Muhammad Sa'id al-Bani, *Tanwir al-basa'ir bi sirah al-shaykh tahir* ([Damascus]: Matba'a al-hukuma al-'arabiyya al-suriyya, 1920), 127–28.

180. Commins, "Religious Reformers," 411, quoting Fakhri al-Barudi, *Mudhakkirat al-barudi* (Beirut: 1951–52), 1:29–32.

181. İbrahim Temo, an Albanian student at the medical school and one of the founders of the Ottoman Union, reports a particular exchange of blows that ended in the imprisonment of the winners, the provincial contingent. Temo, 12.

182. Although many of the Arab students were from prominent families, they were from the less well off branches of these families. See Commins, "Religious Reformers," 412; Khoury, 68.

183. Mardin, *Jön Türklerin*, 40.

184. Ergin, 3:892–94.

185. Ali Çankaya, *Mülkiye Tarihi ve Mülkiyeliler* (Ankara: Örnek, 1954), 356–57.

186. Ibid., 3:892.

187. Ergin, 2:617.

188. Also, an Aşiret Mektebi (Tribal School) was established with this purpose in 1892. Karal, 401. On Abdülhamid's personal relationship with Arab chiefs, see Akarlı, "Abdülhamid II's Attempt," 81, 86.

189. Hourani, *Arabic Thought*, 264–65, 275.

Chapter 2. The Second Constitutional Experiment, 1908–1909

1. Feroz Ahmad, *The Young Turks: The Committee of Union and Progress in Turkish Politics, 1908–1914* (Oxford: Clarendon Press, 1969), 15–18.

2. *Tanin*, 29 August 1908; Ali Cevat, *İkinci Meşrutiyetin İlanı ve Otuz Bir Mart Hadisesi*, ed. Faik Reşit Unat (Ankara: Türk Tarih Kurumu Basımevi, 1960), 167.

3. Sabine Prätor, *Der arabische Faktor in der jungtürkischen Politik: Eine Studie zum osmanischen Parlament der II. Konstitution (1908–1918)* (Berlin: Klaus Schwarz Verlag, 1993), 206. In the early months of the revolution the freedom of the press was unabridged. Even after the enactment of a press law the following year opposition newspapers found ways of circumventing the restrictions. *Tanin* itself was closed and reopened several times under different names in 1912, when the CUP fell from power.

4. Orhan Koloğlu, "Osmanlı Basını: İçeriği ve Rejimi," *TCTA*, 1:90.

5. Kedourie, "Impact," 142.

6. Ergin, 4:1280.

7. Ahmad, *Young Turks*, 15–20.

8. *Tanin*, 14 August 1908.

9. The date corresponded to 31 March 1325 in the official Ottoman calendar.

10. Ahmad, *Young Turks*, 47–57.

11. In the provincial administration of the Hijaz, for instance, the number of government employees went up from 14 to 100 during his reign. Karal, 332–33.

12. According to Sina Akşin, from the First Army Corps alone 1,400 officers were laid off following the revolution. *100 Soruda Jön*, 120.

13. *Tanin*, 14 August 1908. While Hüseyin Cahid's suggestion points to the desperation that the CUP felt at this juncture, it also shows that the Committee was favorably disposed toward cooperation with Europe.

14. *Tanin*, 1 August 1908. He was referred to as Arap İzzet (İzzet the Arab) in the İstanbul press. Upon receiving pleas from Arabs of the empire, who regretted this usage, *Tanin* announced on August 4 that he would henceforth be referred to as "İzzet."

15. Ali Birinci, *Hürriyet ve İtilâf Fırkası* (İstanbul: Dergah, 1990), 222.

16. Taj el-Sir Ahmad Harran, "Syrian Relations in the Ottoman Constitutional Period, 1908–1914" (Ph.D. diss., University of London, 1969), 52–59.

17. *Tanin*, 25 September 1908.

18. Both the centralists and the decentralists advocated *tevsi'-i mezuniyet* (ex-

tension of discretion). For the different interpretations of this principle, see Yıldızhan Yayla, *Anayasalarımızda Yönetim İlkeleri: Tevsi-i Mezuniyet ve Tefrik-i Vezaif* (İstanbul: İstanbul Üniversitesi Siyasal Bilgiler Fakültesi, 1984), 84–94.

19. *Tanin*, 4 September 1908.

20. *Tanin*, 19 September 1908.

21. For example, on the situation in Yemen, see *Tanin*, 16 September 1908.

22. Some officials even managed to arrange to reside at locations where conditions were better than the district of their assignment. Faiz Demiroğlu, *Abdülhamid'e Verilen Jurnaller* (İstanbul: İstanbul Matbaası, 1955), 97.

23. Ratib Pasha had served as governor of the Hijaz since 1893 and had amassed a fortune, mostly through illegal practices, when in office. See also chapter 5.

24. On his dismissal, see *Tanin*, 6 August 1908. See chapter 5 for a detailed account of the political changes in the Hijaz at this time.

25. *Takvim-i Vekai*, 30 January 1909.

26. BBA. BEO 264060. The Grand Vizierate to Osman Pasha (25 March 1909).

27. BBA. BEO 264548. Minister of War to [the Grand Vizierate] (30 March 1909).

28. BBA. BEO 264548. The Grand Vizierate to Hadi Pasha (4 April 1909).

29. PRO. FO 195/2320. Acting Consul Richardson to Lowther, no. 81 (Jidda, 18 July 1909) and no. 92 (30 August 1909).

30. Donald Quataert, "A Provisional Report Concerning the Impact of European Capital on Ottoman Port and Railway Workers, 1888–1909," in Bacqué-Grammont and Dumont.

31. *Takvim-i Vekai*, 1 October 1908.

32. Harran, "Syrian Relations," 42.

33. For example, in December 1909 certain villages near Medina applied to the authorities, pleading to submit their taxes to the government rather than to oppressive tax collectors of Ibn Rashid, who ruled over the Najd. The request was not found feasible. BBA. BEO 276300. The Ministry of the Interior to the Grand Vizierate (22 December 1909).

34. Stephen Hemsley Longrigg, *Iraq, 1900 to 1950* (London: Oxford University Press, 1953), 49.

35. BBA. BEO 265626 (266358). Müşir Osman Fevzi Pasha to the Ministry of War ([Damascus], 15 July 1909). For an account of similar conflicts between the governor of Damascus and commander of the Fifth Army in the Hamidian period, see Akarlı, "Abdülhamid II's Attempt," 82–83.

36. For an account of the repercussions of the revolution in the Arab provinces based on British and American consular sources, see Kedourie, "Impact."

37. Harran, "Syrian Relations," 39.

38. PRO. FO 195/2286. Acting Consul Husain to Lowther (Jidda, 25 August 1908).

39. Khalidi, *British Policy*, 210.

40. HHS. PA 38/341. Zepharovich to Aehrenthal (Jerusalem, 14 August 1908). Ekrem was the son of Namık Kemal, the renowned poet and Young Ottoman activist. According to Zepharovich, he ingratiated himself to Abdül-

hamid in order to build a career for himself. Ekrem immediately initiated a campaign with an eye to assure the election of anti-CUP candidates in the elections that the new charter called for.

In Benghazi, as in Jerusalem, the CUP leadership consisted of administrative officials and not officers. PRO. FO/371/760/325. Consul Raphael A. Fontana to Sir Edward Grey, no. 13 (Benghazi, 21 December 1908).

41. Reeva S. Simon, "The Education of an Iraqi Ottoman Army Officer," in *Origins of Arab Nationalism*, ed. Khalidi et al., 161.

42. *Tanin*, 19 September 1908.

43. Kedourie approaches these demonstrations with skepticism. See his "Impact," 134–35.

44. PRO. FO 371/560/36123. Major J. Ramsay to Government of India, no. 93 (Baghdad, 14 September 1908). Enclosure in Lowther to Grey, no. 62 (Therapia, 19 October 1909).

45. MAE. Turquie, N.S. 6. Bertrand to [Ministère des Affaires Etrangères] (Jidda, 24 August 1908).

46. PRO. FO 195/2286. Acting Consul Husain to Lowther (Jidda, 25 August 1908). The report makes particular mention of a local money changer by the name of Ahmed Hazzazi among the leaders of this mob of extraordinary size for a town like Jidda.

47. BBA. DH-SYS 122/5–1. Cemal Bey (?) to the Ministry of the Interior (2 June 1909).

48. PRO. FO 371/560/37930. Devey to Lowther (Damascus, 1 October 1908). Enclosed in Lowther to Grey, no. 697 (Constantinople, 24 October 1908).

49. *Tanin*, 27 August 1908.

50. PRO. FO 371/560/36123. See note 44.

51. In January 1909, in a speech in Parliament, Kamil Pasha repeated that when he became grand vizier organizations imitating the CUP emerged in the provinces. These organizations, according to Kamil, were devoid of patriotism: they expelled officials and freed criminal prisoners along with political ones. *Takvim-i Vekai*, 15 January 1909.

52. İsmail Hakkı wrote that the CUP realizes the dangers of constituting a government within a government. See *Tanin*, 27 August 1908.

53. PRO. FO 195/2286. See note 38.

54. Danişmend, *İzahlı*, 365.

55. Kamal S. Salibi, "Beirut under the Young Turks: As Depicted in the Political Memoirs of Salim Ali Salam (1868–1938)," in Berque and Chevallier, eds., *Les Arabes par leurs archives* (Paris: CNRS, 1976), 200. President of the Beirut CUP at the time was Rida al-Maqdisi.

56. On delegation to Beirut, see PRO. FO 371/560/37689. Lowther to Grey, no. 705 (Therapia, 24 October 1908); on Benghazi, PRO. FO 371/760/325 (see note 40); on Damascus, see PRO. FO 618/3. Devey to Lowther, no. 1 (Damascus, 2 January 1909).

57. PRO. FO 371/560/37689. See note 56.

58. PRO. FO 618/3. Devey to Lowther, no. 1 (Damascus, 2 January 1909).

59. *Takvim-i Vekai*, 1 November 1908.

60. PRO. FO 371/760/325. See note 40.

61. PRO. FO 371/560/37953. Lieutenant-Colonel Ramsay to the Government of India (Baghdad, 19 October 1908). Enclosed in Lowther to Grey, no. 796 (Constantinople, 23 November 1908).

62. BBA. BEO. Vilayet Defterleri 304: "Hicaz gelen," no. 78; PRO. FO 195/2286. Monahan to Lowther (Jidda, 18 November 1908).

63. MAE. N.S. 6, no. 376. Valdrôme to [Quai d'Orsay ?] (Cairo, 25 November 1908).

64. PRO. FO 618/3. Devey to Lowther, no. 50 (Damascus, 4 October 1909).

65. Kayalı, "Elections," 268–73.

66. For a contemporary appraisal of the evolution of parties, see Lütfi Fikri, *Selanikte Bir Konferans: Bizde Furuk-ı Siyasiye, Hal-i Hazırı, İstikbali* (İstanbul, 1326 [1910]). Fikri mentions the CUP's position in 1908 on p. 35.

67. "Osmanlı İttihat ve Terakki Cemiyeti'nin 1908 (1324) Senesinde Kabul Edilen Siyasal Programı," in Tunaya, *Türkiye'de Siyasal Partiler*, vol. 1, *İkinci Meşrutiyet Dönemi* (İstanbul: Hürriyet Vakfı Yayınları, 1988), 65.

68. Halil Menteşe, *Osmanlı Mebusan Meclisi Reisi Halil Menteşe'nin Anıları*, ed. İsmail Arar (İstanbul: Hürriyet Yayınları, 1986), 11.

69. *Tanin*, 10 September 1908.

70. *Tanin*, 24 September 1908.

71. Suleiman Mousa, *Al-haraka al-ʿarabiyya* (Beirut: Dar al-nahar, 1970), 26; Tawfiq ʿAli Burru, *Al-ʿarab wa al-turk fi al-ʿahd al-dusturi al-ʿuthmani, 1908–1914* (Cairo: Jamiʿa al-Duwal al-ʿArabiyya, 1960), 109; Antonius, 104. The merits of the methods of calculation and of the substance of the charges will be discussed in the next chapter.

72. The CUP took measures in İstanbul to assure proportional representation to Muslims because the Christian communities, and especially the Greeks, were better organized to secure disproportionately large numbers of deputies for their own communities. See Feroz Ahmad, "Unionist Relations with the Greek, Armenian, and Jewish Communities of the Ottoman Empire, 1908–1914," in *Christians and Jews in the Ottoman Empire*, ed. Benjamin Braude and Bernard Lewis (New York: Holmes and Meier Publishers, 1982), 1:407; Akşin, 106.

73. Prätor, 20.

74. *Takvim-i Vekai*, 10 February 1909.

75. Reşat Ekrem Koçu, "Türkiye'de Seçimin Tarihi, 1877–1950," *Tarih Dünyası* 1 (1950): 181–82.

76. PRO. FO 195/2286. Monahan to Lowther, no. 123 (Jidda, 18 December 1908).

77. *Takvim-i Vekai*, 21 December 1908.

78. *Takvim-i Vekai*, 23 December 1908.

79. Demiroğlu, 24; Prätor, 283.

80. Prätor, 278.

81. MMZC, I/1/3 (first term [December 1908–January 1912], first legislative year [December 1908–August 1909], third sitting), 24 December 1908. For al-Muʿayyad, see also I/1/6, 29 December 1908; Prätor, 52–54; Harran, "Syrian Relations," 134–35.

82. MMZC, I/1/4, 25 December 1908.

83. The title of the leader of an Arab town's families that claimed descent from the Prophet Muhammad.

84. He was described by Rashid Rida as a reactionary and a supporter of absolute rule and denounced for his complicity with unlawful elements against the state. *Al-manar* 11:865 (6 January 1909).

85. *Yeni Tasvir-i Efkar*, 13 July 1909.

86. Prätor, 54, 258. Cami had served eight to ten years in Libya before becoming *kaymakam*. Prätor observes that the resignation of the deputy-elect led to reelection in Fezzan but not in Karak.

87. Hüseyin Hatemi, "Tanzimat ve Meşrutiyet Dönemlerinde Derneklerin Gelişimi," *TCTA* 1:202.

88. Harran, "Syrian Relations," 136.

89. Eliezer Tauber, *The Emergence of the Arab Movements* (London: Frank Cass, 1993), 61.

90. Kedourie, "Political Parties in the Arab World," in *Memoirs*, 41.

91. See Taj el-Sir Ahmad Harran, "The Young Turks and the Arabs: The Role of Arab Societies in the Turkish-Arab Relations in the Period 1908–1914," in *Türk-Arap İlişkileri*: (Ankara: Hacettepe Üniversitesi Türkiye ve Orta Doğu Araştırma Enstitüsü, [1980]), 182–85.

92. HHS. PA 12/197, fol. 97, "Le Comité Syrien," 25 December 1908.

93. Burru cites his article (p. 92) in *Correspondance d'Orient*, 15 January 1909.

94. Due to cultural and political interests in Syria, France was likely to have supported the Syrian Committee. It seems, however, that the Committee was not simply an organ of the French government. In April 1909 the Syrian Committee engaged in pro-autonomy propaganda in Iraq and alarmed the French consulate in Baghdad, which viewed the possible outcome of such propaganda not as autonomy but independence under a British protectorate. (MAE. Turquie, N.S. 6. Rouet to [İstanbul ?], no. 17 (Baghdad, 1 April 1909).

95. *Takvim-i Vekai*, 18 January 1909.

96. PRO. FO 618/3. Devey to Lowther, no. 7, "Rashid B. Moutran's proposal for the independence of Syria," (Damascus, 21 January 1909).

97. *Takvim-i Vekai*, 20 January 1909.

98. *Takvim-i Vekai*, 18 and 19 January 1909 (MMZC, I/1/13, 14 and 16 January 1909).

99. *Takvim-i Vekai*, 18 January 1909.

100. The name occurs as Hasan Rushdi in the parliamentary proceedings. This appears to be a mistake, as there was no Beiruti deputy by this name. It is evident, however, that the remarks do belong to one of the Beiruti deputies, and in all likelihood, to Rushdi al-Sham'a. *Takvim-i Vekai*, 19 January 1909.

101. He spoke with specific reference to a telegram by Ahmad al-Sham'a, a member of the Damascus administrative council, who implicated the entire Mutran family.

102. Prätor, 210, 278.

103. Burru, 93.

104. Harran, "Syrian Relations," 145.

105. Prätor, 41–42.

106. Ibid., 41.

107. *Takvim-i Vekai*, 26 January 1909 (MMZC, I/1/16, 21 January 1909).

108. *Takvim-i Vekai*, 16 February 1909 (MMZC, I/1/25, 9 February 1909).

109. *Takvim-i Vekai*, 18 January 1909 (MMZC, I/1/13, 14 January 1909).

110. *Takvim-i Vekai*, 17 and 18 January 1908 (MMZC, I/1/13, 14 January 1909); Prätor, 104.

111. The matter was shelved until the interpellation of the minister of education and does not seem to have been taken up again. *Takvim-i Vekai*, 17 February 1909 (MMZC, I/1/26, 11 February 1909).

112. See also Prätor, 162.

113. See Akşin, 124–30; Ahmad, *Young Turks*, 40–47. There are different interpretations of this incident. Ahmad and Akşin assign the responsibility largely to the Liberal opposition supported by the British Embassy in İstanbul. Danişmend sees it as a scheme of the CUP designed to discredit the old regime and enhance its own powers (*31 Mart Vakası* [İstanbul: İstanbul Kitabevi, 1986], 109–10), as does a contemporary observer Mehmed Selahaddin in *İttihad ve Terakki'nin Kuruluşu ve Osmanlı Devleti'nin Yıkılışı Hakkında Bildiklerim* (İstanbul: İnkilab, 1989), 30. A less than scholarly treatment of the event presents it as a CUP-Jewish-*dönme* conspiracy. Cevat Rıfat Atılhan, *Bütün Çıplaklığıyla 31 Mart Faciası* (İstanbul: Aykurt, 1959).

114. BBA. BEO 266358 (265626). The Grand Vizierate to the Ministries of War and Finance (19 May 1909).

115. PRO. FO 195/2320. Monahan to Lowther, no. 47 (Jidda, 8 May 1909).

116. BBA. BEO 266818. [Governor ?] to the Grand Vizierate (Baghdad, 15 April 1909).

117. Khalidi, *British Policy*, 211; Commins, "Religious Reformers," 416–17.

118. BBA. BEO 265948. Governor Nazım [to the Grand Vizierate] (10 May 1909). Reproduced in Birinci, 251.

119. BBA. BEO 266303. Grand Vizier to the Ministry of War (15 May 1909).

120. His brother Hikmat Sulayman served as prime minister of Iraq in the 1930s.

121. Feroz Ahmad, *Young Turks*, 49, 66.

122. Ibid., 52–53. Talat was a self-made statesman who came from a lower-middle-class, provincial background (a postal employee in Edirne) and rose to become grand vizier during World War I. He had a less flamboyant personality than other prominent CUP leaders like Enver and Cemal, but emerged as the Committee's strongman in the capital, thanks to his political skills. Cavid was the son of a Salonika family also of modest means, but he was able to build on a career in the *Mülkiye* (where he later taught) to emerge as the indispensable economic virtuoso of the CUP.

123. Carter V. Findley, *Bureaucratic Reform in the Ottoman Empire* (Princeton, N.J.: Princeton University Press, 1980), 294–95.

124. AA. Türkei 142/Bd. 31–32. Marschall to Bülow, no. 196 (Therapia, 3 September 1908).

125. Birinci, 25; Hatemi, 207; Tunaya, *Türkiye'de Siyasal Partiler*, vol. 1, *İkinci Meşrutiyet Dönemi*, 206–7.

126. BBA. BEO 262881 (262357, 264987). Governor to the Minister of the Interior (31 January 1909).

127. BBA. BEO 263720 (262357). Governor to the Minister of the Interior (9 February 1909).

128. BBA. BEO 262881 (262357). Grand Vizierate to the Presidency of the Council of State (30 March 1909).

129. Khalidi, *British Policy*, 204.

130. "1908 (1324) Kongresi Kararları," in Tunaya, *Türkiye'de Siyasal Partiler*, 1:65.

131. Ergin, 4:1274.

132. *Tanin*, 25 October 1909.

133. *Tanin*, 8 November 1909.

134. *Tanin*, 26 March 1910.

135. *Takvim-i Vekai*, 14 January 1909. All provincial government employees earning a salary of 300 *kuruş* or above were encouraged to subscribe to the official paper of the province to support its publication.

136. BBA. BEO 258601. Minister of the Interior to the Grand Vizierate, no. 4392 (10 February 1909).

137. Rushdi al-Sham'a (Damascus) proposed the appointment of itinerant teachers for the tribes in this area. *Takvim-i Vekai*, 17 February 1909 (MMZC, I/1/26, 11 February 1909). Also of interest is Rushdi Bey's suggestion that the salaries of five preachers who had been sent to the region but had proved useless should be paid instead to teachers to be appointed. See also Prätor, 174.

138. BBA. BEO 269189 (258601). Ministry of the Interior [to the Grand Vizier] (4 July 1909).

139. *Tanin*, 16 October 1909.

140. *Tanin*, 25 October 1909.

141. *Tanin*, 4 September 1908.

142. Danişmend, *İzahlı*, 368.

143. *Yeni Tasvir-i Efkar*, 29 June 1909.

144. *Tasvir-i Efkar*, 13 June 1909.

145. During a discussion of disturbances in Hawran, a motion by the *sancak*'s only deputy, Sa'd al-Din al-Khalil, was dismissed because those on the floor were unable to understand his imperfect Turkish. *Takvim-i Vekai*, 30 January 1909 (MMZC, I/1/17, 23 January 1909) and 31 January 1909 (MMZC, I/1/18, 26 January 1909).

Chapter 3.   The Opposition and the Arabs, 1910–1911

1. Ahmad describes the Unionists as "representatives of the provincial petty bourgeoisie." Though the Unionists were proponents of administrative centralization and wished to exercise control over state organs, they were suspicious of "cosmopolitan İstanbul." "Vanguard of a Nascent Bourgeoisie: The Social and Economic Policy of the Young Turks, 1908–1918," in *Türkiye'nin Sosyal ve Ekonomik Tarihi, 1071–1920*, ed. Osman Okyar and Halil İnalcık (Ankara: Meteksan, 1980), 336.

2. William Miller, *The Ottoman Empire, 1801–1913* (Cambridge: Cambridge University Press, 1913), 495.

3. Zeine, *Arab Nationalism*, 76.

4. PRO. FO 371/662/17914. Lowther to Grey, no. 584 (Therapia, 21 July 1909).

5. *Tanin*, 31 August 1909.

6. Resignations, reelections, and variant names in the records for the same individuals complicate the tally. Feroz Ahmad and Dankwart Rustow summarized data on Ottoman parliaments provided by previous studies and contributed considerable further useful, though still inconclusive, information to the existing data. "İkinci Meşrutiyet Döneminde Meclisler, 1908–1918," in *Güney-Doğu Avrupa Araştırmaları Dergisi* 4–5 (1976): 247–48. See also Zeine, *Arab Nationalism*, 71–72. Prätor has worked with Ahmad and Rustow's data pertaining to the Arab provinces and offered some amendments and further statistical analysis. See Prätor, 37–48.

7. According to Fargo, there were 152 Turkish and 50 Arab deputies. See Fargo, 205.

8. Especially noteworthy are the figures supplied by the German consul in Beirut. To refute an article titled "The Turkish Hegemony" by Orientalist D[avis] Trietsch in *Osmanischer Lloyd* (24 July 1910), Consul Padel analyzed and adjusted existing census data and estimated the number of Turks at 12.1 million and Arabs at 12.6 million. According to Padel's figures, 9.1 million Turks lived in Anatolia (as opposed to Trietsch's 7.5 million) and 3 million in the European provinces. 5.6 million Arabs (according to Trietsch, 5 million) lived in Syria and Mesopotamia, 6 million in Arabia, and 1 million in Libya. AA Türkei 165/32. Padel to Bethmann-Hollweg, no. 138 (Beirut, 30 September 1910). The inflated figures for Arabia are consistent with official Ottoman estimates. See Kemal Karpat, *Ottoman Population, 1830–1914* (Madison: University of Wisconsin Press, 1985), 150. On various other figures on the number of Arabs and Turks, see Zeine, *Emergence*, 140–43, and Dawn, *Ottomanism*, 153.

9. Karpat, *Ottoman Population*, 164–68.

10. Assignment of parliamentary contingents to regions where an eligible votership did not exist posed a certain incongruity, even in the presence of more or less reliable population estimates. In view of the general disinterest in elections, deputies from many tribal areas could only be "elected" by fiat, as was done in Yemen.

11. Syed Ali El-Edroos, *The Hashemite Arab Army, 1908–1979* (Amman: The Publishing Committee, 1980), 8. Quoted in Linda L. Layne, "Tribesmen as Citizens: 'Primordial Ties' and Democracy in Rural Jordan," in *Elections in the Middle East*, ed. Layne (Boulder, Colo.: Westview, 1987), 114. El-Edroos claims that the Arabs outnumbered Turks three to two (and Layne misquotes him as three to one) in 1908.

12. Prätor tabulates ethnic affiliations largely relying on Ahmad and Rustow's data. See Prätor, 29.

13. Prätor, 203.

14. *Tanin*, 31 August 1909.

15. *Tanin*, 8, 10, 15, 16, and 19 April 1910.

16. Indeed, even under Abdülhamid, who employed many Arabs in the Palace, Arabs had not "permeated" the bureaucracy that had evolved under the Tanzimat. Ruth Roded, "Ottoman Service as a Vehicle for the Rise of New Upstarts among the Urban Elite Families of Syria in the Last Decades of Ottoman Rule," *Asian and African Studies* 17 (1985): 85.

17. *Tanin*, 19 April 1910.

18. For this committee's declaration dated April 1909, see Tunaya, *Türkiye'de Siyasal Partiler*, 1:206–7.

19. See Tauber, *Emergence*, 101–8.

20. Masami Arai, *Turkish Nationalism in the Young Turk Era* (Leiden: E. J. Brill, 1992), 6–20.

21. Orhan Koloğlu, in his preface to Jeltyakov, makes this argument about Young Ottomans (no page number).

22. Arai, "The Genç Kalemler and the Young Turks: A Study in Nationalism," in *Orta Doğu Teknik Üniversitesi Gelişme Dergisi* 12 (1985): 227–30.

23. On Akçura, see François Georgeon, *Aux Origines du nationalisme turc: Yusuf Akçura (1876–1935)* (Paris: ADPF, 1980).

24. Jacob M. Landau, *Pan-Turkism in Turkey* (London: C. Hurst & Company, 1981), 40–41.

25. Tevfik Tarık, *Muaddel Kanun-u Esasi ve İntihab-ı Mebusan Kanunu* (İstanbul: İkbal, 1327 [1911]), 55, 76.

26. Tunaya, *Türkiye'de Siyasal Partiler*, 1:66–67.

27. Knut Eriksen, Andreas Kazamias, Robin Okey, and Janusz Tomiak, "Governments and the Education of Non-Dominant Ethnic Groups in Comparative Perspective," in *Schooling, Educational Policy and Ethnic Identity*, ed. Tomiak (New York: New York University Press, 1991), 392–93.

28. Ibid., 395.

29. Buzpınar, 132.

30. Hüseyin Cahid mentioned that theoretically, and from the point of view of the constitution, the Ministry of Justice was right in implementing Turkish, but "we should confess that a state cannot be administered with theories." *Tanin*, 11 November 1909; also 19 April 1910.

31. *Tanin*, 11 February 1911.

32. Prätor, 167–68.

33. Prätor, 164–65, 169.

34. Ergin, 2:617; Çankaya, 93–95.

35. Hobsbawm, 117.

36. 25 February 1909.

37. This concern is explicitly voiced by Hüseyin Cahid in his article on the language of the courts. *Tanin*, 11 November 1909.

38. PRO. FO 618/3. Devey to Lowther, no. 28 (Damascus, 12 July 1910).

39. Hanna Batatu, *The Old Social Classes and the Revolutionary Movements of Iraq* (Princeton, N.J.: Princeton University Press, 1978), 171.

40. BBA. DH-SYS 64/33. Aleppines to the Grand Vizier and the Ministry of the Interior (6 February 1911).

41. BBA. DH-MTV 19/20. Deputy Governor Cemal to the Ministry of the

Interior (Aleppo, 13 September 1911). These documents suggest that prostitution by non-Muslim women was tolerated in Aleppo.

42. Prätor, 280.

43. BBA. DH-MTV 21–1/51. Sa'id Mu'ayyad al-'Azm and associates to the Ministry of the Interior (Damascus, 10 April 1911).

44. BBA. DH-MTV 6–2/4. The Ministry of the Interior to the *Muhafiz* of Medina (15 April 1911).

45. BBA. DH-SYS 64/27 (15 April 1911).

46. Ahmad, *Young Turks*, 54.

47. Tunaya, *Türkiye'de Siyasal Partiler*, 1:80.

48. For the party's declaration to this effect, see Tunaya, *Türkiye'de Siyasal Partiler*, 1:217.

49. Ibid., 151–52, 170. İsmail Kemal played a leading role in the Albanian movement. See *The Memoirs of İsmail Kemal Bey* (London, 1920).

50. Tunaya, *Türkiye'de Siyasal Partiler*, 1:214–17.

51. "Although a constitutional government necessitates the equal treatment of all Ottoman classes (*sunuf*), the Party will seek special legislation that will enable the administration of those regions backward in their social and material conditions and inhabited by nomadic tribes until such people are settled and are induced to fulfill their civil and political obligations."

52. Ahmad, *Young Turks*, 83.

53. Tunaya, *Siyasi*, 295–96. Tunaya renders the Jerusalem deputy as Sa'id. While Sa'id al-Husayni is the likely signatory because of his oppositional activity at this stage, Hafiz al-Sa'id was another Jerusalem deputy.

54. Fikri, 34–35.

55. Ibid., 25–26. The social composition of these currents, Fikri said, showed variation from one polity to the other. For instance, unlike in Europe, the lower classes [*ayak takımı*] were conservative in the Ottoman Empire.

56. Tunaya, *Siyasi*, 186–87.

57. MMZC, I/3/59, 16 March 1911.

58. Prätor, 47.

59. Roger Owen, *The Middle East in the World Economy, 1800–1914* (London and New York: Methuen, 1981), 181. In 1861 Lynch Brothers established the Euphrates & Tigris Steam Navigation Company. Despite the name, the company operated only on the Tigris, as the Euphrates was not navigable. (I thank Professor Roger Owen for this information.) Holt, 253.

60. Feroz Ahmad, "Great Britain's Relations with the Young Turks, 1908–1914," *Middle Eastern Studies* 2 (1966): 317–18.

61. MMZC, I/2/14, 13 December 1909.

62. İ. Mahmud Kemal İnal, *Osmanlı Devrinde Son Sadrazamlar* (İstanbul: Milli Eğitim Matbaası, 1940–1953), 1161–63.

63. The vote was 163 to 8. Two Arab deputies (Sulayman Bustani of Beirut and Amir Arslan) voted with the majority, while two others (Shafiq al-Mu'ayyad of Damascus and Haji Sa'id of Musul) voted against the grand vizier. MMZC, I/2/14, 13 December 1909.

64. İnal, 1763–64.

65. In his analysis of the incident, Mahmoud Haddad describes the Iraqi

reaction as "proto-nationalist." "Iraq before World War I: A Case of Anti-European Arab Ottomanism," in *Origins of Arab Nationalism*, ed. Khalidi et al., 120–29.

66. BBA. DH-SYS 57–1/9. Governor of the Hijaz Kamil to the Ministry of the Interior (13 November 1910) and the Grand Vizier to Kamil (6 December 1910).

67. See BBA. DH-SYS 57–1/15 for a copy of the poem (7 December 1910). Also see in the same file the Ministry of the Interior to the province of Beirut (8 January 1911).

68. BBA. DH-SYS 64/25 (3 May 1911).

69. BBA. DH-MTV 52–2/20. Aleppo and Urfa deputies to the Ministry of the Interior (9 February 1911).

70. BBA. DH-İ.Um 26/4–8. The Ministry of Imperial Records (*Defter-i Hakani*) to the Ministry of the Interior (13 September 1910).

71. Zahrawi was an *âlim* who had contributed to the Young Turk agitation in Syria before 1908. On Zahrawi, see Ahmed Tarabein, " 'Abd al-Hamid al-Zahrawi: The Career and Thought of an Arab Nationalist," in *Origins of Arab Nationalism*, ed. Khalidi et al., 97–119.

72. MMZC, I/3/47, 25 February 1911.

73. See Neville J. Mandel, *The Arabs and Zionism before World War I* (Berkeley and Los Angeles: University of California Press, 1976), 97ff., for a discussion of the parliamentary debates based on information from British diplomatic and Zionist correspondence. See Ali Nejat Ölçen, *Osmanlı Meclisi Meb'usanında Kuvvetler Ayırımı ve Siyasal İşkenceler* (Ankara: Ayça, 1982), 49–58, for a partial rendering of this debate in modern Turkish.

74. MMZC, I/3/49, 1 March 1911.

75. See Kayalı, "Jewish Representation in the Ottoman Parliaments," in *The Jews of the Ottoman Empire*, ed. Avigdor Levy (Princeton, N.J.: The Darwin Press, 1994), 513–15.

76. Mandel, 107.

77. Ibid., 107–12.

78. MMZC, I/3/99, 16 May 1911.

79. Nisim Masliyah (İzmir) said that neither Ottoman nor foreign Jews could be held responsible for what is written in Jewish scriptures. The Torah, he added, was superseded by the Quran.

80. See also Mandel, 112–14.

81. Ahmad, "Unionist Relations," 426; Mandel, 114; Ölçen, 57–58.

82. MMZC, I/3/100, 17 May 1911.

83. MMZC, I/3/68, 29 March 1911. See also Prätor, 203–4.

84. Prätor, 43; Tauber, *Emergence*, 154.

85. BBA. DH-SYS 64/26 (8 April 1911).

86. Selahaddin, 38.

87. The British high commissioner in Egypt, Kitchener, held this view (Dawn, *Ottomanism*, 62). This helps explain the increased involvement of the British administration in Egypt in the affairs of Syria and Arabia during the next few years.

88. 18 (1912): 214, 220.

89. ATASE. Italian War, 12/34–35, nos. 3, 7–1, 10, 11, 14, 17, 18, 20, 24, 37–1 (September–October 1911).

90. See, for instance, Mousa, *Al-haraka*, 27.

91. Hüseyin Cahid remarked in October 1909 that Hawran had become quiet without the use of force, thanks to the constitution. *Tanin*, 25 October 1909.

92. On Faruq Sami, see Gövsa, 345.

93. US 867.00/307. Vice Consul to Secretary of State (Beirut, 12 August 1910).

94. HHS. PA 38/347. Pinter to Aehrenthal (Beirut, 18 October 1910 and 15 December 1910). Also, Ritter von Zepharovich to Aehrenthal (Jerusalem, 17 December 1910).

95. PRO. FO 618/3. Devey to Marling (Damascus, 13 December 1910).

96. HHS. PA 38/347. Pinter to Aehrenthal (Beirut, 21 December 1910).

97. PRO. FO 618/3. Devey to Marling (Damascus, 19 November 1910).

98. US 867.00/329. Ravndal to Secretary of State (Beirut, 19 December 1910).

99. PRO. FO 618/3. Devey to Lowther (16 March 1911 and 13 July 1911).

100. HHS. PA 38/350. Pinter to Aehrenthal (Beirut, 8 February 1911).

101. BBA. BEO *Defter* 698/28/9, no. 141. Sharif Abdullah to Grand Vizier (25 September 1910). See also no. 146. Husayn to Grand Vizier (7 October 1910).

102. PRO. FO 195/2376. Monahan to Lowther, no. 101 (30 May 1911).

103. Bayur, 2 (pt. 1): 45.

104. Ahmed İzzet Pasha (1864–1937) became war minister in 1912 and served as grand vizier during the Armistice period.

105. BBA. BEO *Defter* 705, no. 89. Grand Vizier Hakkı to the Emirate (19 February 1911).

106. Bayur, 2 (pt. 1): 46–47.

107. PRO. FO 195/2376. Monahan to Lowther, no. 30 (9 February 1911).

108. AA. Türkei 165/Bd. 33/4. Tschirschky to Bethmann-Hollweg, no. 49 (Vienna, 10 February 1911).

109. *Tanin*, 2 July 1910.

110. In 1897, for instance, Russia and Austria discussed the partitioning of the Balkan Peninsula among the Balkan states and the setting up of an Albanian principality (Karal, 152).

111. BBA. DH-SYS 60/3. Al-ʿAsali to the Ministry of the Interior (15 October 1911).

112. BBA. DH-SYS 60/3. Excerpt from *Al-mufid* of 18 November 1911.

113. BBA. BEO 290793 (290672). The Ministry of the Interior to the Grand Vizier (5 April 1911); AA. Türkei 165/Bd. 33. Clipping from *Dresdner Anzeiger*, 18 February 1911, "Die Lage in Arabien."

114. BBA. BEO *Defter* 705, no. 95. Grand Vizier Hakkı Pasha to the Egyptian Commisariat (23 February 1911). The government was of the opinion that the ex-sharif of Mecca ʿAli Pasha and ʿIzzat Pasha played a role in Egypt to incite the Yemenis to rebellion.

115. Bayur, 2 (pt. 1): 38–39.

116. BBA. DH-MTV 25/22 (31 April 1911).

117. Richard Allen, *Imperialism and Nationalism in the Fertile Crescent* (London: Oxford University Press, 1974), 136.

118. Simon, 159.

119. In his memoirs Talat Pasha mentions the reluctance of the Christian, specifically Greek, deputies to cooperate with the CUP toward the achievement of the Ottomanist ideal. See H. Cahit Yalçın, ed., *Talat Paşa'nın Hatıraları* (İstanbul: Bolayır, 1946), 14–15. See also Lewis, 218; Zeine, *Arab Nationalism*, 76.

120. Zeine, *Arab Nationalism*, 77.

121. Ahmad, *Young Turks*, 93.

122. AA. Türkei 165/32. Padel to Bethmann-Hollweg, no. 138 (Beirut, 30 September 1910).

Chapter 4.   The Decentralist Challenge and a New "Arab Policy," 1912–1913

1. See Kayalı, "Elections," 273–77.

2. Selahaddin, 40.

3. HHS. PA 38/355. Pinter to Aehrenthal (Beirut, 10 January 1912).

4. HHS. PA 38/354. Pinter to Berchtold (Beirut, 3 April 1912).

5. MAE. Turquie, N.S. 9. Bompard to MAE, no. 178 (20 March 1912).

6. BBA. BEO 302292. The Ministry of the Interior to Grand Vizier (16 March 1912).

7. PRO. FO 195/2415. Consul J. G. Lorimer to Lowther, fol. 296–304 (Baghdad, 6 March 1912). In contrast, the government encouraged tribes in Basra—presumably won over to the government cause—to register and considered sending delegations to the Peninsula to enable the tribes to participate. See Prätor, 19–20.

8. For measures taken by the government to undermine the Liberal candidate for Sidon, Kamil Bey al-As'ad, and to win him back to the Unionist camp, see HHS. PA 38/354 (see note 4). Similarly, for pressures exerted on the Liberal notable of Damascus, 'Ata Pasha Bakri, see HHS. PA 38/355. Ranzi to Berchtold (Damascus, 24 April 1912).

9. See Rashid Khalidi, "The 1912 Election Campaign in the Cities of *bilad al-Sham*," *IJMES* 16 (1984): 461–71.

10. HHS. PA 12/205. Pallavicini to Aehrenthal (12 March 1912).

11. See Khalidi, "1912 Election," 466, and "'Uraysi,'" in Buheiry, 44–45.

12. Feroz Ahmad, "The Agrarian Policy of the Young Turks, 1908–1918," in Bacqué-Grammont and Dumont, 278.

13. Salibi, 205–6.

14. HHS. PA 38/354 (see note 4).

15. Engin Akarlı, *The Long Peace* (Berkeley and Los Angeles: University of California Press, 1993), 61, 127, 187–192.

16. Salibi, 205.

17. On the role of port workers and their links with the Unionists during the boycott, see Donald Quataert, *Social Disintegration and Popular Resistance in the Ottoman Empire, 1881–1908* (New York: New York University Press, 1983), 141.

18. HHS. PA 38/354. Pinter to Berchtold (Beirut, 14 March 1912). In an earlier report Pinter refers to the CUP's support among the "lowest popular classes" and "unsavory elements" such as boaters and porters. Pinter to Aehrenthal (Beirut, 1 February 1912).

19. Michael Johnson, *Class and Client in Beirut* (London: Ithaca Press, 1986), 17.

20. BBA. DH-SYS 53/46. The Court-Martial General to the Ministry of the Interior (April 17, 1912). The specific pamphlet was titled *Açık Söz: Hürriyet ve İtilâf Fırkasının Makasidini Yanlış Anlayanlara İzahat ve Red-i İtirazat* (Kustantiniye [İstanbul]: Hikmet Matbaası, 1330 [1912]), of which 20,000 copies were printed and distributed. For accusations about Libya, see p. 12.

21. Kayalı, "Elections," 276; Khalidi, "1912 Election," 462.

22. The British consul in Aleppo estimated the size of one such rally in Aleppo at 80,000. PRO. FO 195/2429. Fontana to Lowther (Aleppo, 2 May 1912).

23. Haqqi al-'Azm, *Haqa'iq 'an al-intikhabat al-niyabiyya* (Cairo, 1912); Kurşun, 66–67.

24. See BBA. DH-SYS 83-1/2-16 (31 March 1912) on CUP attempts to censure the governor of Latakia because of violence against Entente supporters in that city.

25. The offer of the Musul candidate and ex-deputy Dawud Yusfani, for example, to be admitted as a Unionist candidate at the eleventh hour was turned down. PRO. FO 195/2415, fol. 323–38. Lorimer to Lowther (Baghdad, 4 June 1912).

26. PRO. FO 195/2389. Lowther to Grey (draft) (Constantinople, 26 March 1912).

27. Sixty-six out of 288 in 1908, 77 out of 284 in 1912 (Prätor, 27–29).

28. Prätor, 47.

29. Ibid., 33.

30. Ahmad, *Young Turks*, 106–7.

31. BBA. BEO 306762 (305252, 305838). Grand Vizier to all state agencies (1 October 1912).

32. Prätor, 62–63.

33. BBA. BEO 310332. Grand Vizier to the Ministry of the Interior (30 January 1913). This document was drafted after the CUP takeover in January and referred to past policy.

34. Among them Dr. Nazım (perennial member of the CUP's central committee), Halil (head of the CUP's parliamentary group), and Rahmi (influential Salonika deputy, later governor of İzmir). Menteşe, 34.

35. Menteşe, 34. The new government suspended martial law but soon had to reinstate it. See Ahmad, *Young Turks*, 109.

36. BBA. BEO *Defter* 112, no. 1123 (24 July 1912).

37. The governor recommended that the request of Shukri al-'Asali and Ah-

mad Kurd 'Ali, coeditor of the closed *Al-muqtabas* with his brother Muhammad, regarding reopening of the seditious paper, be denied. BBA. BEO 305092. Grand Vizier to the Ministry of the Interior (4 August 1912).

38. On the organization and program of the party, see Tauber, *Emergence*, 121–34, and Duri, 277–80.

39. James Paul Thomas, "The Sykes-Picot Agreement of 1916: Its Genesis in British Policy" (Ph.D. diss., Johns Hopkins University, 1971), 4. See Khalidi, *British Policy*, 113–86, on an extensive discussion of Anglo-French railway agreements of 1909–10, which marked the beginnings of the partition of Syria among the two powers.

40. PRO. FO 195/2433. Lowther to consuls of Beirut, Damascus, Jerusalem, Aleppo (confidential), fol. 19 (Pera, 26 June 1912).

41. James Jankowski, "Egypt and Early Arab Nationalism, 1908–1922," in *Origins of Arab Nationalism*, ed. Khalidi et al., 255–56.

42. Thomas Philipp, *The Syrians in Egypt, 1725–1975* (Stuttgart: Franz Steiner Verlag, 1985), 114.

43. PRO. FO 195/2446. Grey to Lowther, fol. 66 (25 November 1912).

44. BBA. BEO 309692 (266893). Governor Edhem to the Grand Vizier (9 November 1912).

45. Ibid. Grand Vizier to Beirut (25 November 1912).

46. PRO. FO 195/2444. Devey to Lowther (14 November 1912).

47. PRO. FO 195/2445. C. Leonard Woolley to Consul Fontana. Enclosure in Fontana to Lowther, no. 78 (14 December 1912). Also PRO. FO 195/2445. Lowther to Foreign Office (İstanbul, 31 December 1912).

48. US 867.00/1455. Theodore J. Stuve to Hollis. Enclosure in Hollis to Secretary of State (23 December 1912).

49. HHS. PA 38/354. Pinter to Berchtold (Beirut, 6 December 1912).

50. PRO. FO 195/2446. Hough to McGregor (8 November 1912). Enclosure in McGregor to Lowther (Jerusalem, 8 November 1912).

51. HHS. PA 38/354. Pinter to Berchtold (23 November 1912).

52. See, for example, PRO. FO 195/2446, fol. 17. Captain Cuthbert Hunter (?) to Lowther (19 November 1912); HHS. PA 38/354. Pinter to Berchtold (28 November 1912).

53. PRO. FO 195/2446. Mallet (for the Secretary of State) to Lowther, fol. 43 (12 December 1912).

54. PRO. FO 195/2446. Cumberbatch to Lowther, fol. 36–42 (4 December 1912).

55. On role of Fa'iq al-Mu'ayyad in pro-Arab caliphate propaganda, see HHS. PA 38/354 (see note 51).

56. Ibid.

57. The authorities cracked down on a committee in Damascus that favored British occupation and arrested six members. Shafiq al-Mu'ayyad and 'Izzat Pasha, who were known to be the originators of this group and were in Damascus at the time of the arrests, fled to Egypt. HHS. PA 38/359. Ranzi to Berchtold (5 January 1913).

58. PRO. FO 195/2446. Cumberbatch to Lowther, fol. 53 (31 December 1912).

The consul was personally involved in establishing contacts between Egyptian authorities and Syrians. See Khalidi, *British Policy*, 266.

59. Shaw and Shaw, 295.

60. BBA. BEO 309692. Governor Edhem to the Grand Vizierate (25 December 1912).

61. Zeine, *Arab Nationalism*, 89.

62. BBA. BEO 309692. The Ministry of the Interior to the provinces of Syria and Aleppo.

63. Tauber, *Emergence*, 135–51; Johnson, 61.

64. HHS. PA 38/359. Ranzi to Berchtold (8 February 1913). See enclosure to same for a list of Damascene reform proposals. For Beirut's proposals, see Tauber, *Emergence*, 138–39.

65. US 867.00/523. Willoughby-Smith to Secretary of State (14 April 1913). Enclosure: "Projet de Reforms à appliquer au Vilayet de Beyrouth" (31 January 1913).

66. Birinci, 202.

67. Ahmad, *Young Turks*, 134.

68. BBA. BEO *Sadaret Defterleri* 922, no. 75 (13 February 1913).

69. HHS. PA 38/359. Ranzi to Berchtold (Damascus, 24 February 1913).

70. HHS. PA 38/358. Dandini to Berchtold (8 March 1913).

71. HHS. PA 38/359 (see note 69).

72. HHS. PA 38/358 (see note 70).

73. On the persistence of the idea of British annexation in Aleppo, see Khalidi, *British Policy*, 284.

74. US 867.00/492. Captain Fletcher to Secretary of Navy (16 February 1913). Enclosure in Navy Department to Secretary of State (8 March 1913); HHS. PA 38/358. Pinter to Berchtold (27 March 1913).

75. PRO. FO 195/2451/484. Cumberbatch to Lowther (Beirut, 27 March 1913).

76. On other resignations from public offices, see Tauber, *Emergence*, 141.

77. PRO. FO 195/2451/484 (see note 75); Salibi, 207; Samir Seikaly, "Shukri al-'Asali: A Case Study of a Political Activist," in *Origins of Arab Nationalism*, ed. Khalidi et al., 89–90.

78. US 867.00/517. Willoughby-Smith (vice consul-general in charge) to Secretary of State (?), no. 426 (14 April 1913).

79. Tauber, *Emergence*, 157–68. The reform movement in Basra strived to unify the *shaykhs* of Mesopotamia in a struggle "for local autonomy, if not for absolute independence of the Turkish government." US 867.00/517. Sauer to Secretary of State (Baghdad, 17 March 1913).

80. HHS. PA 38/356. Ranzi to Berchtold (Damascus, 22 April 1913).

81. HHS. PA 38/358. Pinter to Berchtold (23 April 1913).

82. PRO. FO 195/2414 (31 January 1912).

83. PRO. FO 195/2390. Lowther to Grey (25 September 1912). Enclosed in the report is a clipping from the *Liberté* of the same date reporting on the CUP's consideration of Jawish's case.

84. After the January 1913 takeover of the government by the CUP, Kamil traveled to Egypt, where he waited for his moment to reclaim his former post.

85. *Egyptian Gazette*, 22 April 1913. "The Khalifate." Enclosed in US 867.00/535. Willoughby-Smith to Secretary of State (28 April 1913).

86. *Egyptian Gazette*, 15 April 1913. "Turks and Arabs." Enclosed in US 867.00/527. Willoughby-Smith to Secretary of State, April (?), 1913.

87. Ibid. Quotes Alexandria Consul General Donald Andreas Cameron, *Egypt in the Nineteenth Century* (London: Smith, Elder, & Co., 1898).

88. HHS. PA 38/358. Pinter to Berchtold (Beirut, 23 April 1913).

89. HHS. PA 38/359. Ranzi to Berchtold (Damascus, 22 April 1913). Also, PRO. FO 195/2452/1831. Lowther to the Foreign Office (Pera, 21 April 1913).

90. HHS. PA 12/206. Pallavicini to Berchtold (13 May 1913).

91. See, for instance, the petition from the mayor of the Bab district of Aleppo regarding the removal of the *kadı*. BBA. DH-MTV 60/48 (25 July 1913).

92. BBA. DH-MTV 60/35 (8 May 1913).

93. MAE. Turquie, N.S. 9, fol. 450. Boppe to Ministère des Affaires Etrangères (26 May 1913). See chapter 1 for a similar proposal in 1897 by von der Goltz, who had been responsible for the reorganization of the Ottoman army in the 1890s and was to command Ottoman forces in their Arabian campaigns during World War I.

94. Ibid.

95. AA. Türkei 134/Bd. 32, no. 171. Wangenheim to B. Hollweg (Therapia, 29 May 1913).

96. PRO. FO 195/2453/2368. L[owther] to [FO], no. 475 (Pera, 26 May 1913).

97. BBA. DH-KMS 15/7 (16 February 1913).

98. HHS. PA 38/358. Pering to Berchtold (17 May 1913). Enclosure: *Da'wa ila ebna' al-umma al-'arabiyya*. Signed by 'Awni 'Abd al-Hadi, Jamil Ma'luf, Nadra Mutran, Muhammad al-Mahmasani, 'Abd al-Ghani al-'Uraysi, Sharl Debbas, Shukri Ghanem, Jamil Mardam. See also Tauber, *Emergence*, 179.

99. Tauber, *Emergence*, 183–84.

100. HSS. PA 38/358 (see note 98).

101. Zeine, *Arab Nationalism*, 92; Antonius, 114–17. See *Al-mu'tamar* for the proceedings of the Congress.

102. Salibi, 210.

103. It is interesting and surprising that Midhat Şükrü's memoirs do not mention his own involvement in negotiations with the Arab leaders. Mithat Şükrü Bleda, *İmparatorluğun Çöküşü*, ed. Turgut Bleda (İstanbul: Remzi, 1979).

104. Prätor, 220.

105. Zeine, *Arab Nationalism*, 93; Mousa, *Al-haraka*, 39.

106. Salibi, 210.

107. Fourteen Liberal leaders who had fled the country were sentenced to death in absentia. These included Sabahaddin, Şerif Pasha, and Gümülcineli İsmail. See Ahmad, *Young Turks*, 130; Birinci, 210; Danişmend, *İzahlı*, 397; Fahri Belen, *20. Yüzyılda Osmanlı Devleti* (İstanbul: Remzi, 1973), 178.

108. US 867.00/556. Hollis to Secretary of State (Beirut, 24 June 1913).

109. See, for instance, the letter sent to İstanbul by Osman Nashashibi and other Jerusalem residents. PRO. FO 195/2451/484. Hough to Marling (Jerusalem, 1 July 1913).

110. For his career until 1913, see Bostan, 17–36. Sa'id Halim Pasha's biog-

raphy in a recent modern Turkish edition of his works is largely based on Bostan's M.A. thesis, the precursor of his book. See Sa'id Halim Pasha, *Buhranlarımız ve Son Eserleri*, ed. M. Ertuğrul Düzdağ (İstanbul: İz Yayıncılık, 1991), xiii–xviii. Excerpts of his work and a synoptic biography occur also in İsmail Kara, ed., *Türkiye'de İslâmcılık Düşüncesi*, 2d ed. (İstanbul: Risale, 1987), 1:73–174.

111. Bostan, 34.

112. AA. Türkei 165/Bd. 35/36, no. 93. Loytved-Hardegg to Bethmann-Hollweg (Haifa, 26 July 1913).

113. Mousa, 38.

114. Conservative notables were cajoled with promises such as salary increases to religious students and functionaries, improvement of the waterways in the holy city of Medina, and the opening of a medical school in Damascus. AA. Türkei 177/Bd. 10. Mutius to Bethmann-Hollweg (Beirut, 4 September 1913).

115. HHS. PA 38/359. Ranzi to Berchtold (Damascus, 5 November 1913).

116. HHS. PA 38/359. Ranzi to Berchtold (Damascus, 16 October 1913).

117. AA. Türkei 177/Bd. 10, no. 122. Loytved-Hardegg to Bethmann-Hollweg (Haifa, 26 September 1913).

118. US 867.00/566. Sauer to Embassy (Baghdad, 9 June 1913). Reported by Ravndal to Secretary of State (31 July 1913).

119. US 867.00/592. Vice-consul to Secretary of State (Baghdad, 12 November 1913).

120. The deputy-governor for Basra, İzzeddin, reported the "extraordinary assistance" that Talib rendered in mollifying the crowds who stormed the post office with their petitions. İzzeddin added that great services could be expected from Talib in the upcoming elections. BBA. DH-KMS 63/43 (11 October 1913).

121. Tunaya, *Siyasal Partiler*, 106–10.

122. MAE. Turquie, N.S. 9. Bompard to MAE (Pera, 3 November 1913).

123. HHS. PA 38/358. Dandini to Berchtold (Aleppo, 12 November 1913).

124. *The Egyptian Gazette*, 25 April 1913. "Turks and Arabs." Enclosure in Willoughby-Smith to Secretary of State (Beirut, 6 May 1913). In Baghdad government organs denounced decentralist agitation as being "against the principles of the Muslim religion which stands for unity." US 867.00/548. Sauer to Embassy (Baghdad, 3 May 1913).

125. Landau, *Pan-Islam*, 80–83.

126. William L. Cleveland, *Islam against the West* (Austin: University of Texas Press, 1985), xvii. Shakib Arslan was the brother of Amin Arslan, whom we encountered as the leader of the Turco-Syrian Committee at the end of the nineteenth century. Amin was elected deputy to Parliament for Latakia in the by-election of June 1909.

127. Jawish was the president of the committee entrusted with the mission of establishing the university. BBA. DH-KMS 5/24. The Ministry of the Interior to the *Muhafiz* of Medina (19 November 1913). Martin Strohmeier, *Al-kulliya as-salahiya in Jerusalem* (Stuttgart: Franz Steiner [Deutsche Morgenländische Gesellschaft], 1991), 8–12.

128. BBA. BEO 318545. From 'Abd al-'Aziz Jawish, Shakib Arslan, and Ahmad Zafar to the Grand Vizierate (6 December 1913).

129. On *Teşkilat-ı Mahsusa*, see Philip Hendrick Stoddard, "The Ottoman Government and the Arabs, 1911–1918: A Preliminary Study of the Teşkilat-ı Mahsusa" (Ph.D. diss., Princeton University, 1963); Ergun Hiçyılmaz, *Teşkilat-ı Mahsusa* (İstanbul: Ünsal, 1979).

Chapter 5.   A Case Study in Centralization: The Hijaz under Young Turk Rule, 1908–1914

1. Ernest Dawn's articles on Arab nationalism compiled in his *From Ottomanism to Arabism*, Mary C. Wilson's biography of Sharif ʿAbdullah, *King Abdullah, Britain, and the Making of Jordan*, her essay "The Hashemites, the Arab Revolt, and Arab Nationalism" and William Ochsenwald's "Ironic Origins: Arab Nationalism in the Hijaz," both in *The Origins of Arab Nationalism*, ed. Khalidi et al., provide insights on the Hijaz province during the Young Turk period. The following works focus on the pre-1908 period, but also throw light on the next decade: William Ochsenwald, *Religion, Society, and the State in Arabia: The Hijaz under Ottoman Control, 1840–1908* (Columbus: Ohio State University Press, 1984) and *The Hijaz Railroad* (Charlottesville: University Press of Virginia, 1980); Saleh Muhammad al-Amr, *The Hijaz under Ottoman Rule, 1869–1914: Ottoman Vali, the Sharif of Mecca, and the Growth of British Influence* ([Riyadh]: Riyad University Publications, 1978); and Ufuk Gülsoy, *Hicaz Demiryolu* (İstanbul: Eren, 1994).

2. Suraiya Faroqhi argues this point even for the seventeenth century: "Mecca and Medina['s] enduring religious significance far outweighs their role in the formation of the modern state of which they form a part. In discussing relations of the Ottoman central government with a remote province, we are thus induced to study problems which have little relation to future nation-building, but touch a number of issues crucial for the functioning of the Ottoman Empire during the sixteenth and seventeenth centuries." *Pilgrims and Sultans: The Hajj under the Ottomans, 1517–1683* (London: I. B. Tauris, 1994), 3. The original German version of Faroqhi's book is rich with information on the Hijaz and the pilgrimage after 1908: *Herrscher über Mekka: Die Geschichte der Pilgerfahrt* (München: Artemis Verlag, 1990).

3. On the history of the emirate of Mecca under Ottoman rule, see İsmail Hakkı Uzunçarşılı, *Mekke-i Mükerreme Emirleri* (Ankara: Türk Tarih Kurumu, 1972).

4. Ten percent of the May salary of the deputies in Parliament was allocated toward the subsidies of the people of the holy cities. *Takvim-i Vekai* (13 December 1908).

5. PRO. FO 195/2286. Acting Consul Husain to Lowther (Jidda, 25 August 1908). See also chapter 2.

6. PRO. FO 195/2286. [Acting Consul ?] Mohammad Husain to [Embassy] (Jidda [?], 23 August 1908).

7. PRO. FO 618/3. Devey to Lowther (Damascus, 25 August and 2 September 1908).

8. *Takvim-i Vekai*, 17 October 1908. The first train arrived in Medina on 19 August 1908 (Cevat, 166), but the official ceremony took place on the anniversary of the sultan's accession to the throne on 1 September. See Charles-Eudes Bonin, "Le Chemin de fer du Hedjaz," *Annales de géographie* 18 (1909): 427. According to Bonin, the day of arrival of the first train in Medina was 22 August.

9. PRO. FO 618/3. Devey to Lowther (25 August 1908).

10. Antonius, 103; Andrew Ryan, *The Last of the Dragomans* (London: Geoffrey Bles, 1951), 75–76; James Morris, *The Hashemite Kings* (London: Faber and Faber, 1959), 25; Fargo, 241. Dawn points to Shakib Arslan's viewpoint, but expresses reservations in *Ottomanism*, 5.

11. This view is primarily based on King Abdullah ibn Husayn's *Memoirs* (New York: Philosophical Library, 1950), 43–44; Dawn, *Ottomanism*, 5; al-Amr, 134.

12. Al-Amr, 134.

13. Morris, 25.

14. George Stitt, *A Prince of Arabia: The Emir Shereef Ali Haider* (London: George Allen and Unwin, 1948), 103–4.

15. PRO. FO 685/3. "Haj Report" of the British consulate in Jidda (July 1906).

16. PRO. FO 195/2286. Monahan to Embassy (Jidda, 9 April 1908).

17. The governor of Hijaz, Ratib Pasha, was dismissed at the beginning of August. Sharif 'Ali served as acting governor until Kazım Pasha, who was the inspector of the Hijaz Railway, arrived at the end of September as the newly appointed governor (*Tanin*, 22 September 1908); PRO. FO 195/2286. Acting Consul Husain to Lowther (Jidda, 1 October 1908).

18. PRO. FO/195/2286. Monahan to Lowther (Jidda, 18 November 1908).

19. BBA. BEO 256641 (2 November 1908). I have not found an *irade* in the Başbakanlık Arşivi concerning the appointment of 'Abd al-Ilah. It is likely that the candidate died prior to investiture.

20. BBA. *İrade: Dahiliye* 1326, no. 45 (29 Şevval 1326/24 November 1908) and no. 50 (17 Şevval 1326/12 November 1908). The earlier *irade* called for an audience with Kamil Paşa "on the day when Husayn Pasha, Emir of Mecca, will be received" in the Palace. The audience with the sultan mentioned in Abdullah's memoirs (p. 44) must have been on this occasion.

21. BBA. BEO *Vilayet Defterleri*, 304: *Hicaz (gelen)*, no. 77 (15 November 1908).

22. PRO. FO 195/2286. Monahan to Lowther. (Jidda, 5 December 1908). "A crowd of not more than 1000 were present. . . . The whole spectacle of the landing and reception was not very enthusiastic."

23. Bayur, 1 (pt. 2): 144.

24. BBA. *İrade: Dahiliye* 1326, no. 37 (12 Şevval 1326/7 November 1908).

25. BBA. BEO 258850. The Ministry of War to the Emirate and the Province of the Hijaz (9 December 1908).

26. BBA. BEO 258766. Sharif Husayn to the Grand Vizierate (10 December 1908).

27. BBA. BEO 259627. Sharif Husayn to the Grand Vizierate (9 December 1908).

28. PRO. FO 195/2320. Monahan to Lowther (Jidda, 20 January 1909).

29. *Takvim-i Vekai*, 11, 17, and 19 February 1909.

30. Abdullah, 67; Dawn, *Ottomanism*, 7; Randall Baker, *King Husain and the Kingdom of the Hejaz* (Cambridge: The Oleander Press, 1979), 24.

31. Faroqhi, *Pilgrims*, 53.

32. BBA. BEO 262239 (261661, 262240, 239487). Grand Vizier to the Province of Syria (12 February 1909). Several months after he was relieved of his duty, ʿAbd al-Rahman al-Yusuf won a by-election in Damascus to enter Parliament at the end of 1909. Prätor, 249; Khoury, 57, 87.

33. Dawn argues that the Unionists tried to weaken the sharif by commissioning Yusuf, but that the latter's failure to carry out the task embarrassed the government and enhanced Husayn's prestige. See Dawn, *Ottomanism*, 7.

34. BBA. BEO 262239. Husayn to the Grand Vizierate (12 February 1909).

35. In this first refusal of an appointment desired by the sharif, the grand vizierate replied that the sultan (who selected the members of the Chamber of Notables, or senators) had already made all the appointments and no increase in the number of senators was contemplated. In fact, the size of the Chamber of Notables at the time was short of the constitutionally stipulated one-third of the Chamber of Deputies, and the cabinet could most probably have secured the particular appointment. (One of the newly appointed senators was Sharif ʿAli Haydar.) For İstanbul's reply, see BBA. BEO 262239. The Grand Vizierate to the Emirate (23 February 1909).

36. PRO. FO 195/2320. Monahan to Lowther (3 July 1909).

37. Prätor, 219.

38. BBA. BEO 265549. Husayn to the Grand Vizierate (20 April 1909). İstanbul urged ʿAli to leave the Hijaz as soon as he was dismissed in the fall of 1908, lest he encounter assaults to his person similar to those received by Governor Ratib. BBA. BEO 257222 (11 November 1908).

39. *Takvim-i Vekai*, 8 November 1908. See also MAE. Turquie, N.S. 6. Serie D. Carton: 37. Dossier: 1. "Tableau par vilayets des résultats des elections au parlement ottoman" (13 November 1908).

40. "He is Mufti at Mecca of the Hanefi sect, as his father was before him. His family is of Indian . . . origin, but has been residing in Mecca for more than 200 years. His father died in exile in Egypt about 12 years ago, having incurred the displeasure of Grand Sharif Aun ar-Rafik, which would be a fact in his favor, and he himself (he is now about 35) was living in Constantinople in fear of the Grand Sharif for more than ten years, until he returned two years ago to Mecca. He appears to have a good reputation, intellectually, and morally, and knows Turkish well . . . " (PRO. FO 195/2286. Monahan to Lowther. Jidda, 15 December 1908).

41. PRO. FO 424/231. Monahan to Lowther (Jidda, 7 March 1912), referring to the 1908 elections on the occasion of the second parliamentary election in 1912. Enclosure in Lowther to Grey (Constantinople, 27 March 1912).

42. PRO. FO 195/2320. Monahan to Lowther (Jidda, 5 November 1908).

43. Ibid.

44. His deputyship was endorsed on 3 February 1909. See *Takvim-i Vekai*, 10 February 1909 (MMZC, I/1/22).

45. Zaynal was seen off by a large crowd in Jidda. See PRO. FO 195/2320. Monahan to Lowther (10 November 1908).

46. In his various reports at different times, Consul Monahan reported that Meccans elected *two* deputies in November 1908. That this should be the case stands to reason. The size of Mecca's population may have warranted the election of two deputies. See al-Amr on some estimates of the population of Hijazi towns. Such estimates vary between 70,000 and 150,000 for Mecca; 30,000 to 60,000 for Medina; and 25,000 to 50,000 for Jidda (pp. 17–18). Indeed, in all later elections Mecca did send two representatives.

According to Monahan, one of the deputies-elect "declined to sit" immediately upon election (PRO. FO 195/2286. 5 November 1908) and "refused to leave Mecca" (PRO. FO 195/2350. 23 March 1910). The other one did leave, but "became homesick in Egypt, and would not go on to Constantinople." Monahan does not provide the names of the two deputies. However, from another of his dispatches (PRO. FO 195/2286. 15 December 1908) we know that 'Abdullah Saraj left Jidda on 13 December 1908. Therefore, it can be presumed that it was Saraj who went to Egypt, only to return.

On 29 December 1908 the letter of resignation of "the deputy from Mecca, the Hanafi *müftü* 'Abd al-Rahman" was brought to the floor in Parliament (I/1/9). The discussion suggests that 'Abd al-Rahman never left Mecca and sent his letter of resignation from there, advancing reasons of health. Thus, it is likely that the name of the other deputy-elect was 'Abd al-Rahman and that he was referred to as the *müftü* incorrectly, since we know not only from Monahan's reports but also from Ottoman sources (*Takvim-i Vekai*, 8 November 1908) that the *müftü* was 'Abdullah Saraj.

47. PRO. FO 195/2350. Monahan to Lowther (Jidda, 23 March 1910). Also al-Amr, 138. The second deputy-elect was Hasan al-Shaybi.

48. PRO. FO 195/2320. Monahan to Lowther, no. 25 (Jidda, 16 March 1909).

49. MAE. Turquie, N.S. 6. "Levant Expédié" (?), no. 6 (Paris, 3 June 1909).

50. Ochsenwald, "Ironic Origins," in *Origins of Arab Nationalism*, ed. Khalidi et al., 197; Muhammad A. al-Shamikh, *Al-sihafa fi al-hijaz, 1908–1941* (Beirut, 1972), 37–40.

51. BBA. BEO 274969. Husayn to the Grand Vizierate (17 May 1909); BBA. BEO 267884. Husayn to the Grand Vizierate (10 June 1909).

52. BBA. BEO 274969. Husayn to the Grand Vizierate (20 October 1909).

53. BBA. BEO 273539. Husayn to the Grand Vizierate (30 August 1909).

54. BBA. BEO 268543. The Grand Vizierate to the Ministries of the Interior and Finance (20 June 1909).

55. BBA. BEO 276845. Husayn to the Grand Vizierate (15 January 1910).

56. BBA. BEO 277412. The Ministry of Finance to the Grand Vizierate (3 February 1910).

57. BBA. BEO 273579. The Grand Vizierate to the Ministry of the Interior (13 October 1909).

58. PRO. FO 195/2350. Monahan to Lowther (Jidda, 23 March 1910). Monahan refers to Makki as a Turkish CUP candidate. It is possible that the consul

identified him as a Turk because of his CUP membership. Even if Makki was of Turkish background, his family probably had long been settled in Mecca. His brother, too, presented himself as a candidate in the same election.

59. BBA. BEO 267884 (277412, 278974). From the Ministry of Finance to the Grand Vizierate (15 March 1910).

60. Prätor, 45.

61. PRO. FO 195/2286. Monahan to Lowther (Jidda, 18 November 1908).

62. PRO. FO 195/2350. Monahan to Lowther, no. 67 (Jidda, 7 June 1910). Also BBA. BEO 288114. Husayn to the Grand Vizierate (6 January 1911).

63. PRO. FO 195/2320 (see note 48).

64. PRO. FO 195/2320. Acting Consul Abdurrahman to Lowther, no. 101 (Jidda, 9 August 1910).

65. PRO. FO 195/2350 (see note 62).

66. BBA. BEO 278608 (281797) (3 and 10 March 1910 and 19 May 1912).

67. Ibid. The Ministry of the Interior to the Grand Vizierate (3 March 1910).

68. BBA. BEO 281400 (278608, 281398) (7 May 1910).

69. PRO. FO 195/2320. Monahan to Lowther, no. 25 (Jidda, 16 March 1909). See also Ehud R. Toledano, *The Ottoman Slave Trade and Its Suppression, 1840–1890* (Princeton, N.J.: Princeton University Press, 1982). According to Toledano, the rumors of an impending prohibition of slave trade triggered a revolt in Mecca in 1855–56. When the prohibition was actually issued the Hijaz was exempted (p. 135).

70. BBA. BEO 266444 (263658). The Grand Vizierate to Acting Governor [Sharif Husayn] (17 May 1909); BBA. BEO. 267483. From Acting Governor Husayn to the Grand Vizierate (19 May 1909) and the Grand Vizierate to Acting Governor (24 May 1909).

71. BBA. BEO 277770. Sharif Husayn to the Grand Vizierate (1 February 1910).

72. BBA. BEO 277770 (279932). The Grand Vizierate to the Ministries of the Interior and Finance (14 February 1910). Also, the Ministry of Finance to the Grand Vizierate (26 March 1910).

73. *Tanin*, 7 September 1908.

74. MMZC, I/1/16, 21 January 1909. The Greek deputies Yorgi Boşo and Kozmidi indicated that a railway is a vital economic institution and should belong to all Ottomans.

75. PRO. FO 195/2286. Monahan to Lowther, no. 97 (Jidda, 5 November 1908).

76. PRO. FO 195/2435. Shipley to Lowther, fol. 231–59 (Jidda, 19 July 1912).

77. *Takvim-i Vekai*, 25 January 1909. MMZC, I/1/16, 21 January 1909.

78. PRO. FO 195/2350. Monahan to Lowther, no. 64 (4 June 1910).

79. Memorandum attached to above report by Monahan.

80. PRO. FO 195/2376. Monahan to Lowther, no. 59 (Jidda, 20 March 1911).

81. BBA. BEO *Defter* 698/28/9, no. 3. Husayn to the Grand Vizierate (16 March 1911).

82. BBA. BEO *Defter* 705, no. 101 (12 March 1911).

83. BBA. BEO 279144 (286439). Copy of this letter, dated "1325" (1909), occurs in the file.

84. BBA. BEO *Defter* 698/28/9, no. 3 (see note 81).

85. MAE. Turquie, N.S. 144. [Robert Armez ?] to Ministère des Affaires Etrangères, no. 1 (Jidda, 9 January 1912).

86. BBA. BEO 279144 (286439). The Minister of War to the Grand Vizierate (16 March 1912).

87. BBA. BEO 298959 (279144). The Minister of War to the Grand Vizierate (20 April 1912).

88. Prätor, 184–86; Gülsoy, 223.

89. Al-Amr, 16.

90. M. S. Makki, *Medina, Saudi Arabia: A Geographical Analysis of the City and the Region* (Avebury, 1982), 3; John Sabini, *Armies in the Sun: The Struggle for Mecca and Medina* (London: Thames and Hudson, 1981), 15.

91. As early as 1908 an American report said, "The subjugation of Najd will not be attempted from Baghdad, Basra, or Katif owing to British influence in those regions, but from Damascus and Medina." US 867.00/792. Ravndal to the State Department (23 July 1908).

92. PRO. FO 195/2350 (see note 62); PRO. FO 424/231. Monahan to [Lowther] (Jidda, 7 March 1912). Enclosed in Lowther to Grey (İstanbul, 27 March 1912).

93. BBA. BEO *Defter* 698/28/9. Deputy Emir of Mecca ʿAbdullah to the Grand Vizierate, no. 132 (1 September 1910); BBA. BEO 283879. The Ministry of the Interior to the Grand Vizierate (12 March 1916). The decision was approved by the sultan on 15 July 1910.

94. Dawn, *Ottomanism*, 10; Abdullah, 47–48.

95. Uzunçarşılı, 26.

96. *Tanin*, 4 April 1910.

97. *Tanin*, 26 March 1910.

98. See chapter 2.

99. BBA. BEO 293822 (281797, 278608). The Ministry of the Interior to the Grand Vizierate (9 January 1911).

100. BBA. BEO 298322. The Ministry of Forests, Minerals, and Agriculture to the Grand Vizierate (11 October 1911).

101. BBA. BEO 293822. The Grand Vizierate to the Ministry of Public Works (15 September 1911).

102. BBA. BEO 293822. The Ministry of the Interior to the Grand Vizierate (9 January 1911). Also included in the file are responses of the various ministries to the reform proposal of the *muhafiz*.

103. For a discussion of the "Ottoman order" vs. the "local order" with respect to the administrative and economic incorporation of Transjordan in the late Ottoman period, see Lawrence Eugene Rogan, "Incorporating the Periphery: The Ottoman Extension of Direct Rule over Southeastern Syria (Transjordan), 1867–1914" (Ph.D. diss., Harvard University, 1991), 10–12.

104. *İkdam*, 1 March 1909.

105. PRO. FO 195/2320. Monahan to Lowther (Jidda, 9 April 1909).

106. BBA. BEO 266661 (263047). Husayn to the Grand Vizierate (29 March 1909).

107. BBA. BEO 266661. Husayn to the Grand Vizierate (18 May 1909); PRO. FO 195/2320. Monahan to Lowther (Jidda, 30 May 1909).

108. BBA. BEO *Defter* 698/28/9, no. 11. Husayn to the Grand Vizierate (7 April 1910); PRO. FO 195/2350. Monahan to Lowther, no. 69 (11 June 1910).

109. BBA. BEO *Defter* 698/28/9, no. 98. Husayn to the Grand Vizierate (30 July 1910); PRO. FO 195/2350. Acting Consul Abdurrahman to Lowther, no. 97 (Jidda, 5 August 1910).

110. BBA. BEO 286962. Husayn to *Müşir* (?) (27 August 1910).

111. BBA. BEO 286962 (285568). Deputy Emir Abdullah to the Ministry of War (12 September 1910).

112. BBA. BEO *Defter* 698/28/9, no. 141. ʿAbdullah to the Grand Vizierate (25 September 1910).

113. BBA. BEO 286312 (280413). Muhafiz ʿAli Rida to the Ministry of the Interior (28 October 1910).

114. PRO. FO 195/2376. Acting Consul Abdurrahman to Lowther, no. 173 (Jidda, 11 October 1911).

115. PRO. FO 424/230. Lowther to Grey, no. 9 ([İstanbul], 3 January 1912).

116. BBA. BEO 265661 (266109, 265930, 257308). Governor of Yemen to the Grand Vizierate (24 February 1909).

117. Ibid. (13 May 1909).

118. BBA. BEO 265930 (265661, 257308). Husayn to the Grand Vizierate (12 May 1909).

119. BBA. *Defter* 698/28/9, no. 3. Husayn to the Grand Vizierate (23 March 1910).

120. BBA. BEO. *Defter* 705, no. 6. The Grand Vizierate to the Emirate (25 April 1910).

121. See chapter 3 for the remonstration of Arab deputies against the paper's editor Ubeydullah.

122. BBA. BEO. 269031 (288705). Husayn to the Grand Vizierate (24 November 1910). Also *Defter* 698/28/9, no. 163. Husayn to the Grand Vizierate (6 November 1910).

123. BBA. BEO. 279266. Deputy Commander of the Seventh Army to the Ministry of War (21 March 1910).

124. BBA. BEO. 269031 (288705). Mutasarrıf Sulayman Shafiq to the Province of the Hijaz (28 October 1910).

125. BBA. BEO. 269031 (288705). The Province of the Hijaz to the Emirate (24 November 1910).

126. BBA. BEO. 269031 (288705). The Province of the Hijaz to the Ministry of the Interior (7 November 1910).

127. PRO. FO 195/2350. Monathan to Lowther, no. 135 (Jidda, 13 December 1910).

128. BBA. BEO *Defter* 698/28/9, no. 201. Husayn to the Grand Vizierate (21 February 1911). Abdullah's request for a two-and-a-half-month leave on grounds of "important personal matters that necessitate his presence in the Hijaz" was granted on 23 February 1911 (MMZC, I/3/46).

129. HHS. PA 38/350. Dr. Toncic to Aehrenthal (Jidda, 20 March 1911).

130. PRO. FO 195/2376. Monahan to Lowther, no. 100 (Jidda, 25 May 1911).

131. Ibid. Monahan to Lowther, no. 101 (Jidda, 30 May 1911).

132. PRO. FO 195/2376. Richardson to Lowther, no. 134 (Hodeida, 23 June 1911).

133. PRO. FO 195/2376. Monahan to Lowther, no. 105 (Jidda, 10 June 1911).

134. BBA. BEO 294354. The Grand Vizierate to Sharif Husayn (9 August 1911).

135. PRO. FO 195/2414. Acting Consul Dr. Abdurrahman to Lowther, fol. 304–5 (Jidda, 7 April 1912). Also, Shipley to Lowther, fol. 312 (Jidda, 20 July 1912).

136. PRO. FO 195/2440. Shipley to Lowther, no. 53 (Jidda, 29 July 1912). The consul quotes the commandant of the gendarmerie in Jidda, Haşim Bey, as saying that the government "woke up to the fact that much of the trouble in [Asir] is due to the Sharif's attempt to bring it under his control."

137. BBA. BEO 307945. Husayn to the Grand Vizierate (28 October 1912); and the Grand Vizierate to Husayn (1 November 1912).

138. See, for example, BBA. BEO 272713. Husayn to the Grand Vizierate (13 September 1910); BBA. BEO 285974. Husayn to the Grand Vizierate (14 October 1910).

139. Monahan describes Hazım Bey as a "weak and insignificant person." See PRO. FO 195/2376. Monahan to Lowther (18 September 1911). Sharif Husayn probably had a better idea about his abilities, and hence wanted to see him removed. See chapter 4 on Hazım in his capacity as governor in Beirut during the reform movement.

140. PRO. FO 195/2376. Monahan to Lowther, no. 160 (Jidda, 18 September 1911); Abdurrahman to Lowther, no. 182 (Jidda, 4 November 1911).

141. In 'Abdullah's memoirs the reference is to Nasir ibn Muhsin of the Ghalib "tribe" (pp. 84–85). The name occurs as "Muhammad Nasir, the grandson of the brother of late Sharif 'Abd al-Muttalib" in a letter that Nasir sent to the grand vizier to air his grievance against Sharif Husayn, who publicly affronted him. BBA. BEO 299282 (18 October 1911). For a congratulatory telegram sent by Nasir to the Central Committee of the CUP in Salonika on the occasion of the first anniversary of the revolution and the text of the reply from the Central Committee, see *Shams al-haqiqa*, 30 August 1909.

142. BBA. BEO 285974. Husayn to the Grand Vizierate (14 October 1910); the Grand Vizierate to Husayn (20 October 1910). 'Abdullah Pasha had served as governor and commander in chief in Yemen in 1903 and as governor of Baghdad in 1909.

143. BBA. BEO 313934. Husayn to the Grand Vizierate (21 June 1913). The Grand Vizierate to the Emirate (25 June 1913).

144. For example, his suggestion for the provincial chief secretary (BBA. BEO 300439. The Grand Vizierate to Emirate [22 February 1912]); his plea against the dismissal of the Hanafi *müftü* of Medina (BBA. BEO *Defter* 698/28/9, no. 407 [30 March 1911], no. 539 [5 April 1911], no. 408 [31 March 1911]).

145. BBA. BEO 306372 (308160; 309416). Husayn to the Grand Vizierate (16 December 1912); Şeyhülislam to the Grand Vizierate, no. 148 (28 January 1913).

146. BBA. BEO 286312 (280413). *Muhafiz* of Medina to the Ministry of the

Interior (6 April 1910). Sharif Husayn denied the charges but dismissed Shahat. Yet, when in the summer of 1910 the government took the decision to separate the administration of Medina from that of the province of the Hijaz, the sharif insisted on reinstituting Shahat as his deputy in Medina and sent him back. However, his reappointment was not endorsed by the grand vizierate. See also the Ministry of the Interior to the Grand Vizierate (24 April 1910); the Grand Vizierate to the Emirate (25 April 1910; 2, 8, 15 November 1910); Husayn to the Grand Vizierate (27 April, 9 October 1910); *Muhafiz* to the Ministry of the Interior (27 October 1910).

147. BBA. BEO 281551. Muhafiz ʿAli Rida Pasha to the Ministry of the Interior (20 May 1910).

148. BBA. DH-MTV 3/9 (24 December 1910).

149. Wilson, *King Abdullah*, 21.

150. BBA. BEO *Defter* 698/28/9, no. 164. Husayn to the Grand Vizierate, no. 4868 (12 November 1910).

151. Stitt, 137–41; Dawn, *Ottomanism*, 13.

152. PRO. FO 195/2429. Shipley to Lowther, no. 43 (10 July 1912).

153. Monahan to Lowther (7 March 1912). Enclosure in PRO. FO 424/231. Lowther to Grey (İstanbul, 27 March 1912).

154. Consul Shipley reported in November 1912 that the sharif's influence "now extends from Alwejh in the north to Abha in the south." PRO. FO 195/2446, fol. 391–92 (7 November 1912).

155. BBA. BEO 296673. The Grand Vizierate to the Ministry of the Interior (31 October 1911).

156. BBA. *İrade*: *Dahiliye* 1330, no. 19. The Minister of Interior to the Grand Vizierate (27 January 1912).

157. BBA. BEO 307518. The Emirate to the Grand Vizierate (9 October 1912); the Grand Vizierate to the Emirate (17 October 1912).

158. MAE. Turquie, N.S. 144. Robert Armez to Poincaré, no. 4 (Jidda, 29 January 1912).

159. PRO. FO 195/2429. Shipley to Lowther, no. 43 (10 July 1912).

160. PRO. FO 195/2440. Shipley [to Lowther], no. 27 (6 December 1912).

161. PRO. FO 195/2435. Shipley to Lowther, no. 46 (Jidda, 19 July 1912). Also PRO. FO 195/2410, fol. 386 (23 June 1912); PRO. FO 195/2433, fol. 146–48 (29 June 1912).

162. BBA. BEO 281551. The Emirate to the Grand Vizierate (23 and 26 April, 1913).

163. BBA. BEO 313973. Muhafiz to the Ministry of the Interior (29 May 1913).

164. BBA. BEO 313934. Husayn to the Grand Vizierate (21 June 1913); the Grand Vizierate to the Emirate (25 June 1913).

165. See, for example, Antonius; Kedourie, *England and the Middle East* (London: Bowes and Bowes, 1956); Isaiah Friedman, *The Question of Palestine, 1914–1918: British-Jewish-Arab Relations* (London: Routledge and Kegan Paul, 1973).

166. Morris, 8–9.

Chapter 6.   The War Years, 1914–1918

1. Arai, *Turkish Nationalism*, 70, 83–85.

2. HHS. PA 38/362. Dandini to Berchtold (Aleppo, 12 March 1914).

3. As'ad served during the war as the *müftü* of the Fourth Army in Syria and as an advisor to Cemal Pasha. T. E. Lawrence describes him as a "notorious pro-Turk pimp" (*Seven Pillars of Wisdom* [New York: Doubleday, 1938], 432). As'ad was the father of Ahmad al-Shuqayri, the first chairman of the Palestine Liberation Organization in 1964.

4. AA. Türkei 177/Bd. 11. Loytved-Hardegg to Bethmann-Hollweg, no. 49 (Haifa, 30 March 1914).

5. Khalidi describes deputies-elect from Syrian provinces, among them Amin 'Abd al-Hadi, as "nonentities whose main distinction was that they were of the same families as prominent Arab nationalists." Amin, related to one of the leaders of the Decentralization League, Salim 'Abd al-Hadi, was a graduate of the *Mülkiye* and a prominent functionary. Khalidi, "Arab Nationalism in Syria," 232.

6. BBA. DH-SYS 122/5–1 (2 April 1914).

7. AA. Türkei 177/Bd. 11, no. 49 (see note 4).

8. BBA. DH-SYS 122/2 (5 January 1914).

9. "Désireux de faire échec à l' 'Union arabe,' le Comité *Union et Progrès* de Beyrouth avait provoqué la création d'une société rivale destinée, sous le nom de 'fraternité musulmane,' à amener une entente entre Turcs et Arabes." MAE. Turquie, N.S. 124. Boppe to MAE, no. 91 (Pera, 8 February 1914).

10. US 867.00/603. Richarz (?) to Secretary of State (Baghdad, 11 January 1914).

11. The Austrian consul in Aleppo reported the lack of interest of leading Arab notables in the elections was expected to result in the election of only Unionist candidates. But in Aleppo, too, half of the newly elected deputies were newcomers more accurately identified as independents. See HHS. PA 38/362. Dandini to Berchtold (24 January 1914).

12. See Ahmad and Rustow (p. 247) and Prätor (pp. 28–29) for the basis of these calculations.

13. The royal decree was issued on 4 January 1914. See As'ad Daghir, *Thawrat al-'arab* (Cairo, 1916), 46; Burru, 548.

14. Daghir sees Zahrawi as the only decentralist, yet Bayhum, Sursuq, and possibly the Aleppine senator had been in the same camp. See PRO. FO 195/2457/316. Cumberbatch to Mallet, no. 3 (Beirut, 16 January 1914); AA. Türkei 177/Bd. 11, no. 49 (see note 4). Baruni was one of the leaders of the Libyan resistance against Italy and stayed in Libya despite his new appointment. See Orhan Koloğlu, *Mustafa Kemal'in Yanında İki Libyalı Lider* (Ankara: Libya Arap Halk Sosyalist Cemahiriyesi Ankara Halk Bürosu Kültür Merkezi Yayınları, 1981). Sursuq, too, probably stayed in Beirut. According to Cumberbatch, he was too old to undertake the trip. Sursuq donated his Senate salary to the *Donanma Cemiyeti* (Naval Defense Fund).

15. Prätor, 220.

16. Khalidi, "Arab Nationalism in Syria," 231.

17. MAE. Turquie, N.S. 9. Boppe to MAE, no. 22 (Pera, 16 January 1914).

18. He was reelected in November 1915. Prätor, 62.

19. MAE. Turquie, N.S. 9. Boppe to MAE, no. 115 (17 February 1914).

20. HHS. PA 38/363. Ranzi to Berchtold (Damascus, 11 February 1914). Al-Inkilizi was later employed in the central inspectoral agency in İstanbul.

21. The reassignment was not due to the Syrian governor's objections, İstanbul explained, but due to the fact that al-'Asali was a native of the province of Syria. Aleppo governor Celal threatened to resign, saying that al-'Asali "will poison this province that has so far managed to stay outside of insidious currents." For this correspondence (28 and 29 January 1914) and the regulations governing the new inspectorships (19 November 1913), see BBA. DH-KMS 5/28.

22. Seikaly, 91.

23. Khalidi, "Arab Nationalism in Syria," 232.

24. Seikaly, 91.

25. The author is careful not to compromise al-Zahrawi's Arabist credentials when he writes, "In the end, al-Zahrawi probably accepted membership of the Senate because it did not imply a post in the government; it was, rather, a control on the government, not a service." Tarabein, 107, 114.

26. AA. Türkei 177/Bd. 11, no. 49 (see note 4).

27. BBA. DH-KMS 18/19 (24 March 1914).

28. BBA. DH-KMS 17/24 (19 March 1914).

29. MAE. Turquie, N.S. 9. Bureau des Communications. "Le Grand Chérif Hossein Pacha et la situation en Arabie" (9 February 1914). He is reported to have contributed to Jawish's undertakings and to the *Donanma Cemiyeti*.

30. BBA. DH-KMS 17/4 (5 March 1914). This is the aforementioned *Al-mu'tamar al-'arabi al-awwal*.

31. Cemal reports in his memoirs of such a meeting with al-Zahrawi and 'Abd al-Karim al-Khalil (a Beiruti reformist leader) in the home of 'Abd al-'Aziz Jawish. Cemal Paşa, *Hatıralar*, ed. Behçet Cemal (İstanbul: Çağdaş, 1977), 75–76.

32. HHS. PA 38/363. Ranzi to Berchtold (Damascus, 17 January 1914).

33. AA. Türkei 177/Bd. 10. Rößler to Bethmann-Hollweg, no. 8 (Aleppo, 21 January 1914).

34. In the early months of the war, when on exile in Europe, the Liberal leader Sabahaddin "considered his Party strong in the Smyrna garrison, numerous in Constantinople and popular among the masses of the Turkish people. . . . [But h]e had no communication either with the Arabs in Syria or the Armenians in Zeitun or Eastern Armenia." PRO. FO 371/2486/34982. Mark Sykes to Major General C. E. Callwell, Director of Military Operations, no. 4 (Athens, 12 June 1915).

35. The most comprehensive sources on Arab societies are Eliezer Tauber's previously cited *The Emergence of the Arab Movements* and its companion volume on the war years, *The Arab Movements in World War I* (London: Frank Cass, 1993). See *Emergence*, 90–97, for *Al-fatat* and 198–236 for *Al-'ahd* and *Arab Movements*, 57–78, for the joint activities of the two societies after 1914.

36. Tauber, *Emergence*, 220; Mousa, *Al-haraka*, 33–34. Dawn is skeptical

about the membership figures for the two secret organizations first cited by nationalist-minded Arab authors like Antonius and Amin Sa'id. See his "Origins", 13.

37. For the imperial decree on Enver's promotion and appointment as minister, see BBA. DUIT 4/14–6 (3 January 1914).

38. US 867.00/600. Ambassador Extraordinary and Plenipotentiary Morgenthau to the Secretary of State (İstanbul, 17 January 1914).

39. HHS. PA 38/363. Ranzi to Berchtold (Damascus, 11 February 1914).

40. PRO. FO 195/2456/66. Mallet (?) to Grey, no. 46 ([İstanbul], 25 January 1914).

41. The owner of *Al-iqbal* (Beirut) requested a similar subsidy. BBA. DH-KMS 14/17 (31 January 1914).

42. US 867.00/608. Baghdad Consulate to the Secretary of State and Ambassador (25 February 1914).

43. Fourth Army, *Âliye Divan-ı Harb-i Örfisinde Tedkik Olunan Mesele-i Siyasiye Hakkında İzahat* (İstanbul, 1332 [1916]), 19.

44. AA. Türkei 165/Bd. 36. Hesse to Bethmann-Hollweg, no. 290/A.3 (Baghdad, 19 March 1914).

45. PRO. FO 195/2457/350. Crow to Mallet, no. 9 (Basra, 4 February 1914).

46. These efforts elicited the sarcastic comment from the British consul that Shafiq was bringing electric tramways to "a town whose drinking water is drawn from a filthy creek." PRO. FO 195/2457/350. Acting Consul R. W. Bullard to Mallet, no. 40 (Basra, 25 July 1914).

47. PRO. FO 195/2457/350. Crow to Mallet, no. 26 (Basra, 2 May 1914).

48. PRO. FO 195/2457/350. Acting consul Bullard to Mallet, no. 38 (Basra, 20 June 1914).

49. PRO. FO 195/2457/350. Mallet to [F.O.], no. 205 (draft) ([İstanbul], 25 March [1914]).

50. AA. Türkei 165/Bd. 36. Wangenheim to Bethmann-Hollweg, no. 100 (Pera, 22 March 1914).

51. PRO. FO 371/2140/46261. Major S. G. Knox to the Foreign Secretary to the Government of India, no. 97 (55364) (Bushire, 8 August 1914).

52. PRO. FO 371/2140/51468. Cheetham to [F.O.], no. 167 (Cairo, 21 September 1914).

53. PRO. FO 371/2140/46261, no. 899 (Constantinople, 30 September 1914).

54. HHS. PA 38/366. Ranzi to Burian (Damascus, 6 February and 5 June 1915).

55. MAE. Turquie, N.S. 9. Consul General [Ottawi] to Doumerque, no. 26 (Damascus, 20 March 1914).

56. AA 165/Bd. 36. Wangenheim to Bethmann-Hollweg (22 May 1914). The only possible candidate for the leadership role, according to Wangenheim, was 'Aziz al-Misri, now in Cairo.

57. BBA. BEO 319014 (305428). The Grand Vizierate to the Ministries of the Interior and War (15 January 1914). Vehib had taken command of the forces at the end of 1913.

58. AA. Türkei 165/Bd. 36. (?) to Bethmann-Hollweg, fol. K196357 (Berlin,

25 January 1914); Wangenheim to Bethmann-Hollweg, no. 87 (Pera, 9 March 1914). See chapter 4 on similar rumors during the Balkan Wars.

59. Tauber, *Emergence*, 114.

60. AA. Türkei 165/Bd. 36. Miquel to Bethmann-Hollweg, no. 47 (Cairo, 19 April 1914); PRO. FO 371/2140/46261. Cheetham [to F.O.], no. 149 (7 September 1914).

61. Ahmad, "International Status of Kuwait," 184.

62. Zeine, *Arab Nationalism*, 106.

63. Tauber, *Emergence*, 115.

64. MAE. Turquie, N.S. 9. Bureau des Communications. "Le Grand Chérif Hossein Pacha et la situation en Arabie," no. 15 (Jidda, 9 February 1914).

65. BBA. BEO 319171. Husayn to Grand Vizierate (3 February 1914).

66. AA. Türkei 165/Bd. 36. Miquel (?) to Bethmann-Hollweg, no. 32 (Cairo, 11 March 1914).

67. BBA. BEO 319362. Husayn to the Grand Vizierate (12 February 1914).

68. BBA. BEO 319823 (319564). Husayn to the Grand Vizierate (25 February 1914).

69. BBA. BEO 319823 (319564). Talat Pasha to [the Grand Vizierate] (3 March 1914).

70. MAE. Turquie, N.S. 9. Boppe to [MAE], no. 95 (Pera, 9 February 1914).

71. PRO. FO 195/2457/350. Acting Consul Abdurrahman to Mallet, no. 17 (Jidda, 19 March 1914). According to Stoddard, Vehib Bey was "ordered to make peace with [Sharif Husayn] in the interests of pan-Islamic harmony." Stoddard, 139.

72. PRO. FO 195/2457/350. Devey to [F.O.] (Damascus, 7 May 1914).

73. BBA. DH-KMS 21/54. Vehib to the Ministry of the Interior, no. 58 (6 April 1914).

74. Ibid., no. 66 (9 May 1914).

75. Ibid., no. 51 (5 May 1914).

76. Ibid., no. 65 (9 May 1914).

77. Ibid., no. 71 (11 May 1914).

78. Ibid., no. 70 (11 May 1914).

79. Ibid., no. 138 (18 June 1914).

80. Ibid., no. 72 (13 May 1914).

81. Ibid., no. 181 (10 August 1914).

82. Ibid. (1 June 1914).

83. BBA. DH-KMS 24–1/8 (16 June 1914).

84. BBA. DH-KMS 21/54 (12 July, 9 and 10 August 1914).

85. Most recently, in April ʿAbdullah had asked the British for machine guns. See Dawn, *Ottomanism*, 20.

86. BBA. DH-KMS 21/54, no. 32 (5 August 1914).

87. Ibid., no. 181 (10 August 1914).

88. Ibid. (17 August 1914).

89. A. Emin Yalman, *Turkey in the World War* (New Haven: Yale University Press, 1930), 102.

90. Dawn, *Ottomanism*, 26.

91. Tauber, *World War I*, 15–16.

92. PRO. FO 195/2446. Cumberbatch to Lowther (Beirut, 14 November 1914).

93. Ahmad, *Young Turks*, 157.

94. Tauber, *World War I*, 19.

95. PRO. FO 371/2140, no. 604 (57234) (Therapia, 22 September 1914).

96. PRO. FO 371/2140/46261. Cheetham to [F.O.], no. 149 (Cairo, 7 September 1914).

97. PRO. FO 371/2140/46261. Cheetham to Grey, no. 177 (Cairo, 15 November 1914); PRO. FO 371/2140/46261. Secretary of State [for India] to Viceroy, no. 75460 (19 November 1914).

98. Majid Khadduri, " 'Aziz 'Ali Misri and the Arab Nationalist Movement," in ed. Hourani, *Middle Eastern Affairs*, no. 4 (Oxford: Oxford University Press, 1965), 140–163.

99. Tauber, *World War I*, 83–86.

100. Briton Cooper Busch, *Britain, India, and the Arabs, 1914–1921* (Berkeley and Los Angeles: University of California Press, 1971), 11; PRO. FO 371/2140/46261. Mallet to Grey, no. 942 (57074) (İstanbul, 7 October 1914); Viceroy to India Office, no. 64904 (28 October 1914); Viceroy to India Office, no. 77724 (Bombay [?], 30 November 1914).

101. Danişmend, *İzahlı*, 419.

102. Ulrich Trumpener, *Germany and the Ottoman Empire, 1914–1918* (Princeton, N.J.: Princeton University Press, 1968), 119.

103. AA. Türkei 165/Bd. 37. Wangenheim to [Auswärtiges Amt], no. 1605 (Pera, 13 December 1914).

104. Ibid.

105. Ibid. The latter of these measures no doubt offered certain political advantages by restricting communications.

106. PRO. FO 371/2139/44923. Cheetham to [F.O.], no. 310 (81133) (Cairo, 10 December 1914).

107. Ali Fuat Erden, *Paris'ten Tih Sahrasına* (Ankara: Ulus, 1949), 53–56. On the Kurdish roots of the al-Yusuf family, see Khoury, 35–40.

108. Amin Sa'id, *Al-thawra al-'arabiya al-kubra* (Cairo, 1934 [?]), 1:105–6, quoted in Dawn, *Ottomanism*, 28.

109. Antonius, 150; Dawn, *Ottomanism*, 27; Zeine, *Arab Nationalism*, 108.

110. For the main stipulations of the treaty, see George Lenczowski, *The Middle East in World Affairs* (London: Cornell University Press, 1980), 75.

111. BBA. DUIT 5/1–3–10 (28 February 1915).

112. ATASE. World War I, 553/[] -2150 (8 February 1915).

113. Ibid. Cemal to Deputy Commander-in-Chief [Enver] (20 February 1915).

114. Ibid. Deputy Commander Ahmed to Enver (13 March 1915).

115. BBA. DH-İ.Um. 4–1/2. Muhafiz Basri to the Ministry of the Interior (30 March 1915); ATASE. World War I, 165/159–725. Commander [Ahmed] to Enver (18 May 1915).

116. ATASE. World War I, 165/159–725. Cemal to Enver, no. 5 (29 May 1915).

117. Ibid., no. 5–1 (31 May 1915).

118. ATASE. World War I, 1832/7–21. Sharif Husayn to Enver (10 July 1915).

119. See, for instance, Tauber, *World War I*, and Antonius, 164.

120. ATASE. World War I, 1832/7–21, no. 1–1 (3 August 1915).

121. Ibid. (15 August 1915).

122. Ibid. (28 August 1915).

123. US 867.4016/290. Philip to Secretary of State, no. 1186 (İstanbul, 1 July 1916); US 867.00/777. Hollis to Morgenthau (Beirut, 26 July 1915).

124. See Erden, *Paris'ten*, for a vivid account of the Canal campaign.

125. Tauber provides a detailed account of how the Ottoman authorities obtained the incriminating documents. Cemal Pasha did not make public the documents that were found in the first roundup of the consulates at the end of 1914 and that incriminated those sentenced in 1915. A second raid of the French consulate at the end of 1915 revealed more evidence and led to the executions of 1916. See Tauber, *World War I*, 39–56. *İzahat*, the book published by Cemal Pasha's Fourth Army in 1916, elaborates on the activities of the executed and attempts to justify *ex post facto* the decisions of the military court.

126. Suleiman Mousa, *T. E. Lawrence: An Arab View*, trans. Albert Butros (London: Oxford University Press, 1966), 14.

127. Tauber, *World War I*, 54; Antonius, 186–87.

128. BBA. DH-KMS 36/22 (10 January 1915).

129. US 867.4016/283. Philip to Secretary of State (İstanbul [via Copenhagen], 21 May 1916).

130. Tauber, *World War I*, 45.

131. HHS. PA 38/369. Nedwed to Burian (Beirut, 15 April 1916).

132. Fourth Army, *İzahat*, 6.

133. "Many are known to have been comfortably transported at Government expense as far as Angora, being given to understand that land will be allotted to them equal in extent to that left behind, etc." US 867.4016/283 (see note 129).

134. HHS. PA 38/369 (see note 131).

135. The purpose of the law was to abolish the use of European languages in the conduct of business so that employment opportunities would open up for Muslim elements in public (primarily, utility) and private companies. Zafer Toprak, *Türkiye'de "Milli İktisat," 1908–1918* (Ankara: Yurt, 1982), 79–80. Yalman, 114.

136. HHS. PA 38/369. Ranzi to Burian (Damascus, 30 March 1916).

137. AA. Türkei 177/Bd. 12. Loytved-Hardegg to Embassy (Damascus, 4 April 1916). Enclosed in Metternich to Bethmann-Hollweg, no. 154 (Pera, 7 April 1916).

138. The American ambassador Morgenthau described to the secretary of state Lansing the balance of power within the Committee of Union and Progress party as an "intensely interesting" phenomenon that, in his opinion, differed distinctly "from the Boss Rule in the United States." According to Morgenthau, there were some forty members of the Committee who were influential in the government of the empire. A core of nine was particularly powerful. It included, in addition to Talat, Enver, and Cemal, Central Committee Chairman Dr. Nazım, Foreign Minister Halil, President of the General Assembly Hacı Adil, Eyüp Sabri, and Bahattin Şakir. US 867.00/797. Morgenthau to Lansing (İstanbul, 4 November 1915). See also Trumpener, 71.

139. Feridun Kandemir, *Peygamberimizin Gölgesinde Son Türkler* (İstanbul, 1974), 23; Falih Rıfkı Atay, *Zeytindağı* (İstanbul, 1938), 63; Erden, *Paris'ten*, 22.

140. PRO. FO 371/2486/34982. Statement of Husayn's messenger Mohammed Ibn Arif Oreifan [to the High Commissioner] (Alexandria, 18 August 1915).

141. HHS. PA 38/366. Ranzi to Burian (Damascus, 15 December 1915). Linda Schatkowski Schilcher, "The Famine of 1915–1918 in Greater Syria," in *Problems of the Modern Middle East in Historical Perspective: Essays in Honor of Albert Hourani*, ed. John P. Spagnolo (Reading: Ithaca Press, 1992), 229–58.

142. See Tauber, *World War I*, 54–55; HHS. PA 38/369 (see note 136); and for Zahrawi, in particular, US 867.4016/283 (see note 129).

143. For the text of the declaration, see André Mandelstam, *Le Sort de l'empire ottomane* (Lausanne: Librairie Payot, 1917), 360–62; F. De Jong, "The Proclamations of al-Husayn b. 'Ali and 'Ali Haydar," *Der Islam* 57 (1980): 281–87; Selahaddin, 93–94.

144. AA. Türkei 165/Bd. 39. Metternich to [Auswärtiges Amt], no. 423 (Therapia, 26 July 1916).

145. De Jong, 285. AA. Türkei 165/Bd. 39. Loytved-Hardegg to [Embassy], no. 118 (Damascus, 5 August 1916). Enclosed in Metternich to Bethmann-Hollweg, no. 455 (Therapia, 6 August 1916).

146. AA. Türkei 165/Bd. 41. Loytved-Hardegg to Bethmann-Hollweg, no. 26 (Damascus, 5 January 1917).

147. Konrad Morsey, *T. E. Lawrence und der arabische Aufstand, 1916/18* (Osnabrück: Biblio Verlag, 1976), 84–86. For Max Freiherr von Oppenheim's activities to establish a news center for propaganda in Syria and Arabia, see Gottfried Hagen, *Die Türkei im Ersten Weltkrieg* (Frankfurt: Peter Lang, 1990), 35–44.

148. HHS. PA 38/369. Ranzi to Burian (Damascus, 28 August 1916).

149. HHS. PA 38/369. Ranzi to Burian (Damascus, 29 September 1916).

150. Nicholas Z. Ajay, Jr., "Political Intrigue and Suppression in Lebanon during World War I," *IJMES* 5 (1974): 158.

151. AA. Türkei 165/Bd. 40. Mutius to Metternich quoting Hoffmann (vice-consul in Tripoli), no. 2076 (Beirut, 12 October 1916).

152. Bayur, 3 (pt. 4): 320–21.

153. AA. Türkei 165/Bd. 38 (Damascus, 1 July 1916). Enclosed in Metternich to [the Minister of Foreign Affairs] ([İstanbul], 2 July 1916).

154. AA. Türkei 167/Bd. 11. M. Hartmann to [Auswärtiges Amt ?], no. 4143/444 (Berlin, 17 July 1916).

155. Dawn, *Ottomanism*, 49.

156. Khadduri, 153–54. On al-Misri's unwillingness to subordinate himself to Sharif Husayn's orders, his continued faith in a federal Turco-Arab empire, and his defection, see Tauber, *World War I*, 91–100.

157. AA. Türkei 165/Bd. 40. Romberg to Bethmann-Hollweg, no. 2259 (Bern, 10 October 1916).

158. AA. Türkei 165/Bd. 41. Loytved-Hardegg to Bethmann-Hollweg, no. 26 (Damascus, 5 January 1917).

159. HHS. PA 38/369. Ranzi to Burian (Damascus, 20 December 1916); HHS. PA 38/370. Same to Ottokar Czernin von Chudenitz (Damascus, 10 April 1917). Ranzi mistakenly refers to 'Abdullah as Ahmad.

160. AA. Türkei 165/Bd. 39. Loytved-Hardegg to Wolff-Metternich, no. 826 (Damascus, 6 August 1916).

161. Schilcher, 234.

162. MAE. Guerre 1679. "La Situation en Syrie" (9 July 1916); Atay, 88.

163. AA. Türkei 177/Bd. 3. Dr. Ruppin to Abram I. Elkus (13 October 1916).

164. HHS. PA 38/369. Nedwed to Burian (26 October and 13 December 1916).

165. MAE. Guerre 1680. Bulletin de Renseignements. Ministère de la Guerre, no. 4498–9/11 (14 June 1917).

166. A. D. Novichev, *Ekonomika Turtsii v period mirovoi voin*, 18–19. Cited in Ahmad, "Agrarian Policy," 285.

167. AA. Türkei 134/Bd. 37. Kühlmann (?) to Bethmann-Hollweg (Pera, 4 April 1917).

168. Ali Fuat Erden, *Birinci Dünya Harbinde Suriye Hatıraları* (İstanbul, 1954), 91–92.

169. On the new financial, educational, and health institutions in Aleppo, see HHS. PA 38/370. Dandini to Czernin (Aleppo, 16 February 1917).

170. *Revue du Monde Musulman* 18 (1912): 224.

171. AA. Türkei 165/Bd. 41. Kühlmann to Auswärtiges Amt, no. 269 (Konstantinopel, 20 February 1917).

172. Trumpener, 57, quotes Talat's remark to Austrian Ambassador Pallavicini.

173. See, for instance, Danişmend, *İzahlı*, 434.

174. AA. Türkei 177/Bd. 11. Loytved-Hardegg to Bethmann-Hollweg, no. 49 (Haifa, 30 March 1914).

175. US 867.00/804½. Elkus to Robert Lansing (İstanbul, 2 March 1917). Also, Bayur, 3 (pt. 4): 326–27.

176. US 867.00/796. Sharp to Secretary of State quoting report from Ambassador Elkus (Paris, 10 June 1917).

177. On 5 February 1917 Talat, in his opening speech of Parliament, announced his cabinet's intention to provide "every Osmanli" with all the rights which "the Constitution grants to him and thus to secure the rule of law in the country." Trumpener, 246.

178. US 867.00/804½ (see note 175). Until the entry of the United States into the war, the American Embassy had contacts with Turkish politicians and a good insight into the political situation in the Ottoman Empire. Elkus requested the secretary of state at the end of his report to "consider the present as strictly confidential and to give nothing of this to the press." He added, "If any of the statements of the Ministers or others should be made public they may get into very serious trouble and my position here will be made very difficult."

179. In 1917 Parliament debated the role of Islam in Ottoman institutions, and a new and more secular civil code was passed. Noteworthy in these debates was the argument of a Turkish deputy (Şemseddin Bey representing Ertuğrul [Bilecik]) that the knowledge of Arabic was important for all Ottomans: "There is no need to dwell at length on the necessity to teach Arabic in our schools. Since the noble Arab *millet* (community or nation) constitutes half of our coun-

try (*vatan*) and of our *millet*, we by all means need to know their language."
Ergin, 4:1373.

180. Holt, 276; T. E. Lawrence, *Seven Pillars of Wisdom* (New York: Doubleday, 1938), 554–55.

181. Celal Bayar, *Ben de Yazdım* (İstanbul: Baha, 1965), 1:25.

182. Bayar, 42, quotes C. V. F. Townshend, *Irak Seferi*, 474–88.

183. US 867.00/866. Stowell to the Secretary of State, no. 6582 (Berne, 4 April 1919).

184. US 867.00/948. Grey to Secretary of State via Paris, no. 1475 (4 October 1919).

185. Khayriyya Qasimiyya, *Al-hukumat al-ʿarabiyya fi dimashq* (Cairo: Dar al-Maʿarif, 1971), 80–81.

186. Laurence Evans, *United States Policy and the Partition of Turkey, 1914–1924* (Baltimore: Johns Hopkins Press, 1965), 246–47. Also, Zeine N. Zeine, *The Struggle for Arab Independence* (New York: Caravan, 1977), 134–35.

187. US 867.00/968. Knabenshue to Secretary of State via Paris, no. 29 (19 October 1919).

188. US 867.00/1094. The Supreme Commission of the Palestine Assemblies to the "Great Government of the United States, Care of the Respected American Representative in Jerusalem" (Haifa, 27 November 1919).

189. Shaw and Shaw, 344–50.

190. An article that appeared in the *Morning Post* noted, crediting Enver with the Anatolian resistance, "If Enver has now got the ear of a section of the Arab people it is owing to the mistakes of our diplomacy." *Morning Post*, 20 December 1919. Quoted in Hollis to Secretary of State (23 December 1919).

191. The book was translated by Hamza Tahir and ʿAbd al-Wahhab ʿAzzam. See Landau, *Pan-Islam*, 80.

192. Zeine, *Struggle*, 136.

193. Y. Porath, *The Emergence of the Palestinian-Arab National Movement, 1918–1929* (London: Frank Cass, 1974), 160–65.

194. Bayur, 3 (pt. 4): 360.

Conclusion

1. Benedict Anderson, *Imagined Communities: Reflections on the Origin and Spread of Nationalism* (London: Verso, 1983), 45.

2. In 1877 these provinces sent fewer than 15 percent of all deputies, as opposed to closer to 25 percent in 1908 (20 percent, excluding Turkish deputies from Arab provinces). The rise corresponds to the increased weight of the Arab population in shrinking boundaries.

3. Michael Garleff, "Relations between the Political Representation of the Baltic Provinces and the Russian Government, 1850–1917," in *Governments, Ethnic Groups, and Political Representation*, ed. Geoffrey Alderman in collaboration with John Leslie and Klaus Erich Pollmann (Aldershot: Dartmouth, 1993), 225.

4. Ernest Gellner's foreword to Arjomand, ix.

5. Both Arab nationalists like ʿAbd al-Ghani al-ʿUraysi, who had dwelled on the presumed irreligiosity of the Unionists—if not Turks in general—in order to strike an Arab nationalist chord, and Turkish nationalists like Ziya Gökalp, who had made Islam a cornerstone of their thought, utilized religion as a political vehicle. Yet, "religion played a secondary role in the thinking of al-ʿUraysi," and Ziya Gökalp opposed the CUP leadership, though a member of the Committee, for its Ottomanist and Islamic policies. On al-ʿUraysi, see Khalidi, "al-ʿUraysi," 30, and on Gökalp, Taha Parla, *The Social and Political Thought of Ziya Gökalp, 1876–1924* (Leiden: Brill, 1985), 15.

Bibliography

Archival Sources

Başbakanlık Osmanlı Arşivi (BBA), İstanbul

BAB-I ÂLİ EVRAK ODASI (BEO)

(*Defter*s [registers] surveyed for short descriptions and six-digit
designations of BEO documents)

Gelen-giden Defterleri

108–114 (Dahiliye giden) 1325–1329
75 (Dahiliye gelen) 1325
770/40/2 Mekke-i Mükerreme giden
769/40/1 Mekke-i Mükerreme gelen
698, 705 Arabistan Şifre Defterleri
326, 328, 330 İstizan irade
526, 527 Meclis-i Mebusan (gelen-giden)

Vilayet Defterleri

304 Hicaz

Sadaret Defterleri

922

İRADE TASNİFİ

Dahiliye 1326–1330
Dosya Usulüne Göre İrade Tasnifi (DUIT)

DAHİLİYE NEZARETİ

İdare-i Umumiye (DH-İ.Um.)
Kalem-i Mahsus (DH-KMS)
Muhaberat-ı Umumiye İdaresi Mütenevvia Kısmı (DH-MTV)
Muhaberat-ı Umumiye Dairesi Siyasi Evrakı (DH-SYS)

Askeri Tarih ve Stratejik Etüt Dairesi (ATASE), Ankara
(Archives of the Turkish General Chief of Staff)

İtalyan Harbi (Italian War)
Birinci Cihan Harbi (World War I)

Public Record Office (PRO), London

FO 195: Correspondence between the British Embassy and the British
    Consulates of Aleppo, Baghdad, Beirut, Damascus, Jerusalem, Jidda
    (1908–1914)
FO 371: Correspondence between Foreign Office and British Embassy
    in İstanbul (FO 371/549, 560, 662, 760, 2139, 2140, 2486, 2767)
FO 424/230, 231; FO 618/3; FO 685/3

Haus—, Hof—, und Staatsarchiv (HHS), Vienna.
Politisches Archiv (PA)

Türkei PA 12 (XII)
Türkei PA 38 (XXXVIII)

Auswärtiges Amt (AA), Bonn

Türkei 134, 142, 165, 167, 177

Archives du Ministère des Affaires Etrangères (MAE), Paris

CORRESPONDANCE POLITIQUE ET COMMERCIAL, 1908–1918

Turquie, Nouvelle Série (N.S.)

Jeunes Turcs, etc. 6–9
Syrie, Liban 111–114
Arabie, Yemen 140–145
Pèlerinage de la Mecque 147–148

Guerre 1914–1918

1679, 1680

United States National Archives (US), Washington (on microform through the Center for Research Libraries)

RECORDS OF THE U.S. DEPARTMENT OF STATE RELATING TO INTERNATIONAL AFFAIRS OF TURKEY, 1910–1929

867 Political Affairs

Newspapers

Takvim-i Vekai (İstanbul)
Tanin (İstanbul)
Tasvir-i Efkar (İstanbul)
Selected copies of *The Egyptian Gazette* (Cairo), *İkdam* (İstanbul), *Al-manar* (Cairo), *Revue du Monde Musulman* (Paris), *Shams al-haqiqa (Şems ül-Haki-kat)* (Mecca), and *Sırat-ı Müstakim* (İstanbul)

Parliamentary Proceedings

Records of the Ottoman Parliament published separately from the official paper *Takvim-i Vekai (Meclis-i Mebusan Zabıt Cerideleri* 1908–1912)

Secondary Sources

Abdullah ibn Husayn, King. *Memoirs*. New York, 1950.

Abou-el-Haj, Rifaʿt ʿAli. *Formation of the Modern State: The Ottoman Empire, Sixteenth to Eighteenth Centuries*. Albany, 1991.

Abu Manneh, Butrus. "The Christians between Ottomanism and Syrian Nationalism: The Ideas of Butrus al-Bustani". *IJMES* 11 (1980): 287–304.

———. "The Islamic Roots of the Gülhane Rescript". *Die Welt des Islams* 34 (1994): 173–203.

———. "The Rise of the Sanjak of Jerusalem in the Late Nineteenth Century". In *The Palestinians and the Middle East Conflict*, ed. Gabriel Ben-Dor, 21–32. Ramat Gan, 1978.

———. "Sultan Abdulhamid II and Shaikh Abulhuda al-Sayyadi". *Middle Eastern Studies* 15 (1979): 131–53.

Açık Söz: Hürriyet ve İtilâf Fırkasının Makasidini Yanlış Anlayanlara İzahat ve Red-i İtirazat. İstanbul, 1330 [1912].

Ahmad, Feroz. "The Agrarian Policy of the Young Turks, 1908–1918". In *Economie et sociétés*, ed. Bacqué-Grammont and Dumont, 275–88.

———. "Great Britain's Relations with the Young Turks, 1908–1914". *Middle Eastern Studies* 2 (1966): 302–29.

———. "A Note on the International Status of Kuwait before November 1914". *IJMES* 24 (1992): 181–85.

———. "Unionist Relations with the Greek, Armenian, and Jewish Communities of the Ottoman Empire, 1908–1914". In *Christians and Jews in the Ottoman Empire*, 2 vols., ed. Benjamin Braude and Bernard Lewis, 401–34. New York, 1982.

———. "Vanguard of a Nascent Bourgeoisie: The Social and Economic Policy of the Young Turks, 1908–1918". In *Türkiye'nin Sosyal ve Ekonomik Tarihi, 1071–1920*, ed. Okyar and İnalcık, 329–50.

———. *The Young Turks: The Committee of Union and Progress in Turkish Politics, 1908–1914*. Oxford, 1969.

Ahmad, Feroz, and Dankwart Rustow. "İkinci Meşrutiyet Döneminde Meclisler, 1908–1918". *Güney-Doğu Avrupa Araştırmaları Dergisi* 4–5 (1976): 245–84.

Ajay, Nicholas Z., Jr. "Political Intrigue and Suppression in Lebanon during World War I". *IJMES* 5 (1974): 140–60.

Akarlı, Engin. "Abdülhamid II's Attempt to Integrate Arabs into the Ottoman System". In *Palestine in the Late Ottoman Period: Political, Social, and Economic Transformation*, ed. David Kushner, 74–89. Jerusalem, 1986.

———. *The Long Peace*. Berkeley and Los Angeles, 1993.

———. "The Problems of External Pressures, Power Struggles, and Budgetary Deficits in Ottoman Politics under Abdulhamid II, 1876–1909: Origins and Solutions". Ph.D. diss., Princeton University, 1976.

Akçura, Yusuf. *Üç Tarz-ı Siyaset*. İstanbul, 1327 [1911].

Akşin, Sina. *100 Soruda Jön Türkler ve İttihat ve Terakki*. İstanbul, 1980.

Allen, Richard. *Imperialism and Nationalism in the Fertile Crescent*. London, 1974.

al-Amr, Saleh Muhammad. *The Hijaz under Ottoman Rule, 1869–1914: Ottoman Vali, the Sharif of Mecca, and the Growth of British Influence*. [Riyadh], 1978.

Anderson, Benedict. *Imagined Communities: Reflections on the Origin and Spread of Nationalism*. London, 1983.

Antonius, George. *The Arab Awakening: The Story of the Arab National Movement*. New York, 1979 (first published in 1938).

Arai, Masami. "The Genç Kalemler and the Young Turks: A Study in Nationalism". *Orta Doğu Teknik Üniversitesi Gelişme Dergisi* 12 (1985): 199–230.

———. *Turkish Nationalism in the Young Turk Era*. Leiden, 1992.

Arjomand, Said Amir, ed. *From Nationalism to Revolutionary Islam*. Albany, 1984.

Arsel, İlhan. *Arap Milliyetçiliği ve Türkler*. İstanbul, 1987.

Atay, Falih Rıfkı. *Zeytindağı*. İstanbul, 1938.

Atılhan, Cevat Rıfat. *Bütün Çıplaklığıyla 31 Mart Faciası*. İstanbul, 1959.

al-'Azm, Haqqi. *Haqa'iq 'an al-intikhabat al-niyabiyya*. Cairo, 1912.

Bacqué-Grammont, Jean-Louis, and Paul Dumont, eds. *Economie et sociétés dans l'Empire ottoman*. Paris, 1983.

Baker, Randall. *King Husain and the Kingdom of the Hejaz*. Cambridge, 1979.

al-Bani, Muhammad Sa'id. *Tanwir al-basa'ir bi sirah al-shaykh tahir*. [Damascus], 1920.

al-Barudi, Fakhri. *Mudhakkirat al-barudi*. Beirut, 1951–52.

Batatu, Hanna. *The Old Social Classes and the Revolutionary Movements of Iraq*. Princeton, 1978.

Bayar, Celal. *Ben de Yazdım*. Vol. 1. İstanbul, 1965.

Bayhum, Muhammad Jamil. *Qawafil al-'urubba wa mawakibuha khilal al-'usur*. Beirut, 1948.

———. *Qawafil al-'urubba wa mawakibuha khilal al-'usur*. Pt. 2. Beirut, 1950.

Bayur, Yusuf Hikmet. *Türk İnkilabı Tarihi*. 3 vols. Ankara, 1983 (1st ed. İstanbul, 1940–43).

Belen, Fahri. *20. Yüzyılda Osmanlı Devleti*. İstanbul, 1973.

Berkes, Niyazi. *The Development of Secularism in Turkey*. Montreal, 1964.

Berque, Jacques, and Dominique Chevallier, eds. *Les Arabes par leurs archives*. Paris, 1976.

Birinci, Ali. *Hürriyet ve İtilâf Fırkası*. İstanbul, 1990.

Black, Cyril E., and L. Carl Brown. *Modernization in the Middle East: The Ottoman Empire and Its Afro-Asian Successors*. Princeton, N.J., 1992.

Blake, Corinne. "Training Arab-Ottoman Bureaucrats: Syrian Graduates of the Mülkiye Mektebi 1890–1920". Ph.D. diss., Princeton University, 1991.

Bleda, Mithat Şükrü. *İmparatorluğun Çöküşü*. Ed. Turgut Bleda. İstanbul, 1979.

Blind, Karl. "The Prorogued Turkish Parliament". *North American Review* 175 (1902): 42–52.

———. "Young Turkey". *Fortnightly Review* 66 (1896): 830–43.

Bonin, Charles-Eudes. "Le Chemin de fer du Hedjaz". *Annales de géographie* 18 (1909): 421–29.

Bostan, M. Hanefi. *Said Halim Paşa*. İstanbul, 1992.

Breuilly, John. *Nationalism and the State*. Manchester, 1982.

Buheiry, Marwan R., ed. *Intellectual Life in the Arab East, 1890–1939*. Beirut, 1981.

Burru, Tawfiq ʿAli. *Al-ʿarab wa al-turk fi al-ʿahd al-dusturi al-ʿuthmani, 1908–1914*. Cairo, 1960.

Busch, Briton Cooper. *Britain and the Persian Gulf*. Berkeley and Los Angeles, 1967.

———. *Britain, India, and the Arabs, 1914–1921*. Berkeley and Los Angeles, 1971.

Buzpınar, S. Tufan. "Abdulhamid II, Islam and the Arabs: The Cases of Syria and the Hijaz (1878–1882)". Ph.D. diss., University of Manchester, 1991.

Çankaya, Ali. *Mülkiye Tarihi ve Mülkiyeliler*. Ankara, 1954.

Cemal Paşa. *Hatıralar*. Ed. Behçet Cemal. İstanbul, 1977.

Cevat, Ali. *İkinci Meşrutiyetin İlanı ve Otuz Bir Mart Hadisesi*. Ed. Faik Reşit Unat. Ankara, 1960.

Cleveland, William L. *Islam against the West*. Austin, 1985.

———. *The Making of an Arab Nationalist: Ottomanism and Arabism in the Life and Thought of Satiʿ al-Husri*. Princeton, 1971.

Commins, David. *Islamic Reform: Politics and Change in Late Ottoman Syria*. New York, 1990.

———. "Religious Reformers and Arabists in Damascus, 1885–1914". *IJMES* 18 (1986): 405–25.

Daghir, Asʿad. *Thawrat al-ʿarab*. Cairo, 1916.

Danişmend, İsmail Hami. *İzahlı Osmanlı Tarihi Kronolojisi*. İstanbul, 1961 (1st ed. İstanbul, 1947–55).

———. *31 Mart Vakası*. İstanbul, 1986 (first published in 1961).

Davison, H. Roderic. "The Advent of the Principle of Representation in the Government of the Ottoman Empire". In *Beginnings of Modernization in the Middle East*, ed. Polk and Chambers, 93–108.

———. *Reform in the Ottoman Empire, 1856–1876*. Princeton, 1963.

Dawn, Ernest. *From Ottomanism to Arabism*. Urbana, Ill., 1973.

———. "The Origins of Arab Nationalism". In *Origins of Arab Nationalism*, ed. Khalidi et al., 4–30.

———. "Rise of Arabism in Syria". In *From Ottomanism to Arabism*, by Ernest Dawn.

De Jong, F. "The Proclamations of al-Husayn b. ʿAli and ʿAli Haydar". *Der Islam* 57 (1980): 281–87.

Demiroğlu, Faiz. *Abdülhamid'e Verilen Jurnaller*. İstanbul, 1955.

Deutsch, Karl. *Nationalism and Its Alternatives*. New York, 1969.

Devereux, Robert. *The First Ottoman Constitutional Period*. Baltimore, 1963.

Duri, ʿAbd al-ʿAziz. *The Historical Formation of the Arab Nation*. London, 1987.

el-Edroos, Syed Ali. *The Hashemite Arab Army, 1908–1979*. Amman, 1980.

Erden, Ali Fuat. *Birinci Dünya Harbinde Suriye Hatıraları*. İstanbul, 1954.

————. *Paris'ten Tih Sahrasına*. Ankara, 1949.

Ergin, Osman. *Türk Maarif Tarihi*. 5 vols. continuously paginated. İstanbul, 1977 (1st ed. İstanbul, 1943).

Eriksen, Knut, Andreas Kazamias, Robin Okey, and Janusz Tomiak. "Governments and the Education of Non-Dominant Ethnic Groups in Comparative Perspective". In *Schooling, Educational Policy and Ethnic Identity*, ed. Tomiak, 389–417. New York, 1991.

Evans, Laurence. *United States Policy and the Partition of Turkey, 1914–1924*. Baltimore, 1965.

Fahri, Ali. *Emel Yolunda*. İstanbul, 1328 [1910].

Farah, Caesar. "Censorship and Freedom of Expression in Syria and Egypt". In *Nationalism in a Non-National State*, ed. Haddad and Ochsenwald.

Fargo, Mumtaz Ayoub. "Arab-Turkish Relations from the Emergence of Arab Nationalism to the Arab Revolt, 1848–1916". Ph.D. diss., University of Utah, 1969.

Faroqhi, Suraiya. *Herrscher über Mekka: Die Geschichte der Pilgerfahrt*. München, 1990.

————. *Pilgrims and Sultans: The Hajj under the Ottomans, 1517–1683*. London, 1994.

Fawaz, Leila T. *Merchants and Migrants in Nineteenth-Century Beirut*. Cambridge, Mass., 1983.

Fikri, Lütfi. *Selanikte Bir Konferans: Bizde Furuk-ı Siyasiye, Hal-i Hazırı, İstikbali*. İstanbul, 1326 [1910].

Findley, Carter. *Bureaucratic Reform in the Ottoman Empire*. Princeton, N.J., 1980.

Fourth Army. *Âliye Divan-ı Harb-i Örfisinde Tedkik Olunan Mesele-i Siyasiye Hakkında İzahat*. İstanbul, 1332 [1916].

Friedman, Isaiah. *The Question of Palestine, 1914–1918: British-Jewish-Arab Relations*. London, 1973.

Füredi, Frank. *Mythical Past, Elusive Future: History and Society in an Anxious Age*. London, 1992.

Garleff, Michael. "Relations between the Political Representation of the Baltic Provinces and the Russian Government, 1850–1917". In *Governments, Ethnic Groups, and Political Representation*, ed. Geoffrey Alderman in collaboration with John Leslie and Klaus Erich Pollmann, 201–38. Aldershot, 1993.

Gellner, Ernest. *Nations and Nationalism*. Oxford, 1983.

Georgeon, François. *Aux Origines du nationalisme turc: Yusuf Akçura (1876–1935)*. Paris, 1980.

Gibb, Hamilton, and Harold Bowen. *Islamic Society and the West*. Vol. 1, pt. 2. London, 1963.

Goltz, Colmar F. von der. "Stärke und Schwäche des türkischen Reiches". *Deutsche Rundschau* 93 (1897): 95–119.

Gövsa, İbrahim Alaettin. *Türk Meşhurları Ansiklopedisi*. Ankara, n.d.

Gross, Max L. "Ottoman Rule in the Province of Damascus, 1860–1909". Ph.D. diss., Georgetown University, 1979.

Gülsoy, Ufuk. *Hicaz Demiryolu*. İstanbul, 1994.

Haarmann, Ulrich W. "Ideology and History, Identity and Alterity: The Arab

Image of the Turk from the 'Abbasids to Modern Egypt". *IJMES* 20 (1988): 175–96.

Haddad, Mahmoud. "Iraq before World War I: A Case of Anti-European Arab Ottomanism". In *Origins of Arab Nationalism*, ed. Khalidi et al., 120–50.

———. "The Rise of Arab Nationalism Reconsidered". *IJMES* 26 (1994): 201–22.

Haddad, William, and William Ochsenwald, eds. *Nationalism in a Non-National State*. Columbus, Ohio, 1977.

Hagen, Gottfried. *Die Türkei im Ersten Weltkrieg*. Frankfurt, 1990.

Haim, Sylvia G., ed. *Arab Nationalism: An Anthology*. Berkeley and Los Angeles, 1964.

Halim, Said. *Buhranlarımız ve Son Eserleri*. Ed. M. Ertuğrul Düzdağ. İstanbul, 1991.

Hanioğlu, M. Şükrü. *Doktor Abdullah Cevdet ve Dönemi*. İstanbul, n.d. [1982].

———. *Osmanlı İttihad ve Terakki Cemiyeti ve Jön Türklük, 1889–1902*. İstanbul, 1986.

———. "The Young Turks and the Arabs before the Revolution of 1908". In *Origins of Arab Nationalism*, ed. Khalidi et al., 31–49.

———. *The Young Turks in Opposition*. New York, 1995.

Harran, Taj el-Sir Ahmad. "Syrian Relations in the Ottoman Constitutional Period, 1908–1914". Ph.D. diss., University of London, 1969.

———. "The Young Turks and the Arabs: The Role of Arab Societies in Turkish-Arab Relations in the Period 1908–1914". In *Türk-Arap İlişkileri: Geçmişte, Bugün ve Gelecekte*, 182–202.

Hatemi, Hüseyin. "Tanzimat ve Meşrutiyet Dönemlerinde Derneklerin Gelişimi". In *Tanzimat'tan Cumhuriyet'e Türkiye Ansiklopedisi*, 1:198–204.

Hiçyılmaz, Ergun. *Teşkilat-ı Mahsusa*. İstanbul, 1979.

Hobsbawm, Eric J. *Nations and Nationalism since 1780*. Cambridge, 1990.

Holt, P. M. *Egypt and the Fertile Crescent, 1516–1922: A Political History*. Ithaca, N.Y., 1966.

Hourani, Albert. "*The Arab Awakening*: Forty Years After". In *Emergence of the Modern Middle East*, by Albert Hourani.

———. *Arabic Thought in the Liberal Age, 1798–1939*. London, 1970 (1st ed. 1962).

———. *The Emergence of the Modern Middle East*. Berkeley and Los Angeles, 1981.

———. "The Ottoman Background of the Modern Middle East". In *Emergence of the Modern Middle East*, by Albert Hourani.

———. "Ottoman Reform and the Politics of Notables". In *Emergence of the Modern Middle East*, by Albert Hourani.

Hroch, Miroslav. "From National Movement to the Fully-Formed Nation". *New Left Review* 198 (1993): 3–20.

İnal, İ. Mahmud Kemal. *Osmanlı Devrinde Son Sadrazamlar*. 3 vols. İstanbul, 1940–1953.

İnalcık, Halil. "The Application of the Tanzimat and its Social Effects". *Archivum Ottomanicum* 5 (1973): 97–128.

Itzkowitz, Norman. *Ottoman Empire and Islamic Tradition*. Chicago, 1972.

Jankowski, James. "Egypt and Early Arab Nationalism, 1908–1922". In *Origins of Arab Nationalism*, ed. Khalidi et al.

Jeltyakov [Zheltiakov], A. D. *Türkiye'nin Sosyo-Politik ve Kültürel Hayatında Basın (1729–1908 Yılları)*. İstanbul, n.d.

Johnson, Michael. *Class and Client in Beirut*. London, 1986.

Kandemir, Feridun. *Peygamberimizin Gölgesinde Son Türkler*. İstanbul, 1974.

Kara, İsmail, ed. *Türkiye'de İslâmcılık Düşüncesi*. 2 vols. İstanbul, 1987.

Karal, Enver Ziya. *Osmanlı Tarihi*. Vol. 8. Ankara, 1962.

Karpat, Kemal. "The Ottoman Parliament of 1877 and Its Social Significance". In *Actes du 1er congrès des études balkaniques et sud-est européennes*, 247–57. Sofia, 1969.

———. *Ottoman Population, 1830–1914*. Madison, 1985.

Kawtharani, Wajih. *Al-ittijahat al-ijtima`iyya al-siyasiyya fi jabal lubnan wa al-mashraq al-`arabi, 1860–1920*. Beirut, 1978.

Kayalı, Hasan. "Elections and the Electoral Process in the Ottoman Empire, 1877–1919". *IJMES* 27 (1995): 265–86.

———. "Jewish Representation in the Ottoman Parliaments". In *The Jews of the Ottoman Empire*, ed. Avigdor Levy, 507–17. Princeton, N.J., 1994.

Kedourie, Elie. *Arabic Political Memoirs and Other Studies*. London, 1974.

———. *England and the Middle East*. London, 1956.

———. "The Impact of the Young Turk Revolution on the Arabic-Speaking Provinces of the Ottoman Empire". In *Arabic Political Memoirs and Other Studies*, by Elie Kedourie, 124–61.

———. "Political Parties in the Arab World". In *Arabic Political Memoirs and Other Studies*, by Elie Kedourie.

Kemal, İsmail. *The Memoirs of İsmail Kemal Bey*. London, 1920.

Khadduri, Majid. "`Aziz `Ali Misri and the Arab Nationalist Movement". In *Middle Eastern Affairs*, ed. Hourani. No. 4. Oxford, 1965.

Khalidi, Rashid. "Arab Nationalism in Syria: The Formative Years, 1908–1914". In *Nationalism in a Non-National State*, ed. Haddad and Ochsenwald, 207–38.

———. *British Policy towards Syria and Palestine, 1906–1914*. London, 1980.

———. "The 1912 Election Campaign in the Cities of *bilad al-Sham*". *IJMES* 16 (1984): 461–74.

———. "Ottomanism and Arabism in Syria before 1914: A Reassessment". In *Origins of Arab Nationalism*, ed. Khalidi et al., 50–69.

———. "The Press as a Source for Modern Arab Political History: `Abd al-Ghani al-`Uraysi and *al-Mufid*". *Arab Studies Quarterly* 3 (1981): 22–42. Also in modified form in *Intellectual Life in the Arab East*, ed. Buheiry, 38–61.

———. "Social Forces in the Rise of the Arab Movement in Syria". In *From Nationalism to Revolutionary Islam*, ed. Arjomand, 53–70.

Khalidi, Rashid, Lisa Anderson, Muhammad Muslih, and Reeva S. Simon, eds. *The Origins of Arab Nationalism*. New York, 1991.

Khoury, Philip. *Urban Notables and Arab Nationalism: The Politics of Damascus, 1860–1920*. Cambridge, 1983.

Koçu, Reşat Ekrem. "Türkiye'de Seçimin Tarihi, 1877–1950". *Tarih Dünyası* 1 (1950): 181–82.

Kohn, Hans. "Der arabische Nationalismus". *Zeitschrift der Politik* 17 (1927).

———. *Western Civilization in the Near East*. New York, 1936.

Koloğlu, Orhan. *Mustafa Kemal'in Yanında İki Libyalı Lider*. Ankara, 1981.

———. "Osmanlı Basını: İçeriği ve Rejimi". In *Tanzimat'tan Cumhuriyet'e Türkiye Ansiklopedisi*, 1:67–93.

Kornrumpf, Hans Jürgen. "Hüseyin Hilmi Pascha: Anmerkungen zu seiner Biographie". In *Wiener Zeitschrift für die Kunde des Morgenlandes* 76 (1986): 193–98.

Kuran, Ahmed Bedevi. *İnkılap Tarihimiz ve İttihat ve Terakki*. İstanbul, 1948.

———. *İnkilap Tarihimiz ve Jön Türkler*. İstanbul, 1945.

———. *Osmanlı İmparatorluğunda İnkilap Hareketleri ve Milli Mücadele*. İstanbul, 1956.

Kuran, Ercümend. "The Impact of Nationalism on the Turkish Elite in the Nineteenth Century". In *Beginnings of Modernization in the Middle East*, ed. Polk and Chambers, 109–18.

Kürkçüoğlu, Ömer. *Osmanlı Devleti'ne Karşı Arap Bağımsızlık Hareketi*. Ankara, 1982.

Kurşun, Zekeriya. *Yol Ayırımında Türk-Arap İlişkileri*. İstanbul, 1992.

Kushner, David. *The Rise of Turkish Nationalism, 1876–1908*. London, 1977.

Kutay, Cemal. *Prens Sabahaddin Bey, Sultan II. Abdülhamid, İttihad ve Terakki*. İstanbul, 1964.

Landau, Jacob M. "An Arab Anti-Turk Handbill, 1881". *Turcica* 9 (1977): 215–27.

———. *Pan-Turkism in Turkey*. London, 1981.

———. *The Politics of Pan-Islam*. Oxford, 1994 (first published in 1990).

Lawrence, T. E. *Seven Pillars of Wisdom*. New York, 1938 (first published in 1926).

Layne, Linda L. "Tribesmen as Citizens: 'Primordial Ties' and Democracy in Rural Jordan". In *Elections in the Middle East*, ed. Layne. Boulder, Colo., 1987.

Lenczowski, George. *The Middle East in World Affairs*. London, 1980.

Lewis, Bernard. *The Emergence of Modern Turkey*. London, 1961.

Longrigg, Stephen Hemsley. *Iraq, 1900 to 1950*. London, 1953.

Makki, M. S. *Medina, Saudi Arabia: A Geographical Analysis of the City and the Region*. Avebury, 1982.

Mandel, Neville J. *The Arabs and Zionism before World War I*. Berkeley and Los Angeles, 1976.

Mandelstam, André. *Le Sort de l'empire ottomane*. Lausanne, 1917.

Ma'oz, Moshe, ed. "The Impact of Modernization on Syrian Politics and Society during the Early Tanzimat Period". In *Beginnings of Modernization in the Middle East*, ed. Polk and Chambers, 333–50.

———. *Ottoman Reform in Syria and Palestine, 1840–1861*. Oxford, 1968.

———. *Studies on Palestine during the Ottoman Period*. Jerusalem, 1975.

Mardin, Şerif. "Center-Periphery Relations: A Key to Turkish Politics?" In *Post-Traditional Societies*, ed. S. N. Eisenstadt, 169–90. New York, 1972.

———. *The Genesis of Young Ottoman Thought*. Princeton, 1962.

———. *Jön Türklerin Siyasi Fikirleri, 1895–1908*. Ankara, 1964.

Marsot, Afaf Lutfi al-Sayyid. *A Short History of Modern Egypt*. Cambridge, 1985.

Menteşe, Halil. *Osmanlı Mebusan Meclisi Reisi Halil Menteşe'nin Anıları*. Ed. İsmail Arar. İstanbul, 1986.

Miller, William. *The Ottoman Empire, 1801–1913*. Cambridge, 1913.

Morris, James. *The Hashemite Kings*. London, 1959.

Morsey, Konrad. *T. E. Lawrence und der arabische Aufstand, 1916/18*. Osnabrück, 1976.

Mousa, Suleiman. *Al-haraka al-ʿarabiyya*. Beirut, 1970.

———. *T. E. Lawrence: An Arab View*. Trans. Albert Butros. London, 1966.

Al-muʾtamar al-ʿarabi al-awwal. Cairo, 1913.

Ochsenwald, William. *The Hijaz Railroad*. Charlottesville, 1980.

———. "Ironic Origins: Arab Nationalism in the Hijaz". In *Origins of Arab Nationalism*, ed. Khalidi et al., 189–203.

———. *Religion, Society, and the State in Arabia: The Hijaz under Ottoman Control, 1840–1908*. Columbus, Ohio, 1984.

Okyar, Osman, and Halil İnalcık, eds. *Türkiye'nin Sosyal ve Ekonomik Tarihi, 1071–1920*. Ankara, 1980.

Ölçen, Ali Nejat. *Osmanlı Meclisi Meb'usanında Kuvvetler Ayırımı ve Siyasal İşkenceler*. Ankara, 1982.

Ortaylı, İlber. *İmparatorluğun En Uzun Yüzyılı*. İstanbul, 1987.

Owen, Roger. *The Middle East in the World Economy, 1800–1914*. London, 1981.

Parla, Taha. *The Social and Political Thought of Ziya Gökalp, 1876–1924*. Leiden, 1985.

Petrosyan, I. E. "On the Motive Force of the Reformist and Constitutional Movements in the Ottoman Empire". In *Economie et sociétés*, ed. Bacqué-Grammont and Dumont, 13–24.

Philipp, Thomas. *The Syrians in Egypt, 1725–1975*. Stuttgart, 1985.

Polk, William R., and Richard L. Chambers, eds. *Beginnings of Modernization in the Middle East: The Nineteenth Century*. Chicago, 1968.

Porath, Y. *The Emergence of the Palestinian-Arab National Movement, 1918–1929*. London, 1974.

Prätor, Sabine. *Der arabische Faktor in der jungtürkischen Politik: Eine Studie zum osmanischen Parlament der II. Konstitution (1908–1918)*. Berlin, 1993.

Qasimiyya, Khayriyya. *Al-hukumat al-ʿarabiyya fi dimashq*. Cairo, 1971.

Quataert, Donald. "A Provisional Report Concerning the Impact of European Capital on Ottoman Port and Railway Workers, 1888–1909". In *Economie et sociétés*, ed. Bacqué-Grammont and Dumont, 459–70.

———. *Social Disintegration and Popular Resistance in the Ottoman Empire, 1881–1908*. New York, 1983.

Ramsaur, E. E. *The Young Turks: Prelude to the Revolution of 1908*. Princeton, 1957.

Rıza, Ahmed. *Ahmed Rıza Bey'in Anıları*. İstanbul, 1988.

Roded, Ruth. "Ottoman Service as a Vehicle for the Rise of New Upstarts among the Urban Elite Families of Syria in the Last Decades of Ottoman Rule". *Asian and African Studies* 17 (1985): 63–94.

Rogan, Eugene Lawrence. "Incorporating the Periphery: The Ottoman Extension of Direct Rule over Southeastern Syria (Transjordan), 1867–1914". Ph.D. diss., Harvard University, 1991.

Ryan, Andrew. *The Last of the Dragomans*. London, 1951.

Sabini, John. *Armies in the Sun: The Struggle for Mecca and Medina*. London, 1981.

Sa'id, Amin. *Al-thawra al-'arabiya al-kubra*. Cairo, [1934].

Salibi, Kamal S. "Beirut under the Young Turks: As Depicted in the Political Memoirs of Salim Ali Salam (1868–1938)". In *Les Arabes par leurs archives*, ed. Berque and Chevallier, 193–216.

Schilcher, Linda Schatkowski. "The Famine of 1915–1918 in Greater Syria". In *Problems of the Modern Middle East in Historical Perspective: Essays in Honor of Albert Hourani*, ed. John P. Spagnolo, 229–58. Reading, 1992.

Schölch, Alexander. "Ein Palästinischer Repräsentant der Tanzimat-Periode: Yusuf Diya'addin al-Halidi, 1842–1906". *Der Islam* 57 (1980): 311–22.

Seikaly, Samir. "Shukri al-'Asali: A Case Study of a Political Activist". In *Origins of Arab Nationalism*, ed. Khalidi et al., 73–96.

Selahaddin, Mehmed. *İttihad ve Terakki'nin Kuruluşu ve Osmanlı Devleti'nin Yıkılışı Hakkında Bildiklerim*. İstanbul, 1989 (first published in 1918).

Şeref, Abdurrahman. *Tarih Musahebeleri*. İstanbul, 1923.

al-Shamikh, Muhammad A. *Al-sihafa fi al-hijaz, 1908–1941*. Beirut, 1972.

Shamir, Shimon. "Midhat Pasha and Anti-Turkish Agitation in Syria". *Middle Eastern Studies* 10 (1974): 115–41.

Shaw, Stanford J. "Some Aspects of the Aims and Achievements of the Nineteenth-Century Ottoman Reformers". In *Beginnings of Modernization in the Middle East*, ed. Polk and Chambers, 29–40.

Shaw, Stanford J., and Ezel Kural Shaw. *History of the Ottoman Empire and Modern Turkey*. Vol. 2, *Reform, Revolution, and Republic: The Rise of Modern Turkey, 1808–1975*. Cambridge, 1977.

al-Shihabi, Mustafa. *Muhadarat 'an al-qawmiyya al-'arabiyya*. Cairo [?], 1959.

———. *Muhadarat fi al-isti'mar*. 3 vols. Cairo, 1957.

Shils, Edward. *Center and Periphery: Essays in Macrosociology*. Chicago, 1975.

Simon, Reeva S. "The Education of an Iraqi Ottoman Army Officer". In *Origins of Arab Nationalism*, ed. Khalidi et al., 151–66.

Soysal, Mümtaz. *100 Soruda Anayasa'nın Anlamı*. İstanbul, 1969.

Steppat, Fritz. "Eine Bewegung unter den Notabeln Syriens, 1877–78". In *Zeitschrift der Deutschen Morgenlandischen Gesellschaft*, supplementa I, 2 (1969): 631–49.

Stitt, George. *A Prince of Arabia: The Emir Shereef Ali Haider*. London, 1948.

Stoddard, Philip Hendrick. "The Ottoman Government and the Arabs, 1911–1918: A Preliminary Study of the Teşkilat-ı Mahsusa". Ph.D. diss., Princeton University, 1963.

Strohmeier, Martin. *Al-kulliya as-salahiya in Jerusalem*. Stuttgart, 1991.

Szyliowicz, Joseph S. "Changes in the Recruitment Patterns and Career Lines of Ottoman Provincial Administrators during the Nineteenth Century". In *Studies on Palestine during the Ottoman Period*, ed. Moshe Ma'oz, 249–83.

Talat Paşa. *Talat Paşa'nın Hatıraları*. Ed. Hüseyin Cahid Yalçın. İstanbul, 1946.

Tanzimat'tan Cumhuriyet'e Türkiye Ansiklopedisi. 6 vols. İstanbul, n.d.

Tarabein, Ahmed. "'Abd al-Hamid al-Zahrawi: The Career and Thought of an Arab Nationalist". In *Origins of Arab Nationalism*, ed. Khalidi et al., 97–119.

Tarazi, Filip de. *Tarikh al-sihafa al-'arabiyya*. 4 vols. Beirut, 1913–14.

Tarık, Tevfik. *Muaddel Kanun-u Esasi ve İntihab-ı Mebusan Kanunu*. İstanbul, 1327 [1911].

Tauber, Eliezer. *The Arab Movements in World War I*. London, 1993.

———. *The Emergence of the Arab Movements*. London, 1993.

Temo, İbrahim. *İttihad ve Terakki Cemiyetinin Teşekkülü ve Hidemat-ı Vataniye ve İnkilab-ı Milliye Dair Hatıratım*. Mecidiye, 1939.

Thomas, James Paul. "The Sykes-Picot Agreement of 1916: Its Genesis in British Policy". Ph.D. diss., Johns Hopkins University, 1971.

Tibawi, A. L. *A Modern History of Syria*. London, 1969.

Tibi, Bassam. *Arab Nationalism: A Critical Enquiry*. Ed. and trans. Marion Farouk-Sluglett and Peter Sluglett. 2d ed. New York, 1990.

Toledano, Ehud R. *The Ottoman Slave Trade and Its Suppression, 1840–1890*. Princeton, N.J., 1982.

Toprak, Zafer. *Türkiye'de "Milli İktisat," 1908–1918*. Ankara: Yurt, 1982.

Trumpener, Ulrich. *Germany and the Ottoman Empire, 1914–1918*. Princeton, N.J., 1968.

Tunaya, Tarık Zafer. *Türkiye'de Siyasal Partiler*. Vol. 1, *İkinci Meşrutiyet Dönemi*. İstanbul, 1988.

———. *Türkiye'de Siyasi Partiler, 1859–1952*. İstanbul, 1952.

———. *Türkiye'nin Siyasi Hayatında Batılılaşma Hareketleri*. İstanbul, 1960.

Türk-Arap İlişkileri: Geçmişte, Bugün ve Gelecekte. Ed. Hacettepe Üniversitesi Türkiye ve Orta Doğu Araştırma Enstitüsü. Ankara, [1980].

Us, Hakkı Tarık, ed. *Meclis-i Mebusan, 1293 (1877)*. 2 vols. İstanbul, 1940 and 1954.

Uzunçarşılı, İsmail Hakkı. *Mekke-i Mükerreme Emirleri*. Ankara, 1972.

Weber, Eugene. *Peasants into Frenchmen: The Modernization of Rural France, 1870–1914*. Stanford, Calif., 1976.

Wilson, Mary C. "The Hashemites, the Arab Revolt, and Arab Nationalism". In *Origins of Arab Nationalism*, ed. Khalidi et al., 204–21.

———. *King Abdullah, Britain, and the Making of Jordan*. Cambridge, 1987.

Yalman, A. Emin. *Turkey in the World War*. New Haven, 1930.

Yayla, Yıldızhan. *Anayasalarımızda Yönetim İlkeleri: Tevsi-i Mezuniyet ve Tefrik-i Vezaif*. İstanbul, 1984.

Zeine, Zeine N. *The Emergence of Arab Nationalism*. 3d ed. New York, 1973 (first edition published in 1958).

————. *The Struggle for Arab Independence.* New York, 1977.

Zirikli, Khayr al-Din. *Al-a 'lam: qamus tarajim li ashhar al-rijal wa al-nisa ' min al-'arab wa al-musta 'ribin wa al-mustashriqin.* Cairo, 1954–59.

Zürcher, Erik Jan. *The Unionist Factor: The Role of the Committee of Union and Progress in the Turkish National Movement.* Leiden, 1984.

Index

Index: Pat Deminna
Map: Bill Nelson
Composition: Impressions Book and Journal Services, Inc.
Text: 10/13 Galliard
Display: Galliard
Printing and binding: Edwards Bros.